# The Kid's Address Book

# THE KID'S ADDRESS BOOK

Over 2,500 Addresses of Celebrities, Athletes, Entertainers, and More . . . Just for Kids!

*Fifth Edition*

# MICHAEL LEVINE

A Perigee Book

Every effort has been made to provide the most current addresses.
Addresses, however, do change, and neither the publisher nor the author
is responsible for misdirected or returned mail.

A Perigee Book
Published by The Berkley Publishing Group
A division of Penguin Putnam Inc.
375 Hudson Street
New York, New York 10014

First printing of fifth edition: August 2001
ISBN: 0-399-52688-9
ISSN: 1091-188X

Published simultaneously in Canada.

Visit our website at
www.penguinputnam.com

Printed in the United States of America

10  9  8  7  6  5  4  3  2  1

# CONTENTS

# ACKNOWLEDGMENTS

I'm lucky. I get to say publicly to the special people in my life how much they mean to me. To each of them, my appreciation for their help with this book and, most of all, their unwavering friendship and love.

My literary agent, Alice Martell.

My friends at Perigee, where I have been published since 1984.

My father, Arthur O. Levine; stepmother, Marilyn; and sister, Patty.

My special friends Adam Christing, Richard Imprescia, Karen Karsian, Nancy Mager, John McKillop, Cable Neuhaus, and Alyse Reynolds.

My loyal staff and associates: Jim Erickson, Rebecca Gallegos, Phil Kass, Mark Vega, and David Weiss.

Special thanks to Joe Kaufmann for commitment to excellence in the researching of this book.

# AUTHOR'S NOTE TO KIDS

Dear Kids:

People are taught in America that you get to vote once a year. This is not true. In America you get to vote every day. The decisions about what you buy, where you eat, television shows you watch, and music you listen to are all a form of voting. Additionally, your comments, suggestions, thoughts, and criticisms are a form of voting. It is my hope that young people will use *The Kid's Address Book* as a way of getting involved with the world and sharing opinions with people all over the place.

While researching this book, I found that nearly everyone I spoke with is eager to hear from you. They want to understand how you feel and they don't want it sugarcoated. As you write to people in this book, you may be surprised to learn that people do respond. That's the exciting part, and you'll learn about that soon enough.

Here are several important things to remember in writing to famous people:

- **Always include a self-addressed stamped envelope (SASE).** This is the single most important factor in writing a letter if you want a response. Because of the unusually high volume of mail famous people receive, anything you can do to make it easier for them to respond is going to work in your favor.
- **Keep your letters short and to the point.** Famous people are usually extremely busy, and long letters tend to be set aside for "future" consideration. For instance, if you want an autographed picture of your favorite TV personality, don't write three pages of prose to explain your request.
- **Make your letters as easy to read as possible.** This means type it or, at the very least, handwrite it very neatly. Avoid crayons, markers, or even pencils. And don't forget to leave some margins on the paper. Be sure to include your name and address (on all materials that you include with your letter) in case the materials are separated from your letter. You would be amazed how many people write letters without return addresses and then wonder why they never hear from the person to whom they wrote.
- **Never send food to famous people.** Due to spoilage and security matters, it cannot be eaten anyway. (Would you eat a box of homemade brownies

given to you by a total stranger?) If you send gifts, don't wrap them in large boxes with yards of paper, string, and tape around them. (They may not have a crowbar on hand.)

- Again, don't forget to include your name and address on all material you send. Of course, don't send—or ask for—money.

The most important thing is to get going and have fun with all of this. Keep a chart at home and monitor your results. Drop me a note and let me know how you are doing.

Michael Levine
The Kid's Address Book
Levine Communications Office
10333 Ashton Ave.
Los Angeles, CA 90024
E-mail: levinepr@earthlink.net

P.S. Remember, *a person who writes to another makes more impact than ten thousand who are silent.*

# AUTHOR'S NOTE TO PARENTS

The Kid's Address Book is more than a simple collection of names and addresses. It is actually a tool of empowerment for young people. Contained herein are all the essentials to instill in them a love for the lost art of letter-writing. Adults would be wise to engage in it as well, but how much more significant to inflame the next generation with a passion for writing.

The great American jurist Oliver Wendell Holmes once said, "Pretty much all the honest truth-telling there is, is done by children." But who's listening? Today, we see scholastic test scores at all grade levels on the decline, poverty rates for children on the rise, and increasing numbers of young people falling victim to the modern-day scourges of drugs, teenage pregnancy, crime, and general aimlessness.

Our kids are in trouble.

Or, more to the point, we are all in trouble if we cannot provide young people with a new direction, a sense of purpose, and a safer world in which to live. Most parents mean well and strive to give their children a financial, educational, moral, and spiritual foundation. But today we bear witness to the Nintendo-ization of American youth. Unfortunately, the easiest way to get a kid's attention these days is to stand in front of the TV. Kids who spend an inordinate amount of time watching the tube will surely go down in history—not to mention math, science, and English. Surely we can do better than that.

One way is to acquaint children with their own inherent power. If they can, in some way, help fashion their own fates and make a direct impact on the world around them, then they will come away with a restored sense of self-reliance and capability. They will become who they are, not what the media tell them they should be. One clear and effective way to do that is to teach our kids to write letters.

I call it the lost art of letter-writing. Contemporary essayist Paul Bowles once wrote:

In other centuries this [letter-writing] was taken for granted. Not any longer. Only a few people carry on true correspondences. No time, the rest tell you. Quicker to telephone. Like saying a photograph is more satisfying than a painting. There wasn't all that much time for writing letters in the past either, but time was found, as it generally can for whatever gives pleasure.

The element of pleasure is missing for most people when contemplating writing. If only they experienced the fun and gratification of letter-writing. Writing is nothing more than guiding a dream, and we all know how enjoyable dreams can be.

For kids, the trick is helping them comprehend that letter-writing will bring results. Although writing can be a pure pleasure in and of itself, writing letters is specifically designed to communicate to someone else. Implicit in the act of writing and sending a letter is the expectation that the addressee will read and respond. Corresponding is an active dialogue between the minds of two people. No, it's not as fast as calling, but I daresay the pen is mightier than the car phone.

Kids instinctively grasp this. I've known shy children barely able to look another human being in the eye, who can find wondrous forms of expression when they write to someone. I've seen the thrilled reaction of a third-grader getting a reply after writing a fan letter. In cases like these, kids learn they can control their destiny in a world ruled by big people.

Bu wht kind of letter should they write, and to whom? The answers are as varied as the children. A letter can be a question or a complaint; a request or a declaration of love; a confession or a condemnation. The old axiom, "kids are people, too" is undeniably true, and children comprise no less complex a constellation of feelings, opinions, hopes, and desires than do adults. Not only should we treat them accordingly, but we should encourage them to view themselves that way.

In the following pages, I have listed hundreds of celebrities, companies, institutions, officials, heroes, and villains, all of whom are of particular interest to children of varying ages. Kids who use this book will find that their voices matter; that those they write to will take a strong interest in what they have to say. Not every letter will get a personal response, but many will.

Since I've published my first address book a number of years ago, I've been deluged with letters from individuals who found that by writing to an important legislator, reviled corporate villain, or favorite movie star, they had tapped into a unique source of power. They learned they were not isolated and that they had the wherewithal to communicate directly with those who affected their lives. That can hold true for children as well.

Writing letters is purposeful work. Kids who normally rebel against rote-learning drills will rise to the occasion when it comes to writing to their heroes, especially when they see that their letters are answered. Writing is a great habit to develop and a hard habit to break.

My hope is that The Kid's Address Book will aid children in turning a corner.

If they develop a love and appreciation for writing, for communicating, for interacting, and for taking action, then they'll be well on the way to becoming good citizens, caring adults, and builders of tomorrow's civilization.

—Michael Levine

# FAN MAIL

**A**

**Aadland, Beverly**
PO Box 1115
Canyon Country, CA 91350
*Actress*

**Aaron, Hank**
PO Box 4064
Atlanta, GA 30302
*Ex–baseball player*
*Birthday: 2/5/34*

**Aaron, Tommy**
PO Drawer 545
Buford, GA 30518
*Golfer*

**Abbott and Costello Fan Club**
PO Box 2084
Toluca Lake, CA 91610

**Abbott, Bruce**
4526 Wilshire Blvd.
Los Angeles, CA 90010
*Actor*

**Abbott, Gregory**
PO Box 68
Bergenfield, NJ 07621
*Singer*

**Abdul-Jabbar, Kareem**
2049 Century Park East,
Suite 1200
Century City, CA 90067
*Ex–basketball player*

**Abdullah the Butcher**
1000 S. Industrial Blvd.
Dallas, TX 75207
*Wrestler*

**Abraham, F. Murray**
40 Fifth Ave., #2C
New York, NY 10011
*Actor*
*Birthday: 10/24/39*

**Abramson, Leslie Hope**
4929 Wilshire Blvd., #940
Los Angeles, CA 90010
*Attorney who represented Erik*
*Menendez*

**Acker, Sharon**
6310 San Vicente Blvd., #401
Los Angeles, CA 90048
*Actress*

**Acuff, Roy**
Grand Ole Opry
2804 Opryland Dr.
Nashville, TN 37214
*Country singer*

**Adair, Deborah**
PO Box 1980
Studio City, CA 91614
*Actress*
*Birthday: 5/23/52*

**Adair, Red**
PO Box 747
Bellville, TX 77418
*His company puts out oil-well fires*

**Adams, Cindy**
475 Park Ave., PH-B
New York, NY 10022
*Actress*

**Adams, Don**
2160 Century Park East
Los Angeles, CA 90067
*Actor, writer, director*
*Birthday: 4/19/?*

**Adams, Joey**
8942 Wilshire Blvd.
Beverly Hills, CA 90211
*Actor, writer, director*
*Birthday: 1/06/11*

**Adams, Maria**
247 S. Beverly Dr., #102
Beverly Hills, CA 90212
*Actress*

**Adams, Mason**
570 Park Ave., #9B
New York, NY 10021
*Actor*
*Birthday: 2/26/19*

**Adams, Maude**
11901 Sunset Blvd., #214
Los Angeles, CA 90049
Or
1939 Century Park W., #403
Los Angeles, CA 90067
*Model, actress*
*Birthday: 2/12/45*

**Adams, Dr. Patch**
PO Box 268
Hillsboro, WV 24946
*Doctor portrayed by Robin*
*Williams in the movie* Patch Adams

**Adams, Tom**
29-31 Kings Rd.
London SW3
England
*Actor*

**Adjani, Isabelle**
5 rue Clement Marot
Paris F-75008
France
*Actress*
*Birthday: 6/27/55*

**Affleck, Ben**
405 S. Beverly Dr., #500
Beverly Hills, CA 90212
*Actor*
*Birthday: 8/15/72*

**Agassi, Andre**
ATP Tour North America
200 ATP Tour Blvd.
Ponte Vedra Beach, FL 32082
*Tennis player*
*Birthday: 4/29/70*

**Agee, Marilyn**
8641 Sugar Gum Rd.
Riverside, CA 92508
Website: http://www.kiwi.net/
~mjagee/
*Biblical prophecy author*

**Agony Column**
*Cosmopolitan*
224 W. 54th St.
New York, NY 10019
Attn: Irma Kurtz
*Magazine advice column*

**Aikman, Troy**
PO Box 630227
Irving, TX 75063
*Ex–football player*
*Birthday: 1/21/66*

**Aimee, Anouk**
201 rue du Faubourg-St.-Honoré
Paris, 75008
France
*Actress*
*Birthday: 4/27/32*

**Ainge, Danny**
2910 North Central
Phoenix, AZ 95012
*Basketball player*

**Albano, Capt. Lou**
16 Mechanic St.
Carmel, NY 10512
*Wrestler, manager*

**Albee, Edward**
PO Box 697
Montauk, NY 11954
*Playwright*

**Albert, Eddie**
1930 Century Park West, #403
Los Angeles, CA 90067
*Actor*
*Birthday: 4/22/09*

**Albert, Crown Prince**
Palais De Monaco
Boite Postal 518
Monte Carlo Monaco
*Crown Prince of Monaco*

**Albright, Lola**
PO Box 250070
Glendale, CA 91225
*Actress*
*Birthday: 7/20/24*

**Alda, Alan**
1122 S. Robertson Blvd., #15
Los Angeles, CA 90035
*Birthday: 1/28/36*

**Aldrin, Dr. Buzz**
838 N. Doheny Dr., #1407
West Hollywood, CA 90069
*Former astronaut*

**Alexander, Denise**
270 N. Danon Dr., #1199
Beverly Hills, CA 90210
*Actress*

**Alexander, Jane**
1325 Ave. of the Americas
New York, NY 10019
*Actress*
*Birthday: 10/28/?*

**Alexander, Jason (Jay Scott Greenspan)**
405 S. Beverly Dr., #500
Beverly Hills, CA 90212
*Actor*
*Birthday: 9/23/59*

**Alexander, Lamar**
1109 Owen Pl. NE
Washington, DC 20008
*Politician*

**Alexis, Kim**
343 N. Maple Dr., #185
Beverly Hills, CA 90210
*Supermodel*

**Alfonso, Kristian**
10061 Riverside Dr., #798
Toluca Lake, CA 91602
*Soap opera star*

**Ali, Muhammad (Cassius Clay)**
5456 Wilshire Blvd.
Los Angeles, CA 90036
*Boxing champion*
*Birthday: 1/17/42*

**Alice in Chains**
207½ First Ave. So., #300
Seattle, WA 98104
*Music Group*

**Allen, Corey**
8642 Hollywood Blvd.
Los Angeles, CA 90069
*Actor, writer, director*

**Allen, Elizabeth**
PO Box 243
Lake Peekskill, NY 10537
*Actress*

**Allen, Joan**
40 W. 57th St.
New York, NY 10019
*Actress*

**Allen, Jonelle**
8730 Sunset Blvd., #480
Los Angeles, CA 90069
*Actress, singer*

**Allen, Karen**
PO Box 237
Monterey, MA 01245
Or
PO Box 5617
Beverly Hills, CA 90212
*Actress*
*Birthday: 10/05/51*

**Allen, Marty**
5750 Wilshire Blvd., #580
Los Angeles, CA 90036
*Comedian*

**Allen, Nancy**
8154 Muholland Terr.
Los Angeles, CA 90046
*Actress*
*Birthday: 6/24/50*

**Allen, Robert**
32 Ave. of the Americas
New York, NY 10013
*Business leader*

**Allen, Steve (Stephen Valentine
Patrick William Allen)**
15201-B Burbank Blvd.
Van Nuys, CA 91411
*Television comedian, author,*
*pianist, songwriter*
*Birthday: 12/26/21*

**Allen, Tim (Tim Allen Dick)**
7920 Sunset Blvd., #400
Los Angeles, CA 90046
Or
1122 S. Robertson Blvd., #15
Los Angeles, CA 90035
E-mail: HI.Tim@refuge.cuug.ab.ca
*Actor*
*Birthday: 6/13/53*

**Allen, Woody**
930 Fifth Ave.
New York, NY 10018
*Actor, comedian, director*
*Birthday: 12/01/35*

**Alley, Kirstie**
132 S. Rodeo Dr., #300
Beverly Hills, CA 90212
*Actress*
*Birthday: 1/12/55*

**Allred, Gloria**
6300 Wilshire Blvd., #1500
Los Angeles, CA, 90048
*Attorney*

**Alonso, Maria Conchita**
PO Box 537
Beverly Hills, CA 90213
*Actress*
*Birthday: 11/30/56*

**Alpert, Hollis**
PO Box 142
Shelter Island, NY 11964
*Writer*

**Alpert, Dr. Richard**
Box 1558
Boulder, CO 80306
*Psychologist*

**Alt, Carol**
4526 Wilshire Blvd.
Los Angeles, CA 90010
*Supermodel*

**Altman, Robert**
9200 Harrington Dr.
Potomac, MD 20854
*Financier*

**Altman, Robert**
502 Park Ave., #15G,
New York, NY 10022
*Writer, producer, director*

**Alva, Luigi**
via Moscova 46/3
Mailand 20121
Italy
*Tenor*

**Alvin and the Chipmunks**
122 E. 57th St., #400
New York, NY 10003
*Animated singing group*

**American Gladiators**
10203 Santa Monica Blvd.
Los Angles, CA 90067
Website: http://
www.americangladiators.com/
E-mail: whoever@bellsouth.net
*Television series*

**Amick, Madchen**
8840 Wilshire Blvd.
Beverly Hills, CA 90212
*Actress*

**Amin, Idi**
Box 8948
Jidda 21492
Saudi Arabia
*Former dictator of Uganda*
*Birthday: 1/1/25*

**Amos, John**
PO Box 18764
Encino, CA 91416
Or
Box 587
Califon, NJ 07830
*Actor*
*Birthday: 12/27/41*

**Amos, Tori (Myra Ellen Amos)**
9830 Wilshire Blvd.
Beverly Hills, CA 90212
*Singer, songwriter*
*Birthday: 8/22/64*

**Amos, Wally (Famous)**
PO Box 897
Kailua, HI 96734
*Entrepreneur*

**Anderson, Barbara**
PO Box 10118
Santa Fe, NM 87504
*Actress*

**Anderson, Gillian**
% *The X-Files*
20th Century Fox
10201 Pico Blvd.
Los Angeles, CA 90035
*Actress*
*Birthday: 8/9/68*

**Anderson, John B.**
Nova University Law Center
Ft. Lauderdale, FL 33314
*Former Representative, former*
*independent presidential candidate*

**Anderson, Louie**
2756 N. Green Valley Pkwy., #449
Las Vegas, NV 89014
*Comedian, game show host*

**Anderson, Richard Dean**
1122 S. Robertson Blvd., #15
Los Angeles, CA 90035
*Actor*
*Birthday: 1/23/50*

**Anderson-Lee, Pamela**
151 El Camino Dr.
Beverly Hills, CA 90212
*Actress*
*Birthday: 7/01/67*

**Andress, Ursula**
Via Francesco Siacci 38
Rome 1-00197
Italy
*Actress*
*Birthday: 3/19/36*

**Andretti, John**
PO Box 2104
Davidson, NC 28036
*Race car driver*

**Andretti, Mario**
53 Victory Lane
Nazareth, PA 18604
Or
% Andretti Signature Line
3310 Airport Rd.
Allentown, PA 18103
*Race car driver*
*Birthday: 2/28/40*

**Andrew, HRH Prince**
Suninghill Park
Windsor
England
*Son of Queen Elizabeth*
*Birthday: 2/19/60*

**Andrews, Andy**
PO Box 17321
Nashville, TN 37217
Website: http://
www.andyandrews.com/
E-mail: andy@andyandrews.com/
*Comedian, author*

**Andrews, Julie**
PO Box 491668
Los Angeles, CA 90049
*Actress, singer*
*Birthday: 10/1/35*

**Angelou, Maya (Margueritte Anne Johnson)**
104 B Wingate Hall
PO Box 7314
Winston-Salem, NC 27109
Website: http://www.educeth.ch/
english/readinglist/angeloum/
index.html
*Poet*
*Birthday: 4/4/28*

**Angelyne**
PO Box 3864
Beverly Hills, CA 90212
*Billboard siren*

**Anglade, Jean-Hughes**
151 El Camino Dr.
Beverly Hills, CA 90212
*Actress*

**Aniston, Jennifer**
% Creative Artists Agency
9830 Wilshire Blvd.
Beverly Hills, CA 90212
Or
1122 S. Robertson Blvd., #15
Los Angeles, CA 90035
*Actress*
*Birthday: 2/11/69*

**Anka, Paul**
433 N. Camden Dr.
Beverly Hills, CA 90210
*Singer, songwriter*
*Birthday: 7/30/41*

**Annan, Secy. Gen. Kofi**
799 United Nations Plaza
New York, NY 10017
*Secretary General of the U.N.*

**Anne, HRH Princess**
Gatcombe Park
Glouchestershire
England
*Daughter of Queen Elizabeth*

**Ann-Margret (Ann-Margret Olson)**
5664 Cahuenga Blvd., #336
North Hollywood, CA 91601
*Actress*
*Birthday: 4/28/41*

**Anton, Susan**
40 W. 57th. St.
New York, NY 10019
*Actress*
*Birthday: 10/12/50*

**Anwar, Gabrielle**
253 26th St., #A-203
Santa Monica, CA 90402
*Actress*
*Birthday: 2/4/70*

**Aoki, Rocky**
8685 N.W. 53rd Terr.
Miami, FL 33166
*Food entrepreneur*

**Apollonia (Kotero)**
8831 Wilshire Blvd., #304
Los Angeles, CA 90069
*Actress*

**Applegate, Christina**
% International Creative
Management
8942 Wilshire Blvd.
Beverly Hills, CA 90211
*Actress*
*Birthday: 11/25/72*

**Aquino, ex-President Corazon**
% Pius XVI Center
UN Manila
Philippines
*Former President of the Philippines*

**Arafat, President Yassir**
PO Box 115
Jericho, Palestine
*President of Palestine*

**Archer, Anne**
% Ilene Feldman Agency
8730 Sunset Blvd., #490
Los Angeles, CA 90069
*Actress*
*Birthday: 10/25/50*

**Archerd, Army**
% *Daily Variety*
5700 Wilshire Blvd., #120
Los Angeles, CA 90036
*Columnist*

**Arens, Moshe**
49 Hagderat, Savyon
Israel
*Politician*

**Arias, ex-President Oscar**
AFP Apdo 8-6410-1000
San Jose
Costa Rica
*Former President of Costa Rica
and Nobel Peace Prize winner*

**Arinze, Francis Cardinal**
Piazza San Calisto 16
Rome 00153
Italy

**Arkin, Adam**
2372 Veteran Ave., #102
Los Angeles, CA 90064
*Actor*

**Arkin, Alan**
21 E. 40th St., #1705
New York, NY 10016
Or
% William Morris Agency
151 S. El Camino Dr.
Beverly Hills, CA 90212
*Actor*
*Birthday: 3/26/34*

**Arledge, Roone**
778 Park Ave., #15
New York, NY 10021
*Sports TV innovator of live events,
anthology shows, Olympic
coverage, and* Monday Night
Football
*Birthday: 7/8/31*

**Armani, Giorgio**
Palazzo Durini 24
Milan 1-20122
Italy
Or
650 Fifth Ave.
New York, NY 10019
*Fashion designer*
*Birthday: 7/11/34*

**Armstrong, Anne**
Armstrong Ranch
Armstrong, TX 78338
*Politician*

**Armstrong, Bess**
151 El Camino Dr.,
Beverly Hills, CA 90212
*Actress*

**Arness, James (James Aurness)**
PO Box 49599
Los Angeles, CA 90049
*Actor*
*Birthday: 5/26/23*

**Arnold, Tom**
1122 S. Robertson Blvd., #15
Los Angeles, CA 90035
Or
151 El Camino Dr.
Beverly Hills, CA 90212
*Actor, comedian, producer*
*Birthday: 3/6/59*

**Arquette, Patricia**
1122 S. Robertson Blvd., #15
Los Angeles, CA 90035
*Actress*
*Birthday: 4/8/68*

**Ash, Mary Kay**
16251 Dallas Pkwy.
Dallas, TX 75248
*Cosmetics executive*

**Ashdown, Paddy**
House of Commons
London SW1A AA
England
*Politician*

**Asner, Ed**
3556 Mound View Ave.
Studio City, CA 91604
E-mail:
72726.357@compuserve.com
*Actor*
*Birthday: 11/15/29*

**Assante, Armand**
367 Windsor Hwy.
New Windsor, NY 12553
*Actor*
*Birthday: 10/4/49*

**Astin, John**
PO Box 49698
Los Angeles, CA 90049
*Actor, writer, director*
*Birthday: 3/30/30*

**Astin, Sean**
% Samantha Crisp
William Morris Agency
151 S. El Camino Dr.
Beverly Hills, CA 90212
*Actor*
*Birthday: 2/25/71*

**Atkinson, Rowan**
PBJ Management Ltd.
5 Soho Square
London W1V 5DE
England
*Actor: "Bean"*

**Atlanta Braves**
521 Capitol Ave. SW
Atlanta, GA 30312
Website: http://
www.atlantabraves.com
*Professional baseball team*
*(National League) and winners of*
*the 1995 World Series*

**Atlanta Falcons**
2745 Burnett Rd.
Suwanee, GA 30174
*Professional football team*

**Atlanta Hawks**
1 CNN Center
South Tower, #405
Atlanta, GA 30174
*Professional basketball team*

**Attenborough, Lord Richard**
5 Park Rd.
Richmond Surrey
England
*Writer, producer*
*Birthday: 8/29/23*

**Auberjonois, Rene**
8428 C Melrose Pl.
Los Angeles, CA 90069
*Actor*
*Birthday: 7/1/40*

**Auermann, Nadja**
% Elite Models
111 East 22nd St.
New York, NY 10010
*Supermodel*
*Birthday: 1971*

**Austin, Stone Cold Steve**
% WWF 1241 East Main St.
PO Box 3857
Stamford, CT 06902
Website: stonecold.com
*Wrestler*

**Avery, Margaret**
PO Box 3493
Los Angeles, CA 90078
*Actress*

**Aykroyd, Dan**
8271 Melrose Ave., #110
Los Angeles, CA 90046
Or
9830 Wilshire Blvd.
Beverly Hills, CA 90212
*Actor, writer*
*Birthday: 7/1/52*

**Aznavour, Charles**
76-78 ave. des Champs Elysses
Paris F75008
France
*Singer, called the "Frank Sinatra of France"*
*Birthday: 5/22/24*

**B**

**Babock, Barbara**
10100 Santa Monica Blvd., #2500
Los Angeles, CA 90067
*Actress*

**Babyface (Kenneth Edmonds)**
10231 Charing Cross Rd.
Los Angeles, CA 90024
*Singer, songwriter, producer*
*Birthday: 1958*

**Baby Spice**
35 Parkgate Rd., #32
Ransome Dock
London SW11
England
*Singer, member of the Spice Girls*

**Bacall, Lauren (Betty Perske)**
1 W. 72nd St., #43
New York, NY 10023
Or
151 El Camino Dr.
Beverly Hills, CA 90212
*Actress*
*Birthday: 9/16/24*

**Bacon, Kevin**
9830 Wilshire Blvd.
Beverly Hills, CA 90212
Or
Box 668
Sharon, CT 06069
*Actor*
*Birthday: 7/8/58*

**Bader, Dietrich**
% *The Drew Carey Show*
4000 Warner Blvd.
Burbank, CA 91522
*Actor*

**Badham, John**
% Elkins and Elkins
16830 Ventura Blvd., #300
Encino, CA 91436
*Movie director*

**Baer, Max Jr.**
PO Box 1831
Zephyr Cove, NV 89448
*Actor*
*Birthday: 12/4/37*

**Baez, Joan**
PO Box 1026
Menlo Park, CA 94026
*Singer*
*Birthday: 1/9/41*

**Bailey, F. Lee**
1400 Centre Park Blvd., #909
West Palm Beach, FL 33401
*Attorney*
*Birthday: 6/10/33*

**Bailey, Razzy**
Box 62
Geneva, NE 68361
Or
% Marilyn Schultze, President
PO Box 11950
Nashville, TN 37222
E-mail: razzypres@hotmail.com
*Fan club for country singer*

**Baio, Scott**
4333 Forman Ave.
Toluca Lake, CA 91602
*Actor*
*Birthday: 9/22/61*

**Baker, Carrol**
PO Box 480589
Los Angeles, CA 90048
Birthday: 11/15/25

**Baker, James A. III**
1299 Pennsylvania Ave. N.W.
Washington, DC 20004
*Ex–Secretary of State*

**Baker, Janet Abbott**
450 Edgeware Rd.
London W2
England
*Mezzo-soprano*

**Bakker, Jim (James O.)**
15948 Lancaster Hwy.
Charlotte, NC 28277
*TV evangelist in PTL scandal*
*Birthday: 1/2/40*

**Baker, Lisa**
% Playboy Ent.
9242 Beverly Blvd.
Beverly Hills, CA 90210
*Model*

**Baker, Tom**
PO Box 5877
Nottingham NG159JG
England
Website: http://
www.officialtombakerwebsite.co.uk/
*Actor known as "Dr. Who"*
*Birthday: 1/20/34*

**Bakula, Scott**
9560 Wilshire Blvd., #500
Beverly Hills, CA 90212
Or
15300 Ventura Blvd., #315
Sherman Oaks, CA 91403
*Actor*
*Birthday: 10/9/55*

**Baldwin, Adam**
PO Box 5617
Beverly Hills, CA 90210
*Actor*
*Birthday: 2/27/62*

**Baldwin, Alec (Alexander Rae Baldwin III)**
9830 Wilshire Blvd.
Beverly Hills, CA 90212
Or
132 S. Rodeo Dr., #300
Beverly Hills, CA 90212
*Actor*
*Birthday: 4/3/58*

**Baldwin, Daniel**
% William Morris Agency
151 S. El Camino Dr.
Beverly Hills, CA 90212
*Actor*

**Baldwin, Stephen**
Box 447
Camillus, NY 13031
*Actor*
*Birthday: 1966*

**Baldwin, William**
25 Music Sq. E.
Nashville, TN 37203
Or
955 S. Carrillo Dr., #200
Beverly Hills, CA 90212
*Actor*
*Birthday: 1963*

**Ballard, Kaye**
PO Box 922
Rancho Mirage, CA 92270
*Birthday: 11/20/26*

**Ballard, Roger**
PO Box 46305
Baton Rouge, LA 70895
Or
25 Music Square E.
Nashville, TN 37203
*Country music singer*

**Baltimore Orioles**
333 W. Camden St.
Baltimore, MD 21202
*Professional baseball team*
*(American League)*

**Baltimore Ravens**
11001 Owings Mills Blvd.
Ownings Mills, MD 21117
*Professional football team*

**Baltimore Spirit**
201 West Baltimore St.
Baltimore, MD 21201
E-mail: spiritsoccer@baltimorespirit
*Soccer tean*

**Bancroft, Anne (Anna Maria Italiano)**
20th Century Fox
Box 900
Beverly Hills, CA 90213
*Actress*
*Birthday: 9/17/31*

**Bandar, Prince Sultan-al-saud**
601 New Hampshire NW
Washington, DC 20037

**Banderas, Antonio**
3110 Main St., #205
Santa Monica, CA 90405
*Actor*
*Birthday: 1960*

**Bando, Saul**
% Milwaukee Brewers
Milwaukee County Stadium
Milwaukee, WI 53214


**Bandy, Moe**
2802 Covington Pl.
Nashville, TN 37204
*Musician*


**Bani Sadr, ex-President
Abolhassan**
Auvers-sur-Oise
France


**Banks, Ernie**
% Chicago Cubs
1060 W. Addison St.
Chicago, IL 60613
*Baseball player*


**Banks, Tyra**
1999 Ave. of the Stars, #2850
Los Angeles, CA 90067
*Actress, model*
*Birthday: 12/73*


**Barak, Prime Minister Ehud**
Likud, 38 Rehov King George
Tel-Aviv 61231
Israel
*Prime Minister of Israel*


**Barbeau Adrienne**
PO Box 1839
Studio City, CA 91614
Or
9255 Sunset Blvd., #515
Los Angeles, CA 90069
*Actress*
*Birthday: 6/11/45*


**Barbieri, Paula**
PO Box 20483
Panama City, FL 32411
*Model, O. J. Simpson's ex-girlfriend*


**Bardot, Brigette**
La Madrague F-83990
St. Tropez
France
*Actress*
*Birthday: 9/28/34*


**Barker, Bob (Robert William
Barker)**
5750 Wilshire Blvd., #475
Los Angeles, CA 90036
*Host of* The Price is Right
*Birthday: 12/12/23*


**Barker, Clive**
PO Box 691885
West Hollywood, CA 90069
*Author*


**Barkin, Ellen**
% Creative Artists Agency
9830 Wilshire Blvd.
Beverly Hills, CA 90212
*Actress*
*Birthday: 4/16/54*


**Barkley, Charles**
10 Greenway Plaza E
Houston, TX 77277
*Basketball player*


**Barnard, Dr. Christian**
Box 6143
Weigemoed 7538
Capetown
South Africa
*Heart surgeon*

**Barnes, Priscilla**
8428-C Melrose Pl.
West Hollywood, CA 90069
*Actress*
*Birthday: 12/7/56*

**Barney**
300 E. Bethany Rd., Box 8000
Allen, TX 75002
*Purple dinosaur*

**Bassey, Shirley**
24 Ave. Princess Grace, #1200
Monte Carlo
Monaco
*Singer*
*Birthday: 1/8/37*

**Barr, Julie**
420 Madison Ave., #1400
New York, NY 10017
*Actress*

**Barrichello, Rubens**
% Stewart Grand Prix Ltd.
16 Tanners Dr.
Blakelands
GB-Milton Keynes MK14 5BW
England
*Professional Formula-1 driver*

**Barris, Chuck**
17 E. 76th St.
New York, NY 10021
*TV producer*

**Barrows, Sydney Biddle**
210 W. 70th St.
New York, NY 10023
*Alleged madam*

**Barry, Dave**
1 Herald Plaza
Miami, FL 33101
E-mail:
733314.722@compuserve.com
*Humorist, columnist*

**Barry, Gene**
151 El Camino Dr.
Beverly Hills, CA 90212
*Actor*
*Birthday: 6/14/22*

**Barry, Mayor Marion**
161 Raleigh St. SE
Washington, DC 20032
*Mayor of Washington, D.C.*
*Birthday: 3/6/36*

**Barrymore, Drew**
1122 S. Robertson Blvd., #15
Los Angeles, CA. 90035
*Actress*
*Birthday: 2/22/75*

**Baros, Dana**
151 Merrimac St., 4th Floor
Boston, MA 02114
*Guard, Boston Celtics*
*Height 5-11*
*Birthday: 4/13/67*

**Baryshnikov, Mikhail**
157 W. 57th St., #502
New York, NY 10019
*Ballet dancer, actor*
*Birthday: 1/28/48*

**Basinger, Kim**
9830 Wilshire Blvd.
Beverly Hills, CA 90212
*Birthday: 12/8/53*

**Bateman, Jason**
2628 2nd St.
Santa Monica, CA 90405
*Actor*
*Birthday: 1/14/69*

**Bateman, Justine**
2628 2nd St.
Santa Monica, CA 90405
*Actress*
*Birthday: 2/19/66*

**Bates, Kathy (Kathleen Doyle Bates)**
121 N. San Vicente Blvd.
Beverly Hills, CA 90211
*Actress*
*Birthday: 6/28/48*

**Battle, Kathleen**
165 W. 57th St.
New York, NY 10019
*Opera singer*
*Birthday: 8/13/48*

**Baxter, Meredith**
2049 Century Park E., #2500
Los Angeles, CA 90067
*Actress*
*Birthday: 6/21/47*

**Bayh, ex-Senator Birch**
1575 "I" St., #1025
Washington, DC 20005

**Beals, Jennifer**
14755 Ventura Blvd., #710
Sherman Oaks, CA 91403
*Actress*
*Birthday: 12/19/63*

**Beard, Amanda**
1 Olympic Plaza
Colorado Springs, CO 80909
*Olympic gold medalist swimmer*

**Beatrix, HM Queen**
Kasteel Drakestijn
Lage Vuursche 3744 BA
Holland

**Beatty, Warren**
9830 Wilshire Blvd.
Beverly Hills, CA 90212
*Shirley MacLaine's brother,*
*married to Annette Bening*
*Birthday: 3/30/37*

**Beavis and Butt-Head**
1515 Broadway, #400
New York, NY 10036
*Animated characters*

**Beck**
17835 Ventura Blvd., #310
Encino, CA 91316
*Musican*

**Beck, Jeff**
11 Old Sq. Lincoln's Inn
London WC2
England
*Musician*

**Beck, Marilyn**
PO Box 11079
Beverly Hills, CA 90210
*Columnist, critic*
*Birthday: 12/17/28*

**Beck, Rufus**
Lamontstr. 9
81679 München
Germany
*Actor*

**Becker, Boris**
Nusslocher Str. 51
69181 Leimen
Germany
*Professional tennis player*
*Birthday: 11/22/67*

**Bedelia, Bonnie**
% ICM
8942 Wilshire Blvd.
Beverly Hills, CA 90211
*Actress*

**Beene, Geoffrey**
550 7th Ave.
New York, NY 10018
*Clothes designer*

**Begley, Ed Jr.**
Sterling/Winters Company
1900 Ave. of the Stars, #1640
Los Angeles, CA 90067
*Birthday: 9/16/49*

**Bell, Archie**
PO Box 11669
Knoxville, TN 37939
*Singer*

**Bell, Catherine**
1999 Ave. of the Stars, #2850
Los Angeles, CA 90067
*Actress*

**Bell, Darryl**
9255 Sunset Blvd., #515
West Hollywood, CA 90069
*Actor*

**Bell, Felicia**
12360 Riverside Dr., #317
North Hollywood, CA 91607
*Actress*

**Bell, Wendell**
Yale University
PO Box 208265
New Haven, CT 06520
E-mail: wendell.bell@yale.edu
*Wendell Bell is a professor*
*emeritus of sociology at Yale*
*University and author of*
Foundations of Futures Studies,
Volumes 1 and 2.

**Bellamy, Bill**
9830 Wilshire Blvd.
Beverly Hills, CA 90212
*Musician*

**Belle, Albert**
% Chicago White Sox
324 W. 35th St.
Chicago, IL 60616
*Baseball player*

**Belmundo, Jean-Paul**
9 rue des Sts.-Peres
Paris F-75006
France
*Actor*
*Birthday: 4/9/?*

**Belushi, Jim**
8271 Melrose Ave., #110
Los Angeles, CA 90046
*Birthday: 6/15/?*

**Belzer, Richard**
9000 Sunset Blvd., #122200
Los Angeles, CA 90069
*Comedian, actor*

**Benatar, Pat**
584 North Larchmont Blvd.
Los Angeles, CA 90004
*Singer*
*Birthday: 1/19/52*

**Benedict, Dirk**
4605 Lankershim Blvd., #305
North Hollywood, CA 91602
*Actor*
*Birthday: 1/01/45*

**Bening, Annette**
13671 Muholland Dr.
Beverly Hills, CA 90210
*Actress, married to Warren Beatty*
*Birthday: 5/29/58*

**Benji**
242 N. Canon Dr.
Beverly Hills, CA 90210
*Acting dog*

**Bennett, Bill**
1776 "I" St., NW, #890
Washington, DC 20006
*Author*

**Bennett, Cornelius**
% Buffalo Bills
One Bills Dr.
Orchard Park, NY 14127
*Football player*

**Benson, George**
Turner Management Group
3500 W. Olive Ave., #900
Burbank, CA 91505
*Singer*
*Birthday: 3/2/43*

**Benson, Jodi**
% Special Artists Agency
Attn: Marcia Hurwitz
345 N. Maple Dr., #302
Beverly Hills, CA 90210
*Actress*

**Benson, Joe**
PO Box 12464
La Crescenta, CA 91224
Website: http://www.unclejoe.com
E-mail: unclejoe@unclejoe.com
*Los Angeles radio personality*

**Benson, Robby (Robby Segal)**
PO Box 1305
Woodland Hills, CA 91364
*Actor, writer, director*
*Birthday: 1/21/55*

**Bentsen, Hon. Lloyd**
901 15th St. NW, #700
Washington, DC 20005
*Former vice-presidential candidate,*
*former senator*

**Berenger, Tom**
PO Box 1842
Beaufort, SC 29901
*Actor*
*Birthday: 5/31/50*

**Berenson, Marisa**
80 Av. Charles de Gaulle
Neuilly F92200
France
*Actress*
*Birthday: 2/15/47*

**Bergen, Candice**
1122 S. Robertson Blvd., #15
Los Angeles, CA 90035
*Actress*
*Birthday: 5/9/46*

**Berger, Gerhard**
Europatrans
Radfeld 12a
Kundl A-6250
Austria
*Professional Formula-1 driver*

**Berkeley, Elizabeth**
12400 Ventura Blvd., #122
Studio City, CA 91604
*Actress*

**Berle, Milton**
10490 Wilshire Blvd., #1603
Los Angeles, CA 90024
*Comedian, actor*
*Birthday: 7/12/08*

**Bernadotte af Wisborg, Count Lennart**
Insel Mainau
D-78465
Konstanz
Germany

**Bernadotte, Princess Marianne**
Villagatan 10
Stockholm
Sweden

**Bernard, Crystal**
9830 Wilshire Blvd.
Beverly Hills, CA 90212
*Actress*

**Bernhard, Sandra**
26500 W. Agoura Rd.
Calabasas, CA 91302
*Actress, comedienne*
*Birthday: 6/16/?*

**Bernsen, Corbin**
11075 Santa Monica Blvd., #150
Los Angeles, CA 90025
*Actor*
*Birthday: 9/07/54*

**Berra, Yogi**
PO Box 462
Caldwell, NJ 07006
*Former baseball player*

**Berry, Chuck**
Berry Park
Buckner Rd.
Wentzville, MO 63385
*Singer, songwriter*
*Birthday: 10/18/26*

**Berry, Halle**
1122 S. Robertson Blvd., #15
Los Angeles, CA 90035
*Actress*

**Berry, John**
1211 16th St. S.
Nashville, TN 37212
*Country music singer*

**John Berry's Pack**
1807 N. Dixie, Suite #116
Elizabethtown, KY 42701
*Country music fan club*

**Berry, Ken**
4704 Cahuenga Blvd.
North Hollywood, CA 91602
*Actor*
*Birthday: 11/3/33*

**Bertil, HRH Prince**
Hert av Halland Kungliga Slottet
S-11130 Stockholm
Sweden

**Bertinelli, Valerie**
151 El Camino Dr.
Beverly Hills, CA 90212
*Actress*
*Birthday: 4/23/60*

**Besson, Luc**
76 Oxford St.
London W1N 0AX
England
*Film director*
*Birthday: 3/18/59*

**Best, James**
PO Box 621027
Oviedo, FL 32762
*Actor*
*Birthday: 7/26/26*

**Best, Pete**
#8 Hyman's Green
W. Derby
Liverpool 12
England
*Former Beatle*
*Birthday: 11/24/41*

**B. G. Prince of Rap**
% Allstars Music
Hundshager Weg 30
Hofheim 68623
Germany
*Rap artist*

**Biafra, Jello (Eric Boucher)**
PO Box 419092
San Francisco, CA 94141
*Former lead singer of the punk-rock band Dead Kennedys*

**Bialik, Mayim**
1529 N. Cahuenga Blvd., #19
Los Angeles, CA 90028
*Actress*
*Birthday: 12/12/75*

**Biffi, Giacomo Cardinal**
Archives Covado
Via Altabella 6
Bologna 40126
Italy

**Biggs-Dawsen, Rozann**
1630 Ft. Campbell Blvd., #9143
Clarksville, TN 37042
*Plays Lt. B'Elanna Torres on* Star
Trek: Voyager

**Bijan**
699 5th Ave.
New York, NY 10022
*Designer*

**Bikel, Theodore**
1131 Alta Loma, Suite #523
West Hollywood, CA 90069
*Musician*
*Birthday: 5/2/24*

**Billingsley, Barbara**
PO Box 1588
Pacific Palisades, CA 9072
*Actress, played Beaver's mother on*
Leave It to Beaver
*Birthday: 12/22/22*

**Bingham, Traci**
2029 Century Park E., #3250
Los Angeles, CA 90067
*Actress on* Baywatch

**Bird, Larry**
RR #1 Box 77A
West Baden Springs, IN 47469
*Former Indiana Pacers basketball coach*
*Birthday: 12/7/56*

**Birney, David**
20 Ocean Park Blvd., #11
Santa Monica, CA 90405
*Actor*
*Birthday: 4/23/39*

**Bishop, Stephen**
% Miles Hymes
18321 Ventura Blvd., #580
Tarzana, CA 91356

**Bisset, Jacqueline**
10 av. George V
Paris F-75008
France
Or
Guttman Assoc.
118 S. Beverly Dr.
Beverly Hills, CA 90212
*Actress*
*Birthday: 9/13/44*

**Black, Clint**
8489 W. Third St., #200
Los Angeles, CA 90048
*Country singer/songwriter*
*Birthday: 2/4/62*

**Black, Karen (Karen Ziegler)**
3500 W. Olive Ave., #1400
Burbank, CA 91505
*Actress*
*Birthday: 7/1/42*

**Blackstone, Harry Jr.**
11075 Santa Monica Blvd., #275
Los Angeles, CA 90025
*Magician*

**Blackwood, Nina**
% Angelwood
23705 Vanowen St., #111
West Hills, CA 91307
*Singer*

**Blair, Linda**
15821 Ventura Blvd., #235
Encino, CA 91436
*Actress*
*Birthday: 1/22/59*

**Blair, Honorable Tony**
10 Downing St.
London SWI
England
*Prime Minister*

**Blakely, Susan**
8436 W. Third St., #740
Los Angeles, CA 90048
*Actress*
*Birthday: 9/7/50*

**Blakley, Ronee**
8033 Sunset Blvd., #693
Los Angeles, CA 90046
*Actress, singer*

**Bland, Bobby "Blue"**
1995 Broadway, #501
New York, NY 10023
*Singer*

**Blanda, George**
PO Box 1153
LaQuinta, CA 92253
*Ex-football player*

**Blass, Bill**
550 7th Ave.
New York, NY 10018
*Fashion designer*
*Birthday: 6/22/22*

**Bledsoe, Drew**
% New England Patriots
Route 1
Foxboro, MA 02035
*Football player*

**Bledsoe, Tempestt**
10100 Santa Monica Blvd., #3480
Los Angeles, CA 90067
*Actress*
*Birthday: 8/1/73*

**Bloodsworth-Thomason, Linda**
4024 Radford Ave., Bldg. 5, #104
Studio City, CA 91604
*Film producer*

**Blount, Lisa**
5750 Wilshire Blvd., #580
Los Angeles, CA 90036
*Actress*

**Blount, Mel**
RD 1 Box 91
Claysville, PA 15323
*Ex-football player*

**Blue, Vida**
PO Box 1449
Pleasonton, CA 94566
*Charges $9 for trading card; $5 for
3× 5*

**Blum, Judy**
40 E. 48th St., #100
New York, NY 10017
*Author*
*Birthday: 2/12/38*

**Blyth, Ann**
Box 9754
Rancho Santa Fe, CA 92067
*Actress*
*Birthday: 8/16/28*

**Boaz, David**
Cato Institute
1000 Massachusetts Ave., N.W.
Washington, DC 20001
E-mail: dboaz@cato.org
*Author and executive vice
president of the Cato Institute*

**Bobek, Nicole**
PO Box 4534
Tequesta, FL 33469
*Figure skater*

**Bocho, Steven**
694 Amalfi Dr.
Pacific Palisades, CA 90272
*Producer, screenwriter*
*Birthday: 12/16/43*

**Bogguss, Suzy**
1207 17th. Ave., #101
Nashville, TN 37212
*Country singer*

**Bogues, Mugsy**
% Golden State Warriors
Oakland Col. Arena
7000 Coliseum Way
Oakland, CA 94621
*Basketball player*

**Boice, Dr. James**
1935 Pine St.
Philadelphia, PA 19103
*Theologian*

**Bologna, Joseph**
16830 Ventura Blvd., #326
Encino, CA 91436
*Actor, writer, director*
*Birthday: 12/30/38*

**Bolton, Michael**
PO Box 679
Branford, CT 06516
*Singer*
*Birthday: 2/26/?*

**Bon Jovi, Jon**
248 W. 17th. St. #502
New York, NY 10011
*Rock singer*
*Birthday: 5/10/60*

**Bonaduce, Danny**
651 Washington St.
New York, NY 10014
*Actor, talk show host*

**James Bonamy Fan Club**
PO Box 587
Smyrna, TN 37167
*Country music fan club*

**Bond, Samantha**
1812 Jernyn St., #300
London SW1Y 6HP
England
*Actress*

**Bonds, Bary**
9595 Wilshire Blvd., #711
Beverly Hills, CA 90212
*Baseball player*

**Bonds, Gary "U.S." (Gary Anderson)**
875 Ave. of the Americas, #1906
New York, NY 10001
*Singer*
*Birthday: 6/6/39*

**Bono (Paul Hewson)**
4 Windmill Ln.
Dublin, 2
Ireland
*Singer, songwriter*
*Birthday: 5/10/60*

**Bono, Chastity**
PO Box 960
Beverly Hills, CA 90213
*Sonny and Cher's daughter*
*Birthday: 3/4/69*

**Boone, Debbie**
4334 Kestar Ave.
Sherman Oaks, CA 91403
*Actress, singer*

**Boone, Larry**
% Gene Ferguson
PO Box 23795
Nashville, TN 37212
*Musician*

**Boone, Pat**
904 N. Beverly Dr.
Beverly Hills, CA 90210
*Singer*
*Birthday: 6/1/34*

**Betty Boop Fan Club**
6024 Fullerton Ave., #2
Buena Park, CA 90621

**Boosler, Elayne**
584 N. Larchmont Blvd.
Los Angeles, CA 90004
*Comedienne, actress*

**Boothe, Powers**
PO Box 9242
Calabasas, CA 91372
*Actor*

**Boothroyd, Betty**
House of Commons
London SW1A 0AA
England

**Borg, Bjorn**
1360 E. 9th St., #100
Cleveland, OH 44114
*Tennis player*
*Birthday: 6/7/56*

**Borman, Col. Frank**
PO Box 1139
Fairacres, NM 88033
*Astronaut*

**Bostwick, Barry**
1640 S. Sepulveda Blvd., #218
Los Angeles, CA 90025
*Actor*
*Birthday: 2/24/46*

**Bosworth, Brian**
17383 Sunset Blvd., #250
Pacific Palisades, CA 90272
*Actor*
*Birthday: 3/9/65*

**Bottoms, Ben**
8228 Sunset Blvd., #212
Los Angeles, CA 90046
*Actor*

**Bottoms, Joe**
1015 Gayley Ave., #300
Los Angeles, CA 90024
*Actor*

**Boucher, Phillippe**
Staples Center
1111 S. Figueroa St.
Los Angeles, CA 90015
*Hockey player*

**Boulez, Pierre**
1 Pl. Igor Stravinsky
Paris F75004
France
*Conductor, composer*

**Boutros-Boutros-Ghali**
2 Ave. El nil
Giza
Cairo
Egypt
*Secretary-General of the United
Nations*
*Birthday: 11/14/22*

**Bowen, Christopher**
37 Berwick St.
London W1V 3RF
England
*Actor*

**Bowie, David**
180-182 Tottenham Ct. Rd.
London W1X 7LH
England
*Musician*

**Bowles, Camilla Parker**
Middlewick House
Nr. Corshm., Wiltshire
England
*Longstanding companion and
confidante of Prince Charles*

**Boxcar Willie**
HCR 1, Box 7085
Branson, MO 65616
*Country singer*

**Boxer, Barbara**
2112 Hart Office Bldg.
Washington, DC 20510
*California senator*

**Boxleitner, Bruce**
23679 Calabasas Rd., #181
Calabasas, CA 91302
*Actor*
*Birthday: 5/12/50*

**Boy George (George O'Dowd)**
63 Grosvenor St.
London W1X 9DA
England
*Singer, songwriter, author*
*Birthday: 6/14/61*

**Boyle, Peter**
130 East End Ave.
New York, NY 10024
*Actor*
*Birthday: 1/18/33*

**Bozo the Clown**
% WGN Television
2501 Bradley Place
Chicago, IL 60618

**Bracco, Lorraine**
18 E. 53rd. St., #1400
New York, NY 10022
*Actress*
*Birthday: 11/30/54*

**Bradford, Barbara Taylor**
450 Park Ave., #1903
New York, NY 10022
*Author*

**Brady, James**
1255 "I" St., #1100
Washington, DC 20005
*Ex-Whitehouse Press Secretary*

**Brady, Marsha**
Maureen McCormick Fan Club
22817 Pera Rd.
Woodland Hills, CA 91364

**Brady, Sarah**
1255 "I" St., #1100
Washington, DC 20005
*Gun control advocate*

**Branagh, Kenneth**
Shepperton Studios
Studios Rd.
Shepperton
TW170QD
England
*Actor*
*Birthday: 12/10/60*

**Brandis, Jonathan**
9255 Sunset Blvd., #1010
West Hollywood, CA 90069
*Actor*

**Brando, Marlon**
13828 Weddington
Van Nuys, CA 91401
*Actor*
*Birthday: 4/03/24*

**Brandy (Norwood)**
22817 Ventura Blvd., #432
Woodland Hills, CA 91364
*Actress*

**Branigan, Laura**
1501 Broadway, #1301
New York, NY 10036

**Braxton, Toni**
9255 Sunset Blvd., #610
Los Angeles, CA 90069
*Singer*
*Birthday: 1968*

**Bream, Julian**
122 Wigmore St.
London W1
England
*Guitarist*

**Breedlove, Craig**
200 N. Front St.
Rio Vista, CA 94571
*Land speed record setter*

**Paul Brandt Fan Club**
Box 57144 Sunridge Postal Outlet
Calgary Alberta T1V 5T0
Canada

**BR5-49 Fan Club**
PO Box 23288
Nashville, TN 37202
*Country music fan club*

**Brennan, Eileen**
10110 Emperian Way, #304
Los Angeles, CA 90067
*Actress*
*Birthday: 9/03/35*

**Brenneman, Amy**
9830 Wilshire Blvd.
Beverly Hills, CA 90212
*Actress*
*Birthday: 2/4/45*

**Brenner, David**
17 E. 16th St., #3
New York, NY 10003
*Comedian*
*Birthday: 2/4/45*

**Breslin, Jimmy**
*Newsday*
Park Ave.
New York, NY 10016
*Author, columnist*

**Brett, George**
PO Box 419969
Kansas City, MO 64141
*Ex-baseball player*

**Bridges, Beau**
5525 N. Jed Smith Rd.
Hidden Hills, CA 91302
*Actor*
*Birthday: 12/09/41*

**Bridges, Elisa**
1560 Broadway, #1308
New York, NY 10036
*Model*

**Bridges, Jeff**
% Creative Artists Agency
9830 Wilshire Blvd.
Beverly Hills, CA 90212
Or
5525 N. Jed Smith Rd.
Hidden Hills, CA 91302
*Actor*
*Birthday: 12/4/49*

**Bridges, Todd**
3518 Cahuenga Blvd. W., #216
Los Angeles, CA 90068
*Actor*
*Birthday: 5/27/65*

**Bright, Dr. Bill**
515 North Cabrillo Park Dr., #225
Santa Ana, CA 9270
Or
1111 W. Sunset Blvd., Suite #600
Los Angles CA 90012
*Evangelist*

**Brightman, Sarah**
1 Sussex Pl., #1421
London W6 9XT
England
Website: http://www,sarah-
brightman.com/
*Singer, Lord Lloyd Webber created*
*the role of Christine in* Phantom of
the Opera *especially for Sarah*
*Brightman*

**Brill, Charlie**
% Irv Schechter Agency
9300 Wilshire Blvd., #400
Beverly Hills, CA 90212
*Actor*

**Brillstein, Bernie**
Brillstein-Grey Enterprises
9150 Wilshire Blvd.
Beverly Hills, CA 90212
*Theatrical/literary agent*

**Brimley, Wilford**
B-7 Ranch
Lehi, UT 84043
*Actor*
*Birthday: 9/27/34*

**Brinkley, Christie**
1122 S. Robertson Blvd., #15
Los Angeles, CA 90035
*Model, actress*
*Birthday: 2/2/54*

**Broderick, Beth**
9300 Wilshire Blvd., #555
Beverly Hills, CA 90212
*Actress*

**Broderick, Matthew**
PO Box 69646
Los Angeles, CA 90069
*Actor*
*Birthday: 3/21/62*

**Brokaw, Tom (Thomas John Brokaw)**
NBC News
30 Rockefeller Plaza
New York, NY 10112
E-mail: mailto:nightly@nbc.com
*Television broadcast executive, correspondent*
*Birthday: 2/6/40*

**Brolin, James**
PO Box 56927
Sherman Oaks, CA 91413
*Actor*
*Birthday: 7/18/40*

**Bronson, Charles**
PO Box 2644
Malibu, CA 90265
*Actor*
*Birthday: 11/03/22*

**Brooks, Albert (Albert Einstein)**
1880 Century Park East, #900
Los Angeles, CA 90067
*Actor, writer, director*
*Birthday: 7/22/47*

**Brooks, Foster**
315 S. Beverly Dr., #216
Beverly Hills, CA 90212
*Comedian*

**Brooks, Garth (Troyal Garth Brooks)**
1111 17th. Ave. S.
Nashville, TN 37212
*Country singer*
*Birthday: 2/7/62*

**Brooks, James L.**
8942 Wilshire Blvd.
Beverly Hills, CA 90211
*Producer, director, screenwriter*
*Birthday: 5/9/40*

**Brosnan, Pierce**
PO Box 982
Malibu, CA 90265
*Actor*
*Birthday: 5/15/53*

**Brother, Phelps**
PO Box 849
Goodlettsville, TN 37070
*Country singer*

**Brothers, Dr. Joyce**
235 E. 45th St.
New York, NY 10017
*TV personality, psychologist*
*Birthday: 10/20/28*

**Brown, Bryan**
110 Queen St.
Woollahra NSW 2025
Australia
*Actor*
*Birthday: 6/23/47*

**Brown, Denise**
PO Box 380
Monarch Bay, CA 92629
*Nicole Brown-Simpson's sister*

**Brown, Georg Stanford**
% International Artists
8033 Sunset Blvd., #1800
Los Angeles, CA 90046
*Actor*

**Brown, Jim**
1851 Sunset Plaza Dr.
Los Angeles, CA 90069
*Actor, ex-football player*
*Birthday: 2/17/36*

**Brown, Jim Ed**
PO Box 121089
Nashville, TN 37212
*Country singer*

**Brown, "Downtown" Julie**
250 W. 57th St., #821
New York, NY 10107
*Actress*

**Brown, Junior**
PO Box 180763
Utica, MI 48318
*Country music singer*

**Brown, Marty**
PO Box 70
Maceo, KY 42355
*Country music singer*

**Brown, Olivia**
% David Shapira and Assoc.
15301 Ventural Blvd., Suite #345
Sherman Oaks, CA 91403
*Actress*

**Brown, T. Graham**
PO Box 50337
Nashville, TN 37205
*Country music singer*

**Brown, Mayor Willie Jr.**
401 Van Ness Ave., #336
San Francisco, CA 94102
Email: DaMayor%ci.sf.ca.us
*Mayor of San Francisco*

**Browne, Jann**
PO Box 3481
Laguna Hills, CA 92654
*Musician*

**Browne, Sylvia**
35 Dillon Ave.
Campbell, CA 95008
*Pyschic*

**Browning, Kurt**
11160 River Valley Rd., #3189
Edmonton
Alberta, T5J 2G7
Canada
*Ice skater*

**Bruce, Ed**
PO Box 120428
Nashville, TN 37212
*Country music singer*

**Buchanan, James M.**
George Mason University
4400 University Dr.
Fairfax, VA 22030
*Nobel Prize winner in Economic
Science, 1986. He is best known
for such works as Fiscal Theory
and Political Economy, The
Calculus of Consent, The Limits of
Liberty, Democracy in Deficit, The
Power to Tax, and The Reason of
Rules*

**Buchanan, Pat**
6862 Elm St., #210
McLean, VA 22101
Website: http://
www.gopatgo2000.org/
*Presidential candidate*

**Buckley, Betty**
420 Madison Ave., #1400
New York, NY 10017
*Actress
Birthday: 7/3/47*

**Buckley, William F. Jr.**
150 E. 35th St.
New York, NY 10016
*Author, editor
Birthday: 11/24/25*

**Buffett, Jimmy**
540 S. Ocean Blvd.
Palm Beach, FL 33480
Or
550-B Duval St.
Key West, FL 33040
*Pop singer, his fans are called
"Parrot Heads."*

**Bullock, Sandra**
PO Box 161090
Austin, TX 78716
*Actress*

**Bunning, Jim**
% Baseball Hall of Fame
PO Box 590
Cooperstown, NY 13326
*Baseball player*

**Bure, Pavel**
% Vancouver Canucks
100 N. Renfrew St.
Vancouver, BC V5K 3N7
Canada
*Hockey player*

**Burghoff, Gary**
13834 Magnolia Blvd.
Encino, CA 91423
*Actor
Birthday: 5/25/40*

**Burke, Delta**
1012 Royal St.
New Orleans, LA 70116
*Actress
Birthday: 7/30/56*

**Burnett, Carol**
7800 Beverly Blvd.
Los Angeles, CA 90036
*Actress, comedienne
Birthday: 4/26/33*

**Burnette, Billy**
1025 16th Ave. So., Suite #401
Nashville, TN 37212
*Country music singer*

**Burnin' Daylight Fan Club**
PO Box 180763
Utica, MI 48318
*Country music fan club*

**Burns, Ken**
Maple Grove Rd.
Walpole, NH 03608
*Documentary maker
Birthday: 7/29/53*

**Burstyn, Ellen**
PO Box 217
Palisades, NY 10964
*Actress*

**Burton, LeVar**
13601 Ventura Blvd., #209
Sherman Oaks, CA 91423
*Actor*
*Birthday: 2/16/57*

**Burton, Tim**
445 Redondo Ave., #7
Long Beach, CA 90814

**Bush, George and Barbara**
9 W. Oak Dr.
Houston, TX 77056
*Former President and First Lady*
*Birthday: Barbara Bush: 1/28/25*
*Birthday: George Bush: 1/12/24*

**Bush, President George W.**
The White House
1600 Pennsylvania Avenue
Washington, DC 20500

**Bush, Jeb**
The Capitol
Tallahassee, FL 32399
*Governor of Florida, son of former President George Bush*

**Busey, Gary**
12424 Wilshire Blvd., #840
Los Angeles, CA 90025
Or
18424 Coastline Dr.
Malibu, CA 90265
*Actor*
*Birthday: 6/29/44*

**Butkus, Dick**
% Excalibur Marketing Group
Attn: Paula Maki
523 W. Chapman Ave., #110
Anaheim, CA 92802
*Ex-football player*

**Butler, Brett**
8942 Wilshire Blvd.
Beverly Hills, CA 90211
*Comedienne*

**Butler, Robert**
% William Morris Agency
151 El Camino Dr.
Beverly Hills, CA 90212
*Film director*

**Buttafuoco, Joey**
PO Box 355
Chatsworth, CA 91313
*Convicted in the Amy Fisher case*
*Birthday: 3/11/56*

**Buttafuoco, Mary Jo**
PO Box 355
Chatsworth, CA 91313
*Joey's wife, shot by Amy Fisher*

**Buzzi, Ruth**
% Sesame Street (CTW)
1 Lincoln Plaza
New York, NY 10023
*Comedienne*
*Birthday: 7/24/36*

**Byner, Jon**
1 S. Ocean Blvd., #316
Boca Raton, FL 33432
*Comedian*

**Tracy Byrd Fan Club**
"Byrd Watchers"
PO Box 7703
Beaumont, TX 77726
*Country music fan club*

**Byrnes, Edd**
PO Box 1623
Beverly Hills, CA 90213
*Played Kookie on* 77 Sunset Strip
*Actor*
*Birthday: 7/30/?*

**C**

**Caan, James**
PO Box 6646
Denver, CO 80206
*Actor*
*Birthday: 3/25/39*

**Caballe, Montserrat**
Caball
Via Augusta 59
Barcelona 08006
Spain
*Opera singer*

**Cage, Nicolas (Nicholas Coppola)**
1122 S. Robertson Blvd., #15
Los Angeles, CA 90035
*Actor*
*Birthday: 1/7/64*

**Cain, Dean**
1122 S. Robertson Blvd., #15
Los Angeles, CA 90035
*Actor*

**Caine, Michael**
Rectory Farm House
North Stoke
GB-Oxfordshire
England
Or
% International Creative
Management
8942 Wilshire Blvd.
Beverly Hills, CA 90211
*Actor*
*Birthday: 3/14/33*

**Callas, Charlie**
PO Box 67-B-69
Los Angeles, CA 90067
*Comedian, actor*
*Birthday: 11/30/64*

**Calley, Lt. William**
% V. V. Vicks
Cross Country Plaza
Columbus, GA 31906
*Involved in the Mi Lai Massacre*

**Camacho, Hector "Macho"**
4751 Yardarm Ln.
Boynton Beach, FL 33436
*Prizefighter*

**Cameron, Candace**
PO Box 8665
Calabasas, CA 91372
*Actress*

**Cameron, James**
3500 W. Olive Ave., #1400
Burbank, CA 91505
Or
919 Santa Monica Blvd.
Santa Monica, CA 90401
*Director*

**Cameron, Kirk**
PO Box 8665
Calabasas, CA 91372
*Actor*
*Birthday: 10/12/70*

**Camp, Shawn**
PO Box 121972
Nashville, TN 37212
*Country music singer*

**Campbell, Bruce**
14431 Ventura Blvd., #120
Sherman Oaks, CA 91423
*Actor*

**Bruce Campbell International Fan Club**
BC CENTRAL
8205 Santa Monica Blvd., #1-287
Los Angeles, CA 90046
*Please include a self-addressed
stamped envelope or e-mail
janholbrk@aol.com for information.*

**Campbell, Glen**
10351 Santa Monica Blvd., #300
Los Angeles, CA 90025
*Singer, songwriter*
*Birthday: 4/22/36*

**Campbell, J. Kenneth**
9150 Wilshire Blvd., #175
Beverly Hills, CA 90212
*Actress*

**Campbell, ex-PM Kim**
Canadian Consulate
550 S. Hope St.
Los Angeles, CA 90071
*Former Canadian Prime Minister*

**Campbell, Neve**
% Creative Artists Agency
9830 Wilshire Blvd.
Beverly Hills, CA 90212
*Actress, dancer*
*Birthday: 10/3/73*

**Campbell, Stacy Dean**
1105-C 16th Ave. So.
Nashville, TN 37212
*Country singer*

**Campbell, Tisha**
5750 Wilshire Blvd., #640
Los Angeles, CA 90036
*Actress*

**Candiotti, Tom**
% Los Angeles Dodgers
1000 Elysian Park Ave.
Los Angeles, CA 90012
*Baseball player*

**Cannell, Steven J.**
7083 Hollywood Blvd.
Hollywood, CA 90028
Website: http://www.cannell.com/
*Author, TV producer*

**Cannon, Dyan**
8033 Sunset Blvd., #254
Los Angeles, CA 90046
*Actress*
*Birthday: 1/04/39*

**Cannon, J. D.**
45 W. 60th St., #10J
New York, NY 10023
*Actor*

**Canova, Diana**
1800 Ave. of the Stars, #400
Los Angeles, CA 90067
*Actress*

**Canyon, Christy**
13601 Ventura Blvd., #218
Sherman Oaks, CA 91423
*Actress*

**Capra, Francis**
% WMA
1325 Ave. of the Americas
New York, NY 10019
*Actor*

**Capshaw, Kate**
PO Box 869
Pacific Palisades, CA 90272
*Actress*

**Cara, Irene**
8033 Sunset Blvd., #735
Los Angeles, CA 90046
*Actress*
*Birthday: 3/18/59*

**Cardin, Pierre**
59 Rue du Foubourg
St. Honore
Paris F-75008
France
*Fashion designer*
*Birthday: 7/7/22*

**Carey, Drew**
955 S. Carillo Dr., #100
Los Angeles, CA 90048
*Actor*

**Carey, Harry, Jr.,**
PO Box 3256
Durango, CO 81302
*Actor*

**Carey, Mariah**
345 N. Maple Dr., #300
Beverly Hills, CA 90210
*Singer*
*Birthday: 3/26/70*

**Carey, Philip**
56 W. 66th St.
New York, NY 10023
*Actor*

**Carey, Ron**
419 N. Larchmont Blvd.
Los Angeles, CA 90004
*Actor*

**Carey, Ron**
25 Louisiana Ave., N.W.
Washington, DC 20001
*Teamster president*

**Carli, Claudio**
V. Aldo Banzi, 66
Rome 00128
Italy

**Carlin, George**
11911 San Vicente Blvd., #348
Los Angeles, CA 90049
*Comedian, actor*
*Birthday: 5/12/?*

**Carlos, King Juan**
Palacio de la Carcuela
Madrid
Spain
*King of Spain*

**Carlson, Paulette**
1906 Chet Atkins Pl., #502
Nashville, TN 37212
*Country singer*

**Carlton, Steve**
555 S. Camino Del Rio, #B2
Durango, CO 81301
*Ex-baseball player*

**Carney, Art**
RR #20 Box 911
Westbrook, CT 06498
*Actor*
*Birthday: 11/14/18*

**Caroline, Princess**
Villa Le Clos
St. Pierre ave.
Saint Martin
Monte Carlo
Monaco
*Birthday: 1/23/57*

**Caron, Leslie**
10 av. George V
F-75116 Paris
France
*Actress*
*Birthday: 7/01/31*

**Carpenter, Mary Chapin**
15030 Ventura Blvd., #1–710
Sherman Oaks, CA 91403
*Country singer*

**Carpenter, Richard**
PO Box 1084
Downey, CA 90240
*Singer*

**Carpenter, Lt. Cmdr. Scott**
55 E. 87th St., #4A
New York, NY 10128
*Astronaut*

**Carr, Vikki**
PO Box 780968
San Antonio, TX 78278
*Singer*
*Birthday: 7/19/41*

**Carradine, David**
628 S. San Fernando Rd., #C
Burbank, CA 91505
*Actor*
*Birthday: 12/08/36*

**Carradine, Keith**
PO Box 460
Placerville, CO 81430
*Actor*
*Birthday: 8/8/49*

**Carrera, Barbara**
PO Box 7631
Beverly Hills, CA 90212
*Actress, Bond girl*
*Birthday: 12/31/45*

**Carrere, Tia**
8228 Sunset Blvd., #300
Los Angeles, CA 90048
*Actress*
*Birthday: 1/6/67*

**Carrey, Jim**
% United Talent Agency
9560 Wilshire Blvd., Suite 500
Beverly Hills, CA 90212
Or
PO Box 57593
Sherman Oaks, CA 91403
*Actor, comedian*
*Birthday: 1/17/62*

**Carroll, Diahann**
PO Box 2999
Beverly Hills, CA 90213
*Actress*
*Birthday: 7/17/35*

**Carson, Jeff**
1002 18th Ave. S.
Nashville, TN 37212
*Country singer*

**Jeff Carson International Fan Club**
PO Box 121056
Nashville, TN 37212
*Country music fan club*

**Carter, Carlene**
PO Box 120845
Nashville, TN 37212
*Singer, musician*

**Carter, Dixie**
10635 Santa Monica Blvd., #130
Los Angeles, CA 90025
*Actress*

**Carter, The Honorable President Jimmy**
1 Woodlawn Dr.
Plains, GA 31780
Website: http://
www.cartercenter.org/home.html
*Former President*

**Carter, Jack**
11365 Ventura Blvd., #100
Studio City, CA 91604
Or
1023 Chevy Chase Dr.
Beverly Hills, CA 90210
*Comedian*
*Birthday: 6/25/23*

**Carter, Lynda**
9200 Harrington Dr.
Potomac, MD 20854
*Actress*
*Birthday: 7/24/51*

**Carter, Nell**
8484 Wilshire Blvd., #500
Beverly Hills, CA 90211
*Actress*
*Birthday: 9/13/48*

**Carter, Rosalyn**
1 Woodlawn Dr.
Plains, GA 31780
*Former first lady*

**Carter, Rubin "Hurricane"**
PO Box 295
College Park, MD 20741
*Former boxer, subject of the film*
Hurricane

**Carter-Cash, June**
700 E. Main St.
Hendersonville, TN 38340
*Country singer*
*Birthday: 6/22/29*

**Cartwright, Angela**
10143 Riverside Dr.
Toluca Lake, CA 91602
*Actress*

**Cartwright, Lionel**
27 Music Square E., #182
Nashville, TN 37203
*Country singer*

**Caruso, David**
270 N. Canon Dr., #1058
Beverly Hills, CA 90210
*Actor*

**Carville, James**
209 Pennsylvania Ave. SE, #800
Washington, DC 20003
*Political commentator*

**Casaroli, Agostino Cardinal**
00120 Vatican City State
Vatican

**Case, Steve**
22000 AOL Way
Dulles, VA 20166
Website: http://hometown.aol.com/
stevecase/index.html
E-mail: SteveCase@aol.com
*Chairman and CEO of America
Online*

**Cash, Johnny**
700 E. Main St.
Hendersonville, TN 38340
*Country singer*
*Birthday: 2/26/32*

**Cash, Rosalind**
PO Box 1605
Topanga, CA 90290
*Actress*

**Cash, Rosanne**
326 Carlton Ave., #3
Brooklyn, NY 11205
*Country singer*
*Birthday: 5/24/55*

**Casals, Rosie**
PO Box 537
Sausalito, CA 94966
*Tennis player*

**Casper, Billy**
PO Box 210010
Chula Vista, CA 91921
*Professional golfer*
*Birthday: 6/4/31*

**Cassidy, David**
3799 Las Vegas Blvd. S.
Las Vegas, NV 89109
*Actor, singer*
*Birthday: 4/12/50*

**Cassidy, Shaun**
8484 Wilshire Blvd., #500
Beverly Hills, CA 90212
*Actor, singer*
*Birthday: 9/27/58*

**Cates, Phoebe**
1636 3rd Ave., #309
New York, NY 10128
*Actress*
*Birthday: 7/16/63*

**Cavett, Dick**
109 E. 79th St., #2C
New York, NY 10021
*TV host*
*Birthday: 11/19/36*

**Cetera, Peter**
8900 Wilshire Blvd., #300
Beverly Hills, CA 90211
*Singer, musician*
*Birthday: 9/13/44*

**Chabert, Lacey**
9000 Sunset Blvd., #525
Los Angeles, CA 90069
*Actress*

**Chan, Jackie**
#303–305 Austin Tower, #400
Tsimsatsui
Austin Kowloon
China
*Actor*
*Birthday: 4/7/54*

**Chance, Jeff**
PO Box 2977
Hendersonville, TN 37077
*Country singer*

**Chao, Rosalind**
2211 Corinth, #210
Los Angeles, CA 90064
*Actress*
*Birthday: 9/23/49*

**Chaplin, Ben**
2–4 Noel St.
GB-London W1V 3RB
England
*Actor*

**Charlie Chaplin Fan Club**
300 S. Topanga Canyon
Topanga, CA 90290

**Chapman, Cee Cee**
PO Box 1422
Franklin, TN 37065
*Country singer*

**Chapman, Mark David**
#81 A 3860
Box 149
Attica Correctional Facility
Attica, NY 14011
*Assassinated John Lennon*

**Chapman, Tracy**
120 W. 44th St., #704
New York, NY 10036
*Singer*
*Birthday: 3/20/64*

**Charisse, Cyd**
10724 Wilshire Blvd., #1406
Los Angeles, CA 90024
*Actress*
*Birthday: 3/3/23*

**Charles, Ray (Ray Charles Robinson)**
2107 W. Washington Blvd., #200
Los Angeles, CA 90018
*Singer, songwriter*
*Birthday: 3/23/30*

**Charleson, Leslie**
% *General Hospital*—ABC-TV
4151 Prospect Ave.
Los Angeles, CA 90027
*Soap opera star*

**Charo**
532 Portlock Rd.
Honolulu, HI 96825
Or
% Reef Towers
227 Lewers St.
Honolulu, HI 96814
*Actress, guitarist*
*Birthday: 1/15/51*

**HRH Charles, Prince of Wales (Charles Philip Arthur George Windsor)**
Highgrove House
Doughton
Tetbury GL8 8TN
England
*Heir to the Throne*
*Birthday: 11/14/48*

**Chase, Chevy (Cornelius Crane Chase)**
955 S. Carillo Dr., #200
Los Angeles, CA 90048
*Actor, comedian*
*Birthday: 10/8/43*

**Cheney, Vice President Dick**
Admiral House
34th and Massachusetts
Washington, DC 20005

**Cher (Cherilyn Sarkisian La Piere)**
% William Morris Agency
151 El Camino Dr.
Beverly Hills, CA 90212
Or
PO Box 2425
Milford, CT 06460
*Actress, director, singer*
*Birthday: 5/20/46*

**Chesnutt, Mark**
PO Box 120544
Nashville, TN 37212
*Country singer*

**Chiao, Leroy**
% NASA
Johnson Space Center
Astronaut Office/Mail Code CB
2101 NASA Rd. 1
Houston, TX 77058
*Astronaut*

**Childs, Andy**
PO Box 24563
Nashville, TN 37202
*Country singer*

**Chin, Tsai**
8383 Wilshire Blvd., #550
Beverly Hills, CA 90211
*Actress*

**Chong, Rae Dawn**
% Metropolitan Talent Agency
4526 Wilshire Blvd.
Los Angeles, CA 90010
*Actress*
*Birthday: 2/28/61*

**Chow, Amy**
% West Valley Gymnastics School
1190 Del Ave., #1
Campbell, CA 95008
Or
% US Gymnastics Federation
201 S. Capitol Ave, Suite 300
Indianapolis, IN 46225
*Gymnast*

**Christensen, Helena**
% Marilyn Gaulthiar Agence
62 bd. Sebastopol
Paris F-75003
France
*Supermodel*

**Cristo**
48 Howard St.
New York, NY 10013
*Artist*

**Claiborne, Liz**
650 Fifth Ave.
New York, NY 10019
*Fashion designer*

**Clapton, Eric**
46 Kensington Ct.
London W8 5DP
England
*Musician*
*Birthday: 3/30/45*

**Buddy Clark Fan Club**
2914 Westmoreland Dr.
Houston, TX 77063

**Clark, Dick**
3003 W. Olive Ave.
Burbank, CA 91505
*TV host, producer*
*Birthday: 11/30/29*

**Clark, Joe**
707 7th Ave. SW, #1300
Calgary
Alberta T2P 3H6
Canada
*Birthday: 1939*
*Ex–Prime minister of Canada*

**Clark, Marcia**
151 El Camino Dr.
Beverly Hills, CA 90212
*Prosecutor in the O. J. Simpson criminal trial*

**Clark, Roy**
1800 Forest Blvd.
Tulsa, OK 74114
*Musician*
*Birthday: 8/16/33*

**Terri Clark International Fan Club**
PO Box 1079
Gallatin, TN 37066
*Country singer*

**Clark, Susan**
Georgian Bay Productions
3815 W. Olive Ave., #202
Burbank, CA 91505
*Actress*
*Birthday: 3/08/44*

**Clay, Andrew Dice**
836 N. La Cienega Blvd., #202
Los Angeles, CA. 90069
*Comedian, actor*

**Clayburgh, Jill**
PO Box 18
Lakeville, CT 06039
*Actress*
*Birthday: 4/30/44*

**Claydermann, Richard**
% Delphine Records
150 bd. Haussmann
Paris 75008
France
*Musician*
*Birthday: 12/28/53*

**Cleese, John**
82 Ladbroke Rd.
London W11 3NU
England
*Comedian, actor*
*Birthday: 10/27/39*

**Clemens, Roger**
% New York Yankees
Yankee Stadium
161st St. and River Ave.
Bronx, NY 10451
*Baseball player*
*Birthday: 8/4/62*

**Patsy Cline Fan Club**
Box 244
Dorchester, MA 02125

**Always Patsy Cline**
PO Box 2236
Winchester, VA 22604
*Patsy Cline fan club*

**Clinton, Hillary Rodham**
United States Senate
Washington, DC 20510
*New York Senator, former First
Lady*

**Cloke, Kirsten**
% The Gersh Agency
PO Box 5617
Beverly Hills, CA 90210
*Actress*

**Clooney, George**
4000 Warner Blvd., #B81-117
Burbank, CA 91522
*Actor; aunt is Rosemary Clooney*
*Birthday: 5/6/61*

**Close, Glenn**
9830 Wilshire Blvd.
Beverly Hills, CA 90212
*Actress*
*Birthday: 3/19/47*

**Clovers, The**
Rt. 1, Box 56
Belvedere, NC 90212
*Music group*

**Coca, Imogene**
PO Box 5151
Westport, CT 06881
*Actress*
*Birthday: 11/18/08*

**Cochran, Johnnie L.**
2373 Hobart Blvd.
Los Angeles, CA 90027
*Lawyer in O. J. Simpson trial*

**Cocker, Joe**
16830 Ventura Blvd., #501
Encino, CA 91436
*Singer*
*Birthday: 5/20/42*

**Coe, David Allan**
PO Box 270188
Nashville, TN 37227-0188
*Country singer*

**Coen, Ethan**
% United Talent Agency
9560 Wilshire Blvd., Suite #516
Beverly Hills, CA 90212
*Screenwriter*
*Birthday: 9/21/37*

**Coen, Joel**
% United Talent Agency
9560 Wilshire Blvd., Suite #516
Beverly Hills, CA 90212
*Film director, writer*
*Birthday: 11/29/54*

**Cohn, Mindy**
9300 Wilshire Blvd., #400
Beverly Hills, CA 90212
*Actress*
*Birthday: 5/20/66*

**Cole, Gary**
1122 S. Robertson Blvd., #15
Los Angeles, CA 90035
*Actor*
*Birthday: 9/27/50*

**Cole, Natalie**
955 S. Carillo Dr., #200
Los Angeles, CA 90048
*Singer*
*Birthday: 2/08/50*

**Coleman, Jack**
%Innovative Artists
1999 Ave. of the Stars, #2850
Los Angeles, CA 90067
*Actor*
*Birthday: 2/21/58*

**Collie, Mark**
3322 West End Ave., #520
Nashville, TN 37203
*Country singer*

**Collins, Eileen**
2101 NASA Rd.
Houston, TX 77058
*Astronaut*
*She has the distinction of being the first female space shuttle pilot and the first woman in the United States to command a space shuttle mission*

**Collins, Phil**
30 Ives St.
London SW3 2nd
England
*Musician*
*Birthday: 1/30/?*

**Colvin, Shawn**
30 West 21st St., 7th Floor
New York, NY 10010
*Website: http://www.shawncolvin.com/flashsplash.html*
*Musician*
*Birthday: 1/10/58*

**Combs, Jeffrey**
13601 Ventura Blvd., #349
Sherman Oaks, CA 91423
*Actor*

**Combs, Sean "Puff Daddy"**
8436 W. 3rd. St., #650
Los Angeles, CA 90048
*Musician*
*Birthday: 11/9/69*

**Conlee, John**
38 Music Sq. E., #117
Nashville, TN 37203
*Country music singer*

**Conley, Earl Thomas**
657 Baker Rd.
Smyrna, TN 37167
*Country singer*

**Conn, Didi**
1901 Ave. of the Stars, #1450
Los Angeles, CA 90067
*Actress*
*Birthday: 7/13/57*

**Connery, Jason**
% Joy Jameson Ltd.
The Plaza
535 Kings Road, #19
London SW10 OSZ
England
*Actor, son of Sean Connery*
*Birthday: 1/11/63*

**Connery, Sean**
% Creative Artists Agency
9830 Wilshire Blvd.
Beverly Hills, CA 90212
*Birthday: 8/25/30*

**Conrad-Hefner, Kimberly**
% Playmate Promotions
9492 Beverly Blvd.
Beverly Hills, CA 90210

**Conrad, Robert**
PO Box 5067
Bear Valley, CA 95223
*Actor*
*Birthday: 3/1/35*

**Constantine, Kevin**
% Pittsburgh Penguins
Civic Arena, Gate 9
Pittsburgh, PA 15219
Website: http://
www.pittsburghpenguins.com/
E-mail:
coaches@
mail.pittsburghpenguins.com
*Head coach of the Pittsburgh
Penguins*

**Constantin, HRH**
4 Linnell Dr., Hampstead Way
London NW11
England
*Ex-King*

**Constantine, Michael**
1800 Ave. of the Stars, #400
Los Angeles, CA 90067
*Actor*
*Birthday: 5/22/27*

**Conway, Tim**
PO Box 17047
Encino, CA 91416
*Actor*
*Birthday: 11/14/33*

**Coolio**
6733 Sepulveda Blvd., #270
Los Angeles, CA 90045
*Rap artist*
*Birthday: 8/1/63*

**Copperfield, David (David Kotkin)**
1122 S. Robertson Blvd., #15
Los Angeles, CA 90035
Or
515 Post Oak Blvd., #300
Houston, TX 77027
Website: http://
www.dcopperfield.com
*Magician*
*Birthday: 9/15/56*

**Corea, Chick**
2635 Grifith Park Blvd.
Los Angeles, CA 90039
E-mail: CCoreaProd@aol.com
*Musician*
*Birthday: 6/12/41*

**Corgan, Billy**
9830 Wilshire Blvd.
Beverly Hills, CA 90212
*Musician, lead singer of Smashing Pumpkins*
*Birthday: 3/17/67*

**The Official Danielle Cormack Fan Club**
Ephiny of the Amazons
PO Box 459
Hermosa Beach, CA 90254
Website http://members.aol.com/dancorfans/index.html
E-mail: DanCorFans@aol.com

**Corman, Roger**
11611 San Vicente Blvd.
Los Angeles, CA 90049
*Film producer*

**Cornelius, Helen**
PO Box 121089
Nashville, TN 37212
*Country singer*

**Cort, Bud**
955 S. Carillo Dr., #300
Los Angeles, CA 90048
*Actor*

**Cortese, Dan**
15250 Ventura Blvd., #900
Sherman Oaks, CA 91403
*Actor*

**Cosby, Bill**
Box 88
Greenfield, MA 01301
*Comedian, actor*
*Birthday: 7/11/37*

**Cossette, Pierre**
8899 Beverly Blvd., #100
Los Angeles, CA 90036
*Producer*

**Costello, Elvis (Declan Patrick McManus)**
9028 Gr. Guest Rd.
Middlesex TW8 9EW
England
*Musician*
*Birthday: 8/25/54*

**Costner, Kevin**
PO Box 275
Montrose, CA 91021
*Actor, director, producer*
*Birthday: 1/18/55*

**Coulier, David**
9150 Wilshire Blvd., #350
Beverly Hills, CA 90212
*Actor*

**Coulthard, David**
% McLaren Int'l Ltd.
Woking Business Park
Albert Dr.
Woking
GB-Surrey GU21 5JS
*Professional Formula-1 driver*

**Couric, Katie**
NBC
30 Rockefeller Plaza
New York, NY 10122
*Broadcast journalist*
*Birthday: 1/7/57*

**Courier, Jim**
% IMG
1 Erieview Plaza, #1300
Cleveland, OH 44114
*Professional tennis player*
*Birthday: 8/17/70*

**Cox Arquette, Courtney**
1122 S. Robertson Blvd., #15
Los Angeles, CA 90035
*Actress*
*Birthday: 6/15/64*

**Cox, DeAnna**
818 18th Ave. S.
Nashville, TN 37203
*Country singer*

**Craddock, Billy "Crash"**
21 Laconwood Dr.
Springfield, IL 62707
*Country singer*

**Craig, Jenny**
PO Box 387190
La Jolla, CA 92038
*Diet company founder*

**Craig, Yvonne**
PO Box 827
Pacific Palisades, CA 90272
*Actress*

**Craven, Wes**
8491 Sunset Blvd., #375
West Hollywood, CA 90069
*Film director*
*Birthday: 8/2/39*

**Crawford, Cindy**
1122 S. Robertson Blvd., #15
Los Angeles, CA 90035
*Model, actress*
*Birthday: 2/20/66*

**Crawford, Michael**
10 Argyle St.
London W1V 1AB
England
*Singer*
*Birthday: 1/19/52*

**Cray, Robert**
Box 170429
San Francisco, CA 94117
*Musician*

**Creme, Benjamin**
59 Darmouth Park Rd.
London
NW5 1SL
England
*New Age speaker, author*

**Creole, Kid**
42 Molyneaux St.
London W1
England
*Musician*

**Crenna, Richard**
% Creative Artists Agency
9830 Wilshire Blvd.
Beverly Hills, CA 90212
*Actor*
*Birthday: 11/30/27*

**Cronenberg, David**
217 Avenue Rd.
Toronto
Ontario M5R 2J3
Canada
*Film director*
*Birthday: 3/15/43*

**Cronkite, Walter**
51 W. 52nd. St., #1934
New York, NY 10019
*News broadcaster*
*Birthday: 11/4/16*

**Crook, Lorianne**
% Jim Owens Assoc.
1515 McGavock
Nashville, TN 37203
*TV host*

**Crook and Chase**
1525 McGavock St.
Nashville, TN 37203
*Talk show hosts*

**Bing Crosby Fan Club**
% W. Martin
435 S. Holmes Ave.
Kirkwood, MO 63122

**Bing Crosby Historical Society**
PO Box 216
Tacoma, WA 98403

**Crosby, David**
PO Box 9008
Solvang, CA 93464
*Musician*
*Birthday: 8/14/41*

**Crosby, Norm**
% Jono Productions, Inc.
5750 Wilshire Blvd., #580
Los Angeles, CA 90036
*Comedian*
*Birthday: 9/15/27*

**Crosby, Rob**
PO Box 121551
Nashville, TN 37212
*Country musician*

**Crosby, Stills and Nash**
9830 Wilshire Blvd.
Beverly Hills, CA 90212
*Music group*

**Cross, Christopher**
PO Box 5156
Santa Barbara, CA 93150
Website: http://
www.christophercross.com/
*Singer*
*Birthday: 5/12/48*

**Crow, Sheryl**
10345 W. Olympic Blvd., #200
Los Angeles, CA 90064
*Singer, songwriter*

**Crowe, Cameron**
9830 Wilshire Blvd.
Beverly Hills, CA 90212
*Director*
*Birthday: 7/13/?*

**Crowded House**
3 Mitchell Rd.
Rose Bay
Sydney NSW 2929
Australia
*Music group*

**Crowell, Rodney**
1514 South St., #100
Nashville, TN 37212
*Musician*
*Birthday: 8/17/50*

**Fans of Rodney Crowell**
PO Box 120576
Nashville, TN 37212
*Country music singer fan club*

**Cruise, Tom**
955 S. Carillo Dr., #200
Los Angeles, CA 90048
*Actor*
*Birthday: 7/3/62*

**Cryner, Bobbie**
PO Box 2147
Hendersonville, TN 37077
*Country singer*

**Crystal, Billy**
9830 Wilshire Blvd., #500
Beverly Hills, CA 90212
*Actor, comedian, director, producer*
*Birthday: 3/14/47*

**Culkin, Macaulay**
9560 Wilshire Blvd., #516
Beverly Hills, CA 90212
*Actor*
*Birthday: 8/26/80*

**Cuomo, ex-Gov. Mario**
50 Sutton Pl. S., #11-G
New York, NY 10022
*Former governor of New York*
*Birthday: 6/15/?*

**Curtin, Jane**
PO Box 1070
Sharon, CT 06069
*Actress*
*Birthday: 9/06/47*

**Curtis-Hall, Vondie**
PO Box 5617
Beverly Hills, CA 90210
*Actress*

**Curtis, Jamie Lee**
% Creative Artists Agency
9830 Wilshire Blvd.
Beverly Hills, CA 90212
*Actress, author*
*Birthday: 11/22/58*

**Cusack, John**
% William Morris Agency
151 S. El Camino Dr.
Beverly Hills, CA 90212
*Actor, producer, stage director*
*Birthday: 6/28/66*

**Cyrus, Billy Ray**
PO Box 1206
Franklin, TN 37115
*Country singer*
*Birthday: 8/25/61*

# D

**D'Abo, Maryam**
9255 Sunset Blvd., #515
Los Angeles, CA 90069
*Actress*

**D'Abo, Olivia**
1122 S. Robertson Blvd., #15
Los Angeles, CA 90035
*Actress*
*Birthday: 1/22/67*

**Daddo, Kathryn**
151 El Camino Dr.
Beverly Hills, CA 90212
*Actress*

**Dahl, Arlene**
% Dahlmark Prod.
PO Box 116
Sparkill, NY 10976
*Actress*
*Birthday: 8/11/28*

**Dallas Cowboy Cheerleaders**
1 Cowboys Pkwy.
Irving, TX 75063

**Dalton, Abby**
PO Box 100
Mammoth Lakes, CA 03546
*Actress*
*Birthday: 8/11/27*

**Dalton, Lacy J.**
820 Cartwirght Rd.
Reno, NV 89511
*Country singer*

**Daltry, Roger**
18/21 Jermyn St., #300
London SW1Y 6hP
England
*Musician*
*Birthday: 3/1/45*

**Daly, Carson**
% MTV
1515 Broadway
New York, NY 10036
*MTV VJ*

**Dana**
4500 Dorr St., PO Box 1000
Toledo, OH 43697
Website: http://www.dana.com
*Joseph M. Magliochetti, Chairman,*
*president, and CEO*
*Motor vehicles and parts*

**Dana, Bill**
PO Box 1792
Santa Monica, CA 90406
*Comedian, actor*

**Dangerfield, Rodney**
10580 Wilshire Blvd., #21-NE
Los Angles, CA 90024
Website: http://www.rodney.com/
*Comedian*

**Daniel, Davis**
PO Box 120186
Nashville, TN 37212
*Country singer*

**Daniels, Charlie**
17060 Central Pike
Lebanon, TN 37087
*Country singer*

**Danza, Tony**
10202 W. Washington Blvd.
David Lean Bldg.
Culver City, CA 90232
*Actor*
*Birthday: 4/21/51*

**Dark Shadows Fan Club**
PO Box 69A04
West Hollywood, CA 90069

**Darren, James**
PO Box 1088
Beverly Hills, CA 90213
*Actor*
*Birthday: 6/9/36*

**Davis, Daniel**
% TriStar (*The Nanny*)
9336 W. Washington Blvd.
Culver City, CA 90232
*Actor*

**Davis, Danny**
38 Music Square E, #300
Nashville, TN 37203
*Country singer*

**Davis, ex-Gov. Jimmie**
PO Box 15826
Baton Rouge, LA 70896
*Former Governor of Louisiana;*
*country singer*

**Davis, Josie**
10635 Santa Monica, Blvd., #130
Los Angeles, CA 90025
*Actress*

**Davis, Linda**
2100 West End Ave., #1000
Nashville, TN 37203
*Musician*

**Davis, Skeeter**
PO Box 1288
Brentwood, TN 37209
*Country singer*

**Davis, Stephanie**
PO Box 121495
Nashville, TN 37212
*Country singer*

**Davies, Gail**
PO Box 150586
Nashville, TN 37221
*Country singer*

**Dawson, Marco**
% PGA Tour
112 TPC Blvd.
Ponte Vedra Beach, FL 32082
*Golfer*

**Day, Doris (Doris von Kappelhoff)**
PO Box 223163
Carmel, CA 93922
*Actress*
*Birthday: 4/1/24*

**Day, Lee**
278 Aspen Ct., Bldg. 15
Stanhope, NJ 07874
*Pet hairstylist, pet entertainer, and
creator of the pet "barkmitzvah"*

**Day-Lewis, Daniel**
46 Albemarle St.
London W1X 4PP
England
*Actor*
*Birthday: 4/20/58*

**De Niro, Robert**
9830 Wilshire Blvd.
Beverly Hills, CA 90212
*Actor*
*Birthday: 8/17/43*

**Dean, Billy**
3310 West End Ave., #500
Nashville, TN 37203
*Country singer*

**Dean, Jimmy**
8000 Centerview Pkwy., #400
Cordova, TN 38018
*Country singer*

**DeAngelis, Barbara**
15332 Antioch St., #504
Pacific Palisades, CA 90272
*Author*

**DeBakey, Dr. Michael**
One Baylor Plaza, #A-902
Houston, TX 77030
*Heart surgeon*

**Dee, Sandra**
% Mr. Larry Martindale Agency
18915 Nordhoff St., Suite #5
Northridge, CA 91324
*Actress*
*Birthday: 4/23/42*

**Dees, Rick**
3400 Riverside Dr., #800
Burbank, CA 91505
*Radio personality*

**DeGeneres, Ellen**
9465 Wilshire Blvd., #444
Beverly Hills, CA 90211
*Actress, comedienne*
*Birthday: 1/26/58*

**DeKlerk, Frederik W.**
120 Plain St.
Priv. Bag X-999
Capetown 8000
Republic of South Africa
*Former South African president
and Nobel laureate*

**Delaney, Kim**
3435 Ocean Park Blvd., Suite
201N
Santa Monica, CA 90405
*Actress*

**DeLuise, Dom**
% Page and Ma Business
Management
11661 San Vicente Blvd. #910
Los Angeles, CA 90049
*Actor*

**DeMornay, Rebecca**
1122 S. Robertson Blvd., #15
Los Angeles, CA 90035
*Actress*

**Dench, Dame Judith**
% Julien Belfrage & Assoc.
46 Albemarle Street, GB
London W1X 4PP
England
*Actress*

**Dennehy, Brian**
121 N. San Vicente Blvd.
Beverly Hills, CA 90211
*Actor*

**Denver, Bob**
PO Box 269
Princeton, WV 24740
*Actor*

**DePalma, Brian**
9830 Wilshire Blvd.
Beverly Hills, CA 90212
*Director*

**Depp, Johnny**
% United Talent Agency
9560 Wilshire Blvd., Suite 500
Beverly Hills, CA 90212
Or

2049 Century Park East, #2500
Los Angeles, CA 90067
*Actor, director, musician,
screenwriter*
*Birthday: 6/9/63*

**Dern, Bruce**
PO Box 1581
Santa Monica, CA 90406
*Actor*

**Dern, Laura**
2401 S. Main St.
Santa Monica, CA 90405
*Actress*
*Birthday: 2/10/67*

**Dershowitz, Alan**
1563 Massachusetts Ave.
Cambridge, MA 02138
*Attorney*

**Deukmejian, ex-Gov. George**
555 W. 5th St.
Los Angeles, CA 90013
*Former governor of California*

**DeVito, Danny**
PO Box 491246
Los Angeles, CA 90049
*Actor*

**DeWitt, Joyce**
101 Ocean Ave., #L-4
Santa Monica, CA 90402
*Actress*
*Birthday: 4/7/?*

**Dey, Susan**
10390 Santa Monica Blvd., #300
Los Angeles, CA 90025
*Actress*
*Birthday: 12/10/52*

**DeYoung, Cliff**
626 Santa Monica Blvd., #57
Santa Monica, CA 90401
*Actor*

**Diana, Princess of Wales
Memorial Fund**
PO Box 1
London WC1B 5HW
England

**Diaz, Cameron**
955 S. Carrillo Dr., #300
Los Angeles, CA 90048
*Actress, model*
*Birthday: 8/30/72*

**Dicaprio, Leonardo**
955 S. Carrillo Dr., #300
Los Angeles, CA 90048
Website: http://www.dicaprio.com
E-mail:
webmaster@pde.paramount.com
*Actor*
*Birthday: 11/11/74*

**Dickens, Little Jimmy (James Cecil
Dickens)**
Grand Ole Opry
PO Box 131
Nashville, TN 37214
*Country musician*

**Dietl, Helmut**
% Diana Film
Ainmillerstr. 33
80801 München
Germany
*Film director*

**Diffie, Joe**
50 Music Square W., #300
Nashville, TN 37203
*Country singer*

**Diller, Phyllis**
11365 Ventura Blvd., #100
Studio City, CA 91604
*Comedienne*

**Dillon, Dean**
PO Box 935
Round Rock, TX 78680
*Country singer*

**Dillon, Matt**
9465 Wilshire Blvd., #419
Beverly Hills, CA 90212
*Actor*
*Birthday: 2/18/64*

**Diniz, Pedro**
% Arrows/TWR Formula One Ltd.
Leafield Technical Centre
Leafield
Whitney
GB-Oxon OX8 5PF
*Professional Formula-1 driver*

**Dinkins, ex-Mayor David**
625 Madison Ave.
New York, NY 10022
*Former mayor of New York*

**Dion, Céline**
4 Place Laval, #500
Laval PQ H7N
Canada
Or
9830 Wilshire Blvd.
Beverly Hills, CA 90212
*Singer*
*Birthday: 3/30/68*

**Dior, Christian**
St. Anna Platz 2
Munich 80538
Germany
*Designer*

**Disney, Roy E.**
% Shamrock Broadcasting Co.
4444 Lakeside Dr.
Burbank, CA 91505
Or
500 S. Buena Vista St.
Burbank, CA 91521
*Broadcasting executive*

**Doherty, Shannen**
9560 Wilshire Blvd., #516
Beverly Hills, CA 90212
*Actress*
*Birthday: 4/12/71*

**Dole, Bob**
700 New Hampshire Ave. NW
Washington, DC 20037
Or
810 First St. NE, #300
Washington, DC 20002
*Former senator from Kansas,*
*senate majority leader, and 1996*
*presidential candidate*

**Dole, Mrs. Elizabeth**
700 New Hampshire Ave. NW
Washington, DC 20037
*Former head of the American Red*
*Cross, former Secretary of*
*Transportation*

**Dolenz, Mickey**
9200 Sunset Blvd., #1200
Los Angeles, CA 90069
*Musician, member of The*
*Monkees*
*Birthday: 3/19/45*

**Domingo, Placido**
157 W. 57th. St. #502
New York, NY 10019
*Tenor*
*Birthday: 1/21/41*

**Donahue, Elinor**
400 S. Beverly Dr., #101
Beverly Hills, CA 90212
*Actress*
*Birthday: 4/19/37*

**Donahue, Phil**
420 E. 54th St., #22F
New York, NY 10022
*Talk show host*
*Birthday: 12/31/35*

**Donner, Richard**
4000 Warner Blvd., #102
Burbank, CA 91522
*Film director*

**Donovan (Leich)**
PO Box 106
Rochdale OL16 4HW
England

**Dorn, Michael**
% Agency for the Performing Arts
9000 Sunset Blvd., Suite 1200
Los Angeles, CA 90069
*Actor*
*Birthday: 12/19/52*

**Douglas, Donna**
PO Box 1511
Huntington Beach, CA 92647
*Actress*
*Birthday: 9/26/39*

**Dow, Tony**
13317 Ventura Blvd., #1
Sherman Oaks, CA 91423
*Actor*

**Downey, Robert Jr.**
20 Waterside Plaza, #28D
New York, NY 10010
*Actor*
*Birthday: 4/4/65*

**Downey, Roma**
55 W. 900 South
Salt Lake City, UT 84101
*Actresss*

**Dr. Alban**
% Dr. Records
Drottningholmsvägen 35
S-11242 Stockholm
Sweden
*Singer*

**Dre, Dr.**
10900 Wilshire Blvd., #1230
Los Angeles, CA 90024
*Musician, rapper, record producer*
*Birthday: 2/18/66*

**Drescher, Fran**
405 S. Beverly Dr., #500
Beverly Hills, CA 90212
*Actress*

**Dreyfus, Richard**
% Addis-Weschler and Assoc.
955 S. Carillo Dr., #300
Los Angeles, CA 90048
*Actor*
*Birthday: 10/29/47*

**Driever, Klaus**
Medienallee 4
Unterföhring 85774
Germany
*Inventor*
*Birthday: 12/10/70*

**Driver, Minnie**
1122 S. Robertson Blvd., #15
Los Angeles, CA 90035
Or
9701 Wilshire Blvd., 10th Floor
Beverly Hills, CA 90212
*Actress*
*Birthday: 1/31/71*

**Dryer, Fred**
1122 S. Robertson Blvd., #15
Los Angeles, CA 90035
Website: http://www.fdprods.com/
*Actor, producer*

**Duchovny, David**
10201 W. Pico Blvd.
Los Angeles, CA 90035
*Actor*
*Birthday: 8/7/60*

**Duffy, Julia**
9255 Sunset Blvd., #1010
Los Angeles, CA 90069
*Actress*

**Duffy, Patrick**
PO Box D
Tarzana, CA 91356
*Actor*
*Birthday: 3/19/49*

**Duke, David**
PO Box 577
Metairie, LA 70004
Or
Box 188
Mandeville, LA 70470
Website: www.davidduke.org
E-mail: davidduke@davidduke.net
*Former Klu Klux Klan leader*
*turned politician*

**Dunaway, Faye**
2311 W. Victory Blvd., #384
Burbank, CA 91506
*Actress*

**Dunn, Holly**
209 10th Ave. South, #347
Nashville, TN 37203
*Singer*

**Dunne, Dominick**
155 E. 49th St.
New York, NY 10017
*Author*

**Dunne, Griffin**
1501 Broadway, #2600
New York, NY 10036
*Actor*
*Birthday: 6/8/55*

**Duvall, James**
% APA
9000 Sunset Blvd., #1200
Los Angeles, CA 90069
*Actor*

**Duvall, Robert**
1122 S. Robertson Blvd., #15
Los Angeles, CA 90035
*Actor*
*Birthday: 1/15/31*

**Duvall, Shelley**
Rt. #1 Box 377-A
Blanco, TX 78606
*Actress, producer*

**Dylan, Bob**
PO Box 870
Cooper Station
New York, NY 10276
*Singer, songwriter*
*Birthday: 5/24/41*

**Dylan, Jakob**
H. K. Management
8900 Wilshire Blvd.
Beverly Hills, CA 90211
*Singer*

**E**

**Eakin, Thomas C.**
2728 Shelley Rd.
Shaker Heights, OH 44122
*Sports promotion executive*
*Birthday: 12/16/33*

**Earl, Steve**
1815 Division St., #295
Nashville, TN 37203
*Country singer*

**Easton, Sheena**
7095 Hollywood Blvd., #469
Hollywood, CA 90028
Website: http://
www.sheenaeaston.com/
*Singer, actress*
*Birthday: 4/29/59*

**Eastwood, Clint**
4000 Warner Blvd., #16
Burbank, CA 91522
*Actor*
*Birthday: 5/29/30*

**Eban, Abba**
PO Box 394
Hertzelia
Israel
*Israel politician and foreign
minister*

**Ebert, Roger**
PO Box 146366
Chicago, IL 60614
*Movie critic*
*Birthday: 6/18/42*

**Ebsen, Buddy**
PO Box 2069
Palos Verdes Peninsula, CA 90274
*Actor*
*Birthday: 4/2/08*

**Eden, Barbara**
PO Box 5556
Sherman Oaks, CA 91403
*Actress*
*Birthday: 8/22/34*

**Edwards, Anthony**
15260 Ventura Blvd., #1420
Sherman Oaks, CA 91403
*Actor*

**Edwards, Blake**
PO Box 491668
Los Angeles, CA 90049
*Producer*

**Eggar, Samantha**
12304 Santa Monica Blvd., #104
Los Angeles, CA 90025
*Actress*

**Eggert, Nicole**
% William Caroll Agency
120 S. Victory Blvd.
Burbank, CA 91502
*Supermodel*

**Eichhorn, Lisa**
1501 Broadway, #2600
New York, NY 10036
*Actress*
*Birthday: 2/4/52*

**Eisner, Michael**
500 S. Buena Vista St.
Burbank, CA 91521
*Entertainment executive*
*Birthday: 4/21/26*

**Ekland, Britt**
280 S. Beverly Dr., #300
Beverly Hills, CA 90212
*Actress*

**Electra, Carmen**
1122 S. Robertson Blvd., #15
Los Angeles, CA 90035
*Actress*

**Elfman, Danny**
345 N. Maple Dr., #385
Beverly Hills, CA 90210
*Musician, composer*

**Elfman, Jenna**
7920 Sunset Blvd., #401
Los Angeles, CA 90069
*Actress*
*Birthday: 9/30/71*

**Elizabeth, HRH Queen II**
Buckingham Palace
London SW1
England

**Elizabeth, HRH Queen Mother**
Clarence House
London SW1
England

**Elizondo, Hector**
15030 Ventura Blvd., #751
Sherman Oaks, CA 91403
*Actor*

**Elliot, Chris**
151 El Camino Dr.
Beverly Hills, CA 90212
*Actor*

**Elliott, David James**
9560 Wilshire Blvd., #516
Beverly Hills, CA 90212
*Actor*

**Elliott, Sam**
151 El Camino Dr.
Beverly Hills, CA 90212
*Actor*

**Elvira (Cassandra Peterson)**
PO Box 38246
Los Angeles, CA 90038
Website: http://www.elvira.com
*Television personality*

**Ely, Joe**
% Campfire Nightmares
7101 Hwy. 71W., Suite A9
Austin, TX 78735
*Country singer*

**Ely, Ron**
151 El Camino Dr.
Beverly Hills, CA 90212
*Actor*

**Embery, Joan**
San Diego Zoo
Park Blvd.
San Diego, CA 92104
*Animal expert, television
personality*

**Emery, Ralph**
PO Box 916
Hendersonville, TN 37033
*Television personality, Nashville
Network talk show host*

**Emilio**
209 10th Ave., #347
Nashville, TN 37077
*Country singer*

**Eminem**
Shady Records
270 Lafayette St., Suite 805
New York, NY 10012
*Rapper*

**Energizer Bunny, The**
800 Chouteau Ave.
St. Louis, MO 63164
*Battery spokesrabbit*

**Engels, Marty**
11365 Ventura Blvd., #100
Studio City, CA 91604
*Comedian*

**England, Ty**
3322 West End Ave., #520
Nashville, TN 37213
*Musician*

**Ty England Fan Club**
PO Box 120964
Nashville, TN 37212

**Engvall, Bill**
8380 Melrose Ave., #310
Los Angeles, CA 90069
*Country comedian*

**Eno, Brian**
330 Harrow Rd.
London W9
England
*Musician*

**Entwhistle, John**
PO Box 241
Lake Peekskill, NY 10537
*Musician*

**Erving, Julius**
PO Box 914100
Longwood, FL 32791
*Basketball player*

**Estefan, Gloria**
151 El Camino Dr.
Bevelry Hills, CA 90212
*Musician, singer*
*Birthday: 9/1/57*

**Estevez, Emilio**
PO Box 4041
Malibu, CA 90264
*Actor*
*Birthday: 5/12/62*

**Eszterhas, Joe**
8942 Wilshire Blvd.
Beverly Hills, CA 90211
*Screenwriter*

**Etheridge, Melissa**
4425 Riverside Dr., #102
Burbank, CA 91505
*Singer*
*Birthday: 5/29/61*

**Eubanks, Bob**
11365 Ventura Blvd., #100
Studio City, CA 91604
*TV game show host*
*Birthday: 1/8/38*

**Eubanks, Kevin**
% *Tonite Show*
NBC Entertainment
3000 W. Alameda Ave.
Burbank, CA 91527

**Eure, Wesley**
PO Box 69405
Los Angeles, CA 90069
*Actor*

**Evangelista, Linda**
% Elite Model Management
111 East 22nd St., 2nd Floor
New York, NY 10010
*Model*

**Everett, Jim**
PO Box 609609
San Diego, CA 92160
*Football player*

**Ewing, Skip**
PO Box 17254
Nashville, TN 37217
*Country singer*

**F**

**Fabares, Shelly (Michelle Marie Fabares)**
PO Box 6010-909
Sherman Oaks, CA 91413
*Actress*
*Birthday: 1/19/42*

**Fahey, Jeff**
8942 Wilshire Blvd.
Beverly Hills, CA 90211
*Actor*

**Fairchild, Barbara**
1078 Skyview Dr.
Branson, MO 65616
*Country singer*

**Falk, Peter**
100 Universal City Plaza
Universal City, CA 91608
*Actor*
*Birthday: 9/26/27*

**Falwell, Rev. Jerry**
PO Box 6004
Forest, VA 24551
*Minister, founder of the Moral Majority, founder of Liberty University*

**Farentino, Debrah**
1199 Ave. of the Stars, #2850
Los Angeles, CA 90067
*Actress*

**Fargo, Donna**
P.O. Box 150527
Nashville, TN 37215
*Country singer*
*Birthday: 11/10/45*

**Farina, Dennis**
955 S. Carrillo Dr., #300
Los Angeles, CA 90048
*Actor*

**Farnsworth, Richard**
PO Box 215
Lincoln, NM 88338
*Actor*
*Birthday: 9/1/20*

**Farrakhan, Rev Louis**
4855 S. Woodlawn Ave.
Chicago, IL 60615
Or
734 W 79th St.
Chicago, IL 60620
*Spokesman for the Nation of Islam*

**Farell, Mike**
MSC 826 PO Box 6010
Sherman Oaks, CA 91413-6010
*Actor*
*Birthday: 2/6/39*

**Farrell, Sharon (Sharon Forthman)**
360 S. Doheny Dr.
Beverly Hills, CA 90211
*Actress*
*Birthday: 12/24/46*

**Farrell, Shea (Edward Leo Farrell III)**
10000 Santa Monica Blvd., #305
Los Angeles, CA 90067
*Actor*
*Birthday: 10/21/57*

**Farrell, Terry**
6500 Wilshire Blvd., #2200
Los Angeles, CA 90648
*Actress*
*Birthday: 11/19/63*

**Faustino, David**
11350 Ventura Blvd., #206
Studio City, CA 91604
*Actor*
*Birthday: 3/7/74*

**Favre, Brett**
% Green Bay Packers
PO Box 10628
Green Bay, WI 54307
*Football player*

**Feiffer, Jules**
RR #1 Box 440
Vineyard Haven, MA 02568
*Political cartoonist*

**Felder, Don**
PO Box 6051
Malibu, CA 90265
*Musician*

**Feldman, Corey**
10960 Wilshire Blvd., #1100
Los Angeles, CA 90024
*Actor*
*Birthday: 3/16/71*

**Feldon, Barbara**
14 East 74th St.
New York, NY 10021
*Birthday: 3/12/?*

**Felix the Cat**
12020 Chandler Blvd., #200
North Hollywood, CA 91607
*Cartoon cat*

**Fender, Freddie**
PO Box 530
Bel Aire, OH 43906
*Country singer*
*Birthday: 6/4/37*

**Ferguson, Marilyn**
PO Box 42211
Los Angeles, CA 90042
*New Age author*

**Ferguson, Tom**
PO Box 50249
Austin, TX 78763
Website: http://www.doctom.com/
E-mail: doctom@doctom.com
*Tom Ferguson is the author of*
Health Online *(Addison-Wesley)*
*and editor and publisher of* The
Ferguson Report: The Newsletter
of Consumer Health Informatics
and Online Health.

**Ferraro, Chris**
% Pittsburgh Penguins
Civic Arena
66 Mario Lemieux Pl.
Pittsburgh, PA 15219
*Hockey player*

**Ferrigno, Lou**
PO Box 1671
Santa Monica, CA 90402
*Actor, bodybuilder*
*Birthday: 11/9/51*

**Field, Sally**
9830 Wilshire Blvd.
Beverly Hills, CA 90212
*Actress*
*Birthday: 11/6/46*

**Fielder, Cecil**
% New York Yankees
Yankee Stadium
E. 161 St. and River Ave.
Bronx, NY 10451
*Baseball player*

**Fierstein, Harvey**
232 N. Canon Dr.
Beverly Hills, CA 90210
*Actor*

**Fiorentino, Linda**
% C.A.A.
9830 Wilshire Blvd.
Beverly Hills, CA 90212
*Actress*
*Birthday: 3/9/30*

**Fishburne, Laurence**
% Paradigm
10100 Santa Monica Blvd., 25th
Floor
Los Angeles, CA 90067
*Actor, playwright, screenwriter,*
*stage director*
*Birthday: 7/30/61*

**Fishel, Danielle**
% Boy Meets World
ABC-TV
2040 Ave. of the Stars
Los Angeles, CA 90064
*Actress*
*Birthday: 5/5/81*

**Fisher, Carrie**
1700 Coldwater Canyon
Beverly Hills, CA 90210
Or
9830 Wilshire Blvd.
Beverly Hills, CA 90212
*Actress, author, daughter of Eddie*
*Fisher and Debbie Reynolds*
*Birthday: 1/1/56*

**Fisher, Frances**
7920 Sunset Blvd., #401
Los Angeles, CA 90046
*Actress*

**Fisher, Joely**
9485 Wilshire Blvd., #430
Beverly Hills, CA 90212
*Actress, singer, half-sister of Carrie
Fisher*

**Fisichella, Giancarlo**
% Jordan Formula-One Ltd.
Silverstone Circuit
Towcester
GB-Northhamptonshire NN12 8TN
England
*Professional Formula-1 driver*

**Flack, Roberta**
1 W. 72nd St.
New York, NY 10022
*Singer*
*Birthday: 2/10/39*

**Flanery, Sean Patrick**
3500 W. Olive Ave., #920
Burbank, CA 91505
*Actor*

**Flatt, Lester**
PO Box 647
Hendersonville, TN 37215
*Musician*

**Fleetwood, Mick**
4905 S. Atlantic Ave.
Daytona Beach, FL 32127
*Musician*

**Fleming, Peggy**
% Studio Fan Mail
1122 S. Robertson Blvd., Suite #15
Los Angeles, CA 90035
*Actress, ice skater*
*Birthday: 7/27/48*

**Fletcher, Louise**
PO Box 64656
Los Angeles, CA 90064
*Actress*

**Flintstones, The**
3400 Cahuenga Blvd.
Los Angeles, CA 90068
*A modern stoneage family*

**Flockhart, Calista**
PO Box 5617
Beverly Hills, CA 90210
*Actress*
*Birthday: 11/11/64*

**Foch, Nina (Nina Consuelo Maud
Fock)**
PO Box 1884
Beverly Hills, CA 90213
*Actress*
*Birthday: 4/20/24*

**Fogelberg, Dan**
PO Box 2399
Pagosa Springs, CO 81147
*Singer*
*Birthday: 8/31/51*

**Fogerty, John**
PO Box 375
Granada Hills, CA 91364
*Singer, songwriter*
*Birthday: 5/28/45*

**Foley, David**
% NBC
3000 W. Alameda Ave.
Burbank, CA 91523
*Actor*
*Birthday: 1/4/63*

**Fonda, Bridget**
9560 Wilshire Blvd., #516
Beverly Hills, CA 90212
*Actress, Jane Fonda's niece*
*Birthday: 1/27/64*

**Fonda, Jane**
9830 Wilshire Blvd.
Beverly Hills, CA 90212
*Actress*
*Birthday: 12/21/37*

**Fonda, Peter (Peter Seymour Fonda)**
Rt. 38 Box 2024
Livingston, MT 59047
*Actor, Bridget's father, Jane's brother*

**Fontaine, Joan**
PO Box 222600
Carmel, CA 93922
*Actress*

**Forbes, Malcome Jr. (Steve)**
60 Fifth Ave.
New York, NY 10011
*Magazine publisher*

**Force, John**
% John Force Racing
23253 East LaPalma Ave.
Yorba Linda, CA 92687
Website: http://
www.johnforceracing.com/
splash1.htm
*Race car driver*

**John Force Fan Club**
1480 South Hohokam Dr.
Tempe, AZ 85281

**Ford, Betty**
1801 Ave. of the Stars, #902
Los Angeles, CA 90067
*Former First Lady*

**Ford, Chris**
% Milwaukee Bucks
1001 N. 4th St.
Milwaukee, WI 53203
*Basketball player*

**Ford, Faith**
9460 Wilshire Blvd., #7
Beverly Hills, CA 90212
*Actress*
*Birthday: 9/14/64*

**Ford, The Honorable Gerald R.**
40365 San Dune Rd.
Rancho Mirage, CA 92270
Or
PO Box 927
Rancho Mirage, CA
*Former President*
*Birthday: 7/14/13*

**Ford, Harrison**
% United Talent Agency
9560 Wilshire Blvd., Suite 500
Beverly Hills, CA 90212
*Actor*
*Birthday: 7/13/42*

**"Ford Model Name"**
% Ford Model Mgmt.
344 E. 59th St.
New York, NY 10022
*Address to write to Ford models*

**Ford, Patricia**
% Playmate Promotions
9242 Beverly Blvd.
Beverly Hills, CA 90210
*Model*

**Ford, Whitey**
38 Schoolhouse Ln.
Lake Success, NY 11020
*Former baseball player*

**Forman, Milos**
150 Central Park So.
New York, NY 10019
*Director*

**Forte, Fabian**
6671 Sunset Blvd., #1502
Los Angeles, CA 90028
*Singer*

**Foss, General Joe**
PO Box 566
Scottsdale, AZ 85252
*The first American to tie Eddie
Rickenbacker's World War I record
of 26 aerial combat victories, he
was the World War II Marine Corp
Ace of Aces, Congressional Medal
of Honor winner, and former
governor of South Dakota.*

**Foster, Jodie**
8942 Wilshire Blvd.
Beverly Hills, CA 90211
*Actress, director, producer*
*Birthday: 11/19/62*

**Foster, Meg**
606 N. Larchmont Blvd., #309
Los Angeles, CA 90004
*Actress*

**Foster, Radney**
1908 Wedgewood
Nashville, TN 37212
*Country singer*

**Fountain, Pete**
237 N. Peters St., #400
New Orleans, LA 71030
*Musician*

**Fox, Michael J.**
% Creative Artists Agency
9830 Wilshire Blvd.
Beverly Hills, CA 90212
Website: www.michaeljfox.org/
*Actor*
*Birthday: 6/9/61*

**Foxx, Jamie**
15445 Ventura Blvd., #790
Sherman Oaks, CA 91403
*Actor*

**Foxworthy, Jeff**
8380 Melrose Ave., #310
Los Angeles, CA 90069
*Comedian, actor*

**Francis, Cleve**
PO Box 15258
Alexandria, VA 22309
*Country singer*

**Francis, Ron**
% Pittsburgh Penguins
66 Mario Lemieux Pl.
Pittsburgh, PA 15219
*Hockey player*

**Franken, Al**
345 N. Maple Dr., #302
Beverly Hills, CA 90210
*Actor, writer*

**Franklin, Bonnie**
10635 Santa Monica Blvd., #130
Los Angeles, CA 90025
*Actress*

**Franz, Dennis**
2300 Century Hill, #75
Los Angeles, CA 90067
*Actor*

**Fraser, Brendan**
2118 Wilshire Blvd., #513
Santa Monica, CA 90403
*Actor*

**Freberg, Stan**
10450 Wilshire Blvd., #1A
Los Angeles, CA 90024
*Writer, comedian*

**Freeh, Louis**
FBI 9th and Pennsylvania Ave. NW
Washington, DC 20035
*FBI director*

**Frentzen, Heinz-Harald**
% Williams GP Engineering Ltd.
Grove
Wantage
GB Oxfordshire OX12 0DQ
*Professional Formula-1 driver*

**Frey, Glenn**
8900 Wilshire Blvd., #300
Beverly Hills, CA 90211
*Musician*

**Fricke, Janie**
PO Box 798
Lancaster, TX 75146
*Country singer*

**Friedman, Milton**
Hoover Institute
Stanford University
Palo Alto, CA 94305
*Economist, Nobel Prize winner*

**Frizzell, David**
% Christina Frazer
PO Box 120964
Nashville, TN 37212
*Country singer*

**Fujita, Dr. Yoshio**
6-21-7 Renkoji
Tama-shi 206
Japan
*Astronomer*

**Fuhrman, Mark**
PO Box 141
Sandpoint, ID 83864
*Police witness in O. J. Simpson trial*

**G**

**G., Kenny**
9830 Wilshire Blvd.
Beverly Hills, CA 90212
*Musician*
*Birthday: 6/5/?*

**Gabriel, Peter**
Box 35
Corsham
Wiltshire
London SW13 8SZ
England
*Musician*

**Gagne, Eric**
% Los Angeles Dodgers
1000 Elysian Park Ave.
Los Angeles, CA 90012
*Baseball player*

**Gail, Max**
PO Box 4160
Malibu, CA 90265
*Actor*

**Galbraith, John Kenneth**
Department of Economics
Littauer Center, Room 206
Harvard University
Cambridge, MA 02138
*Economist*

**Gallagher, Danny**
49 Crouch Hill, Finsbury Park
London N4
England
*Healer*

**Galloway, Joey**
% Dallas Cowboys
1 Cowboys Pkwy.
Irving, TX 75063
*Football player*

**Gantin, Bernardin Cardinal**
Piazza S. Calisto 16
Rome 00153
Italy

**Gantner, Jim**
% Milwaukee Brewers
Milwaukee County Stadium
Milwaukee, WI 53214
*Baseball player*

**Garcia, Andy**
% Paradigm
10100 Santa Monica Blvd.,
25th Floor
Los Angeles, CA 90067
*Actor*
*Birthday: 4/12/56*

**Garofalo, Janeane**
1122 S. Robertson Blvd., #15
Los Angeles, CA 90035
*Actress*

**Garr, Terri**
9200 Sunset Blvd., #428
Los Angeles, CA 90069
Or
9150 Wilshire Blvd. #350
Beverly Hills, CA 90212-3427
*Actress*
*Birthday: 12/11/45*

**Garrison, David**
9229 Sunset Blvd., #710
Los Angeles, CA 90069
*Actor*

**Gates, Bill**
1 Microsoft Way
Redmond, WA 98052
*Founder of Microsoft*
*Birthday: 10/28/55*

**Gatlin, Larry**
Fantasy Harbour
Waccamaw
Myrtle Beach, SC 29577
*Musician*

**Gayle, Crystal**
51 Music Square East
Nashville, TN 37203
*Country singer*
*Birthday: 1/9/51*

**Gaynor, Gloria**
% Cliffside Music
PO Box 374
Fairview, NJ 07010
Or
Longford Ave.
Southall
Middlesex UB1 3QT
England
*Singer*
*Birthday: 9/7/48*

**Geary, Tony**
% General Hospital—ABC-TV
4151 Prospect Ave.
Los Angeles, CA 90027
*Soap opera star*

**Geffen, David**
100 Universal Plaza
Lakeridge Bldg., #601
Universal City, CA 91608
*Founder of Geffen Records, co-founder of DreamWorks Studios*

**Geldof, Sir Bob**
Davington Priory
Priory Rd.
Faversham ME13 7EJ
England
*Musician*

**Gellar, Sarah Michelle**
% *Buffy the Vampire Slayer*
% The Warner Brothers Television
Network
4000 Warner Blvd.
Burbank, CA 91522
Or
1122 S. Robertson Blvd., #15
Los Angeles, CA 90035
*Actress, model*
*Birthday: 4/14/77*

**Geller, Uri**
Sonning-on-Thames
Berkshire
England
*Psychic*

**Gentry, Bobbie**
269 S. Beverly Dr., #368
Beverly Hills, CA 90212
*Singer*

**George, Wally**
14155 Magnolia Blvd., #127
Sherman Oaks, CA 91423
*TV talk show host*

**Gerard, Gil**
23679 Calabasas Rd., #325
Calabasas, CA 91302
*Actor*

**Gere, Richard**
22 W. 15th. St.
New York, NY 10011
*Actor*

**Getty, Estelle**
10960 Wilshire Blvd., #2050
Los Angeles, CA 90024
*Actress*

**Gibb, Barry**
20505 US 19 North, #12–290
Clearwater, FL 33624
*Musician*

**Gibb, Maurice and Robin**
20505 US 19 North, #12–290
Clearwater, FL 33624
*Musicians*

**Gibbons, Leeza**
PO Box 4321
Los Angeles, CA 90068
*Talk show host*

**Gibson, Don**
PO Box 50474
Nashville, TN 37205
*Country singer*

**Gibson, Mel**
4000 Warner Blvd., #139-17
Burbank, CA 91522
*Actor*
*Birthday: 1/7/56*

**Gifford, Frank**
625 Madison Ave., #1200
New York, NY 10022
*Sportscaster, four-time All Pro*
*(1955–57, 1959), NFL MVP in*
*1956; led NY Giants to three NFL*
*title games, married to Kathy Lee*
*Gifford*
*Birthday: 8/16/30*

**Gifford, Kathy Lee**
625 Madison Ave., #1200
New York, NY 10022
*Singer, married to Frank Gifford*
*Birthday: 8/16/53*

**Gilbert, Melissa**
PO Box 57593
Sherman Oaks, CA 91403
*Actress*
*Birthday: 5/8/64*

**Gill, Vince**
PO Box 1407
White House, TN 37188
*Country singer*
*Birthday: 4/12/57*

**Gilley, Mickey**
PO Box 1242
Pasadena, TX 77501
*Country singer*
*Birthday: 3/9/36*

**Gilliam, Terry**
The Old Hall
South Grove
Highgate
London N6
England
*Comedian, actor, director*
*Birthday: 1/22/40*

**Gilmore, Jimmie Dale**
% Main Grand Stand Prom.
122 Longwood Ave.
Austin, TX 78734
*Country singer*

**Gimble, Johnny**
PO Box 347
Dripping Springs, TX 78620
*Country singer*

**Ginger Spice**
35 Parkgate Rd., #32
Ransome Dock
London SW11 4NP
England
*Singer, member of the Spice Girls*

**Ginsberg, Ruth Bader**
700 New Hampshire Ave. NW
Washington, DC 20037
*Supreme Court Justice*

**Ginsburg, Att. William**
10100 Santa Monica Blvd., #800
Los Angeles, CA 90067
*Former attorney for Monica Lewinsky*

**Givens, Robin**
PO Box 118
Stone Ridge, NY 12484
*Actress, talk show host, former wife of Mike Tyson*

**Goen, Bob**
5555 Melrose Ave., #1
Los Angeles, CA 90038
*Co-host of Entertainment Tonight*

**Goldberg, Whoopi**
9171 Wilshire Blvd., #300
Beverly Hills, CA 90210
*Comedienne, actress, producer*

**Goldblum, Jeff**
955 S. Carrillo Dr., #399
Los Angeles, CA 90048
*Actor*

**Golden, William Lee**
RR 2 Saundersville Rd.
Hendersonville, TN 37075
*Country singer*

**Goldsboro, Bobby**
PO Box 5250
Ocala, FL 32678
*Country singer*

**Goldwait, Bobcat**
10061 Riverside Dr., #760
Toluca Lake, CA 91602
*Comedian*

**Gonzales, Juan**
% Texas Rangers
1000 Ballpark Way
Arlington, TX 76011
*Baseball player*

**Goodall, Dr. Jane**
PO Box 41720
Tucson, AZ 85717
Or
PO Box 14890
Silver Spring, MD 20911
Website: http://
www.janegoodall.org/
*Chimpanzee researcher*
*Birthday: 4/3/34*

**Gooding, Cuba Jr.**
1122 S. Robertson Blvd., #15
Los Angeles, CA 90035
*Actor*
*Birthday: 1/2/68*

**Goodman, John**
619 Amalfi Dr.
Pacific Palisades, CA 90272
*Actor*

**Goodrich, Gail**
% Basketball Hall of Fame
1150 W. Columbus Ave.
Springfield, MA 01101
*Basketball player*

**Gorbachev, Michail**
49 Leningradsky prospekt 209
Moscow
Russia
*Ex-President*
*Birthday: 3/2/31*

**Gordeeva, Ekaterina**
% Intl Skating Ctr.
1375 Hopmeadow St.
Simsbury, CT 06070
*Figure skater*

**Gorme, Edie**
10560 Wilshire Blvd., #601
Los Angeles, CA 90024
*Singer*

**Gorshin, Frank**
% Gor Publications
PO Box 17731
West Haven, CT 06516
Or
11365 Ventura Blvd., #100
Studio City, CA 91604
*Actor*
*Birthday: 4/5/34*

**Gosdin, Vern**
2509 W. Marquette Ave.
Tampa, FL 33614
*Country singer*

**Gossett, Lou**
8306 Wilshire Blvd., #438
Beverly Hills, CA 90211

**Gotti, John**
#18261-053
Rt. 5
PO Box 2000
Marion, IL 62959
*Nickname: The Teflon Don,*
*convicted of murdering Paul*
*Castellano, alleged boss of the*
*Gambino Family and his driver,*
*Thomas Bilotti*
*Birthday: 10/27/40*

**Gowdy, Curt**
Box 559
Salisbury, NC 28144
*Sportscaster*
*Birthday: 7/31/19*

**Graf, Steffi**
Mallaustr. 75
68219 Mannheim
Germany
*Tennis player*

**Graham, The Rev. Billy**
PO Box 779
Minneapolis, MN 55440
*Evangelist*
*Birthday: 11/7/18*

**Graham, Gerrit**
8730 Sunset Blvd., #480
Los Angeles, CA 90069
*Actor*

**Graham, Heather**
9839 Wilshire Blvd.
Beverly Hills, CA 90212
*Actress, model*
*Birthday: 1/29/70*

**Grammer, Kelsey**
9560 Wilshire Blvd., #516
Beverly Hills, CA 90212
*Actor*
*Birthday: 2/20/55*

**Granger, Farley**
15 W. 72nd St.
New York, NY 10023
*Actor*
*Birthday: 7/1/25*

**Grant, Amy**
25 Music Square W.
Nashville, TN 37203
*Singer*
*Birthday: 11/25/60*

**Grant, Hugh**
76 Oxford St.
London W1N 0aX
England
*Actor*

**Graves, Peter**
1122 S. Robertson Blvd., #15
Los Angeles, CA 90035
*Actor*

**Gray, Erin**
11288 Ventura Blvd.
Studio City, CA 91604
*Actress*

**Gray, Linda**
1680 N. Vine St., #617
Hollywood, CA 90028
*Actress*
*Birthday: 9/12/41*

**Green, Al**
PO Box 456
Millington, TN 38083
*Singer, minister*

**Greenwood, Lee**
PO Box 6537
Sevierville, TN 37864
*Country singer*

**Greer, Germaine**
29 Fernshaw Rd.
London SW10 0TG
England
*Feminist author*
*Birthday: 1/29/39*

**Gregg, Ricky Lynn**
PO Box 8924
Bossier City, LA 71113
*Country singer*

**Gregory, Clinton**
PO Box 707
Hermitage, TN 37076
*Country singer*

**Gretzky, Wayne**
9100 Wilshire Blvd., #10000W
Beverly Hills, CA 90212
*Hockey player, 10-time NHL
scoring champion, 9-time regular
season MVP
(1979–87, 89), and 9-time All-NHL
first team
Birthday: 1/26/61*

**Grey, Jennifer**
91 Fifth Ave.
New York, NY 10003
*Actress*

**Grey, Joel**
141 Fifth Ave., #300
New York, NY 10011
*Actor
Birthday: 4/11/32*

**Griese, Bob**
% Pro Football Hall of Fame
2121 George Halas Dr. NW
Canton, OH 44708
*Football player*

**Griffey, Ken Jr.**
Cinergy Field
100 Cinergy Field
Cincinnati, OH 45202

**Griffin, Merv**
9876 Wilshire Blvd.
Beverly Hills, CA 90210

**Griffith, Andy**
PO Box 1968
Manteo, NC 27954
Or
9 Music Square S., #146
Nashville, TN 37203
*Actor
Birthday: 6/2/26*

**Griffith, Melanie**
3110 St., #205
Santa Monica, CA 90405
*Actress
Birthday: 8/9/57*

**Griffith, Nanci**
PO Box 128037
Nashville, TN 37212
*Singer*

**Grimes, Dorothy**
128 Roberts Rd.
Aston, PA 19014
*Healer*

**Grisham, John**
PO Box 1780
Oxford, MS 38655
*Author*

**Gritz, Bo**
% Talk America Radio Network
1455 East Tropicana, Suite #700
Las Vegas, NV 89119
*America's most decorated Green
Beret*

**Grizzard, Lewis**
2951 Piedmont Rd. NE, #100
Atlanta, GA 30305
*Country singer*

**Groening, Matt**
10201 West Pico Blvd.
Los Angeles, CA 90035
*Creator and developer of*
The Simpsons
*Birthday: 2/15/54*

**Gross, Michael**
9200 Sunset Blvd., #900
Los Angeles, CA 90069
*Actor*

**Guest, Christopher**
PO Box 2358
Running Springs, CA 92382
Or
9830 Wilshire Blvd.
Beverly Hills, CA 90212
*Actor*

**Guidry, Ron**
PO Box 278
Scott, LA 70583
*Baseball player*
*Birthday: 8/28/50*

**Guisewite, Cathy**
4900 Main St.
Kansas City, MO 64112
*Comic strip creator*

**Gumbel, Bryant**
524 W. 57th St.
New York, NY 10019
*TV show host*
*Birthday: 9/29/48*

**Gumbel, Greg**
524 W. 57th St.
New York, NY 10019
*TV show host*

**Guthrie, Arlo**
The Farm
Washington, MA 01223
*Singer, songwriter*
*Birthday: 7/10/47*

**Guy, Jasmine**
21243 Ventura Blvd., #101
Woodland Hills, CA 91364
*Actress, dancer*
*Birthday: 3/10/64*

**Gwynn, Tony**
% San Diego Padres
PO Box 2000
San Diego, CA 92112
*Baseball player*

**H**

**Haas, Lukas**
10683 Santa Monica Blvd.
Los Angeles, CA 90025
*Actor*
*Birthday: 4/16/76*

**Hackman, Gene**
118 S. Beverly Dr., #1201
Beverly Hills, CA 90212
*Actor*
*Birthday: 1/30/30*

**Hagar, Sammy**
Box 5395
Novato, CA 94948
*Musician*
*Birthday: 10/13/47*

**Haggard, Merle**
3009 Easy St.
Sevierville, TN 37862
*Country singer*

**Haig, Gen. Alexander M. Jr.**
1155 15th St. NW., #800
Washington, DC 20005
*Former Secretary of State*

**Haim, Corey**
150 Carlton St. 2nd Floor
Toronto
Ontario M5A 2K1
Canada
*Actor*
*Birthday: 12/23/72*

**Häkkinen, Mika**
% McLaren Int'l Ltd.
Woking Business Park
Albert Dr.
Woking
GB-Surrey GU21 5JS
*Professional Formula-1 driver*
*Birthday: 9/28/68*

**Halal, William E.**
Dept. of Management Science
School of Business and Public
Management
George Washington University
Washington, DC 20052
Website: http://gwis2.circ.gwu.edu/
~halal/
E-mail: halal@gwu.edu
*Professor of management in the*
*Department of Management*
*Science at George Washington*
*University*

**Hale, Alan Spencer**
5476 St. Paul Rd.
Morristown, TN 37813
*Country singer*

**Hale, Barbara**
PO Box 6061-261
Sherman Oaks, CA 91413
*Actress*
*Birthday: 2/18/21*

**Hall, Arsenio**
9560 Wilshire Blvd., #516
Beverly Hills, CA 90212
*Actor, comedian*

**Hall, Monty**
519 North Arden Dr.
Beverly Hills, CA 90210
*TV game show host*
*Birthday: 8/23/97*

**Hall, Tom T.**
PO Box 1246
Franklin, TN 37065
*Country singer*

**Hamil, Dorothy**
PO Box 16286
Baltimore, MD 21210
*Former figure skater*

**Hamill, Mark**
PO Box 55
Malibu, CA 90265
*Actor*
*Birthday: 9/25/51*

**Hamilton, George**
139 S. Beverly Dr., #330
Beverly Hills, CA 90212
*Actor*

**Hamilton, George IV**
203 SW Third Ave.
Gainesville, FL 32601
*Country singer*

**Hamilton, Scott**
20 First St.
Colorado Springs, CA 80909
*Figure skater, sports commentator*

**Hanks, Tom**
PO Box 900
Beverly Hills, CA 90213
*Actor*

**Hanna, William**
4000 Warner Blvd.
Burbank, CA 91522
*Animation executive*

**Hardaway, Anfernee**
% Orlando Magic
One Magic Pl.
Orlando, FL 32801
*Basketball player*

**Harding, Tonya**
5113 NE 39th Ave.
Vancouver, WA 98661
*Figure skater*
*Birthday: 11/12/70*

**Hargitay, Mariska**
7920 Sunset Blvd., #400
Los Angeles, CA 90046
*Actress*

**Harlem Globe Trotters**
1000 S. Fremont Ave.
Alhambra, CA 91803
*Basketball team*

**Harling, Keith**
PO Box 1304
Goodlettsville, TN 37070
E-mail: fanclub@keithharling.com
*Country music singer*

**Harmon, Angie**
Pier 62
Hudson River and W. 23rd St.
New York, NY 10011
*Actress*

**Harper, Tess**
8484 Wilshire Blvd., #500
Beverly Hills, CA 90211
*Actress*
*Birthday: 11/30/51*

**Harper, Valerie**
PO Box 7187
Beverly Hills, CA 90212
*Actress*
*Birthday: 8/22/?*

**Harrelson, Woody**
16133 Ventura Blvd., #560
Encino, CA 91436
*Actor*

**Harris, Emmylou**
PO Box 159007
Nashville, TN 37215
*Singer*
*Birthday: 4/2/48*

**Harris, Mel**
6300 Wilshire Blvd., #2110
Los Angeles, CA 90048
*Actress*

**Harris, Neal Patrick**
1122 S. Robertson Blvd., #15
Los Angeles, CA 90035
*Actor*
*Birthday: 6/15/73*

**Harrison, A. J.**
% Romaha Records
PO Box 823
Snellville, GA 30078
Web page: http://www.aj-harrison.com/
E-mail: fan-mail@aj-harrison.com
*Singer, actor, writer*

**Harrison, George**
5 Park Rd.
Henley-on-Thames
RG9 1DB
England
*Musician, former Beatle*

**Harry, Deborah**
1325 Ave of the Americas
New York, NY 10019
Or
% Crave
Axis: Theatre
1 Sheridan Square
New York, NY 10014
*Singer*

**Harry, HRH Prince**
Highgrove House
Gloucestershire
England
*Son of Prince Charles*

**Hart, ex-Senator Gary**
950 17th St., #2050
Denver, CO 80202
*Former senator, former
presidential candidate*

**Hart, Mary**
9000 Sunset Blvd., #16
Los Angeles, CA 90069
*TV hostess*
*Birthday: 11/8/51*

**Hart, Melissa Joan**
10880 Wilshire Blvd., #1101
Los Angeles, CA 90024
*Actress*

**Harvey, Steve**
9100 Wilshire Blvd., #700 E.
Tower
Beverly Hills, CA 90212
*Actor*

**Hatch, Richard**
3349 Cahuenga Blvd. W.
Los Angeles, CA 90068
*Actor*

**Hatcher, Teri**
10100 Santa Monica Blvd., #410
Los Angeles, CA 90067
*Actress*

**Hauer, Rutger**
9560 Wilshire Blvd., #516
Beverly Hills, CA 90212
*Actor*

**Haven, Annette**
PO Box 1244
Sausalito, CA 94966
*Porn star*

**Havens, Ritchie**
223 E 48th St.
New York, NY 10017
*Musician*

**Hawking, Professor Stephen**
University of Cambridge
Applied Math Department
Cambridge
CB3 9EW
England
E-mail:
S.W.Hawking@damtp.cam.ac.uk
*Stephen Hawking is perhaps best
known for his discovery, in 1974,
that black holes emit radiation.
Stephen Hawking has two popular
books published: his best-seller, A
Brief History of Time, and his later
book, Black Holes and Baby
Universes and Other Essays.*
*Birthday: 1/8/42*

**Hawn, Goldie**
955 S. Carrillo Dr., #200
Los Angeles, CA 90048
*Actress*
*Birthday: 11/2/45*

**Hayden, Tom**
10951 W. Pico Blvd., #202
Los Angeles, CA 90064
*Politican*

**Hayek, Salma**
PO Box 57593
Sherman Oaks, CA 91403
*Actress*

**Hayes, Isaac**
2635 Griffith Park Blvd.
Los Angeles, CA 90039
*Singer*
*Birthday: 8/20/42*

**Hayes, Wade**
PO Box 128546
Nashville, TN 37212

**Rita Hayworth Fan Club**
3943 York Ave. South
Minneapolis, MN 55410

**Heche, Anne**
10960 Wilshire Blvd., #1100
Los Angeles, CA 90024
*Actress*

**Hedren, Tippi**
Box 189
Acton, CA 93510
*Actress, animal activist*

**Hefner, Christie**
680 N. Lake Shore Dr.
Chicago, IL 60611
*Chairman and CEO of Playboy*
*Enterprises*

**Hefner, Hugh**
680 N. Lake Shore Dr.
Chicago, IL 60611
*Founder, Chairman Emeritus, and*
*Editor-in-Chief of* Playboy
*magazine*

**Heft, Bob**
PO Box 131
Napoleon, OH 43545
*Designed the 50-star U.S. flag*

**Helm, Levon**
315 S. Beverly Dr., #206
Beverly Hills, CA 90212
*Musician*

**Helms, Bobby**
% Tessier March Talent, Inc.
505 Canton Pass
Madison, TN 37115
*Country singer*

**Heloise**
PO Box 795000
San Antonio, TX 78279
*Newspaper columnist, author*

**Hemingway, Mariel**
Box 2249
Ketchum, ID 83340
*Actress, granddaughter of Ernest*
*Hemingway*

**Hemsley, Sherman**
PO Box 5344
Sherman Oaks, CA 91413

**Henderson, Florence**
Box 11295
Marina del Rey, CA 90295
*Actress*

**Henderson, Tareva**
PO Box 17303
Nashville, TN 37217
*Country singer*

**Hendricks, Ted**
% Pro Football Hall of Fame
2121 George Halas Dr. NW
Canton, OH 44708
*Football player*

**Henley, Don**
3500 W. Olive Ave., #1400
Burbank, CA 91505
*Musician*

**Henry, Buckl**
117 E. 57th. St.
New York, NY 10019
*Actor, writer*

**Herman, Pee-Wee (Paul Reubens)**
PO 29373
Los Angeles, CA 90029
*Actor, comedian*

**Hershey, Barbara**
% CAA
9830 Wilshire Blvd.
Beverly Hills, CA 90212
*Actress*
*Birthday: 2/5/48*

**Herzigova, Eva**
20 West 20th St., #600
New York, NY 10011
*Supermodel*
*Birthday: 3/10/73*

**Hewitt, Jennifer Love**
151 El Camino Dr.
Beverly Hills, CA 90212
*Actress, dancer, singer*
*Birthday: 2/21/79*

**Heyerdahl, Thor**
E-38500 Guimar
Tenerife
Spain
*Anthropologist, adventurer, author*
*Birthday: 10/6/14*

**Hickman, Dwayne**
PO Box 3352
Santa Monica, CA 90403
Website: http://www.dobietv.com/
E-mail: dwayne@dobieart.com
*Actor, artist, author*

**Hicks, Catherine**
1122 S. Robertson Blvd., #15
Los Angeles, CA 90035
*Actress*

**Hilfiger, Tommy**
25 W. 39th St., #1300
New York, NY 10018
Website: http://www.tommypr.com/
index1.jhtml
*Fashion designer*
*Birthday: 1952*

**Hill, Dr. Anita**
300 Timberdell Rd.
Norman, OK 73109
*Attorney, author, witness in the*
*Thomas Clarence confirmation*
*hearings*

**Hill, Faith (Audrey Faith Perry Hill)**
3310 West End Ave., #500
Nashville, TN 37203
Website: http://www.faith-hill.com/
*Singer*
*Birthday: 9/21/67*

**Hill, Kim**
% Blanton Harrell
2910 Poston Ave.
Nashville, TN 37203
*Country singer*

**Hill, Lauryn**
151 El Camino Dr.
Beverly Hills, CA 90212
*Singer*

**Hillary, Sir Edmund (Percival)**
278A Remuera Rd.
Auckland SE 2
New Zealand
*Mountain climber and Antarctic explorer, who, with Tenzing Norgay, a Sherpa from Nepal, was the first to reach the summit of Mount Everest, the world's highest peak.*
*Birthday: 7/20/19*

**Hillerman, John**
PO Box 218
Blue Jay, CA 92317
*Actor*

**Hinckley, John Jr.**
2700 Martin Luther King Ave.
Washington, DC 20005
*Attempted to assassinate President Ronald Reagan*
*Birthday: 5/29/55*

**Hines, Gregory**
377 W. 11th St., #PH-4
New York, NY 10014
Or
4009 Ocean Front Walk
Venice, CA 90292
*Dancer, actor*
*Birthday: 2/14/46*

**Hirsch, Judd**
137 W. 12th St.
New York, NY 10011
*Actor*

**Hirschfield, Al**
122 E. 95th St.
New York, NY 10028
*Caricaturist, he always hides his niece's name, Nina, in his drawings. You can usually find NINA in the subject's hair or sleeves.*
*Birthday: 6/21/03*

**Hite, Shere**
PO Box 1037
New York, NY 10028
*Author*

**Hobbs, Becky**
PO Box 121974
Nashville, TN 37212
*Country singer*

**Hockney, David**
2029 Century Park E., #300
Los Angeles, CA 90067
*Artist*

**Hogan, Paul**
515 N. Robertson Blvd.
Los Angeles, CA 90048
*Actor*

**Holbrook, Hal**
9200 Sunset Blvd., #1130
Los Angeles, CA 90069
*Actor*

**Holden, Rebecca**
PO Box 23504
Nashville, TN 37202
*Country singer*

**Buddy Holly Memorial Society**
PO Box 6123
Lubbock, TX 79413

**Holly, Lauren**
955 S. Carrillo Dr., #300
Los Angeles, CA 90048
*Actress*
*Birthday: 10/28/63*

**Holly, Mrs. Buddy (Maria Díaz)**
PO Box 6123
Lubbock, TX 79493
*Buddy Holly's widow*

**Holmes, Katie**
9830 Wilshire Blvd.,
Beverly Hills, CA 90212

**Holmes, Larry**
91 Larry Holmes Dr., #101
Aston, PA 18042
*Boxer*
*Birthday: 11/3/49*

**Sherlock Holmes Society**
221B Baker St.
London W1
England

**Hooker, John Lee**
PO Box 170429
San Francisco, CA 94117
*Musician*

**Hope, Bob**
10346 Moorpark
North Hollywood, CA 91602
*Comedian, actor*

**Hopkins, Sir Anthony**
15250 Ventura Blvd., #710
Sherman Oaks, CA 91403
*Actor*

**Hopper, Dennis**
% Creative Artists Agency
9830 Wilshire Blvd.
Beverly Hills, CA 90212
*Actor*

**Horne, Lena**
23 E. 74th St., #5A
New York, NY 100221
*Singer*

**Hornsby, Bruce**
Box 3545
Williamsburg, VA 23187
*Musician*

**Horowitz, David**
PO Box 49915
Los Angeles, CA 90049
*Consumer activist*

**Horton, Peter**
9560 Wilshire Blvd., #500
Beverly Hills, CA 90212
*Actor, director, producer*
*Birthday: 8/20/53*

**Hoskins, Bob**
200 Fulham Rd.
London SW10 9PN
England
*Actor*

**Howard, Jan**
Grand Ole Opry
2804 Opryland Dr.
Nashville, TN 37214
*Country singer*

**Howard, Jayne**
PO Box 95
Upperco, MD 21155
*Author*

**Howard, Ron**
9465 Wilshire Blvd., #700
Beverly Hills, CA 90212
*Director*
*Birthday: 3/1/54*

**Huddleston, David**
3518 Cahuenga Blvd. W., #216
Los Angeles, CA 90068
*Actor*

**Huffington, Arianna**
1250 "H" St., NW #550
Washington, DC 20005
*Political commentator, author*

**Hulce, Tom**
175 5th Ave., #2409
New York, NY 10010
*Actor*
*Birthday: 12/6/53*

**Humperdinck, Engelbert**
PO Box 5734
Beverly Hills, CA 90209
*Singer*
*Birthday: 5/2/36*

**Hunt, Dave**
PO Box 7019
Bend, OR 97708
*Religious author*

**Hunt, Helen**
9830 Wilshire Blvd.
Beverly Hills, CA 90212
*Actress*
*Birthday: 6/15/63*

**Hunt, Linda**
% WMA
1325 Ave. of the Americas
New York, NY 10019
*Actress*
*Birthday: 4/2/45*

**Hunter, Holly**
9460 Wilshire Blvd., 7th Floor
Beverly Hills, CA 90212
Or
% ICM
8942 Wilshire Blvd.
Beverly Hills, CA 90211
*Actress*
*Birthday: 3/20/58*

**Hunter, Rachael**
1122 S. Robertson Blvd., #15
Los Angeles, CA 90035
*Supermodel*

**Hunter, Tommy**
2806 Opryland Dr.
Nashville, TN 37214
*Country singer*

**Hurley, Elizabeth**
3 Cromwell Pl.
London SW7 2JE
England
Or
% United Talent Agency
9560 Wilshire Blvd., Suite 500
Beverly Hills, CA 90212
*Actress*

**Hurt, William**
151 El Camino Dr.
Beverly Hills, CA 90212
*Actor*

**Husky, Ferlin**
38 Music Square East
Nashville, TN 37203
*Country singer*
*Birthday: 12/3/25*

**Hussein, President Saddam**
Office of the President
Baghdad
Iraq

**Hussey, Olivia**
PO Box 2131
Crestline, CA 92008

**Hutton, Lauren**
382 Lafayette St., #6
New York, NY 10003
*Model, actress*

**Hutton, Sylvia**
PO Box 158467
Nashville, TN 37215
*Country singer*

**Hutton, Timothy**
RR #2
Box 3318
Cushman Rd.
Patterson, NY 12563
*Actor*

**Hyland, Brian**
PO Box 101
Helendale, CA 92342
*Musician*

**Hynde, Chrissie**
30 Ives St.
GB-London SW3 2ND
England
*Singer*
*Birthday: 9/7/51*

**I**

**Ice-T**
2287 Sunset Plaza Dr.
Los Angeles, CA 90069
*Rapper, actor*
*Birthday: 2/16/58*

**Idol, Billy**
7314 Woodrow Wilson Dr.
Los Angels, CA 90046
*Singer*

**Iman**
180-182 Tottingham Ct. Rd.
London W1P9LE
England
*Singer, model, wife of David Bowie*
*Birthday: 7/25/55*

**Imus, Don**
34-12 36th St.
Astoria, NY 11106
*Radio personality*

**Ingle, John**
% General Hospital–ABC-TV
4151 Prospect Ave.
Los Angeles, CA 90027
*Soap opera star*

**Ingels, Marty**
Suite One Prod.
8127 Melrose Ave., #1
Los Angeles, CA 90046
*Actor*

**Ireland, Kathy**
1122 S. Robertson Blvd., #15
Los Angeles, CA 90035
*Model, actress*

**Irons, Jeremy**
200 Fulham Rd.
London SW10 9PN
England
*Actor*

**Irving, Amy**
7920 Sunset Blvd., #401
Los Angeles, CA 90046
*Actress*

**Irwin, Tom**
PO Box 5617
Beverly Hills, CA 90210
*Actor and founding member of the
acclaimed Chicago-based
Steppenwolf Theater Company*

**Ito, Judge Lance A.**
Criminal Courts Building
210 W. Temple St., #M-6
Los Angeles, CA 90012
*Judge who presided over the O. J.
Simpson trial*

**Ivey, Judith**
11500 W. Olympic Blvd., #510
Los Angeles, CA 90046
*Actress*
*Birthday: 9/4/51*

**J**

**Jackson, Alan**
1101 17th Ave. So.
Nashville, TN 37212
*Country singer*
*Birthday: 10/17/?*

**Jackson, Bo**
PO Box 158
Mobile, AL 36601
*Professional baseball and football
player*

**Jackson, Glenda**
51 Harvey Rd.
London SE3
England
*Actress*
*Birthday: 5/9/36*

**Jackson, Janet**
9830 Wilshire Blvd.
Beverly Hills, CA 90212
*Singer, actress*
*Birthday: 5/16/66*

**Jackson, Jeremy**
% Mary Grady Agency
4444 Lankershim Blvd., #207
North Hollywood, CA 91602
*Actor*
*Birthday: 10/16/80*

**Jackson, Rev. Jesse**
400 "T" St., NW
Washington, DC 20001
*Political activist*
*Birthday: 10/8/41*

**Jackson, Jonathan**
9830 Wilshire Blvd.
Beverly Hills, CA 90212
*Actor*

**Jackson, Kate**
PO Box 57593
Sherman Oaks, CA 91403
*Actress*

**Jackson, Michael**
Neverland Ranch
Los Olivos, CA 93441
Or
% The Firm
9100 Wilshire Blvd., Suite 400
West
Beverly Hills, CA 90212
*Singer, actor, songwriter*
*Birthday: 8/29/58*

**Jackson, Stonewall**
PO Box 463
McMinnville, TN 37110
*Country singer*

**Jagger, Bianca**
530 Park Ave., #18D
New York, NY 10021
*Actress, former wife of Mick Jagger*
*Birthday: 5/2/45*

**Jagger, Mick**
304 W. 81st St.
New York, NY 10024
*Singer, songwriter*

**James, Art**
11365 Ventura Blvd., #100
Studio City, CA 91604
Website: http://
www.corpgameshow.com/
E-mail:
artjames@corpgameshow.com
*TV host*

**James, Brian**
PO Box 1207
Pineville, WV 24874
*Country singer*

**James, Dalton**
303 N. Buena Vista, #209
Burbank, CA 91505
*Actor*
*Birthday: 3/19/71*

**James, Sonny**
818 18th Ave. South
Nashville, TN 37212
*Country singer*

**Jardine, Al**
Box 39
Big Sur, CA 93920
*Musician*

**Jarreau, Al**
9830 Wilshire Blvd.
Beverly Hills, CA 90212
*Singer*

**Jarrett, Keith**
PO Box 2728
Bala Cynwyd, PA 19004
*Musician*

**Jean, Norma**
1300 Division St.
Nashville, TN 37203
*Country singer*

**Jenner, Bruce**
PO Box 11137
Beverly Hills, CA 90213
*Olympic track and field medalist*
*Birthday: 10/28/49*

**Jennings, Peter**
7 W. 66th St.
New York, NY 10023
*News anchor*
*Birthday: 7/29/38*

**Jennings, Waylon**
824 Old Hickory Blvd.
Brentwood, TN 37027
*Country singer*
*Birthday: 6/15/37*

**Jeter, Derek**
% New York Yankees
Yankee Stadium
161 St. and River Ave.
Bronx, NY 10451
*Baseball player*

**Jett, Joan**
155 E. 55th St., #6H
New York, NY 10022
*Musician*

**Jewel**
PO Box 33494
San Diego, CA 92163
*Singer*

**Jillian, Ann**
PO Box 57739
Sherman Oaks, CA 91413
*Actress*

**John Paul II, Pope**
Palazzo Apostolico Vaticano
1-00120 Citta del Vaticano
Italy

**John, Sir Elton**
Woodside
Crump Hill Rd.
Old Windsor
Berkshire
England
*Singer*

**Johns, Glynis**
121 N. San Vicente Blvd.
Beverly Hills, CA 90211
*Actress*

**Johnson, Beverly**
8485-E Melrose Pl.
Los Angeles, CA 90046
*Model*

**Johnson, Davey**
% Baltimore Orioles
333 W. Camden St.
Baltimore, MD 21201
*Baseball player*

**Johnson, Don**
1122 S. Robertson Blvd., #15
Los Angeles, CA 90035
*Actor*
*Birthday: 12/15/49*

**Johnson, Dr. Virginia**
Campbell Plaza 59th and Arsenel
St. Louis, MO 63118
*Sex researcher*

**Johnson, Earvin Magic**
9100 Wilshire Blvd., #1060 W.
Tower
Beverly Hills, CA 90212
Or
% William Morris Agency
151 El Camino Dr.
Beverly Hills, CA 90212
*Athlete, businessman*
*Birthday: 8/14/59*

**Johnson, Jimmy**
Pro Player Stadium
2269 N.W. 199th St.
Miami, FL 33056
*Head coach of the Miami Dolphins*
*Birthday: 7/16/43*

**Johnson, Keyshawn**
% New York Jets
1000 Fulton Ave.
Hempstead, NY 11550
*Football player*

**Johnson, Lady Bird**
% LBJ Presidential Library
2313 Red River St.
Austin, TX 78705
Or
LBJ Ranch
Stonewall, TX 78671
*Former First Lady*

**Johnson, Michael**
818 18th Ave. S., 3rd Floor
Nashville, TN 37211
*Country singer*

**Jolie, Angelina**
% Industry Entertainment
955 Carrillo Dr., 3rd Floor
Los Angeles, CA 90048
*Actress*
*Birthday: 6/4/75*

**Al Jolson International Society**
2981 Westmoore Dr.
Columbus, OH 43204

**Jones, David Lynn**
% Mercury
901 18th Ave. South
Nashville, TN 37203
*Country singer*

**Jones, Davy**
PO Box 400
Beavertown, PA 17813
*Musician, member of the Monkees*

**Jones, Dean**
500 S. Buena Vista
Burbank, CA 91521
*Actor*

**Jones, George**
Rt. 3, Box 150
Murphy, NC 28906
*Country singer*

**Jones, James Earl**
PO Box 610
Pawling, NY 12564
*Actor, voice of CNN*

**Jones, Jenny**
454 N. Columbus Dr., 4th Floor
Chicago, IL 60611
Website: http://
www.jennyjones.com
*Talk show host*

**Jones, Parnelli**
PO Box "W"
Torrance, CA 90507
*Race car driver*

**Jones, Paula**
% General Delivery
Cabot, AR 72923
*Accused President Bill Clinton of sexual harassment*

**Jones, Quincy**
Quincy Jones/David Salzman
Entertainment
3800 Barham Blvd., #503
Los Angeles, CA 90068
*Composer, musician*

**Jones, Randy**
% San Diego Padres
PO Box 2000
San Diego, CA 92112
*Baseball player*

**Jones, Shirley**
Suite One Productions
8127 Melrose Ave., #1
Los Angeles, CA 90046
Or
11365 Ventura Blvd., #100
Studio City, CA. 91604
*Actress*

**Jones, Tom**
10100 Santa Monica Blvd., #225
Los Angeles, CA 90067
*Singer*

**Jordan, Michael**
676 Michigan Ave., #2940
Chicago, IL 60611
Website:http://cbs.sportsline.com/u/
jordan/
*Actor, athlete, businessman*
*Birthday: 2/17/63*

**Scott Joss Fan Club**
PO Box 6208
Santa Rosa, CA 95406

**Judd, Ashley**
% William Morris Agency
151 El Camino Dr.
Beverly Hills, CA 90212
Or
PO Box 680339
Franklin, TN 37068
*Actress*
*Birthday: 4/19/68*

**Judd, Naomi**
PO Box 682068
Nashville, TN 37217
*Country singer*

**Judd, Wynonna**
PO Box 682068
Nashville, TN 37217
E-mail: fanclub@wynonna.com
*Country singer*

**Jump, Gordon**
PO Box 2526
Costa Mesa, CA 92628

**Jurgenson, Sonny**
PO Box 53
Mt. Vernon, VA 22121

**K**

**Kaelin, Brian "Kato"**
6404 Wilshire Blvd., #950
Los Angeles, CA 90048
*Talk show host, actor, onetime
O. J. Simpson houseguest*

**Kalb, Marvin**
79 John F. Kennedy St.
Cambridge, MA 02138
*Broadcaster*

**Kane Bob**
% DC Comics
1325 Ave. of Americas
New York, NY 10019
*Batman creator*

**Kane, Big Daddy**
151 El Camino Dr.
Beverly Hills, CA 90212
*Old-school rapper, whose name
stands for King Asiatic No Equal*

**Kane, Carol**
8205 Santa Monica Blvd., #1426
West Hollywood, CA 90046
*Actress*
*Birthday: 6/18/52*

**Karolyi, Bela**
RR #12
Box 140
Huntsville, TX 77340
*Gymnastics coach*

**Karras, Alex**
Georgian Bay Productions
3815 W. Olive Ave., #202
Burbank, CA 91505
*Actor*
*Birthday: 7/15/35*

**Kasem, Casey**
% Global Satellite Network
14958 Ventura Blvd.
Sherman Oaks, CA 91403
*Radio and TV host*

**Katayama, Ukyo**
% Minardi Team S.p.A.
Via Spellanzani 21
I-48018 Faenza/RA
*Professional Formula-1 driver*

**Katzenberg, Jeffrey**
100 Universal City Plaza, #10
Universal City, CA 91608
*Co-founder of DreamWorks*

**Kauffman, David**
5826 IH 10 West, Suite #101
San Antonio, TX 78201
Website: http://
www.davidkauffman.com/
E-mail: david@davidkauffman.com
*Christian musician*

**Kawasaki, Guy**
PO Box 21631
Santa Barbara, CA 93121
Website: http://www.umsl.edu/~
sbmeade/macway/
E-mail: Mac Way@aol.com
*Mac guru*

**Kazan, Lainie**
9903 Santa Monica Blvd., #283
Beverly Hills, CA 90212
*Actress*

**Keaton, Michael**
11901 Santa Monica, #547
Los Angeles, CA 90025
*Actor*
*Birthday: 9/9/51*

**Keel, Howard**
% Clifford Prods.
394 Red River Rd.
Palm Desert, CA 92211
*Actor*
*Birthday: 4/13/17*

**Keel, John A.**
PO Box 351
Murray Hill Station
New York, NY 10016
*UFO researcher*

**Keeshan, Bob**
40 W. 57th St., #1600
New York, NY 10019
*Captain Kangaroo*
*Birthday: 6/27/27*

**Keillor, Garrison**
45 E. 7th St.
St. Paul, MN 55101
E-mail: gkeillor@madmax.mpr.org
*Radio host*

**Keitel, Harvey**
9560 Wilshire Blvd., #516
Beverly Hills, CA 90212
*Actor*

**Keith, Toby**
PO Box 8739
Rockford, IL 61126
*Country singer*

**Keener, Catherine**
PO Box 5617
Beverly Hills, CA 90210
*Actress*

**Keller, Marthe**
5 rue Saint Dominique
Paris 75007
France
*Actress*
*Birthday: 2/28/45*

**Kemp, Shawn**
% Seattle Supersonics
190 Queen Anne Ave., N. Suite
#200
Seattle, WA 98109
*Basketball player*

**Kendalls, The**
2802 Columbine Pl.
Nashville, TN 37204
*Singing group*

**Kennedy, Jamie**
9465 Wilshire Blvd., #212
Beverly Hills, CA 90212
*Actor*

**Kennedy, Ray**
PO Box 158309
Nashville, TN 37215
*Country singer*

**Kennedy, Senator Edward M.
(Ted)**
2416 Tracy Pl. NW
Washington, DC 20008

**Kennedy, Tom**
11365 Ventura Blvd., #100
Studio City, CA 91604
*TV game show host, Jack Narz's
brother*
*Birthday: 2/26/27*

**Kenzle, Leila**
151 El Camino Dr.
Beverly Hills, CA 90212
*Actress*

**Kercheval, Ken**
PO Box 325
Goshen, KY 40026
*Actor*
*Birthday: 7/15/35*

**Kerns, Joanna**
PO Box 49216
Los Angeles, CA 90049
*Actress*
*Birthday: 2/12/53*

**Kerr, Deborah**
Wyherut
7250 Klosters
Grisons
Switzerland
*Actress*

**Kerr, Graham**
300 S. 1st St., #C-2
Mt. Vernon, WA 98273
*The Galloping Gourmet*

**Kershaw, Doug**
Rt. 1
Box 34285
Weld County Rd. 47
Eaton, CO 80615
*Cajun singer and musician*

**Kershaw, Sammy**
PO Box 121739
Nashville, TN 37212
*Country singer*

**Ketchum, Hal**
1700 Hayes St., #304
Nashville, TN 37203
*Country singer*

**Ketchum, Hank**
PO Box 1997
Monterey, CA 93942
*Cartoonist*

**Kevorkian, Dr. Jack**
4870 Lockhart St.
W. Bloomfield, MI 48323
*Suicide assistance doctor*

**Key, Jimmy**
% Baltimore Orioles
333 West Camden St.
Baltimore, MD 21201
*Baseball player*

**Keyes, Dr. Alan**
1030 115th St. NW, #700
Washington, DC 20005
*Presidential candidate, talk show
host*
*Birthday: 8/7/50*

**Keysey, Ken**
Rt. 8 Box 477
Pleasant Hill, OR 97401
*Author*

**Khamani, Pres. Mohammad**
The Majilis
Tehran
Iran

**Khan, The Aga Iv**
Aga Ailemont
60270 Gouvieux
France

**Khan, Chaka**
PO Box 16680
Beverly Hills, CA 90209
*Singer*
*Birthday: 3/23/53*

**Khan, Prince Sadruddin Aga**
CH-1245
Collonge-Bellerive
Switzerland

**Khan, Princess Yasmin**
146 Central Park W.
New York, NY 10023

**Khruschev, Sergei**
PO Box 1948
Providence, RI 02912
*Son of the former Soviet premiere*
*Nikita Khruschev*

**Kidd, Jason**
% Phoenix Suns
PO Box 1369
Phoenix, AZ 85001
*Basketball player*

**Kidder, Margot**
220 Pine Creek Rd.
Livingstone, MT 59047
*Actress*
*Birthday: 10/17/48*

**Kidman, Nicole**
5555 Melrose Ave.
Lucille Ball Bldg., #00
Los Angeles, CA 90038
Or
9830 Wilshire Blvd.
Beverly Hills, CA 90212
*Actress*
*Birthday: 6/20/67*

**Killebrew, Harmon**
PO Box 14550
Scottsdale, AZ 85267
*Ex-baseball player*

**Killy, Jean-Claude**
13 Chemin ellefontaine
1223 Cologny
GE Switzerland
*Olympic skier*

**Kilmer, Val**
PO Box 362
Tesuque, NM 87574
Or
9830 Wilshire Blvd.
Beverly Hills, CA 90212
*Actor*
*Birthday: 12/31/59*

**Kimes, Royal Wade**
PO Box 128038
Nashville, TN 37212
*Country singer*

**King, Alan**
888 7th Ave., #3800
New York, NY 10106
*Comedian*

**King, B. B.**
1414 Sixth Ave.
New York, NY 10019
*Musician*

**King, Carole**
Robinson Bar Ranch
Box 146
Stanley, ID 83278
*Singer, songwriter*

**King, Don**
% Don King Enterprises
871 W. Oakland Park Ave.
Fort Lauderdale, FL 33311
*Impressario*
*Birthday: 8/20/31*

**King, Pee Wee**
% CMA
1 Music Circle South
Nashville, TN 37203
*Country singer*

**King, Perry**
1033 Gayley Ave., #201
Los Angeles, CA 90024
*Actor*

**King, Rodney**
9100 Wilshire Blvd., #250W
Beverly Hills, CA 90212
Website: http://www.rodney-
king.com/altapazz/default.htm

**King, Stephen**
47 W. Broadway
Banfor, ME 04401
*Author*

**Kingsley, Ben**
76 Oxford St.
London W1N OAX
England
*Actor*

**Kinmont, Kathleen**
6404 Wilshire Blvd., #950
Los Angeles, CA 90048
*Actress*

**Kinnear, Greg**
3000 W. Alameda Ave., #2908
Burbank, CA 91523
Or
9150 Wilshire Blvd., #350
Beverly Hills, CA 90212
*Talk show host*

**Kinney, Kathy**
10061 Riverside Dr., #777
North Hollywood, CA 91607

**Kinski, Nastassja**
% William Morris Agency
151 El Camino Dr.
Beverly Hills, CA 90212
*Actress, model*

**Kinsley, Michael**
5602 Lakeview Dr., #J
Kirkland, WA 98033
*Editor of* Slate Magazine

**Kirby, Durwood**
PO Box 3054
N. Ft. Myers, FL 33918
*Actor, announcer*

**Kirkconnell, Clare**
Box 63
Rutherford, CA 94573
*Actress*

**Kirkland, Sally**
11300 W. Olympic Blvd., #610
Los Angeles, CA 90064
*Actress*
*Birthday: 10/31/44*

**Kirsebom, Vendela**
151 El Camino Dr.
Beverly Hills, CA 90212
*Actress*

**Kissinger, Dr. Henry**
435 E. 52nd St.
New York, NY 10022
*Nobel laureate, statesman,
secretary of state under presidents
Richard M. Nixon and Gerald R.
Ford*

**Klasky, Arlene**
1258 N. Highland Ave.
Hollywood, CA 90038
Website: http://
www.klaskycsupo.com
*Creator of* Rugrats

**Klein, Calvin**
205 W. 39th St.
New York, NY 10018
*Fashion designer*

**Klemp, Cardinal Josef-Koiski**
U1Miodowa 17
PL-00-583
Warsaw
Poland

**Klemperer, Werner**
44 W. 62nd St., 10th Floor
New York, NY 10023
*Actor*
*Birthday: 3/29/19*

**Klensch, Elsa**
1050 Techwood Dr. NW
Atlanta, GA 30318
*Fashion commentator*

**Kline, Kevin**
151 El Camino Dr.
Beverly Hills, CA 90212
*Actor*
*Birthday: 10/24/47*

**Kline, Richard**
4530 Balboa Blvd.
Encino, CA 91316
*Comedian*

**Klum, Heidi**
% Elite Model Managemt
111 East 22nd St.
New York, NY 10010
*Model*

**Knievel, Evel**
2375 E. Tropicana Ave., #178
Las Vegas, NV 89119
*Daredevil*

**Knight, Shirley**
19528 Ventura Blvd., #559
Tarzana, CA 91356
*Actress*

**Knotts, Don**
1854 S. Beverly Glenn, #402
Los Angeles, CA 90025
*Actor*

**Kober, Jeff**
13333 Ventura Blvd., #205
Sherman Oaks, CA 91423
*Actor*

**Koch, ex-Mayor Edward**
1290 Ave. of the Americas
New York, NY 10104
*Former Mayor of New York*

**Kodjoe, Boris**
% Ford Model Agency
344 E. 59th St.
New York, NY 10022
*Model*

**Koenig, Walter**
PO Box 4395
North Hollywod, CA 91607
*Actor*

**Kohl, ex-Chancellor Helmut**
Marbacher Str. 11
D-67071 Ludwighsfen
Germany
*Former Chancellor of West
Germany*

**Kool Moe Dee**
151 El Camion Dr.
Beverly Hills, CA 90212
*Musician*

**Koontz, Dean R.**
PO Box 9529
New Port Beach, CA 92658
*Author*

**Koop, Dr. Everett**
3 Ivy Point Way
Hanover, NH 03755
*Former Surgeon General*

**Korda, Michael**
1230 Ave. of the Americas
New York, NY 10019
*Author and Editor-in-chief at Simon
& Schuster*

**Knight, Wayne**
10061 Riverside Dr., #1043
Toluca Lake, CA 91602
*Actor*

**Kournikova, Anna**
5500 34th St.
West Bradenton, FL 34210
*Tennis player*

**Kozlowski, Linda**
5757 Wilshire Blvd., #1
Los Angeles, CA 90036
*Actress*

**Krakowski, Jane**
8271 Melrose Ave., #110
Los Angeles, CA 90046
*Actress*

**Kramer, Stefanie**
8271 Melrose Ave., #110
Los Angeles, CA 90046
*Actress*

**Krauss, Alison**
PO Box 121711
Nashville, TN 37212
Website: http://
www.alisonkrauss.com/
*Singer*

**Kreskin**
PO Box 1383
West Caldwell, NJ 07006
*Mentalist*

**Kristen, Marta**
3575 Cahuenga Blvd., W. #500
Los Angeles, CA 90068
*Actress*

**Kristofferson, Kris**
PO Box 2147
Malibu, CA 90265
Or
313 Lakeshore Dr.
Marietta, GA 30067
*Songwriter, actor*

**Kruger, Hardy**
Box 726
Crestline, CA 92325
*Actor*

**Kstsulas, Andreas**
% Innovative Artists
1999 Ave. of the Stars, #2850
Los Angeles, CA 90067
*Plays Commander Tomalak on*
Star Trek: The Next Generation

**Kudrow, Lisa**
1122 S. Robertson Blvd., #15
Los Angeles, CA 90035
*Actress*

**Kumantunga, President Chandrika**
President Secretariat
Columbo 1
Sri Lanka

**Kurtz, Swoozie**
320 Central Park W.
New York, NY 10025
*Actress*
*Birthday: 9/6/44*

**Kwan, Michelle**
% Proper Marketing Assoc.
44450 Pinetree Dr., #103
Plymouth, MI 48170

**Kwan, Nancy**
PO Box 50747
Santa Barbara, CA 93150
*Actress*

**L**

**Labelle, Patti**
1212 Grennox Rd.
Wynnewood, PA 19096
*Singer*
*Birthday: 10/4/44*

**Labonte, Terry**
PO Box 9
Harrisburg, NC 28075
*Race car driver*
*Birthday: 11/16/56*

**Ladd, Cheryl**
8942 Wilshire Blvd.
Beverly Hills, CA 90211
*Actress*
*Birthday: 7/2/51*

**Ladd, Diane**
PO Box 1859
Ojai, CA 93024
*Actress, Laura Dern is her daughter*
*Birthday: 11/29/32*

**Laffer, Dr. Arthur**
5375 Executive Square, #330
La Jolla, CA 92037
*Economist*

**Lagerfeld, Karl**
14 blvd. De la Madeleine
Paris F-75008
France
*Fashion designer and*
*photographer*
*Birthday: 1938*

**Lahti, Christine**
1122 S. Robertson Blvd., #15
Los Angeles, CA 90035
*Birthday: 4/5/50*

**Lai, Francis**
4146 Lankershim Blvd., #401
North Hollywood, CA 91602
Website:http://www.francis-lai.com/
*Composer*

**Laine, Dame Cleo**
The Old Rectory
Wavendon
Milton Keynes MK17 8LT
England
*Singer*

**Laine, Frankie**
PO Box 6910
San Diego, CA 92166
*Singer*

**Laird, Melvin**
1730 Rhode Island Ave. NW
Washington, DC 20036
*American politician, U.S. Secretary of Defense*

**Lake, Ricki**
226 W. 26th St., #400
New York, NY 10010
*Actress, talk show host*
*Birthday: 9/21/68*

**Laker, Sir Freddie**
138 Chapside
London Ec2V 6BL
England
*Founder of original Laker Airways*

**Lakin, Christine**
*Step by Step* Fan Mail
2040 Ave. of the Stars
Los Angeles, CA 90067
*Actress*
*Birthday: 1/25/79*

**Lama, Dalai**
Thekchen Choling
McLeod Gunji
Dharamsala
Himachal Pradesh
India
*Religious leader*
*Birthday: 7/6/35*

**Lamas, Lorenzo**
3727 W. Magnolia Blvd., #807
Burbank, CA 91505
*Actor*
*Birthday: 1/20/58*

**Lambert, Christopher**
1901 Ave. of the Stars, #1245
Los Angeles, CA 90067
*Actor*
*Birtday: 3/29/57*

**Lamm, ex-Gov. Richard**
University of Denver
Center for Public Policy
Denver, CO 80208
*Former Governor of Colorado*

**Landers, Ann**
435 N. Michigan Ave.
Chicago, IL 60611
*Advice columnist*

**Landers, Audrey**
4048 Las Palmas Dr.
Sarasota, FL 34238
*Actress*
*Birthday: 7/18/59*

**Landers, Judy**
3933 Losillas Dr.
Sarasota, FL 34238
*Actress*
*Birthday: 10/7/61*

**Lando, Joe**
% William Morris Agency
151 S. El Camino Dr.
Beverly Hills, CA 90212
*Actor*
*Birthday: 12/9/61*

**Landry, Tom**
8411 Preston Rd., Suite 720-LB3
Dallas, TX 75225
Or
% Football Hall of Fame
2121 George Halas Dr. NW
Canton, OH 44708
*Ex-football player*

**Lane, Cristy**
LS Records
120 Hickory St.
Nashville, TN 37115
*Country singer*

**Lane, Diane**
25 Sea Colony Dr.
Santa Monica, CA 90405
*Actress*
*Birthday: 1/22/63*

**Lane, Nathan**
PO Box 1249
White River Junction, VT 05001
*Actor*

**lang, k. d.**
% Burnstead Prod.
PO Box 33800
Station D
Vancouver BC V6J 5C7
Canada
*Singer*
*Birthday: 11/2/61*

**Lange, Hope**
1801 Ave. of the Stars, #902
Los Angeles, CA 90067
*Actress*

**Lange, Jessica**
8942 Wilshire Blvd.
Beverly Hills, CA 90211
*Actress*

**Lange, Ted**
17801 Victory Blvd.
Reseda, CA 91335
*Actor*

**Langella, Frank**
151 El Camino Dr.
Beverly Hills, CA 90212
*Actor*
*Birthday: 1/1/40*

**Langenkamp, Heather**
9229 Sunset Blvd, #311
Los Angeles, CA 90069

**Lansbury, Angela**
100 Universal City Plaza, Bldg.,
426
Universal City, CA 91608
*Actress*

**LaPaglia, Anthony**
955 S. Carrillo Dr., #300
Los Angeles, CA 90048
*Actor*

**Larroquette, John**
PO Box 6910
Malibu, CA 90264
*Actor*

**Larson, Gary**
Box 36A
Denver, CO 80236
*Cartoonist*

**Larson, Nicolette**
3818 Abbot Martin Rd.
Nashville, TN 37215
*Singer*

**La Salle, Eriq**
PO Box 2396
Beverly Hills, CA 90213
*Actor*

**Lasorda, Tommy**
% L.A. Dodgers
1000 Elysian Park Blvd.
Los Angeles, CA 90012
*Ex-manager of the Dodgers*

**Lassie**
16133 Soledad Canyon Rd.
Canyon Country, CA 91351
*Acting dog*

**Latifah, Queen**
% William Morris Agency
151 El Camino Dr.
Beverly Hills, CA 90212
Or
155 Morgan St.
Jersey City, NJ 07302
*Actress, singer, talk show host*
*Birthday: 3/18/70*

**Lauer, Matt**
30 Rockefeller Plaza, #701
New York, NY 10112
Today Show *host*

**Laughlin, Tom**
PO Box 25355
Los Angeles, CA 90025
*Actor, director*

**Lauper, Cyndi**
826 Broadway, #400
New York, NY 10003
*Singer, songwriter*
*Birthday: 6/20/53*

**Lauren, Ralph**
1107 5th Ave.
New York, NY 10128
*Fashion designer*
*Birthday: 10/14/39*

**Laurie, Piper**
PMB 931
2118 Wilshire Blvd.
Santa Monica, CA 90403
*Actress*

**Laurie, Hugh**
% Hamilton Asper Management
Ground Floor
24 Hanway St.
London W1P 9DD
United Kingdom
*Actor*

**Laver, Rod**
Box 4798
Hilton Head Island, SC 29928
*Tennis player*
*Birthday: 8/9/38*

**Lavin, Linda**
PO Box 2847
Wilmington, NC 28402
*Actress*

**Lawless, Lucy**
100 Universal City Plaza, #415A
Universal City, CA 91608
*Actress*

**The Lucy Lawless Fan Club**
65 Edwin Rd.
Waltham, MA 02154

**Lawrence, Martin**
9560 Wilshire Blvd., #516
Beverly Hills, CA 91212
Or
PO Box 7304, Suite 440
North Hollywood, CA 91603
*Actor*

**Lawrence, Sharon**
PO Box 462048
Los Angeles, CA 90046
*Actress*

**Lawrence, Steve**
10560 Wilshire Blvd., #601
Los Angeles, CA 90046
*Singer*

**Lawrence, Tracy**
2100 West End Ave., #1000
Nashville, TN 37203
*Country singer*

**Lawson, Dennis**
21 Golden Sq.
London W1R 3PA
England
*Actor*

**Leach, Robin**
342 Madison Ave., #950
New York, NY 10173
*Television host*

**Leakey, Dr. Richard**
PO Box 24926
Nairobi
Kenya
*Paleontologist*

**Lear, Norman**
1999 Ave. of the Stars, #500
Los Angeles, CA 90067
*TV producer*

**Learned, Michael**
1600 N. Beverly Dr.
Beverly Hills, CA 90210
*Actress*

**Leary, Denis**
9560 Wilshire Blvd., #516
Beverly Hills, CA 90212
*Comedian*

**Le Blanc, Matt**
1122 S. Robertson Blvd., #15
Los Angeles, CA 90035
*Actor*

**Le Brock, Kelly**
PO Box 57593
Sherman Oaks, CA 91403
Website: http://
www.kellylebrock.net/
*Actress*

**LeDoux, Chris**
PO Box 253
Sumner, IA 50674
*Country singer*

**Lee, Brenda (Brenda Mae Tarpley)**
Brenda Lee Productions, Inc.
PO Box 101188
Nashville, TN 37210
Website: http://
www.brendalee.com/
*Singer*
*Birthday: 12/11/44*

**Lee, Christopher**
21 Golden Square
GB-London W12 3PA
England

**Lee, Johnny**
PO Box 1644
Dickinson, TX 77539
*Country singer*

**Lee, Spike**
40 Acres and A Mule Filmworks
124 DeKalb, 2nd Floor
Brooklyn, NY 11217
*Film director*

**Lee, Stan**
% Marvel Films
1440 S. Sepulveda, Suite #114
Los Angeles, CA 90025
Or
% Marvel Comics
387 Park Ave. South
New York, NY 10016
E-mail: stanzfanz@aol.com
*Publisher of Spider Man*

**Leick, Hudson**
PO Box 775
Fair Oaks, CA 95628
Website: http://
www.hudsonleickfan.com
*Actress*

**Leigh, Jennifer Jason**
% International Creative
Management
8942 Wilshire Blvd.
Beverly Hills, CA 90211
*Actress*
*Birthday: 2/5/62*

**Leisure, David**
8428-C Melrose Pl.
Los Angeles, CA 90046
*Actor*
*Birthday: 11/16/?*

**Lemmon, Jack**
955 S. Carrillo Dr., #300
Los Angeles, CA 90048
*Actor*
*Birthday: 2/8/25*

**Lennon, Julian**
30 Ives St.
London SW3 2ND
England
*Musician*

**Lennox, Annie**
35-37 Park Gate Rd.
Unit 2
Ransome's Docks
London SW11 4NP
England
*Singer*
*Birthday: 12/25/54*

**Leno, Jay**
PO Box 7885
Burbank, CA 91510
Tonight Show *host*
*Birthday: 4/20/50*

**Leonard, Robert Sean**
PO Box 103
Waldwick, NJ 07463
*Actor*
*Birthday: 2/28/69*

**Leoni, Tea**
2300 West Victory Blvd., #384
Burbank, CA 91506
*Actress, married to David
Duchovny*

**Leto, Jared**
1999 Ave. of the Stars, Suite 2850
Los Angeles, CA 90067
*Actor*

**Letterman, David**
1697 Broadway
New York, NY 10019
Or
9830 Wilshire Blvd.
Beverly Hills, CA 90212
*Comedian, talk show host*
*Birthday: 4/12/47*

**Levine, Michael**
Levine Communications Office
10333 Ashton Ave.
Los Angeles, CA 90024
E-mail: levinepr@earthlink.net
*Author, of The Address Book,*
*media specialist*
*Birthday: 4/17/54*

**Lewinsky, Monica**
660 Greenwich St.
New York, NY 10014
*Former White House intern*

**Lewis, Al**
612 Lighthouse Ave., #220
Pacific Grove, CA 93951
*Actor, played Grandpa on the*
Munsters

**Lewis, Carl**
PO Box 571990
Houston, TX 77082
*Olympic competitor in track and*
*field*

**Lewis, Huey**
PO Box 819
Mill Valley, CA 94942
*Singer*
*Birthday: 7/5/50*

**Lewis, Jerry**
3160 W. Sahara Ave., #816
Las Vegas, NV 89102
Or
% William Morris Agency
151 El Camino Dr.
Beverly Hills, CA 90212
*Actor, comedian*
*Birthday: 3/16/26*

**Lewis, Jerry Lee**
PO Box 23162
Nashville, TN 37202
*Singer*

**Liddy, G. Gordon**
PO Box 3649
Washington, DC 20007
Website: http://www.rtis.com/liddy/
E-mail: gordonliddy@aol.com
*Watergate conspirator and talk*
*show host*

**Lien, Jennifer**
% Paramount Pictures
5555 Melrose Ave.
Los Angeles, CA 90038
*Actor, plays Kes or* Star Trek:
Voyager

**Limbaugh, Rush**
PO Box 2182
Palm Beach, FL 33480
Or
366 Madison Ave., #700
New York, NY 10017
Website: http://
www.rushlimbaugh.com/home/
guest.html
E-mail: rush@eibnet.com
*Talk show host*
*Birthday: 1/12/51*

**Linden, Hal**
9100 Sunset Blvd., #4530TE
Beverly Hills, CA 90212
*Actor*
*Birthday: 3/20/31*

**Lindenberg, Udo**
% Kempinski Hotel Atlantic
Am der Alster 72
Hamburg D20099
Germany
*Singer*

**Lindsey, George**
% Avon Books
1350 Ave. of the Americas
New York, NY 10019
*Country singer*

**Liotta, Ray**
955 S. Carrillo Dr., #300
Los Angeles, CA 90048
*Actor*
*Birthday: 12/18/?*

**Lipinski, Tara**
PO Box 472288
Charlotte, NC 28247
*Ice skater*

**Lipnicki, Jonathan**
% Brillstein-Greg Ent.
9150 Wilshire Blvd., #350
Beverly Hills, CA 90212
*Actor*
*Birthday: 10/22/90*

**Little Richard (Richard Wayne Penniman)**
8401 Sunset Blvd.
Los Angeles, CA 90069
*Singer*
*Birthday: 12/5/32*

**Livingston, Ron**
1180 S. Beverly Dr., #608
Los Angeles, CA 90035
*Actor*

**LL Cool J**
% Rush Mgmt.
298 Elisabeth St.
New York, NY 10012
*Rap artist*

**Lloyd, Christopher**
PO Box 491246
Los Angeles, CA 90049
*Actor*

**Lloyd, Kathleen**
10100 Santa Monica Blvd., #2500
Los Angeles, CA 90067
*Actress*

**Lo Bianco, Tony**
15821 Ventura Blvd., #235
Encino, CA 91436
*Actor*

**Locke, Sandra**
15821 Ventura Blvd., #235
Encino, CA 91436
*Actress*
*Birthday: 5/28/48*

**Lockhart, June**
PO Box 3207
Santa Monica, CA 90403
*Actress*

**Locklear, Heather**
139 S. Beverly Blvd., #230
Bevelry Hills, CA 90212
*Actress*
*Birthday: 9/25/61*

**Loeb, Lisa**
98930 Wilshire Blvd.
Bevelry Hills, CA 90212
*Actress, singer*

**Lollobrigida, Gina**
Via Appia Antica 223
Roma I-00179
Italy
*Actress*
*Birthday: 7/4/27*

**London, Jason**
151 El Camino Dr.
Beverly Hills, CA 90212
*Actor*

**Long, Kathy**
1800 Ave. of the Stars, Suite #400
Los Angeles, CA 90067
*Actress*

**Long, Shelley**
15237 Sunset Blvd.
Pacific Palisades, CA 90272
*Actress*
*Birthday: 8/23/49*

**Lopez, Jennifer**
PO Box 57593
Sherman Oaks, CA 91403
*Actress, singer*
*Birthday: 7/24/70*

**Lopez, Mario**
PO Box 4736
Chatsworth, CA 91311
*Actor*
*Birthday: 10/10/73*

**Lords, Traci (Norma Kuzma)**
100 Universal City Plaza Bldg. 507, #3D
Universal City, CA 91608
*Actress*
*Birthday: 5/7/68*

**Loren, Sophia (Sophia Scicolone)**
1151 Hidden Valley Rd.
Thousand Oaks, CA 91361
*Actress*
*Birthday: 9/20/34*

**Louganis, Greg**
PO Box 4130
Malibu, CA 90264
*Olympic diver*

**Louis-Dreyfus, Julia**
5757 Wilshire Blvd., #1
Los Angeles, CA 90036
*Actress*
*Birthday: 1/13/61*

**Louise, Tina**
310 E. 46th St., #18T
New York, NY 10017
*Actress*

**Louvin, Charlie**
PO Box 140324
Nashville, TN 37214
*Country singer*

**Love, Courtney**
8942 Wilshire Blvd.
Beverly Hills, CA 90211
*Actress, musician*
*Birthday: 7/9/64*

**Loveless, Patty**
PO Box 1423
White House, TN 37188
*Country singer*

**Lovett, Lyle**
% General Delivery
Klein, TX 77391
*Singer*

**Lowe, Rob**
270 N. Canon Dr., #1072
Beverly Hills, CA 90210
Or
% Celebrity Merchandise
PMB 710
15030 Ventura Blvd.
Sherman Oaks, CA 91403
*Actor*
*Birthday: 3/17/64*

**Lowell, Carey**
8942 Wilshire Blvd.
Beverly Hills, CA 90211
*Actress*

**Lucas, George**
PO Box 2009
San Rafael, CA 94912
*Director, producer*
*Birthday: 5/14/44*

**Lucci, Susan**
PO Box 621
Quogue, NY 11959
*Soap opera star*
*Birthday: 12/23/45*

**Luchsinger, Susie**
PO Box 990
Atoka, OK 74525
*Country singer*

**Lumbly, Carl**
8730 Sunset Blvd., #480
Los Angeles, CA 90069
*Actor*

**Lundgren, Dolph**
1999 Ave. of the Stars, #2100
Los Angeles, CA 90067
*Actor*
*Birthday: 10/18/59*

**Lundy, Jessica**
151 El Camino Dr.
Beverly Hills, CA 90212
*Actress*

**Lütgenhorst, David**
% Agentur Goosmann
Fichtenstr. 33
Unterföhring 85774
Germany
*Actor*

**Lydon, John (Johnny Rotten)**
14724 Ventura Blvd., #410
Sherman Oaks, CA 91403
*Musician*

**Lynch, David**
PO Box 93624
Los Angeles, CA 90093
*Director*

**Lynley, Carol**
% Pierce and Shelly
612 Lighthouse Ave., #275
Pacific Grove, CA 93951
E-mail: carolynley@aol.com
*Actress*
*Birthday: 2/13/42*

**Lynn, Amber**
12400 Ventura Blvd., #329
Studio City, CA 91604
*Actress*

**Lynn, Loretta**
PO Box 120369
Nashville, TN 37212
*Country singer*

**Lynne, Shelby**
PO Box 190
Monroeville, AL 36461
*Country singer*

# M

**MacAnally, Mac**
% T. K. Kimbrell
TKO Management
4205 Hillsboro Rd., Suite. #208
Nashville, TN 37215
*Country singer*

**MacDowell, Andie**
939 8th Ave., #400
New York, NY 10019
*Actress*
*Birthday: 5/4/58*

**MacGraw, Ali**
% Provident Financial Mgmt.
10345 W. Olympic Blvd., #200
Los Angeles, CA 90064
*Actress*
*Birthday: 4/1/38*

**MacIntire, Reba**
30 Music Sq. W.
Nashville, TN 37203
Or
511 Fairground Ct.
Nashville, TN 37204
*Country singer*

**MacKenzie, Gisele**
3500 W. Olive Ave., #1400
Burbank, CA 91505
*Actress*

**Mackie, Bob**
1400 Broadway
New York, NY 10018
*Fashion designer*

**MacLaine, Shirley**
25200 Old Malibu Rd., #4
Malibu, CA 90265
*Actress*

**MacLeod, Gavin**
1025 Fifth Ave.
New York, NY 10028
*Actor*

**Macnee, Patrick**
PO Box 1685
Palm Springs, CA 92263
*Actor*
*Birthday: 2/6/22*

**MacPherson, Elle**
414 E. 52nd St. PH B
New York, NY 10022
*Model, actress*

**Macy, William H.**
8383 Wilshire Blvd., #550
Beverly Hills, CA 90211
*Actor*

**Madden, John**
31/32 Soho SQ
London W1V 5DG
England
*Director*
*Birthday: 4/10/36*

**Madden, John**
5095 Coronado Blvd.
Pleasanton, CA 94588
*Sportscaster*

**Madigan, Amy**
151 El Camino Dr.
Beverly Hills, CA 90212
*Actress*

**Madonna**
8491 Sunset Blvd., #485
Los Angeles, CA 90069
*Actress, singer, mother of daughter*
*Lourdes (born 10/14/96) and son*
*Rocco Ritchie (born 8/11/00)*
*Birthday: 8/16/58*

**Mae, Vanessa**
% PO Box 363
Bournmouth
Dorset
BH76LA
United Kingdom
*Singer*
*Birthday: 10/27/78*

**Magnussenn, Jan**
% Stewart Grand Prix Ltd.
16 Tanners Dr.
Blakelands
GB-Milton Keynes MK14 5BW
Or
% Team AMG Mercedes
Daimlerstr. 1
Affalterbach D-71563
*Professional Formula-1 driver*
*Birthday: 7/4/73*

**Mahal, Taj**
PO Box 429090
San Francisco, CA 94142
*Musician*

**Maher, Bill**
% *Politically Incorrect*
CBS Television City
7800 Beverly Blvd.
Los Angeles, CA 90036
*Actor, TV host of* Politically
Incorrect

**Mahony, Cardinal Roger**
1531 W. 9th St.
Los Angeles, CA 90015

**Majorino, Tina**
1640 S. Sepulveda
PMB 530
Los Angeles, CA 90025
*Actress*

**Makkena, Wendy**
PO Box 5617
Beverly Hills, CA 90212
*Actress*

**Malkovich, John**
PO Box 5106
Westport, CT 06881
*Actor*
*Birthday: 12/9/53*

**Mamet, David**
PO Box 381589
Cambirde, MA 02238
*Director*

**Mancuso, Nick**
3500 W. Olive Ave., #1400
Burbank, CA 91505
*Actor*

**Mandel, Howie**
8942 Wilshire Blvd.
Beverly Hills, CA 90211
*Comedian, actor*

**Mandela, President Nelson**
51 Plain St.
Johannesburg 2001
South Africa
*President of South Africa*

**Mandela, Winnie**
Orlando West
Soweto
Johannesburg
South Africa

**Mandrell, Barbara**
PO Box 100
Whites Creek, TN 37189
*Singer*

**Erlene Mandrell Friend's Club**
2046 Parkway
Pigeon Forge, TN 37863
*Singer*

**Mandrell, Louise**
2046 Parkway
Pigeon Forge, TN 37863
*Singer*

**Manetti, Larry**
% Epstein/Wyckoff
280 S. Beverly Dr., #400
Beverly Hills, CA 90212
*Actor*

**Manheim, Camryn**
9057-C Nemo St.
West Hollywood, CA 90069
Or
*The Practice*
% 20th Century Fox
10201 W. Pico Blvd.
Los Angeles, CA 90035
E-mail: camrynmail@aol.com
*Actress*

**Mann, Michael**
13746 Sunset Blvd.
Pacific Palisades, CA 90272
*Director*

**Manners, Miss**
1651 Harvard St. NW
Washington, DE 20009
*Etiquette specialist*

**Manoff, Dinah**
21244 Ventura Blvd., #101
Woodland Hills, CA 91364
*Actress*
*Birthday: 1/25/58*

**Manson, Charles**
#B33920
Pelican Bay Prison
Box 7000
Crescent City, CA 95531-7000
*Convicted serial killer/cult leader*
*Birthday: 11/11/34*

**Manson, Marilyn**
25935 Detroit Rd.
Westlake, OH 44145
*Musician*

**Mantegna, Joe**
% Peter Strain
1500 Broadway, 2001
New York, NY 10036
*Actor*

**Manzarek, Ray**
1900 Ave. of the Stars, #1040
Los Angeles, CA 90067
*Actor*

**Maples, Marla**
725 Fifth Ave.
New York, NY 10022
*Donald Trump's ex-wife*

**Maradona, Diego**
% FC Boca Juniors
Brandsen 805
1161 Capital Federal
Argentina
*Professional soccer player*
*Birthday: 10/30/60*

**Marceau, Marcel**
PO Box 411197
San Francisco, CA 94141
*Mime*

**March, Barbara**
% Judy Schoen Assoc.
606 N. Larchmont Blvd., #309
Los Angeles, CA 90004
*Plays Lursa on* Star Trek: The Next
Generation *and* Star Trek:
Deep Space Nine

**March, Jane**
5 Jubilee Pl., #100
London SW3 3TD
United Kingdom
*Actress*

**Marcos, Imelda**
Leyte Providencia Dept.
Tolosa, Leyte
Philippines
*Former First Lady*

**Marcy, Dr. Geoffrey**
Department of Physics and
Astronomy
San Francisco State University
1600 Holloway
San Francisco, CA 94132

**Margolin, Stuart**
10000 Santa Monica Blvd., #305
Los Angeles, CA 90067
*Actor*

**Margolis, Cindy**
345 N. Maple Dr., #185
Beverly Hills, CA 90212
Website: http://
www.cindymargolis.com/index.cfm
*Model, actress*

**Margulies, Julianna**
405 S. Beverly Dr., #500
Beverly Hills, CA 90212
*Actress*

**Marin, Richard (Cheech)**
1122 S. Robertson Blvd., #15
Los Angeles, CA 90035
*Actor*

**Marley, Ziggy**
Jack's Hill
Kingston
Jamaica
*Musician*

**Marrs, Texe**
1708 Patterson Rd.
Austin, TX 78733
*Religious author*

**Marsden, Jason**
10753 Santa Monica Blvd., #130
Los Angeles, CA 90025
*Actor*

**Marshall Tucker Band**
100 W. Putnam
Greenwich, CT 06830
*Music group*

**Marshall, Penny**
9465 Wilshire Blvd., #419
Beverly Hills, CA 90212
*Actress, director*

**Marshall, Peter**
11365 Ventura Blvd., #100
Studio City, CA 91604
*TV game show host*
*Birthday: 3/20/27*

**Martell, Donna**
PO Box 3335
Granada Hills, CA 91394
*Actress*

**Martin, Dick**
30765 Pacific Coast Hwy., #103
Malibu, CA 90265
*Actor, television personality*

**Martin, Pamela Sue**
℅ Pierce and Shelly
612 Lighthouse Ave., #275
Pacific Grove, CA 93951
E-mail: PAMSUEMART@aol.com
*Actress*
*Birthday: 1/5/54*

**Martin, Ricky**
℅ CCA
9830 Wilshire Blvd.
Beverly Hills, CA 90212
*Singer*
*Birthday: 12/24/71*

**Martin, Steve**
PO Box 929
Beverly Hills, CA 90213
*Actor, comedian*

**Martindale, Wink**
11365 Ventura Blvd., #100
Studio City, CA 91604
*TV game show host*
*Birthday: 12/4/34*

**Masekela, Hugh**
230 Park Ave., #1512
New York, NY 10169
*Musician*

**Maske, Henry**
℅ Sauerland Promotion
Hochstadenstr. 1–3
Köln 50674
Germany
Or
℅ WLT Sport Int.
Römerstr. 108
Trier 54293
Germany
*Former professional boxer*
*Birthday: 1/6/64*

**Mason, Marsha**
320 Galiston St., #402B
Santa Fe, NM 87501
*Actress*
*Birthday: 4/3/42*

**Masterson, Mary Stuart**
℅ Constellation
PO Box 1249
White River Junction, VT 05001
*Actress*

**Mastrantonio, Mary Elizabeth**
℅ Hofflund-Tolone
9465 Wilshire Blvd., #620
Beverly Hills, CA 90212
*Actress*
*Birthday: 11/17/64*

**Masur, Richard**
121 N. San Vicente Blvd.
Beverly Hills, CA 90211
*Actor*

**Mathers, Jerry**
30290 Rancho Viejo Rd., #122
San Juan Capistrano, CA 92675
*Actor*

**Matheson, Tim**
10290 Santa Monica Blvd., #300
Los Angeles, CA 90025
*Actor*
*Birthday: 12/31/48*

**Mathis, Johnny**
3500 W. Olive Ave., #750
Burbank, CA 91505
*Singer*
*Birthday: 9/30/35*

**Matlin, Marlee**
7920 Sunset Blvd., #400
Los Angeles, CA 90046
*Actress*
*Birthday: 8/24/65*

**Mattea, Kathy**
900 Division St.
Nashville, TN 37203
*Singer, songwriter*

**Mattingly, Don**
RR #5
Box 74
Evansville, IN 47711
*Ex–baseball player*

**Maven, Max**
PO Box 3819
La Mesa, CA 92044
Or
7095 Hollywood Blvd., #382
Hollywood, CA 90028
Website: http://
www.maxmaven.com/
E-mail: MaxMaven@aol.com
*Mentalist, magician*

**Max, Peter**
118 Riverside Dr.
New York, NY 10024
*Artist*

**Maxwell**
1325 Ave. of the Americas
New York, NY 10019
Website: http://
www.sonymusic.com/artists/
Maxwell/index2.html
*R&B singer*

**May, Elaine**
145 Central Park West
New York, NY 10023
*Actress*

**Mayhew, Peter**
% *Star Wars* Fan Club
PO Box 111000
Aurora, CO 80042
*Actor*
*Played Chewbacca in* Star Wars

**Mays, Willie**
PO Box 2410
Menlo Park, CA 94026
*Retired baseball player*
*Birthday: 5/6/31*

**Mcallister, Dawson**
PO Box 8123
Irving, TX 75016
*Christian talk show host*

**McBride, Martina**
406-68 Water St.
Vancouver, BC
V6B 1A4
*Country singer*

**McCain, Senator John**
1300 Crystal Dr.
Arlington, VA 22202
*Senator and former presidential candidate*

**McCambridge, Mercedes**
156 Fifth Ave., #820
New York, NY 10010
*Actress*

**McCarter Sisters**
PO Box 121551
Nashville, TN 37212
*Musical group*

**McCarthy, Andrew**
8942 Wilshire Blvd.
Beverly Hills, CA 90211
*Actor*
*Birthday: 11/29/62*

**McCarthy, Jenny**
8424A Santa Monica Blvd., #804
West Hollywood, CA 90069
*She was 1994 Playmate of the Year*
*Birthday: 11/2/72*

**McCartney, Sir Paul**
1 Soho Square
London W1
England
*Former Beatle*

**McCaughey Septuplets, The**
615 N. First
Carlisle, IA 50047

**McClain, Charly**
PO Box 198888
Nashville, TN 37219
*Country singer*

**McClanahan, Rue**
9454 Wilshire Blvd., #405
Beverly Hills, CA 90212
*Actress*
*Birthday: 2/21/34*

**Delbert McClinton Int'l.**
47 Music Square E.
Nashville, TN 37203
*Country singer's fan club*

**McConaughey, Matthew**
PO Box 1145
Malibu, CA 90265
*Actor*
*Birthday: 11/4/69*

**McCord, Kent**
15301 Ventura Blvd., #345
Sherman Oaks, CA 91403
*Actor*

**McCormack, Mary**
PO Box 67335
Los Angeles, CA 90067
*Actress*

**McCormick, Carolyn**
Box 250
Seal Beach, CA 90740
*Actress*

**McCormick, Kelly**
Box 250
Seal Beach, CA 90740
*Musician*

**McCormick, Maureen**
1925 Century Park E., #2320
Los Angeles, CA 90067
*Actress, played Marsha Brady*

**McCormick, Pat**
23388 Mulholland Dr.
Woodland Hills, CA 91364
*Comedian, writer*

**McCormick, Pat**
Box 250
Seal Beach, CA 90740
*Swimmer*

**McCoy, Charlie**
1300 Division St., #304
Nashville, TN 37203
*Musician*

**McCoy, Matt**
4526 Wilshire Blvd.
Los Angeles, CA 90010
*Actor*

**McCoy, Neal**
3878 Oaklawn Ave., #620
Dallas, TX 75219
*Country singer*

**McCracken, Jeff**
15760 Ventura Blvd., #1730
Encino, CA 91436
*Actor*

**McCromack, Catherine**
9830 Wilshire Blvd.
Beverly Hills, CA 90212
*Actress*

**McCullough, Julie**
% Pierce and Shelly
612 Lighthouse Ave., #275
Pacific Grove, CA 93951
E-mail: JulieMcCul@aol.com
*Actress*

**McDaniel, Mel**
PO Box 2285
Hendersonville, TN 37077
Or
2802 Columbine Pl.
Nashville, TN 37204
*Country singer*

**McDermott, Dylan**
PO Box 25516
Los Angeles, CA 90025
*Actor*

**McDonald, Audra**
130 W. 42nd St., #1804
New York, NY 10036
*Singer*

**McDonald "Country" Joe**
PO Box 7054
Berkeley, CA 94707
Or
17337 Ventura Blvd., #208
Encino, CA 91316
Website: http://
www.countryjoe.com/
*Singer, songwriter*

**McDonnell, Mary**
PO Box 6010-540
Sherman Oaks, CA 91413
*Actress*

**McDormand, Frances**
333 West End Ave., Suite #12-C
New York, NY 10023
*Actor*

**McDowell, Malcolm**
4 Windmill St.
London W1P 1HF
England
*Actor*
*Birthday: 6/19/43*

**McDowell, Ronnie**
20 Music Square W., #200
Nashville, TN 37203
*Country singer*

**McEntire, Reba**
40 Music Square West
Nashville, TN 37203
*Country singer*
*Birthday: 3/28/55*

**McEuen, John**
6044 Deal Ave.
Nashville, TN 37209
*Country singer*

**McFadden, Gates**
% Innovative Artists
1999 Ave. of the Stars, #2850
Los Angeles, CA 90067
*Actress, played Dr. Beverly Crusher*
on Star Trek: The Next Generation
*Birthday: 8/28/49*

**McFerrin, Bobby**
826 Broadway, #400
New York, NY 10003
*Musician*

**McGavin, Darren**
PO Box 2939
Beverly Hills, CA 90213
*Actor*

**McGinley, Ted**
1925 Century Park E., Suite #2320
Los Angeles, CA 90067
*Actor*
*Birthday: 5/30/58*

**McGovern, Elizabeth**
17319 Magnolia Blvd.
Encino, CA 91316
*Actress*

**McGovern, ex-Sen. George**
PO Box 5591
Friendship Sta.
Washington, DC 20016

**McGovern, Maureen**
163 Amsterdam Ave., #174
New York, NY 10023
Website: http: //
www.maureenmcgovern.com/
*Singer*

**McGraw, Tim**
209 10th Ave., #229
Nashville, TN 37203
*Country singer*

**McGregor, Ewan**
503/504 Lotts Rd.
The Cambers
Chesea Harbour SWIO OXF
England
*Actor*
*Birthday: 3/31/71*

**McGwire, Mark**
6615 E. Pacific Coast Hwy., #260
Long Beach, CA 90803
*Baseball player*

**McKeon, Nancy**
PO Box 6778
Burbank, CA 91510
*Actress*
*Birthday: 4/4/66*

**McLean, Don**
450 7th Ave., #603
New York, NY 10123
*Singer, songwriter*
*Birthday: 10/2/45*

**McMurtry, Tom**
PO Box 273
Edwards AFB, CA 93523
*Test pilot*

**McNeill, Robert Duncan**
% Paramount Pictures Productions
*Star Trek: Voyager*
5555 Melrose Ave.
Los Angeles, CA 90038
*Actor, plays Lt. Tom Paris on* Star
Trek: Voyager

**McNeil, Kate**
9229 Sunset Blvd., #710
Los Angeles, CA 90069
*Actress*

**McRaney, Gerald**
1012 Royal St.
New Orleans, LA 70116
*Actor, married to Delta Burke*
*Birthday: 8/19/48*

**Meadows, Jayne**
15201-B Burbank Blvd.
Van Nuys, CA 91411
*Actress*

**Meara, Anne**
% Innovative Artists
1999 Ave. of the Stars, #2850
Los Angeles, CA 90067
*Comedienne, actress, married to*
*Jerry Stiller*

**Meatloaf (Marvin Lee Aday)**
9255 Sunset Blvd., #200
Los Angeles, CA 90069
*Singer*
*Birthday: 9/27/51*

**Mellencamp, John**
Rt 1 Box 361
Nashville, IN 47448
*Rock singer, songwriter, guitarist*
*Birthday: 10/7/51*

**Mellons, Ken**
PO Box 756
Hermitage, TN 37076
*Singer*

**Menendez, Erik**
#1878449
CSP-Sac
Box 290066
Represa, CA 95671
*Convicted of killing his parents*

**Menendez, Lyle**
#1887106
California Correctional Institute
CCI-Box 1031
Tehachapi, CA 93581
*Convicted of killing his parents*

**Mensy, Tim**
PO Box 128007
Nashville, TN 37212
*Country singer*

**Meriwether, Lee**
2555 E. Colorado Blvd.
Pasadena, CA 91107
*Actress, former Miss America*
*Birthday: 5/27/35*

**Meyer, Dina**
% UTA
9560 Wilshire Blvd.
Beverly Hills, CA 90212
*Actress*
*Birthday: 6/15/69*

**Midler, Bette**
9701 Wilshire Blvd., 10th Floor
Beverly Hills, CA 90212
*Actress, singer*
*Birthday: 12/1/45*

**Mickey Mouse**
500 S. Buena Vista St.
Burbank, CA 92521
Website: http://www.disney.com/
*Cartoon character, Steamboat*
*Willie—First Mickey Mouse cartoon*
*released 11/18/28*

**Milano, Alyssa**
5700 Wilshire Blvd., #575
Los Angeles, CA 90036
*Actress*
*Birthday: 12/19/73*

**Miles, Vera**
Box 1704
Big Bear Lake, CA 92315
*Actress*
*Birthday: 8/23/30*

**Milius, John**
8942 Wilshire blvd.
Beverly Hills, CA 90211
*Director*

**Miller, Bill**
% Sherry Halton
1223 17th Ave. S.
Nashville, TN 37212
*Singer*

**Miller, Dennis**
7800 Beverly Blvd.
Los Angeles, CA 90036
*TV host, comedian, actor*
*Birthday: 10/5/43*

**Glenn Miller Birthplace Society**
PO Box 61
Clarinda, IA 51632

**Miller, Glenn Society**
18 Crendon St.
High Wycombe
Bucks
England

**Miller, Penelope Ann**
9569 Wilshire Blvd., #516
Bevelry Hills, CA 90212
*Actress*
*Birthday: 1/13/64*

**Mills, Donna**
253 26th St., #259
Santa Monica, CA 90402
*Actress*

**Mills, Sir John**
Hill House
Denham Village
GB-Buckinghamshire
*Actor*
*Birthday: 2/22/08*

**Milner, Martin**
10100 Santa Monica Blvd., #2490
Los Angeles, CA 90067
*Actor*

**Milsap, Ronnie**
PO Box 40665
Nashville, TN 37204
*Country singer*

**Minghella, Anthony**
122 Wigmore St.
London W1H 9FE
England
*Film director*

**Minnelli, Liza**
160 Central Park S.
New York, NY 10019
*Actress, singer, Judy Garland's
oldest daughter*
*Birthday: 3/12/46*

**Mitchell, Dennis**
% US Olympic Comm.
1750 E. Boulder St.
Colorado Springs, CO 80909
*Olympic sprinter*

**Mitchell, George**
8280 Greensboro Dr.
McLean, VA 22102
*Former Senator*

**Mitchell, Waddie**
PO Box 268
Elko, NV 89801
Or
PO Box 9188
Colorado Springs, CO 80932
*Cowboy poet*

**Moceanu, Dominique**
17911 Fall River Circle
Houston, TX 77090
*Olympic gymnast*

**Modine, Mathew**
8942 Wilshire Blvd.
Beverly Hills, CA 90211
*Actor*
*Birthday: 3/22/59*

**Moffat, Donald**
151 El Camino Dr.
Beverly Hills, CA 90212
*Actor*

**Moll, Richard**
1119 M. Amalfi Dr.
Pacific Palisades, CA 90272
*Actor*
*Birthday: 1/13/43*

**Montalban, Ricardo**
13701 Riverside Dr., #500
Sherman Oaks, CA 91423
*Actor*

**Montana, Joe**
21515 Hawthorne Blvd., #1250
Torrance, CA 90503
*Football quarterback*

**Montana, Patsy**
3728 Highway 411
Madisonville, TN 37354
*Country singer*

**Montgomery, George**
PO Box 2187
Rancho Mirage, CA 92270
*Actor*
*Birthday: 8/29/?*

**Montgomery, John Michael**
1905 Broadway
Nashville, TN 37203
*Country singer*

**Moore, Demi**
955 S. Carrillo Dr., #200
Los Angeles, CA 90048
E-mail: DemiM2@aol.com
*Actress*
*Birthday: 11/11/62*

**Moore, Mary Tyler**
510 E. 86th St., #21A
New York, NY 10028
Or
% William-Morris
1325 Ave. of the Americas
New York, NY 10019
*Birthday: 12/29/36*

**Moore, Melba**
% Hush
231 W. 58th St.
New York, NY 10019
*Actress*

**Moore, Sir Roger**
2–4 Noel St.
London W1V 3RB
United Kingdom
*Actor*
*Birthday: 10/14/27*

**Moran, Erin**
PO Box 3261
Quartz Hill, CA 93586
*Actress*
*Birthday: 10/18/61*

**Moreno, Rita (Rosita Dolores Alverio)**
160 Gravatt Dr.
Berkeley, CA 94705
*Actress*
*Birthday: 12/11/31*

**Morgan, Lorrie**
1906 Acklen Ave.
Nashville, TN 37212
*Country singer*

**Morissette, Alanis**
75 Rockefeller Plaza, #2100
New York, NY 10019
*Singer, songwriter*

**Morita, Noriuki "Pat"**
PO Box 491278
Los Angeles, CA 90049
*Actor*
*Birthday: 6/28/30*

**Morris, Garret**
8436 Third St., #740
Los Angeles, CA 90048
*Actor*

**Morris, Gary**
2829 Dogwood Pl.
Nashville, TN 37204
*Singer, songwriter*

**Morrison, Van**
1AS
London W1A 1AS
England
*Singer, songwriter*
*Birthday: 8/31/45*

**Moses, Rick**
% The Calder Agency
19919 Redwing St.
Woodland Hills, CA 91364
*Actor*
*Birthday: 9/5/52*

**Moss, Kate**
% Storm Model Mgmt.
1st Floor 5 Jubilee Pl.
London SW3 3TD
England
*Model*
*Birthday: 1/16/74*

**Mowrey, Dude**
11 Music Circle S.
Nashville, TN 37203
*Musician*

**Mueller-Stahl, Armin**
% ZBF-Agentur
Ordensmeisterstr. 15
12099 Berlin
Germany
*Actor*
*Birthday: 12/17/30*

**Muldaur, Diana**
10100 Santa Monica Blvd., #2490
Los Angeles, CA 90006
*Actress*
*Birthday: 8/19/38*

**Muldoon, Patrick**
% Gallin-Morey Assoc.
345 N. Maple Dr., #300
Beverly Hills, CA 90210
*Actor*

**Mulgrew, Kate**
612 N. Sepulveda Blvd., #10
Los Angeles, CA 90049
*Actress*
*Birthday: 4/29/45*

**Mulroney, Dermot**
1180 S. Beverly Dr., #618
Los Angeles, CA 90035
*Actor*
*Birthday: 10/31/63*

**Murphey, David Lee**
PO Box 12168
Nashville, TN 37212
*Country singer*

**Murphey, Michael Martin**
PO Box 777
Taos, NM 87571
*Country and cowboy singer*

**Murphy, Eddie**
PO Box 1028
Englewood Cliffs, NJ 07632
Or
% Int'l Creative Mgmt.
8942 Wilshire Blvd.
Beverly Hills, CA 90211
Or
1400 Tower Grove Dr.
Beverly Hills, CA 90210
*Actor, comedian*
*Birthday: 4/3/61*

**Murray, Anne**
4950 Yonge St., #2400
Toronto, Ontario M2N 6K1
Canada
Or
Box 69030
12 St. Clair Ave. East
Toronto, Ontario M4T 1K0
Canada
Or
Balmur Entertainment Ltd.
35 Alvin Ave.
Toronto, Ontario M4T 2A7
Canada
Website: http://
www.annemurray.com/
E-mail: anne@annemurray.com
*Singer*

**Murray, Bill**
% Creative Artists Agency
9830 Wilshire Blvd.
Beverly Hills, CA 90212
*Actor, comedian, writer*
*Birthday: 9/21/50*

**Muster, Thomas**
% AMJ Pro Mgmt.
Steinfeldstr. 17
2351 Wiener Neudorf
Austria
*Professional tennis player*
*Birthday: 10/2/67*

**Myers, Mike**
9150 Wilshire Blvd., #350
Beverly Hills, CA 90212
*Actor*
Birthday: 5/25/63

**N**

**'N Sync**
7616 Soundland Blvd., #115
Orlando, FL 32809
*Music group*

**Nabors, Jim**
215 Kulamanu Pl.
Honolulu, HI 96816
*Actor, singer*
*Birthday: 6/11/33*

**Nader, Ralph**
1600 20th St. NW
Washington, DC 20009
*Green Party presidential candidate*

**Nakano, Shinji**
% Prost Grand Prix
Technopole de la Nièvre
Magny Cours F-58470
France
*Professional Formula-1 driver*

**Nana**
% Booya Music
Marlowring 3
Hamburg D-22525
Germany
*Singer*
*Birthday: 10/5/71*

**Nannini, Alessandro**
Via del Paradiso 4
Siena 53100
Italy
*Race car driver*
*Birthday: 7/7/59*

**Narz, Jack**
11365 Ventura Blvd., #100
Studio City, CA 91604
*TV game show host, Tom
Kennedy's brother*
*Birthday: 11/13/22*

**Nash, Graham**
14930 Ventura Blvd., #205
Sherman Oaks, CA 91403
*Rock musician*

**Naughton, David**
11774-B Moorpark St.
Studio City, CA 91604
*Actor*
*Birthday: 2/13/51*

**Navratilova, Martina**
% WTA Tour
1266 E. Main St., #4
Stamford, CT 06902
*Professional tennis player*
*Birthday: 10/18/56*

**Neal, Patricia**
45 East End Ave., #4C
New York, NY 10028
*Actress*
*Birthday: 1/20/26*

**Nealon, Kevin**
9363 Wilshire Blvd., #212
Beverly Hills, CA 90210
*Actor*

**Needham, Tracey**
*J*A*G*
% Badgley + Connor
9229 Sunset Blvd., #311
Los Angeles, CA 90069
*Actress*

**Neeson, Liam**
76 Oxford St.
London W1N 0AX
England
*Actor*
*Birthday: 6/7/52*

**Neil, Sam**
PO Box 153
Noble Park
Victoria 3174
Australia
*Actor*
*Birthday: 9/14/47*

**Nelligan, Kate**
% IA
1999 Ave. of the Stars, #2850
Los Angeles, CA 90067
*Actress*
*Birthday: 3/16/51*

**Nelson, Willie**
Rt #1
Briarcliff TT
Spicewood, TX 78669
*Singer, songwriter*
*Birthday: 4/30/33*

**Neville, Aaron**
Box 750187
New Orleans, LA 70175
*Singer*
*Birthday: 1/24/41*

**Nevins, Jason**
% Sony Music/epic
Stephanstr. 15
60313 Frankfurt
Germany
*Member of Run-D.M.C.*

**Newman, Jimmy C.**
2804 Opryland Dr.
Nashville, TN 37214
*Country singer*

**Newman, Paul**
40 W. 57th St.
New York, NY 10019
*Actor, married to Joanne*
*Woodward*
*Birthday: 1/26/25*

**Newman, Randy**
21241 Ventura Blvd., #241
Woodland Hills, CA 91364
*Singer*
*Birthday: 11/28/43*

**Newton, Juice**
PO Box 3035
Rancho Santa Fe, CA 92067
*Singer*

**Newton-John, Olivia**
PO Box 2710
Malibu, CA 90265
*Singer, actress*
*Birthday: 9/26/47*

**Nichols, Nichelle**
22647 Ventura Blvd.
Woodland Hills, CA 91364
*Actress, plays Lt. Uhura on* Star
Trek

**Nicholson, Jack**
11500 W. Olympic Blvd., #510
Los Angeles, CA 90064
*Actor*
*Birthday: 4/22/37*

**Nicklaus, Jack**
11760 US Hwy., #1–6
North Palm Beach, FL 33408
*Professional golfer*
*Birthday: 1/21/40*

**Nicollier, Claude**
% NASA
Johnson Space Center
Dept. CB
Houston, TX 77058
*Astronaut*

**Nicks, Stevie**
PO Box 7855
Alhambra, CA 91802
*Member of Fleetwood Mac*

**Nielsen, Brigitte**
PO Box 57593
Sherman Oaks, CA 91403
*Actress*
*Birthday: 7/15/63*

**Nielsen, Leslie**
1622 Viewmont Dr.
Los Angeles, CA 90069
*Actor*
*Birthday: 2/11/26*

**Nimoy, Leonard**
2300 W. Victory Blvd., #C-384
Burbank, CA 91506
*Actor, director*
*Birthday: 3/26/31*

**Nolte, Nick**
% Kingsgate Films
6153 Bonsall Dr.
Malibu, CA 90265
*Actor*
*Birthday: 2/8/40*

**Nomo, Hideo**
% Los Angeles Dodgers
1000 Elysian Park Ave.
Los Angeles, CA 90012
*Pitcher*

**Norris, Chuck (Carlos Ray)**
PO Box 872
Navasota, TX 77868
*Actor, athlete, producer,*
*screenwriter, stunt choreographer*
*Birthday: 3/10/40*

**North, Oliver**
RR #1
Box 560
Bluemont, VA 22012
*Former presidential aide, senatorial*
*candidate, radio talk show host*

**Norville, Deborah**
Box 426
Mill Neck, NY 11765
*TV personality*

**Norwood, Daron**
PO Box #674659
Nashville, TN 37203
*Country singer*

**Novello, Don**
PO Box 245
Fairfax, CA 94930
*Comedian known as Father Guido
Sarducci*
*Birthday: 1/1/43*

**Nye, Bill**
% KCTS TV
401 Mercer St.
Seattle, WA 98109
*The Science Guy*

**O**

**O'Brien, Conan**
30 Rockefeller Plaza
New York, NY 10112
*Talk show host*
*Birthday: 4/18/63*

**O'Brien, Tim**
PO Box 458
Nevada City, CA 95959
*Country singer*

**O'Connell, Jerry**
151 El Camino Dr.
Beverly Hills, CA 90212
*Actor*
*Birthday: 2/17/74*

**O'Connor, Sinead**
43 Brook Green
London W6 7EF
England
*Musician*
*Birthday: 12/8/67*

**O'Donnell, Chris**
8912 Burton Way
Beverly Hills, CA 90211
*Actor*
*Birthday: 1970*

**O'Donnell, Rosie**
666 Fifth Ave., #288
New York, NY 10103
Web: http://www.rosieo.com
*Talk show host*
*Birthday: 1962*

**O'Hara, Maureen**
Box 1400
Christiansted
St. Croix, VI 00820
*Actress*
*Birthday: 8/17/20*

**Olajuwon, Hakeem**
10 Greenway Plaza
East Houston, TX 77046
*Basketball player*

**Oldman, Gary**
% J.C.M.
Oxford House
76 Oxford St.
London W1N 0AX
England
*Actor*
*Birthday: 3/21/58*

**Olin, Ken**
5855 Topanga Canyon, #410
Woodland Hills, CA 91367
*Actor*
*Birthday: 7/30/54*

**Olin, Lena**
40 W. 57th St.
New York, NY 10019
*Actress*
*Birthday: 3/22/55*

**Olmos, Edward James**
2020 Ave. of the Stars, #500
Los Angeles, CA 90067
*Actor*
*Birthday: 2/24/47*

**Olsen, Ashley**
8916 Ashcroft Ave.
Los Angeles, CA 90048
*Actress*
*Birthday: 6/13/86*

**Olsen, Mary Kate**
8916 Ashcroft Ave.
Los Angeles, CA 90048
*Actress*
*Birthday: 6/13/86*

**O'Neal, Tatum**
300 Central Park W., #16-G
New York, NY 10024
*Actress*
*Birthday: 11/5/63*

**O'Neal, Shaquille**
Los Angeles Lakers
Staples Center
1111 S. Figueroa St.
Los Angeles, CA 90015
*L.A. Laker center, Ht. 7' 1" Wt. 315
lbs.*
*Birthday: 3/6/72*

**Ormond, Julia**
9465 Wilshire Blvd., #517
Beverly Hills, CA 90212
*Actress*
*Birthday: 1/4/65*

**Orrall, Robert Ellis**
PO Box 121274
Nashville, TN 37212
*Country singer*

**Osborn, Super Dave**
10 Universal City Plaza, Suite 3100
Universal City, CA 91606
*Actor*

**Osbourne, Ozzy (John Michael
Osbourne)**
9 Highpoint Dr.
Gulf Breeze, FL 32561
*Singer, songwriter*
*Birthday: 12/3/46*

**Oslin, K. T.**
1102 18th Ave. S.
Nashville, TN 37212
*Singer*
*Birthday: 5/15/42*

**Osmond, Marie (Olive Marie
Osmond)**
3325 N. University Ave., Suite 375
Provo, UT 84604
*Singer, actress*
*Birthday: 10/13/59*

**Oteri, Cheri**
315 S. Beverly Dr., #216
Beverly Hills, CA 90212
*Comedian*

**O'Toole, Peter**
% Veerline Ltd.
8 Baker St.
GB-London WAA 1DA
England
*Actor*
*Birthday: 8/2/32*

**Overstreet, Paul**
PO Box 320
Pregram, TN 37143
*Country singer*

**Owens, Buck (Alvis Edgar Jr.)**
3223 Sillect Ave.
Bakersfield, CA 93308
*Country singer*

**Owens, Gary**
18034 Ventura Blvd.
Encino, CA 91316
*Radio and TV personality*

**Oz, Frank (Frank Oznovicz)**
PO Box 20750
New York, NY 10023
*Muppeteer*

**P**

**Pacino, Al (Alfredo James Pacino)**
301 W. 57th St., #16-C
New York, NY 10017
*Actor*
*Birthday: 4/25/40*

**Palance, Jack**
PO Box 6201
Tehachapi, CA 93561
*Actor, director*
*Birthday: 2/18/20*

**Palin, Michael**
68A Delancey St.
London NW1 7RY
England
*Actor, writer*
*Birthday: 5/5/43*

**Palmer, Arnold**
9000 Bay Hill Blvd.
Orlando, FL 32819
*Golfer*

**Palmer, Robert**
% Dera Assoc.
584 Broadway, #1201
New York, NY 10012
*Singer, songwriter*
*Birthday: 1/19/49*

**Palminteri, Chazz**
375 Greenwich St.
New York, NY 10013
*Actor*
*Birthday: 5/15/51*

**Paltrow, Gwyneth**
% Creative Artists Agency
9830 Wilshire Blvd.
Beverly Hills, CA 90212
*Actress*

**Panis, Olivier**
% Prost Grand Prix
Technopole de la Nièvre
F-58470 Magny Cours
*Professional Formula-1 driver*

**Parazynski, Scott**
Astronaut Office
Mail Code CB
NASA, Johnson Space Center
Houston, TX 77058
*Astronaut*

**Parker, Andrea**
% Susan Smith + Assoc.
121 N. San Vicente Blvd.
Beverly Hills, CA 90211
*Actress*

**Parker, Mary-Louise**
151 El Camino Dr.
Beverly Hills, CA 90212
*Actress*
*Birthday: 8/2/64*

**Parker, Ray Jr.**
1025 N. Roxbury Dr.
Beverly Hills, CA 90210
*Musician, songwriter*

**Parker, Sarah Jessica**
PO 69646
Los Angeles, CA 90069
*Actress*
*Birthday: 3/25/65*

**Parnell, Lee Roy**
PO Box 120073
Nashville, TN 37212
*Country singer*

**Parrish, Julie**
PO Box 247
Santa Monica, CA 90406
*Actress*
*Birthday: 10/21/40*

**Parsons, Karyn**
104-106 Bedford St., #4D
New York, NY 10014
*Actress*

**Parton, Dolly**
PO Box 15037
Nashville, TN 37215
*Country singer, actress*
*Birthday: 1/19/46*

**Parton, Stella**
PO Box 120295
Nashville, TN 37212
*Country singer*

**Patkin, Max**
211 Mitchell Rd.
Exton, PA 19341
*Actor*

**Patric, Jason (Jason Patrick Miller)**
% Dolores Robinson Ent.
10683 Santa Monica Blvd.
Los Angeles, CA 90025-4807
*Actor*
*Birthday: 6/17/66*

**Patterson, Floyd**
Box 336
New Paltz, NY 12561
*Former boxer*

**Patty, Sandi**
PO Box 2940
Anderson, IN 46018
*Singer of religious music*

**Pavarotti, Luciano**
Via Giardini
I-41040 Saliceto Panaro
Italy
*Opera singer and member of the Three Tenors*
*Birthday: 10/12/35*

**Paxton, Bill**
8000 Sunset Blvd., #300
Los Angeles, CA 90046
*Actor, director, musician, producer, screenwriter*
*Birthday: 5/17/55*

**Paycheck, Johnny**
PO Box 916
Hendersonville, TN 37077
*Country singer*

**Payne, John**
Hoogstraat 161
3131 BB Vlaardingen
The Netherlands
Website: http://www.spiritweb.org/Spirit/omni.html
*Trance channeller*

**Payton, Walter**
300 N. Martingale Rd., #340
Schaumburg, IL 60173
*Ex-football player*
*Birthday: 6/25/54*

**Pearce, Guy**
Box 4778
Kings Cross NSW 2011
Australia
*Actor*
*Birthday: 10/5/67*

**Peeples, Nia**
7800 Beverly Blvd.
Los Angeles, CA 90036
*Actress*

**Pei, I. M.**
600 Madison Ave.
New York, NY 10022
*Architect*

**Pele**
% Minist. Extraordinario de
Esporte
Praca dos Tres Poderes
70150-900 Brasilia D. F.
Brasilia
*Former soccer player*
*Birthday: 10/21/40*

**Penn, Sean**
2049 Century Park E., #2500
Los Angeles, CA 90067
*Actor*

**Penn and Teller**
4132 S. Rainbow Blvd., #377
Las Vegas, NV 89103
Website: http://www.sincity.com/
*Magicians*

**Peres, Shimon**
10 Hayarkon St., #3263
Tel Aviv 63571
Israel

**Perkins, Elizabeth**
9150 Wilshire Blvd., #340
Beverly Hills, CA 90212
*Actress*
*Birthday: 11/18/60*

**Perlman, Rhea**
PO Box 491246
Los Angeles, CA 90049
*Actress*
*Birthday: 3/31/?*

**Perlman, Ron**
275 S. Beverly Dr., #215
Beverly Hills, CA 90212
*Actor*
*Birthday: 4/13/50*

**Perot, Ross**
1700 Lakeside Square
Dallas, TX 75251
*Businessman, former presidential*
*candidate*

**Perrine, Valerie**
% Soli + Associati
Via Toscana 1
Roma I-00187
Italy
*Actress*
*Birthday: 9/3/43*

**Perry, Luke (Coy Perry III)**
1122 S. Robertson Blvd., #15
Los Angeles, CA 90035
*Actor*
*Birthday: 10/11/66*

**Pesci, Joe**
PO Box 6
Lavallette, NJ 08735
*Actor*
*Birthday: 2/9/43*

**Pestova, Daniela**
% Next Models
23 Watts St.
New York, NY 10013
*Model*

**Peters, Bernadette (Bernadette Lazzara)**
323 W. 80th St.
New York, NY 10024
*Actress*
*Birthday: 2/28/48*

**Petersen, William L.**
3330 Cahuenga Blvd. W., #400
Los Angeles, CA 90068
*Actor*

**Petersen, Wolfgang**
% C.A.A.
9830 Wilshire Blvd.
Beverly Hills, CA 90212
*Director*
*Birthday: 3/14/41*

**Petty, Lori**
400 W. Alameda Ave., #301
Burbank, CA 91505
*Actress*

**Petty, Richard**
1028 E. 22nd St.
Kannapolis, NC 28083
*Race car driver*

**Phair, Liz**
811 Broadway, #730
New York, NY 10012
*Singer, songwriter*
*Birthday: 4/17/67*

**Philbin, Regis**
101 W. 67th St., #51A
New York, NY 10023
*Talk show host, Game show host*
*Birthday: 8/25/34*

**Phillips, Ethan**
4212 McFarlane Ave.
Burbank, CA 91505
*Actor, plays Neelix on* Star Trek: Voyager

**Phillips, Julianne**
1999 Ave. of the Stars, #2850
Los Angeles, CA 90067
*Actress, model*

**Phillips, Lou Diamond (Lou Upchurch)**
1122 S. Robertson Blvd., #15
Los Angeles, CA 90035
*Actor*
*Birthday: 2/17/62*

**Picardo, Robert**
PO Box 5617
Beverly Hills, CA 90210
*Actor, plays the Doctor on* Star Trek: Voyager

**Pierce, David Hyde**
8730 Sunset Blvd., #480
Los Angeles, CA 90069
*Actor*

**Pietz, Amy**
PO Box 81
Oak Creek, WI 53134
*Actress*

**Pinkett, Jada**
% United Talent Agency
9560 Wilshire Blvd., #516
Beverly Hills, CA 90212
*Actress*

**Piraro, Dan**
% "Bizzaro"
1119 N. Edgefield Ave.
Dallas, TX 75208
Or
% Universal Press Syndicate
4520 Main St.
Kansas City, MO 64111
*Cartoonist*

**Pitt, Brad**
% Creative Artists Agency
9830 Wilshire Blvd.
Beverly Hills, CA 90212
*Actor*
*Birthday: 12/18/64*

**Plant, Robert**
46 Kensington C. St.
London W85DP
England
*Singer, songwriter*
*Birthday: 8/20/48*

**Platt, Oliver**
29 E. 9th St.
New York, NY 10003
*Actor*

**Pleshette, Suzanne**
PO Box 1492
Beverly Hills, CA 90210
*Actress*

**Plumb, Eve**
5757 Wilshire Blvd., #510
Los Angeles, CA 90036
*Actress*

**Plummer, Amanda**
1925 Century Park E., #2320
Los Angeles, CA 90067
*Actress*
*Birthday: 3/23/57*

**Poitier, Sidney**
9255 Doheny Rd.
Los Angeles, CA 90069
*Actor, writer, prodcuer*
*Birthday: 2/20/27*

**Pollack, Kevin**
8942 Wilshire Blvd.
Beverly Hills, CA 90211
*Actor*

**Popcorn, Faith**
% BrainReserve
59 E. 64th St.
New York, NY 10021-7003
Website: http://
www.faithpopcorn.com/
E-mail:
Webmistress@faithpopcorn.com
*Futurist and author of* The Popcorn
Report *and* Clicking

**Official Popeye Fan Club**
1001 State St.
Chester, IL 62233

**Porizkova, Paulina**
% IMG
304 Park Ave. South, 12th Floor
New York, NY 10010
*Model*

**Portman, Natalie**
8942 Wilshire Blvd.
Beverly Hills, CA 90210
*Actress*

**Post, Markie**
10153 1/2 Riverside Dr., #333
Toluca Lake, CA 90049
*Actress*
*Birthday: 11/4/50*

**Poston, Tom**
1 North Venice Blvd., #106
Venice, CA 90291
Or
% International Creative
Management
8942 Wilshire Blvd.
Beverly Hills, CA 90211
*Actor*
*Birthday: 10/17/?*

**Potts, Annie**
PO Box 29400
Los Angeles, CA 90027
*Actress*
*Birthday: 10/27/52*

**Potts, M. C.**
818 18th Ave. S.
Nashville, TN 37203
E-mail: mcfanclub@aol.com

**Powell, General Colin**
909 N. Washington St., Suite #767
Alexandria, VA 22314
*Military leader, author, Secretary of State*
*Birthday: 4/5/37*

**Powers, Stefanie (Jennifer Hart)**
15821 Ventura Blvd. #235
Encino, CA 91436
*Actress*
*Birthday: 11/2/42*

**Presley, Lisa-Marie**
1167 Summit Dr.
Beverly Hills, CA 90210
*Daughter of Elvis and Priscilla Presley*
*Birthday: 2/1/68*

**Presley, Priscilla**
1167 Summit Dr.
Beverly Hills, CA 90210
*Actress*
*Birthday: 5/24/45*

**Preston, Kelly**
15020 Ventura Blvd., #710
Sherman Oaks, CA 91403
*Actress*
*Birthday: 10/13/62*

**Price, Ray**
10-31 Battlefield St., #224
Springfield, MO 65807
*Singer*

**Pride, Charley**
PO Box 670507
Dallas, TX 75367
*Country singer*

**Priestley, Jason**
11766 Wilshire Blvd., #1610
Los Angeles, CA 90025
*Actor*
*Birthday: 8/28/69*

**Prince Charles**
Highgrove House
Tetbury
Gloucestershire
England
*Birthday: 11/14/48*

**Princess Margaret**
Kensington Palace
GB-London N5
England
*Birthday: 8/21/30*

**Principal, Victoria**
120 S. Spalding Dr., #205
Beverly Hills, CA 90212
*Actress*
*Birthday: 1/3/50*

**Prinze, Freddie Jr.**
9830 Wilshire Blvd.
Beverly Hills, CA 90212
*Actor*

**Prosky, Robert**
306 9th Ave.
Washington, DC 20003
*Actor*

**Prowse, David "Dave"**
7 Leicester Ct.
London WC2H 7BP
England
*Actor who played Darth Vader*

**Prudhomme, Chef Paul**
2424 Chartres
New Orleans, LA 70117
Website: http//www.chefpaul.com/
*Louisiana chef*

**Pruett, Jeanne**
1906 Chet Atkins Pl., #502
Nashville, TN 37212
*Country singer*

**Puckett, Kirby**
% Minnesota Twins
501 Chicago Ave S.
Minneapolis, MN 55415
*Ex-baseball player*

**Puff Daddy (Sean Combs)**
% Arista Records
9975 Santa Monica Blvd.
Beverly Hills, CA 90212
*Rap artist*

**Pullman, Bill**
1122 S. Robertson Blvd., #15
Los Angeles, CA 90035
*Actor, producer*
*Birthday: 12/17/54*

**Putin, President Putin**
Krasnopresenskaya 2
Moscow,
Russia

# Q

**Quaid, Dennis**
8942 Wilshire Blvd.
Beverly Hills, CA 90211
Or
PO Box 742625
Houston, TX 77274
*Actor, Randy's brother*
*Birthday: 4/9/54*

**Quaid, Randy**
PO Box 17572
Beverly Hills, CA 90209
*Actor*
*Birthday: 10/1/50*

**Quayle, Dan**
2929 E. Camelback Rd., #124
Phoenix, AZ 85016
*Former vice president of the United States*
*Birthday: 2/4/47*

**Quinn, Aidan**
9830 Wilshire Blvd.
Beverly Hills, CA 90212
*Actress*
*Birthday: 3/8/59*

**Quinn, Anthony**
420 Poppasquash Rd.
Bristol, RI 02809
*Actor*

**Quivers, Robin**
WXRK-FM
600 Madison Ave.
New York, NY 10022
*Radio personality*

**R**

**Rachins, Alan**
1274 Capri Dr.
Pacific Palisades, CA 90272
*Actor*

**Rae, Cassidy**
1801 Ave. of the Stars, #902
Los Angeles, CA 90067
*Actress*

**Rae, Charlotte**
10790 Wilshire Blvd., #903
Los Angeles, CA 90024-4448
*Actress*
*Birthday: 4/22/26*

**Ted Raimi International Fan Club**
Club Ted
2032 Hickory Hill
Argyle, TX 76226
Website: http://
www.tedraimifan.com/
clubmain.html

**Rampling, Charlotte**
1 av. Emile Augier
Croissy-sur-Seine 78290
France
*Actress*
*Birthday: 2/4/46*

**Ramsay, Bruce**
% Brillstein-Grey Ent.
9150 Wilshire Blvd., #350
Beverly Hills, CA 90212
*Actor*

**Ramsey, John and Patsy**
1426 Pearl St.
Boulder, CO 80302

**Randall, Bobby**
PO Box 208
Unicoi, TN 37692
*Country singer*

**Randall, Tony (Leonard Rosenberg)**
1 W. 81st St., #6D
New York, NY 10024
*Actor, director*
*Birthday: 2/26/20*

**Randolph, Boots**
541 Richmar Dr.
Nashville, TN 37211
*Musician*

**Rapaport, Michael**
1610 Broadway
Santa Monica, CA 90404
*Actor*

**Ratzenberger, John**
13563 Ventura Blvd., #200
Sherman Oaks, CA 91423
*Actor*
*Birthday: 4/16/47*

**Ratzinger, Joseph Cardinal**
00120 Vatican City State
Vatican

**Raven, Eddy**
1071 Bradley Rd.
Gallatin, TN 37066
*Country singer*

**Ray, Jimmy**
% Sony Music
10 Great Marlborough St.
London W1V 2LP
England
*Singer*

**Raye, Collin**
612 Humboldt St.
Reno, NV 89509
*Country singer*

**Read, James**
9229 Sunset Blvd., Suite #315
Los Angeles, CA 90069
*Actor*
*Birthday: 7/3/54*

**Reagan, Nancy**
668 St. Cloud Rd.
Los Angeles, CA 90077
*Former First Lady, actress*
*Birthday: 7/6/21*

**Reagan, Ronald**
668 St. Cloud Rd.
Los Angeles, CA 90077
*Former president of the United
States, actor*
*Birthday: 2/6/11*

**Redford, Robert**
1101 East Montana Ave.
Santa Monica, CA 90403
*Actor, director, producer*
*Birthday: 3/8/43*

**Reece, Gabrielle**
5111 Ocean Front Walk, #4
Marina del Rey, CA 90291
*Model*

**Reed, Jerry**
153 Rue De Grande
Brentwood, TN 37027
*Musician*

**Reed, Pamela**
10390 Santa Monica Blvd., #300
Los Angeles, CA 90025
*Actress*

**Reed, Willis**
% Basketball Hall of Fame
1150 W. Columbus Ave.
Springfield, MA 01101

**Reese, Della**
55 West 900 South
Salt Lake City, UT 84101
*Actress*

**Reeve, Christopher**
RR #2
Bedford, NY 10506
*Actor*
*Birthday: 9/25/52*

**Reeves, Del**
1300 Division St., #102
Nashville, TN 37203
*Country singer*

**Reeves, Keanu**
9460 Wilshire Blvd., #700
Beverly Hills, CA 90212
*Actor*
*Birthday: 9/4/64*

**Reeves, Ronna**
PO Box 80424
Midland, TX 79709
*Country singer*

**Regalbuto, Joe**
724 24th St.
Santa Monica, CA 90402
*Actor*

**Regina Regina Fan Club**
PO Box 428
Marshville, NC 28103

**Reid, Mike**
PO Box 218142
Nashville, TN 37203
*Country singer*

**Reich, Dr. Robert**
Brandeis University
The Heller School
MS 035
Brandeis University
PO Box 9110
Waltham, MA 02454
E-mail: reich@brandeis.edu
*Former Secretary of Labor, founder
and national editor of The
American Prospect*

**Reilly, Charles Nelson**
11365 Ventura Blvd., #100
Studio City, CA 91604
*Actor*
*Birthday: 1/13/31*

**Reiner, Carl**
714 North Rodeo Dr.
Beverly Hills, CA 90210
*Actor, writer, director, Rob's dad*
*Birthday: 3/20/22*

**Reiner, Rob**
335 Maple Dr., #135
Beverly Hills, CA 90212
*Actor, director, producer*
*Birthday: 3/16/45*

**Reinhold, Judge**
626 Santa Monica Blvd., #113
Santa Monica, CA 90405
*Actor*
*Birthday: 5/21/56*

**Reiser, Paul**
% Culver Studios
9336 W. Washington
Culver City, CA 90232
*Actor*
*Birthday: 3/30/57*

**Reitman, Ivan**
% Creative Artists Agency
Attn: Rand Holston
9830 Wilshire Blvd.
Beverly Hills, CA 90212
*Director*
*Birthday: 10/27/46*

**Renfro, Brad**
PO Box 53454
Knoxville, TN 37950
*Actor*
*Birthday: 7/25/82*

**Reubens, Paul**
PO Box 29373
Los Angeles, CA 90029
*Actor who played Pee-Wee
Herman*

**Reynolds, Burt**
PO Box 3288
Teqyesta, FL 33469
*Actor*
*Birthday: 2/11/36*

**Reynolds, Debbie**
6415 Lankershim Blvd.
North Hollywood, CA 91606
*Actress, Carrie Fisher's mom*
*Birthday: 4/1/32*

**Rhys-Davies, John**
8033 Sunset Blvd., #29
Los Angeles, CA 90046
*Actor*

**Ricci, Christina**
% ICM
8942 Wilshire Blvd.
Beverly Hills, CA 90211
*Actress*

**Rice, Anne**
1239 First St.
New Orleans, LA 70130
Website: http://www.annerice.com/
*Author*
*Birthday: 10/14/41*

**Rich, Katie**
10100 Santa Monica Blvd., #2490
Los Angeles, CA 90067
*Actress*

**Richard, Sir Cliff (Harry Webb)**
Queen Ann House
Weybridge, Surrey
England
*Singer*
*Birthday: 10/14/40*

**Richards, Ariana**
5918 Van Nuys Blvd.
Van Nuys, CA 91401
*Actress*

**Richards, Denise**
PO Box 4590
Oceanside, CA 92052
*Actress*

**Richardson, Joely**
Oxford House
76 Oxford St.
London WIN 0AX
England
*Actress*

**Richardson, Patricia**
253 26th St., #A-312
Santa Monica, CA 90402
*Actress*

**Richie, Lionel**
PO Box 9055
Calabasas, CA 91372
Or
5750 Wilshire Blvd., Suite #590
Los Angeles, CA 90039
*Singer*

**Rickles, Don**
Premier Artist Services
% Eliot Weisman
1401 University Dr., Suite #305
Coral Springs, FL 33071
Website: http://
www.thehockeypuck.com/
E-mail: dj@hifrontier.com
*Comedian*
*Birthday: 5/8/26*

**Richter, Jason James**
10683 Santa Monica Blvd.
Los Angeles, CA 90025
*Actor*
*Birthday: 1/29/80*

**Rickman, Alan**
76 Oxford St.
London W1N 0AX
United Kingdom
*Actor*
*Birthday: 2/21/46*

**Riley, Jeannie C.**
906 Granville Rd.
Franklin, TN 37064
*Country singer*

**Rimes, LeAnn**
2945 Fondren Dr., #816
Dallas, TX 75205
*Country singer*

**Ringwald, Molly**
1999 Ave. of the Stars, #850
Los Angeles, CA 90067
*Actress*
*Birthday: 2/28/68*

**Ripa, Molly**
7800 Beverly Blvd., #3305
Los Angeles, CA 90036
*Actress*

**Ripkin, Cal Jr.**
2330 W. Juppa Rd., #333
Lutherville, MD 21093
Or
Camden Yards @ Oriole Park
333 W. Camden St.
Baltimore, MD 21201
*Baseball player*

**Ritter, John**
15030 Ventura Blvd., #806
Sherman Oaks, CA 91403
*Actor*
*Birthday: 9/17/48*

**Tex Ritter Fan Club**
Sharon L. Sweeting, Pres.
15326 73rd Ave. SE
Snohomish, WA 98290

**Rivera, Geraldo**
524 W 57th St., #1100
New York, NY 10019
*TV show host*
*Birthday: 7/4/43*

**Rivers, Joan (Joan Alexandra Molinsky)**
1 E. 62nd St.
New York, NY 1021
Or
PO Box 49774
Los Angeles, CA 90049
*Comedienne*
*Birthday: 11/7/37*

**Rizzuto, Phil**
12 Westminster Ave.
Hillside, NJ 07205
*Ex-baseball player*

**Robbins, Tim**
% I.C.M.
40 W. 57th St.
New York, NY 10019
*Actor*
*Birthday: 10/16/58*

**Roberts, Eric**
132 S. Rodeo Dr., #300
Beverly Hills, CA 90212
*Actor, Julia's brother*
*Birthday: 4/18/56*

**Roberts, Julia (Julie Fiona Roberts)**
% ICM
8942 Wilshire Blvd.
Beverly Hills, CA 90211
*Actress*
*Birthday: 10/28/67*

**Roberts, Tanya**
1122 S. Robertson Blvd., #15
Los Angeles, CA 90035
*Actress*

**Robinson, Brooks**
36 S. Charles St., #2000
Baltimore, MD 21201
*Actor*

**Robinson, David**
% San Antonio Spurs
600 E. Market St., Suite #102
San Antonio, TX 78205
*Basketball player*

**Robinson, Holly**
% Dolores Robinson
Entertainment
10683 Santa Monica Blvd.
Los Angeles, CA 90025
*Actress*
*Birthday: 9/18/64*

**Rock, Chris**
527 N. Azusa Ave., #231
Covina, CA 91722
Or
ML Management Associates, Inc.
1740 Broadway, 15th Floor
New York, NY 10019
*Comedian*

**Rocky Horror Fan Club**
220 W. 19th St.
New York, NY 10011

**Rodgers, Jimmie**
PO Box 685
Forsyth, MO 65653
*Singer*

**Rodrique, George**
721 Royal St.
New Orleans, LA 70016
*Artist known for "The Blue Dog"*
*paintings*

**Rodriguez, Chi Chi**
1720 Merriman Rd.
PO Box 5118
Akron, OH 44313
*Golfer*

**Rodriguez, Johnny**
PO Box 23162
Nashville, TN 37202
*Country singer*

**Roe, Tommy**
PO Box 26037
Minneapolis, MN 55426
*Singer, songwriter*

**Rogers, Fred**
% Family Communications Inc.
4802 Fifth Ave.
Pittsburgh, PA 15213
*Children's TV show host,*
*Presbyterian minister*
*Birthday: 3/20/28*

**Rogers, Kenny**
9 Music Square S., #99
Nashville, TN 37203
*Singer, songwriter*
*Birthday: 8/21/38*

**Kenny Rogers Int'l Fan Club**
PO Box 769
Hendersonville, TN 37077

**Rogers, Mimi**
11693 San Vicente Blvd., Suite
#241
Los Angeles, CA 90049
*Actress*
*Birthday: 1/27/56*

**Roggin, Fred**
3000 W. Alameda Ave.
Burbank, CA 91505
*TV show host*

**Rohner, Clayton**
8271 Melrose Ave., #110
Los Angeles, CA 90046
*Actor*

**Roman, LuLu**
PO Box 8178
Hermitage, TN 37076
*Country singer*

**Roseanne (formerly Barr, formerly Arnold)**
5664 Cahuenga Blvd., #433
North Hollywoood, CA 91601
*Actress, comedienne*
*Birthday: 11/3/52*

**Ross, Diana**
PO Box 11059
Glenville Stadion
Greenwich, CT 06831
*Singer, actress*
*Birthday: 3/26/44*

**Ross, Marion**
20929 Ventura Blvd., #47
Woodland Hills, CA 91364
*Birthday: 10/25/38*

**Ross, Natanya**
1000 Universal Studios Plaza Blvd.,
Bldg. 22
Orlando, FL 32819
*Actress*

**Rossellini, Isabella**
575 Lexington Ave., #2000
New York, NY 10022
*Actress*
*Birthday: 6/18/42*

**Rothrock, Cynthia**
2633 Lincoln Blvd., #103
Santa Monica, CA 90405
*Actress*

**Rourke, Mickey**
9150 Wilshire Blvd., #350
Beverly Hills, CA 90212
*Actor*
*Birthday: 7/16/53*

**Rowland, Rodney**
PO Box 5617
Beverly Hills, CA 90210
*Actor*

**Royal, Billy Joe**
PO Box 50572
Nashville, TN 37205
*Singer*

**Ruehl, Mercedes**
Box 178
Old Chelsea Station
New York, NY 10011
*Actress*
*Birthday: 2/28/48*

**Ruini, Camillo Cardinal**
00120 Vatican City State
Vatican

**Rumsfeld, Donald, Secretary of Defense**
The Pentagon
Rm. 2E779, #1400
Washington, D.C. 20201

**Run-D.M.C.**
160 Varick St.
New York, NY 10013
*Music group*

**RuPaul**
902 Broadway, #1200
New York, NY 10010
*Entertainer*

**Rush**
189 Carlton St.
Toronto, Ontario M5A 2K7
Canada
*Music group*

**Rush, Geoffrey**
% Creative Artists Agency
9830 Wilshire Blvd.
Beverly Hills, CA 90212
*Actor*

**Russell, Johnny**
PO Drawer 37
Hendersonville, TN 37077
*Country singer*

**Russell, Kurt**
1900 Ave. of the Stars, #1240
Los Angeles, CA 90067
*Actor*
*Birthday: 3/17/51*

**Russell, Nipsey**
1650 Broadway, #1410
New York, NY 10019
*Comedian, writer, director*
*Birthday: 10/13/24*

**Rutherford, Kelly**
PO Box 492266
Los Angeles, CA 90049
*Actress*

**Ryan, Jeri**
% Paramount Pictures
*Star Trek Voyager*
5555 Melrose Ave.
Los Angeles, CA 90038
*Actress*

**Ryan, Nolan**
200 W. South St., #B
Alvin, TX 77511
*Baseball great*

**Ryan, Tim**
335 N. Maple Dr., #360
Beverly Hills, CA 90210
*Country singer*

**Ryder, Winona (Winona Laura Horowitz)**
350 Park Ave., #900
New York, NY 10022
*Actress*
*Birthday: 10/29/71*

**S**

**Sabatini, Gabriella**
217 E. Redwood St., #1800
Baltimore, MD 21202
*Former professional volleyball player*

**Sabato, Antonio Jr.**
PO Box 480012
Los Angeles, CA 90048
*Actor*

**Sagal, Katey**
7095 Hollywood Blvd., #792
Hollywood, CA 90028
*Actress*
*Birthday: 1956*

**Saget, Bob**
1122 S. Robertson Blvd., #15
Los Angeles, CA 90035
*Actor, TV host*
*Birthday: 5/17/56*

**Sajak, Pat**
10202 W. Washington Blvd.
Culver City, CA 90232
*TV game show host*
*Birthday: 10/26/46*

**Sambora, Richie**
248 W. 17th St., #501
New York, NY 10011
*Musician, married to Heather Locklear*
*Birthday: 7/11/59*

**Samms, Emma**
2934 1/2 N. Beverly Glen Cir.,
Suite #417
Los Angeles, CA 90077
*Actress*
*Birthday: 8/28/60*

**Sandler, Adam**
9701 Wilshire Blvd., 10th Floor
Beverly Hills, CA 90212
*Actor, comedian*
*Birthday: 9/9/66*

**Santana, Carlos**
121 Jordon St.
San Rafael, CA 94901
Or
PO Box 881630
San Francisco, CA 94188
*Musician*

**Sara, Mia**
PO Box 5617
Beverly Hills, CA 90210
*Actress*

**Sara, Duchess of York**
Birch Hall
Windlesham, Surrey GU2O6BN
England

**Sarandon, Susan (Susan Abigail Tomalin)**
40 W. 57th. St.
New York, NY 10019
*Actress*
*Birthday: 10/4/46*

**Savage, Fred**
1122 S. Robertson Blvd., #15
Los Angeles, CA 90035
*Actor*
*Birthday: 7/9/76*

**Sawa, Devon**
101–1001 W. Broadway, #148
Vancouver BC V6H 4B1
Canada
*Actor*
*Birthday: 9/7/78*

**Saxon, John**
PO Box 492480
Los Angeles, CA 90049
*Actor, writer*
*Birthday: 8/5/35*

**Scacchi, Greta**
18–21 Jermyn St., #300
London SW1Y 6HP
England
*Birthday: 2/18/60*

**Scarabelli, Michele**
4720 Vineland Ave., #216
North Hollywood, CA 91602
*Actress*

**Scatman, John**
% RCA Records
1133 Ave. of the Americas
New York, NY 10036
*Singer*

**Schaech, Jonathon**
1122 S. Roxbury Dr.
Los Angeles, CA 90035
*Actor*
*Birthday: 9/10/69*

**Scheider, Roy**
PO Box 364
Sagaponack, NY 11962
*Actor*
*Birthday: 11/10/35*

**Schell, Maria**
A-9451
Preitenegg
Austria
*Actress*
*Birthday: 1/15/26*

**Schiffer, Claudia**
342 Madison Ave., #1900
New York, NY 10173
*Supermodel, actress*
*Birthday: 8/24/71*

**Schlessinger, Dr. Laura**
% Premiere Radio Network
15260 Ventura Blvd., #500
Sherman Oaks, CA 91403
Or
PO Box 8120
Van Nuys, CA 91409
Website: drlaura.com
*Advice columnist, radio and
television talk show host*

**Schneider, John**
8436 W. 3rd St., #740
Los Angeles, CA 90048
*Singer*

**Schroeder, Rick**
9560 Wilshire Blvd., #500
Beverly Hills, CA 90212
*Actor*
*Birthday: 4/13/70*

**Schumacher, Joel**
4000 Warner Blvd., Bldg. 81, #117
Burbank, CA 91522
*Director*

**Schumacher, Michael**
Forthausstr
92 Kepen/Manheim
Germany
*Professional Formula-1 driver,*
*Birthday: 1/3/69*

**Schwartz, Sherwood**
The Sherwood Schwartz Co.
1865 Carla Ridge Dr.
Beverly Hills, CA 90210
*Creator of* Gilligan's Island

**Schwarzenegger, Arnold**
3110 Main St., #300
Santa Monica, CA 90039
*Actor, author, director, restaurateur*
*Birthday: 7/30/47*

**Scott, Ridley**
% CAA
9830 Wilshire Blvd.
Beverly Hills, CA 90210
Or
632 N. La Peer Dr.
Los Angeles, CA 90040
*Director*
*Birthday: 11/30/37*

**Scott, Tom Everett**
% UTA
9560 Wilshire Blvd., #516
Beverly Hills, CA 90212
*Actor*

**Scully, Vin**
% Los Angeles Dodgers
1000 Elysian Park Ave.
Los Angeles, CA 90012
*Sportscaster*

**Seal**
% Beethoven Street Mgmt.
56 Beethoven St.
GB-London W10 4LG
England
*Singer*
*Birthday: 2/19/63*

**Seals, Brady**
2100 West End Ave., #1000
Nashville, TN 37203
*Singer*

**Seals, Dan**
153 Saunders Ferry Rd.
Hendersonville, TN 37075
*Singer*

**Sedaka, Neil**
201 E. 66th St., #3N
New York, NY 10021
*Singer, songwriter*
*Birthday: 3/13/39*

**Seinfeld, Jerry**
211 Central Park W.
New York, NY 10024
*Actor, comedian*
*Birthday: 4/29/54*

**Selleca, Connie**
15030 Ventura Blvd., #355
Sherman Oaks, CA 91403
*Actress, married to John Tesh*
*Birthday: 5/25/55*

**Selleck, Tom**
331 Sage Ln.
Santa Monica, CA 90402
*Actor*

**Semmelrogge, Martin**
Terhallest II
Munich D-81545
Germany
*Actor, director of Das Boot*

**Setzer, Brian**
10900 Wilshire Blvd., #1230
Los Angeles, CA 90024
*Musician*

**Severance, Joan**
9200 Sunset Blvd., #900
Los Angeles, CA 90069
*Actress*

**Seymour, Jane (Joyce Frankenberger)**
PO Box 548
Agoura, CA 91376
*Actress*
*Birthday: 2/15/51*

**Seymour, Stephanie**
% IT Model Mgmt.
526 N. Larchmont Blvd.
Los Angeles, CA 90004
Or
5415 Oberlin Dr.
San Diego, CA 92121
*Model*

**Shaffer, Paul**
1697 Broadway
New York, NY 10019
*Musical director of The David
Lettterman Show*
*Birthday: 11/28/49*

**Shaggy**
% Virgin Records
338 N. Foothill Rd.
Beverly Hills, CA 90212
*Singer*
*Birthday: 10/26/68*

**Shandling, Garry**
9590 Wilhire Blvd., #516
Beverly Hills, CA 90212
*Actor, comedian*
*Birthday: 11/29/49*

**Sharif, Omar (Michael Shaloub)**
% Anne Alvares Correa
18 rue Troyon
Paris 75017
France
*Actor*
*Birthday: 4/10/32*

**Sharp, Kevin**
PO Box 22105
Nashville, TN 37202
*Country singer*

**Shatner, William**
11288 Ventura Blvd., #725
Studio City, CA 91604
*Actor*
*Birthday: 3/22/31*

**Shaugnessy, Charles**
1999 Ave. of the Stars, #2850
Los Angeles, CA 90067
*Actor*
*Birthday: 2/9/55*

**Shearer, Harry**
119 Ocean Park Blvd.
Santa Monica, CA 90405
*Comedian, writer, director*
*Birthday: 12/23/43*

**Sheedy, Ali**
132 S. Rodeo Dr., #300
Beverly Hills, CA 90212
*Actress*
*Birthday: 6/13/62*

**Sheen, Charlie (Carlos Irwin Estevez)**
10580 Wilshire Blvd.
Los Angeles, CA 90024
*Actor*
*Birthday: 9/3/65*

**Sheldrake, Dr. Rupert**
20 Willow Rd.
London NW3 1TJ
England
Website: http://www.sheldrake.org/
*Biochemist*

**Shelton, Ricky Van**
PO Box 683
Lebannon, TN 37087
Website: http://
www.rickyvanshelton.com/
*Country singer*

**Shepard, Jean**
PO Box 428
Portland, TN 37148
*Country singer*

**Shepherd, Cybill**
% Studio Fan Mail
1122 S. Robertson Blvd., #15
Los Angeles, CA 90035
*Actress, model*
*Birthday: 2/18/50*

**Sheppard, T. G.**
PO Box 510
Dundee, IL 60118
*Country singer*

**Sheridan, Jamey**
% ICM
8942 Wilshire Blvd.
Beverly Hills, CA 90211
*Actor*

**Shields, Brooke**
10061 Riverside Dr., #1013
Toluca Lake, CA 91602
*Actress*
*Birthday: 5/31/65*

**Shimerman, Armin**
1999 Ave. of the Stars, #2850
Los Angeles, CA 90067
*Actor, plays Quark on Star Trek: Deep Space Nine*

**Shirley, Mariah**
% Cinema Talent Agency-Taylor
2609 W. Wyoming Ave., Suite. A
Burbank, CA 91505
*Actress*

**Shore, Pauly**
8491 Sunset Blvd., #700
West Hollywood, CA 90069
*Actor*

**Short, Martin**
760 N. La Cienega Blvd., #200
Los Angeles, CA 90069
*Actor*
*Birthday: 3/26/50*

**Shriver, Pam**
401 Washington Ave., #902
Baltimore, MD 21204
*Tennis player*

**Shue, Elisabeth**
PO Box 464
South Orange, NJ 07079
*Actress*
*Birthday: 10/6/63*

**Siegfried and Roy**
1639 N. Valley Dr.
Las Vegas, NV 89109
*Circus act*

**Silver, Ron**
955 S. Carillo Dr., #300
Los Angeles, CA 90048
*Actor*
*Birthday: 7/2/46*

**Silverman, Fred**
12400 Wilshire Blvd., #920
Los Angeles, CA 90025
*Television producer*

**Silverman, Jonathan**
7920 Sunset Blvd., #401
Los Angeles, CA 90046
Or
4024 Radford Ave., Bldg. 6
Studio City, CA 91604
*Actor*
*Birthday: 8/5/66*

**Silverstone, Alecia**
1122 S. Robertson Blvd., #15
Los Angeles, CA 90035
*Actress*
*Birthday: 1/4/76*

**Simmons, Gene (Chaim Witz)**
8730 Sunset Blvd., #175
Los Angeles, CA 90069
*Singer, bassist of Kiss*
*Birthday: 8/25/49*

**Simon, Paul**
1619 Broadway, #500
New York, NY 10019
*Singer, songwriter*
*Birthday: 10/13/41*

**Simpson, O. J.**
11661 San Vicente Blvd., #600
Los Angeles, CA 90049
*Ex-football player, actor*

**Sin, Jaime Cardinal**
PO Box 132
Manila 10099
Philippines

**Sinatra, Nancy**
1121 N. Beverly Dr.
Beverly Hills, CA 90210
*Singer, Frank's daughter*
*Birthday: 6/8/40*

**Sinbad**
21704 Devonshire, #13
Chatsworth, CA 91311
*Actor, comedian*

**Sinise, Gary**
% CAA
9830 Wilshire Blvd.
Beverly Hills, CA 90212
*Actor*
*Birthday: 3/17/55*

**Singer, Lori**
1465 Linda Crest Dr.
Beverly Hills, CA 90210
*Actress*
*Birthday: 5/6/62*

**Singletary, Daryle**
1610 16th Ave. S.
Nashville, TN 37212
*Country singer*

**Sirhan, Sirhan**
#B21014
Corcoran State Prison
Box 8800
Corcoran, CA 93212
*Assasinated Robert Kennedy*

**Sirtis, Marina**
4526 Wilshire Blvd.
Los Angeles, CA 90010
*Actress*

**Sizemore, Tom**
9830 Wilshire Blvd.
Beverly Hills, CA 90212
*Actor*

**Skaggs, Ricky**
PO Box 150871
Nashville, TN 37215
*Country singer*

**Skerritt, Tom**
1122 S. Robertson Blvd., #15
Los Angeles, CA 90035
*Actor*
*Birthday: 8/25/33*

**Slash (Sol Hudson)**
PO Box 93909
Los Angeles, CA 90093
*Guns 'N Roses guitar player*

**Slater, Christian (Christian Hawkins)**
9150 Wilshire Blvd., #350
Beverly Hills, CA 90210
*Actor*
*Birthday: 8/18/69*

**Slater, Kelly**
% The *Baywatch* Prod. Co.
5433 Beethoven St.
Los Angeles, CA 90066
*Actress: 11/2/72*

**Sledge, Percy**
% Artists Int. Mgmt.
9850 Sandalfoot Blvd., #458
Boca Raton, FL 33428
*Singer*
*Birthday: 11/25/40*

**Smalley, Richard E.**
Dept of Chemistry
Rice University
6100 Main St.
Houston, TX 77005
Website: http://cnst.rice.edu/
reshome.html
*1996 Nobel Prize winner in chemistry*

**Smart, Jean**
151 El Camino Dr.
Beverly Hills, CA 90212
*Actress*

**Smith, Anna Nicole**
10927 Santa Monica Blvd., #136
Los Angeles, CA 90025
*Model*

**Smith, Connie**
PO Box 428
Portland, TN 37148
*Country singer*

**Smith, Jaclyn**
10398 Sunset Blvd.
Los Angeles, CA 90077
*Actress*
*Birthday: 10/26/47*

**Smith, Kevin**
Box 90-409
Auckland Mail Center
Auckland
New Zealand
*Actor*

**Smith, Lou**
11365 Ventura Blvd., #100
Studio City, CA 91604
*Widow of Wolfman Jack*

**Smith, Shawnee**
Innovative Artists
1999 Ave. of the Stars, Suite
#2850
Los Angeles, CA 90069
*Actress*
*Birthday: 7/3/70*

**Smith, Will**
% Creative Artists Management
9830 Wilshire Blvd.
Beverly Hills, CA 90212
Or
303 Bob Hope Dr.
Burbank, CA 91523
*Actor*
*Birthday: 9/25/68*

**Smits, Jimmy**
PO Box 49922 Barrington Station
Los Angeles, CA 90049
*Actor*
*Birthday: 7/9/55*

**Snider, Mike**
PO Box 140710
Nashville, TN 37214
*Country singer*

**Snipes, Wesley**
1888 Century Park East, #500
Los Angeles, CA 90067
*Actor*

**Snow**
% S. L. Feldman
1505 W. 2nd Ave., #200
Vancouver, BC V6H 3Y4
Canada
*Singer*
*Birthday: 10/30/69*

**Sodano, Angelo Cardinal**
00120 Vatican City State
Vatican

**Somers, Suzanne**
23852 Pacific Coast Hwy., #916
Malibu, CA 90265
*Actress*
*Birthday: 11/5/40*

**Sonnier, Joel**
PO Box 120845
Nashville, TN 37212
*Singer*

**Soraya**
% Mercury Records
11150 Santa Monica Blvd., 10th
Floor
Los Angeles, CA 90025
*Singer*
*Birthday: 3/11/69*

**Sorbo, Kevin**
PO Box 410
Buffalo Center, IA 50424
Or
5664 Cahuenga Blvd., Suite #437
North Hollywood, CA 91601
*Actor*

**Sorenson, Heidi**
% Pierce and Shelly
612 Lighthouse Ave., #275
Pacific Grove, CA 93951
E-mail: HeidiSoren@aol.com
*Model*

**Sorvino, Mira**
110 E. 87th St.
New York, NY 10128
*Actress*

**Sorvino, Paul**
110 E. 87th St.
New York, NY 10128
*Actor*
*Birthday: 4/13/49*

**Sothern, Ann**
Box 2285
Ketchum, ID 83340
*Actress*
*Birthday: 1/22/09*

**Soto, Talisa**
9200 Sunset Blvd., #900
Los Angeles, CA 90069
*Model*

**Soul, David**
8306 Wilshire Blvd., #438
Beverly Hills, CA 90211
*Actor*

**Spacek, Sissy (Mary Elizbeth Spacek)**
Rt. 2 #640
Cobham, VA 22929
*Actress*
*Birthday: 12/25/49*

**Spacey, Kevin**
151 El Camino Dr.
Beverly Hills, CA 90212
*Actor*
*Birthday: 7/26/49*

**Spade, David**
9150 Wilshire Blvd., #350
Beverly Hills, CA 90212
Or
% Jonas P R
240 26th St., Suite 3
Santa Monica, CA 90402
*Actor*

**Spears, Billie Jo**
2802 Columbine Pl.
Nashville, TN 37204
*Country singer*

**Spears, Britney**
137 W. 25th St.
New York, NY 10001
E-mail: britney@britney.com
*Singer, actress*
*Birthday: 12/2/81*

**Spelling, Aaron**
5700 Wilshire Blvd.
Los Angeles, CA 90036
*Television producer*

**Spelling, Tori**
5700 Wilshire Blvd.
Los Angeles, CA 90036
Or
% SFM
1122 S. Robertson Blvd., #15
Los Angeles, CA 90035
*Actress, daughter of Aaron Spelling*
*Birthday: 5/16/73*

**Spencer, Bud**
Via Cortina d'Apezzo 156
Rome 00191
Italy
*Actor*

**Spielberg, Steven**
PO Box 8520
Universal City, CA 91608
*Producer, director, co-founder of*
*Dreamworks*
*Birthday: 12/18/47*


**Spiner, Brent**
PO Box 5617
Beverly Hills, CA 90210
*Actor*
*Birthday: 2/2/55*


**Spinks, Leon**
PO Box 88771
Carol Stream, IL 60188
*Boxer*


**Springer, Jerry**
454 N. Columbus Dr., #200
Chicago, IL 60611
*Talk show host, former Mayor of*
*Cincinnati, Ohio*


**Springfield, Rick**
9200 Sunset Blvd., #900
Los Angeles, CA 90069
*Singer, actor*
*Birthday: 8/23/49*


**Squier, Billy**
PO Box 1251
New York, NY 10023
*Singer, musician*
*Birthday: 5/12/50*


**St. Laurent, Yves**
5 Av. Marceau
Paris F-75116
France
*Fashion designer*
*Birthday: 8/4/?*

**Stack, Robert**
415 N. Camden Dr., #121
Beverly Hills, CA 90210
*Actor*
*Birthday: 1/13/19*


**Stafford, Jim**
PO Box 6366
Branson, MO 65616
*Country singer*


**Stahl, Lisa**
% Shelly and Pierce
612 Lighthouse Ave., #275
Pacific Grove, CA 93951
E-mail: LISASTAHL1@aol.com
*Actress*


**Stallone, Sylvester**
9150 Wilshire Blvd., #340
Beverly Hills, CA 90212
*Actor, writer, director*
*Birthday: 7/6/46*


**Stamos, John**
270 N. Canon Dr., #1064
Beverly Hills, CA 90210
*Actor, musician*
*Birthday: 8/19/63*


**Stapleton, Jean**
% Bauman, Hiller and Associates
5757 Wilshire Blvd., 5th Floor
Los Angeles, CA 90036
*Actress*


**Starr, Ringo (Richard Starkey)**
1541 Ocean Ave., #200
Santa Monica, CA 90401
*Drummer, actor*
*Birthday: 7/7/40*


**Staubach, Roger**
6912 Edelweiss Cr.
Dallas, TX 75240
*Football player*

**Steel, Danielle**
PO Box 1637
Murray Hill Station
New York, NY 10156
*Author*

**Steen, Jessica**
% Somers Teitelbaum David (Chris Henze)
1925 Century Park East, #2320
Los Angeles, CA 90067
Web site: http://
www.jessicasteen.com/
*Actress*

**Steinbrenner, George**
PO Box 25077
Tampa, FL 33622
*Baseball executive*

**Stern, Daniel**
PO Box 6788
Malibu, CA 90264
*Actor*
*Birthday: 8/28/57*

**Stern, Howard**
40 W. 57th St., #1400
New York, NY 10019
*Radio personality*

**Stevens, Brinke**
PMB #556
8033 Sunset Blvd.
Hollywood, CA 90046
*Actress*

**Stevens, Connie (Concetta Ann Ingolia)**
426 S. Robertson Blvd.
Los Angeles, CA 90048
*Actress, singer*
*Birthday: 8/8/38*

**Stevens, Ray (Ray Ragsdale)**
1708 Grand Ave.
Nashville, TN 37212
*Singer, songwriter*
*Birthday: 1/24/39*

**Stevens, Stella (Estelle Eggleston)**
2180 Coldwater Cyn.
Beverly Hills, CA 90210
*Actress*
*Birthday: 10/1/36*

**Stevenson, Parker**
% Metropolitan Talent Agency
4526 Wilshire Blvd.
Los Angeles, CA 90010
*Actor*
*Birthday: 6/4/51*

**Stewart, Martha**
19 Newton Turnpike
Westport, CT 06880
*TV personality, lifestyle consultant, writer, publisher*
*Birthday: 8/3/41*

**Stewart, Patrick**
PO Box 93999
Los Angeles, CA 90093
*Actor, writer*
*Birthday: 7/13/40*

**Stewart, Rod**
1122 S. Robertson Blvd., #15
Los Angeles, CA 90035
*Singer, songwriter*
*Birthday: 1/10/45*

**Stich, Michael**
Bayerstr 383
A-5071
Salzburg/Wals-Siezenheim
Austria
*Professional tennis player*

**Stiers, David Ogden**
121 N. San Vicente Blvd.
Beverly Hills, CA 90211
*Actor*
*Birthday: 10/31/42*

**Sting (Gordon Matthew Sumner)**
2 The Grove
Highgate Village
London N6
England
*Singer, songwriter, actor*
*Birthday: 10/2/51*

**Stockwell, Dean**
PO Box 6248
Malibu, CA 90264
*Birthday: 3/5/35*

**Stone, Cliffie**
PO Box 710
Los Angeles, CA 90078
*Country singer*

**Stone, Doug**
PO Box 943
Springfield, TN 37172
*Country singer*

**Stone, Sharon**
PO Box 7304
North Hollywood, CA 91603
*Actress*

**Stone, Sly**
6467 Sunset Blvd., #110
Hollywood, CA 90028
*Musician*

**Storch, Larry**
330 West End Ave.
New York, NY 10023
*Actor*
*Birthday: 1/8/23*

**Stowe, Madeleine**
9560 Wilshire Blvd., #516
Beverly Hills, CA 90212
*Actress*
*Birthday: 1958*

**Strait, George**
1000 18th Ave. S.
Nashville, TN 37212
*Country singer*

**Strange, Curtis**
% Kingsman Golf Club
100 Golf Club Rd.
Williamsburg, VA 23185
*Golfer*

**Streep, Meryl (Mary Louise Streep)**
% Creative Artists Agency
9830 Wilshire Blvd.
Beverly Hills, CA 90212
*Actress*
*Birthday: 4/22/49*

**Streisand, Barbra (Barbara Joan)**
320 Central Park W.
New York, NY 10025
*Singer, actress, director*
*Birthday: 4/24/42*

**Stringfield, Sherry**
9560 Wilshire Blvd., #516
Beverly Hills, CA 90212
*Actress*

**Stroker, Dr. Carol**
Ames, Moffett
Field, CA 94035
*NASA scientist with the Mars mission*

**Strugg, Kerry**
1122 S. Robertson Blvd., #14
Los Angeles, CA 90035
*Gymnast*

**Struthers, Sally**
8721 Sunset Blvd.
Los Angeles, CA 90046
*Actress*
*Birthday: 7/28/48*

**Stuart, Marty**
119 17th Ave. S.
Nashville, TN 37203
*Singer, songwriter*

**Marty Stuart Fan Club**
PO Box 24180
Nashville, TN 37202

**Sunny**
% WWF
PO Box 3859
Stamford, CT 06905
*Professional wrestler*

**Supernaw, Doug**
56 Lindsley Ave.
Nashville, TN 37210
*Country singer*

**Sutherland, Donald**
760 N. La Cienega Blvd., #300
Los Angeles, CA 90069
*Actor*
*Birthday: 7/17/36*

**Sutherland, Kiefer**
132 S. Rodeo Dr., #300
Beverly Hills, CA 90212
*Actor, Donald's son*
*Birthday: 12/18/66*

**Swank, Hilary**
3500 W. Olive Ave., #920
Burbank, CA 91505
*Actress*

**Swanson, Kristy**
2934 N. Beverly Glen Circle, #416
Los Angeles, CA 90077
*Actress*
*Birthday: 12/19/69*

**Swayze, Patrick**
% Wolf/Kasteler Inc.
132 S. Rodeo Dr., #300
Beverly Hills, CA 90212
*Actor*
*Birthday: 8/18/52*

**T**

**Tabuchi, Shoji**
HCR Rt.1
Box 755
Branson, MO 65616
*Musician*

**Takei, George**
419 N. Larchmont Blvd., #41
Los Angeles, CA 90004
*Actor, plays Lt. Sulu on Star Trek*

**Tarantino, Quentin**
7966 Beverly Blvd., #300
Los Angeles, CA 90048
*Director, actor, writer*
*Birthday: 3/27/63*

**Taupin, Bernie**
450 N. Maple Dr., #501
Beverly Hills, CA 90210
*Songwriter*

**Taylor, Elizabeth**
PO Box 55995
Sherman Oaks, CA 91413
*Actress*
*Birthday: 2/27/32*

**Taylor, James**
1250 6th St., #401
Santa Monica, CA 90401
*Singer, songwriter, musician*
*Birthday: 3/12/48*

**Taylor, Niki**
8326 Pines Blvd., #334
Hollywood, FL 33024
*Model*

**Taylor, Les**
177 Northwood Dr.
Lexington, KY 40505
*Country singer*

**Taylor-Young, Leigh**
6500 Wilshire Blvd., #2200
Los Angeles, CA 90048
*Actress*

**Tennant, Victoria**
% Metropolitan Talent Agency
4526 Wilshire Blvd.
Los Angeles, CA 90010
*Actress*
*Birthday: 9/30/53*

**Tenney, Jon**
1122 S. Roxbury Dr.
Los Angeles, CA 90035
*Actor*

**Tesh, John**
PO Box 6010
Sherman Oaks, CA 91413
*Musician*
*Birthday: 7/1/53*

**Thiessen, Tiffani-Amber**
3500 W. Olive Ave., #1400
Burbank, CA 91505
*Actress*
*Birthday: 1/23/74*

**Thomas, B. J.**
PO Box 120003
Arlington, TX 76012
*Singer*

**Thomas, Dave**
429 Santa Monica Blvd., #500
Santa Monica, CA 90401
*Comedian, actor*

**Thomas, Fred Dalton**
401 Church St., 12th Floor
Nashville, TN 37219
*Actor*

**Thomas, Heather**
1122 S. Robertson Blvd., #15
Los Angeles, CA 90035
*Actress*
*Birthday: 9/8/57*

**Thomas, Irma**
PO Box 26126
New Orleans, LA 70186
*Musician*

**Thomas, Jay**
6500 Wilshire Blvd., #2200
Los Angeles, CA 90048
*Actor, radio personality*
*Birthday: 7/12/48*

**Thomas, Jonathan Taylor**
PO Box 64846
Los Angels, CA 90064
*Actor*
*Birthday: 9/8/81*

**Thomas, Kristin Scott**
9830 Wilshire Blvd.
Beverly Hills, CA 90212
*Actress*

**Thomas, Michael Phillip**
PO Box 611222
Miami, FL 33261
*Actor*
*Birthday: 5/26/49*

**Thompson, Andrea**
14431 Ventura Blvd., #260
Sherman Oaks, CA 91423
*Actress*

**Thompson, Emma**
31/32 Soho Sq.
London W1V 5DG
England
*Actress*

**Thompson, Hank**
5 Rushing Creek Ct.
Roanoke, TX 76262
*Country singer*

**Thompson, Lea**
PO Box 5617
Beverly Hills, CA 90210
*Actress*
*Birthday: 5/31/62*

**Thompson, Sada**
PO Box 490
Southebury, CT 06488
*Actress*
*Birthday: 9/27/29*

**Thorne-Smith, Courtney**
11693 San Vicente Blvd., #266
Los Angeles, CA 90049
*Actress*

**Thornton, Billy Bob**
11777 San Vicente Blvd., #880
Los Angeles, CA 90049
*Actor*

**Thurman, Uma**
% Creative Artists Agency
9830 Wilshire Blvd.
Beverly Hills, CA 90212
*Actress*

**Tiegs, Cheryl**
15 E. Putnam Ave., #3260
Greenwich, CT 06830
*Model*

**Tighe, Kevin**
PO Box 453
Sedro Woolley, WA 98284
*Actor*
*Birthday: 8/13/44*

**Tillis, Mell**
2527 State Hwy. #248
Box 1630
Branson, MO 65615
*Country singer*

**Tillis, Pam**
PO Box 128575
Nashville, TN 37212
*Country singer*

**Tilly, Jennifer**
270 N. Canon Dr. #1582
Beverly Hills, CA 90210
Or
% ICM
8942 Wilshire Blvd.
Beverly Hills, CA 90211
*Actress, Meg's sister*
*Birthday: 9/10/58*

**Tilly, Meg**
321 S. Beverly Dr. #M
Beverly Hills, CA 90212
*Actress*
*Birthday: 2/14/60*

**Tilton, Charlene**
PO Box 1309
Studio City, CA 91614
*Actress*

**Tippin, Aaron**
PO Box 121709
Nashville, TN 37212
*Country singer*

**Toblowsky, Stephen**
% William Morris Agency
151 El Camino Dr.
Beverly Hills, CA 90212
*Actor*

**Tomei, Marisa**
120 W. 45th St., #3600
New York, NY 10036
*Actress*
*Birthday: 12/4/64*

**Tomlin, Lily**
PO Box 27700
Los Angeles, CA 90027
*Comedienne, actress*
*Birthday: 9/1/39*

**Tone Loc**
1650 Broadway, #508
New York, NY 10019
*Musician*

**Top, Carrot**
420 Sylvan Dr.
Winter Park, FL 32789
*Comedian*

**Tork, Peter**
1551 S. Robertson Blvd.
Los Angeles, CA 90035
*Musician, actor*
*Birthday: 2/13/42*

**Tracy, Paul**
% Penske Motorsports
Penske Plaza
Reading, PA 19603
*Race car driver*

**Travis, Randy (Randy Traywick)**
PO Box 121137
Nashville, TN 37212
*Country singer*
*Birthday: 5/4/59*

**Travanti, Daniel J.**
1077 Melody Rd.
Lake Forest, IL 60045
*Actor*
*Birthday: 3/7/40*

**Travolta, John**
15821 Ventura Blvd., #460
Studio City, CA 91436
*Actor*
*Birthday: 2/18/54*

**Trebek, Alex**
10210 W. Washington
Culver City, CA 90232
*Game show host*

**Tritt, Travis**
PO Box 2044
Hiram, GA 40141
*Singer, songwriter*
*Birthday: 2/9/63*

**Travis Tritt Country Club**
Attn: Liz
PO Box 2044
Hiram, GA 30141

**Trudeau, Garry (Garretson Beckman Trudeau)**
% United Press Media
200 Madison Ave
New York, NY 10016
*Cartoonist, married to Jane Pauley*
*Birthday: 1948*

**Trulli, Jarno**
% Minardi Team S.p.A.
Via Spellanzani 21
I-48018 Faenza/RA
*Professional Formula-1 driver*

**Trump, Donald**
721 5th Ave.
New York, NY 10022
*Real estate executive*
*Birthday: 6/14/46*

**Tubb, Justin**
PO Box 500
Nashville, TN 37202
*Country singer*

**Tucker, Tanya**
109 Westpark Dr., #400
Brentwood, TN 37027
*Country singer*
*Birthday: 10/10/58*

**Tudor, Tasha**
PO Box 503
Marlboro, VT 05344
Website: http://
www.tashatudorandfamily.com/
E-mail: ensingm@together.net
*One of America's most beloved author/illustrators, has written, illustrated or been the subject of over 90 books spanning more than half a century. Her 91st book, The Great Corgiville Kidnapping, was published in 1997.*

**Tune, Tommy**
50 E. 89th St.
New York, NY 10128
*Dancer, director, actor*
*Birthday: 2/28/39*

**Turlington, Christy**
% United Talent Agency
9560 Wilshire Blvd.
Beverly Hills, CA 90212
Or
% Celebrity Merchandise
PMB 710
15030 Ventura Blvd.
Sherman Oaks, CA 91403
*Model, actress*

**Turner, Grant**
PO Box 414
Brentwood, TN 37027
*Country singer*

**Turner, Ted (Robert Edward Turner III)**
1050 Techwood Dr., NW
Atlanta, GA 30318
*Media executive, owner of Atlanta Braves and Atlanta Hawks*
*Birthday: 11/26/39*

**Tutu, Archbishop Desmond**
7981 Orlando West
Box 1131
Johannesburg
Rep. of South Africa

**Twain, Shania**
410 W. Elm St.
Greenwich, CT 06830
*Country singer*

**Tweed, Shannon**
9300 Wilshire Blvd., #410
Beverly Hills, CA 90212
*Actress*

**Twiggy (Leslie Hornby)**
4 St. George's House
15 Hanover Square
GB-London W1R 9AJ
England
*Model, actress*
*Birthday: 9/19/49*

**Tyler, Liv**
233 Park Ave. S., 10th Floor
New York, NY 10003
Or
1999 Ave. of the Stars, Suite
#2850
Los Angeles, CA 90067
*Actress daughter of Steven Tyler,*
*lead singer of Aerosmith*

**Tyler, Steven (Steven Tallarico)**
584 Broadway, #1009
New York, NY 10012
Or
% Monterey Pennisula Artists
509 Hartnell St.
Monterey, CA 93940
*Lead singer of Aerosmith*
*Birthday: 3/26/48*

**Tylo, Hunter**
11684 Ventura Blvd., #910
Studio City, CA 91604
*Actress*

**Tyson, Cicely**
315 W. 70th St.
New York, NY 1023
*Actress*
*Birthday: 12/19/33*

**Tyson, Mike**
10100 Santa Monica Blvd., #1300
Los Angeles, CA 90067
*Boxer*
*Birthday: 7/1/66*

# U

**Ullrich, Jan**
% Team Deutsche Telekom
Königstr. 97
Bonn 53115
Germany
*Winner of the 1997 Tour de France*
*Birthday: 11/2/73*

**Ulrich, Skeet (Brian Ray Ulrich)**
8942 Wilshire Blvd.
Beverly Hills, CA 90211
*Actor*
*Birthday: 1/20/69*

**Underwood, Blair**
4116 N. Magnolia Blvd., #101
Burbank, CA 91505
*Actor*
*Birthday: 8/25/64*

**Unitas, Johnny**
% Pro Football Hall of Fame
2121 George Halas Dr. NW
Canton, OH 44708
*Former football player*

**Unser, Al, Jr.**
PO Box 25047
Albuquerque, NM 87125
*Race car driver*

**Upshaw, Gene**
% Pro Football Hall of Fame
2121 George Halas Dr. NW
Canton, OH 44708
*Professional football player*

**Urich, Robert**
10061 Riverside Dr., #1026
Toluca Lake, CA 91602
*Actor*
*Birthday: 12/19/47*

# V

**Van Horn, Patrick**
9200 Sunset Blvd., #1130
Los Angeles, CA 90069
*Actor*

**Van Houten, Leslie**
#W13378
Bed #1B314U
California Inst. for Women
16756 Chino Corona
Frontera, CA 91720
*Member of the Manson "Family,"*
*convicted murderer*

**Van Peebles, Mario**
853 7th Ave., #3E
New York, NY 10019
*Actor, writer, director*
*Birthday: 1/15/57*

**Van Shelton, Ricky**
6424 Bresslyn Rd.
Nashville, TN 37205
*Country singer*

**Vanilla Ice**
250 W. 57th St., #821
New York, NY 10107
*Rapper*

**Vargas, Elizabeth**
% ABC-TV News Dept.
77 W. 66th St.
New York, NY 10023
*Journalist*

**Vedder, Eddie**
1423 34th Ave.
Seattle, WA 98122
*Singer, songwriter*
*Birthday: 12/23/64*

**Ventura, Gov. Jesse**
75 Constitution Ave., #130
St. Paul, MN 55155
*Governor, former Navy Seal,*
*former wrestler*

**Vereen, Ben**
9255 Sunset Blvd., #804
Los Angeles, CA 90069
*Actor*
*Birthday: 1/13/25*

**Verstappen, Jos**
% Tyrrell Racing Organization Ltd.
Long Reach
Ockham
Woking
GB-Surrey GU23 6PE
*Professional Formula-1 driver*

**Vigoda, Abe**
8500 Melrose Ave. #208
West Hollywood, CA 90069
*Actor*
*Birthday: 2/24/21*

**Vila, Bob**
Box 749
Marstons Mills, MA 02648
*TV host*

**Villeneuve, Jaques**
% Williams GP Engineering Ltd.
Grove
Wantage
GB Oxfordshire OX12 0DQ
*Professional Formula-1 driver,*
*1997 World Cup winner*

**Vincent, Jan Michael**
27856 Pacific Coast Hwy.
Malibu, CA 90265
*Actor*

**Vincent, Rhonda**
PO Box #31
Greentop, MO 63546
*Country singer*

**Vincent, Rick**
Box #323
1336 North Moorpark Rd.
Thousand Oaks, CA 91360
*Country singer*

**Vinton, Bobby**
PO Box 6010
Branson, MO 65615
*Singer*
*Birthday: 4/16/35*

**Visitor, Nana**
*% Star Trek: Deep Space Nine*
*5555 Melrose Ave.*
*Los Angeles, CA 90036*
*Or*
*9016 Wilshire Blvd., #363*
*Beverly Hills, CA 90211*
*Actress, plays Major Kira on* Star
Trek: Deep Space Nine
*Birthday: 2/26/57*

**Vitale, Dick**
*% ESPN Plaza*
935 Middlestreet
Bristol, CT 06010
*Sportscaster*

**Vonnegut, Kurt Jr.**
Box 27
Sagaponack, NY 11962
*Author*

**Voorhies, Lark**
10635 Santa Monica Blvd., Suite
130
Los Angeles, CA 90025
*Actress*
*Birthday: 3/25/74*

**W**

**Wade, Virginia**
Sharstead Ct.
Sittingbourne, Kent
England
*Tennis player*

**Wagner, Lindsay**
PO Box 5002
Sherman Oaks, CA 91403
*Actress*
*Birthday: 6/22/49*

**Wagner, Robert**
1500 Old Oak Rd.
Los Angeles, CA 90049
*Actor*
*Birthday: 2/10/30*

**Wagoner, Porter**
PO Box 290785
Nashville, TN 37229
*Country singer*

**Wai-hing, Emily Lau**
Suite #602, Citibank Tower
3 Garden Road
Central
Hong Kong
or
No 12-13, g/f
Hok Sam House
Lung Hang Estatne
Shatin, New Territories
Hong Kong
Website: http://
www.emilylau.org.hk/
E-mail: Elau@hknet.com
*Hong Kong legislator and*
*democracy advocate*
*Birthday: 1/2/52*

**Waits, Tom**
PO Box 498
Valley Ford, CA 94972
*Singer, songwriter, actor*
*Birthday: 12/7/49*

**Walker, Ally**
10390 Santa Monica Blvd., #300
Los Angeles, CA 90025
*Actress*

**Walker, Billy**
PO Box 618
Hendersonville, TN 37077
*Country singer*

**Walker, Charles**
National Space Society
600 Pennsylvania Ave., #201
Washington, DC 20003
*Astronaut*

**Walker, Charlie**
Grand Ole Opry
2804 Opryland Dr.
Nashville, TN 37214
*Country singer*

**Walker, Clay**
PO. Box 8125
Gallatin, TN 37066
*Country singer*

**Walker, Jerry Jeff**
PO Box 39
Austin, TX 78767
*Country singer, songwriter*

**Walker, Marcy**
9107 Wilshire Blvd., #700
Beverly Hills, CA 90210
*Birthday: 11/26/61*

**Walker, Mort**
% King Features
235 E. 45th St.
New York, NY 10017
*Cartoonist*

**Wallach, Eli**
200 W. 57th St., #900
New York, NY 10019
*Actor*
*Birthday: 12/7/15*

**Wallendas, The Great**
138 Frog Hollow Rd.
Churchville, PA 18966
*The most famous highwire family
in history*

**Walston, Ray**
423 S. Rexford Dr., #205
Beverly Hills, CA 90212
*Actor*
*Birthday: 11/2/24*

**Walters, Barbara**
33 W. 60th. St.
New York, NY 10023
*TV hostess*
*Birthday: 9/25/31*

**Wang, Garret**
1440 Veteran Ave., #212
Los Angeles, CA 90024
*Actor, plays Ensign Harry Kim on
Star Trek: Voyager*

**Ward, Megan**
PO Box 481210
Los Angeles, CA 90036
*Actress*
*Birthday: 9/24/69*

**Ward, Rachel**
PO Box 5617
Beverly Hills, CA 90210
*Actress*
*Birthday: 9/12/57*

**Wariner, Steve**
PO Box 1647
Franklin, TN 37065
*Country singer*

**Warlock, Billy**
9229 Sunset Blvd., #315
Los Angeles, CA 90069
*Actor*
*Birthday: 3/26/60*

**Waters, John**
1018 N. Charles St.
Baltimore, MD 21201
*Actor, director, writer*
*Birthday: 4/22/49*

**Waters, Roger**
% Ten Tenth Mgmt.
106 Gifford St.
England-London N1 0DF
*Actor*
*Birthday: 9/6/44*

**Waterson, Sam**
RR1, Box 232
West Cornwall, CT 06796
*Actor*
*Birthday: 11/15/40*

**Watson, Gene**
PO Box 2210
Nashville, TN 37202
*Country singer*

**Weathers, Carl**
10960 Wilshire Blvd., #826
Los Angeles, CA 90024
*Actor*
*Birthday: 1/14/48*

**Weaver, Dennis**
PO Box 257
Ridgeway, CO 81432
*Actor*
*Birthday: 6/4/25*

**Weaver, Sigourney**
200 W. 57th St.
New York, NY 10019
*Actress*

**Webber, Andrew Lloyd**
725 Fifth Ave.
New York, NY 10022
*Composer, producer*
*Birthday: 3/22/48*

**Weber, Steven**
% ICM
8942 Wilshire Blvd.
Beverly Hills, CA 90211
*Actor*

**Weinger, Scott**
9255 Sunset Blvd., #1010
West Hollywood, CA 90069
*Actor*

**Weir, Peter**
Post Office
Palm Beach 2108
Australia
*Director*

**Welch, Kevin**
Warner Bros.
1815 Division
Nashville, TN 37212
*Country singer*

**Welch, Rachquel (Racquel Tejada)**
9903 Santa Monica Blvd., #514
Beverly Hills, CA 90212
*Actress*
*Birthday: 9/5/40*

**Weld, Tuesday**
711 West End Ave., #5k-N
New York, NY 10025
*Actress*

**Wells, Dawn**
11684 Ventura Blvd., #985
Studio City, CA 91604
*TV actress, played Marianne on
Gilligan's Island*

**Wells, Kitty**
240 Old Hickory Blvd.
Madison, TN 37115
*Country singer*

**Wenders, Wim**
% Wim Wenders Produktion
Segitzdamm 2
Berlin 10969
Germany
*Director*
*Birthday: 8/14/45*

**Wendt, George**
9150 Wilshire Blvd.
Beverly Hills, CA 90212
*Actor*
*Birthday: 10/17/48*

**West, Adam**
PO Box 3477
Ketchum, ID 83340
*TV actor played Batman*
*Birthday: 9/19/29*

**West, Jerry**
% Basketball Hall of Fame
1150 W. Columbia Ave.
Springfield, MA 01101
*Basketball player*

**Whalley, Joanne**
9830 Wilshire Blvd.
Beverly Hills, CA 90212
*Actress*
*Birthday: 8/25/64*

**Wheaton, Wil**
2820 Honolulu, #255
Verdugo City, CA 91403
*Actor*

**White, Barry**
% WMA
1325 Ave. of the Americas
New York, NY 10019
*Musican*

**White, Betty**
PO Box 491965
Los Angeles, CA 90049
*Actress*
*Birthday: 1/17/22*

**White, Bryan**
2100 West End Ave., #1000
Nashville, TN 37203
*Country singer*

**White, Jaleel**
1122 S. Robertson Blvd., #15
Los Angeles, CA 90035
*Actor*
*Birthday: 1/26/76*

**White, Joy Lynn**
1101 17th Ave. S.
Nashville, TN 37212
*Country singer*

**White, Lari**
1028-B 18th Ave. S.
Nashville, TN 37212
*Country singer*

**White, Michael**
5420 Camelot Rd.
Brentwood, TN 37027
*Country singer*

**White, Reggie**
% Green Bay Packers
PO Box 10628
Green Bay, WI 54307
*Football player*

**White, Vanna (Vanna Rosich)**
10202 W. Washington Blvd.
Culver City, CA 90232
*TV personality*
*Birthday: 2/8/57*

**White House for Kids**
Website: http://
www.whitehouse.gov/WH/kids/
html/home.html

**Whitman, Slim**
505 Canton Pass
Madison, TN 37115
*Singer*

**Wilburn, Teddy**
Grand Ole Opry
2804 Opryland Dr.
Nashville, TN 37214
*Country singer*

**Wilder, Gene (Jerome Silberman)**
1511 Sawtelle Blvd., #155
Los Angeles, CA 90025
*Actor, writer director, married to
the late Gilda Radner*
*Birthday: 6/11/35*

**William, HRH Prince**
Highgrove House
Gloucestershire
England

**Williams, Andy**
2500 W. Hwy 76
Branson, MO 65616
*Singer*
*Birthday: 12/30/30*

**Williams, Hank Jr.**
PO Box 850
Paris, TN 38242
*Country singer, son of Hank
Williams*

**Williams, Hank III**
PO Box 121736
Nashville, TN 37212
*Country singer*

**Williams, Jason D.**
819 18th Ave. S.
Nashville, TN 37203
*Country singer*

**Williams, Jett**
PO Box 177
Hartsville, TN 37074
*Country singer*

**Williams, Jobeth**
9465 Wilshire Blvd., #430
Beverly Hills, CA 90212
*Actress*
*Birthday: 1953*

**Williams, John**
Boston Symphony Orchestra
Symphony Hall
301 Massachusetts Ave.
Boston, MA 02115
*Composer, conductor*
*Birthday: 2/8/32*

**Williams, Robin**
9465 Wilshire Blvd., #419
Beverly Hills, CA 90212
*Actor, comedian*
*Birthday: 7/21/52*

**Williams, Serena**
U.S. Tennis Assoc.
70 W. Red Oaks Lane
White Plains, NY 10604
*Tennis player*

**Williams, Treat (Richard Williams)**
% Gladys-Marie Hart
1244 11th St., #A
Santa Monica, CA 90401
*Actor*
*Birthday: 12/1/51*

**Williams, Vanessa**
4526 Wilshire Blvd.
Los Angeles, CA 90010
*Actress*

**Williams, Vanessa**
Box 858
Chappaqua, NY 10514
*Singer*

**Williams, Venus**
U.S. Tennis Assoc.
70 W. Red Oaks Lane
White Plains, NY 10604
*Tennis player*

**Williams, Walter E.**
George Mason University
4400 University Dr.
Fairfax, VA 22030-4444
Website: http://www.gmu.edu/
departments/economics/wew/
index.html
E-mail: wwilliam@gmu.edu
*John M. Olin Distinguished*
*Professor of Economics, his most*
*recent book is* Do the Right Thing:
The People's Economist Speaks

**Willis, Bruce (Walter Bruce Willis)**
1122 S. Robertson Blvd., #15
Los Angeles, CA 90035
*Actor*
*Birthday: 3/19/55*

**Wilson, Carnie**
13601 Ventura Blvd., #286
Sherman Oaks, CA 91423
*Singer*
*Birthday: 4/29/68*

**Wilson, Mara**
3500 W. Olive Ave., #1400
Burbank, CA 91506
*Actress*

**Wilson, Rita**
PO Box 900
Beverly Hills, CA 90213
*Actress*

**Windom, William**
PO Box 1067
Woodacre, CA 94973
*Actor*
*Birthday: 9/28/23*

**Winfrey, Oprah**
PO Box 909715
Chicago, IL 60690
*Talk show host, actress*
*Birthday: 1/29/54*

**Winger, Debra (May Debra Winger)**
PO Box 9078
Van Nuys, CA 91409
*Actress*
*Birthday: 5/17/55*

**Winkler, Henry**
1122 S. Robertson Blvd., #15
Los Angeles, CA 90035
*Actor, director, played The Fonz on*
Happy Days
*Birthday: 10/30/45*

**Winslet, Kate**
503/504 Lotts Rd.
The Chambers
Chelsea Harbour
London SWIO OXF
England
*Actress*

**Winwood, Steve**
PO Box 261640
Encino, CA 91426
*Musician*

**Witt, Katarina**
Reichenhaner Str.
D-09023
Chemnitz
Germany
*Actress*
*Birthday: 12/3/65*

**Wolf, Scott**
1122 S. Robertson Blvd., #15
Los Angeles, CA 90035
*Actor*

**Wonder, Stevie**
4616 Magnolia Blvd.
Burbank, CA 91505
*Singer, songwriter*

**Wong, B. D.**
% Innovative Artists
1999 Ave. of the Stars, #2850
Los Angeles, CA 90067
*Actor*

**Woo, John**
450 Roxbury Dr., #800
Beverly Hills, CA 90210
*Director*

**Wood, Elijah**
2300 W. Victory Blvd., #384
Burbank, CA 91506
*Actor*
*Birthday: 1/28/81*

**Woodard, Alfre**
% ICM
8942 Wilshire Blvd.
Beverly Hills, CA 90211
*Actor*

**Woods, James**
760 N. La Cienega Blvd.
Los Angeles, CA 90069
*Actor*
*Birthday: 4/18/47*

**Woods, Tiger**
4281 Katella Ave., #111
Los Alamitos, CA 90720
Website: http://www.clubtiger.com/
*Professional golf-player*

**Woodward, Joanne**
1120 5th Ave., #1C
New York, NY 10128
*Actress, married to Paul Newman*
*Birthday: 10/27/30*

**Wooley, Sheb**
123 Walton Ferry Rd., 2nd Floor
Hendersonville, TN 37075
*Singer*

**Wopat, Tom**
PO Box 128031
Nashville, TN 37212
Website: http://www.wopat.com/
*Actor, singer*

**Worley, Joanne**
PO Box 2054
Toluca Lake, CA 91610
*Actress*

**Wright, Bobby**
PO Box 477
Madison, TN 37116
*Country singer*

**Wright, Johnny**
PO Box 477
Madison, TN 37116
*Country singer*

**Wright, Michelle**
PO Box 152
Morpeth,
Ontario N0P 1X0
Canada
*Country singer*

**Wyman, Bill**
344 Kings Rd.
Chelsea
London SW3 5UR
England
*Bass player in The Rolling Stones*
*Birthday: 10/24/36*

**Wynonna**
325 Bridge St.
Franklin, TN 37064
*Musician*

**X**

**Official Xena: Warrior Princess**
**Fan Club**
100 W. Broadway, Suite 1200
Glendale, CA 91204

**Y**

**Yankovic, "Weird Al"**
% Close Personal Friends of Al
8033 Sunset Blvd.
Los Angeles, CA 90046
Website: http://www.weirdal.com/
*Musician*

**Yasbeck, Amy**
2170 Century Park East, #1111
Los Angeles, CA 90067
*Actress*

**Yearwood, Trisha**
4836-316 Lebanon Pike
Nashville, TN 37076
*Country singer*

**Yeltsin, Boris**
Ulliza Twerskaya
Jamskayaw
Moscow
Russia
*Russian political leader*
*Birthday: 2/1/31*

**York, Michael**
9100 Cardell Dr.
Los Angeles, CA 90069
*Actor*
*Birthday: 3/27/42*

**Young, Burt**
9300 Wilshire Blvd., #410
Beverly Hills, CA 90212
*Actor*

**Young, Faron**
1300 Division
Nashville, TN 37203
*Country singer*

**Young, Jesse Colin**
Box 31
Lancaster, NH 03584
*Musician*

**Young, John**
% NASA
Houston, TX 77058
*Astronaut*
*Birthday: 9/24/30*

**Young Neil**
8501 Wilshire Blvd., #220
Beverly Hills, CA 90211
*Singer, songwriter*

**Young, Nina**
% Narrow Road Company
22 Poland St.
London W1V 3DD
England
*Actress*

**Young, Sean**
PO Box 20547
Sedona, AZ 86341
*Actress*
*Birthday: 11/20/59*

**Z**

**Zadora, Pia**
9560 Wilshire Blvd.
Beverly Hills, CA 90212
*Actress, singer*
*Birthday: 5/4/56*

**Zahn, Steve**
1964 Westwood Blvd., #400
Los Angeles, CA 90025
*Actor*

**Zane, Billy**
450 N. Rossmore Ave., #1001
Los Angeles, CA 90004
Or
% Celebrity Merchandise
PMB 710
15030 Ventura Blvd.
Sherman Oaks, CA 91403
*Actor*
*Birthday: 2/24/66*

**Zappa, Dweezil**
PO Box 5265
North Hollywood, CA 91616
*Musician, Frank Zappa's son*
*Birthday: 9/5/69*

**Zappa, Moon Unit**
PO Box 5265
North Hollywood, CA 91616
*Frank Zappa's daughter, actress,*
*singer, Dweezil's sister*
*Birthday: 9/28/68*

**Zeman, Jackie**
% General Hospital—ABC-TV
4151 Prospect Ave.
Los Angeles, CA 90027
*Soap opera actress*

**Zemeckis, Robert**
1880 Century Park E., Suite #900
Los Angeles, CA 90067
*Director, producer, screenwriter*
*Birthday: 5/14/51*

**Ziering, Ian**
1122 S. Robertson Blvd., #15
Los Angeles, CA 90035
*Actor*

**Zimbalist, Stephanie**
1925 Century Park E., #2320
Los Angeles, CA 90067
*Actress*

**Zucchero**
% Prima Pagina
Via Hayech 41
Milano I-20100
Italy
*Singer*

**Zuniga, Daphne**
% Contellation
PO Box 1249
White River Junction, VT 05001
*Actress*

**Zydeco, Buckwheat**
PO Box 561
Rhinebeck, NY 12572
*Musician*

# MUSIC MAKERS

**ABBA**
Postbus3079
NL4700 GB
Roosendaal
Holland
*Pop group*

**Abdul, Paula**
14755 Ventura Blvd., #1-710
Sherman Oaks, CA 91403
Or
12434 Wilshire Blvd., #770
Los Angeles, CA 90024
*Singer, dancer, choreographer*
*Birthday: 6/19/62*

**Acadiana Symphony Assoc.**
412 Travis St.
Lafayette, LA 70503
Website: http://cust.iamerica.net/
symphony/
E-mail: symphony@iamerica.net
Maestro Xiao-Lu Li, Conductor

*The Acadiana Symphony (ASO)
was founded in 1984. Maestro
Xiao-Lu Li became the fourth
conductor of the Symphony in
1992. They have been featured
several times in Symphony
magazine, the official journal of the
American Symphony Orchestra
League, and on CBS News /
Sunday Morning.*

**AC/DC**
46 Kensington Ct. St.
London W8 5DP
England
*Rock group*

**Ace of Base**
Sibyllegatan 81
Stockholm 114433
Sweden
*Music group*

**Acid Test**
83 Riverside Dr.
New York, NY 10024
*Music group*

**Adams, Bryan**
406-68 Water St.
Vancouver BC V6B 14A
Canada
Website: http://
www.bryanadams.com/
*Singer, songwriter*
*Birthday: 11/5/59*

**ADC Band**
17397 Santa Barbara
Detroit, MI 48221
*Music group*

**Trace Adkins Fan Club**
PO Box 121889
Nashville, TN 37212

**Adrian Symphony Orchestra**
Cornelius House
110 S. Madison
Adrian, MI 49221
Website: http://www.aso.org/
E-mail: aso@lni.net
*David Katz, conductor*

**Aerosmith**
PO Box 4668
San Francisco, CA 94101
Or
584 Broadway, #1009
New York, NY 10012
*Rock group*

**Air Supply**
9200 Sunset Blvd.
Los Angeles, CA 90069
*Music group*

**Alabama**
PO Box 529
Ft. Payne, AL 35967
*Country music group*

**Alice in Chains**
207 1/2 First Ave. So., #300
Seattle, WA 98104
*Rock group*

**Alexander, Daniele**
PO Box 23362
Nashville, TN 37202
*Country music singer*

**Alexandria Symphony Orchestra**
PO Box 11014
Alexandria, VA 22312
Website: http://www.cais.com/
webweave/symphony.htm
Kim Allen Kluge, Music Director/
Conductor
Marcia N. Speck, Executive
Director

**Deborah Allen's Front Row
Friends**
PO Box 120849
Nashville, TN 37212
*Fan club*

**All 4 One**
11693 San Vicente Blvd., #550
Los Angeles, CA 90049
Website:http://www.otb1.com/all-4-
one/
*Music group*

**Allen, Rex, Jr.**
PO Box 120501
Nashville, TN 37212
*Country music singer*

**Allen, Rex Sr.**
Box 430
Sonoita, AZ 85637
*Country music singer*

**Allman Brothers**
40 West 57th St.
New York, NY 10019
*Music group*

**Allman, Greg**
40 West 57th St.
New York, NY 10019
*Musician*
*Birthday: 12/07/47*

**Aerospace**
584 Broadway, #1009
New York, NY 10012
*Rock group*

**All Saints**
72 Chancellor's Rd.
London W6 9SG
*England*
*Music group*

**Almost Persuaded**
PO Box 727
Rossville, GA 30741
*Country music group*

**Amazing Rhythm Aces**
1010 16th St. So.
Nashville, TN 37212
*Music group*

**Ambrosia**
245 E. 54th St.
New York, NY 10022
*Music group*

**America**
345 N. Maple Dr., #300
Beverly Hills, CA 90210
*Music group*

**American Society of Composers,**
**Authors and Publishers—ASCAP—**
**Atlanta**
ASCAP Membership—Atlanta
PMB 400
541 10th St. NW
Atlanta, GA 30318
Website: http://www.ascap.com/

**American Society of Composers,**
**Authors and Publishers—ASCAP—**
**London**
8 Cork St.
London W1X1PB
England
Website: http://www.ascap.com

**American Society Of Composers,**
**Authors and Publishers—ASCAP—**
**Los Angeles**
7920 Sunset Blvd., Suite #300
Los Angeles, CA 90046
Website: http://www.ascap.com/

**American Society of Composers,**
**Authors and Publishers—ASCAP—**
**Miami**
844 Alton Rd., Suite #1
Miami Beach, FL 33139
Website: http://www.ascap.com

**American Society of Composers,**
**Authors and Publishers—ASCAP—**
**Nashville**
Two Music Square West
Nashville, TN 37203
Website: http://www.ascap.com/

**American Society of Composers,**
**Authors and Publishers—ASCAP—**
**Midwest**
1608 W. Belmont Avenue, Suite
200
Chicago, IL 60657
Website: http://www.ascap.com/

**American Society of Composers, Authors and Publishers—ASCAP—New York**
One Lincoln Plaza
New York, NY 10023
Website: http://www.ascap.com/
Marilyn Bergman, ASCAP President and Chairman of the Board
*The only performing rights licensing organization in the United States whose Board of Directors is made up entirely of writers and music publishers elected by and from its membership.*

**American Society of Composers, Authors and Publishers—ASCAP—Puerto Rico**
1519 Ponce de Leon Ave., Suite #505
Santurce, PR 00909
Website: http://www.ascap.com/

**Anderson, Bill**
PO Box 888
Hermitage, TN 37076
*Country music singer*

**Anderson, John**
PO Box 810
Smithville, TN 37166
*Country music singer*

**Anderson, Lynn**
PO Box EE
Taos, NM 87571
*Singer*
*Birthday: 9/26/47*

**Angels, The**
PO Box 3864
Beverly Hills, CA 90212
*Music group*

**Ant, Adam (Stewart Goddard)**
503 The Chambers
Chelsea Harbour
Lots Rd.
London SW10 0XF
England
*Singer*
*Birthday: 11/3/54*

**Anthrax**
15 Haldane Crescent
Piners Heath
Wakefield Heath
Wakefield WF1 4TE
England
*Heavy metal group*

**Armatrading, Joan**
2 Ramillies St.
London W1V 1DF
England
*Singer, guitarist*
*Birthday: 12/9/50*

**Armstrong, Billie Joe**
% Warner Brothers Recording
3300 Warner Blvd.
Burbank, CA 91505
*Musician*
*Birthday: 2/17/72*

**Army of Lovers**
78 Stanley Gardens
London W3 7SN
England
*Musical group*

**Arnold, Eddy**
PO Box 97
Brentwood, TN 37024
*Country singer*

**Arrested Development**
9380 SW 72nd St., #B-220
Miami, FL 33174
*Musical group*

**Art of Noise, The**
Box 119
London W11 4AN
England
*Music group*

**Asheville Symphony Orchestra**
PO Box 2852
Asheville, NC 28802
Website: http://
www.ashevillesymphony.org/
George M. Bilbrey, M.D., President
Robert Hart Baker, Music Director

**Ashford and Simpson**
254 W. 72nd St., #1A
New York, NY 10023
*Music group*

**Asleep at the Wheel**
PO Box 463
Austin, TX 78767
*Country music group*

**Atkins, Chet**
1013 17th Ave. So.
Nashville, TN 37212
*Guitarist*
*Birthday: 6/20/24*

**Average White Band**
One Water Lane
Camden Town
London NW1 8N2
England
*Music group*

**Awsome**
10 Bourlit Close
London W1T 7PJ
England
*Music group*

**B-52's, The**
947 N. La Cienega Blvd., #G
Los Angeles, CA 90069
*Music group*

**Baby's**
1545 Archer Rd.
Bronx, NY 10462
*Music group*

**Bach Week Festival in Evanston**
PO Box 466
Deerfield, IL 60015-0466
Website: http://
www.bachweek.org.
E-mail: bachwk@aol.com
Mr. Richard Webster, Music
Director
*Bach Week has earned the
reputation as one of the Midwest's
most highly regarded and
respected concert series.*

**Bachman Turner Overdrive**
1505 W. 2nd Ave., #299
Vancouver BC V6h 3Y4
Canada
*Music group*

**Backstreet Boys**
7380 Sand Lake Rd., #350
Orlando, FL 32819
*Music group*

**Baillie and The Boys**
PO Box 121185
Arlington, TX 76012
Or
% The Bobby Roberts Company
PO Box 1547
Goodlettsville, TN 37070
*Country music group*

**Bama Band**
% Rob Battle, Ent. Artists
819 18th Ave. So.
Nashville, TN 37203
*Country music group*

**Bananarama**
1 Sussex Pl.
London W6
England
*Music group*

**Band, The**
121 N. San Vicente Blvd.
Beverly Hills, CA 90211
*Musical group*

**Banshees, The**
127 Aldersgate St.
London EC1
England
*Music group*

**Bates, The**
Sickinger Str. 6–8
Kassel D-34117
Germany
*Music group*

**Bay City Rollers**
21a Clifftown Rd.
Southend-on-Sea
Essex SSL 1AB
England
*Rock band*

**Beach Boys, The**
8942 Wilshire Blvd.
Beverly Hills, CA 90211
*Music group*

**Beastie Boys**
% EMI
1290 Ave. of the Americas
New York, NY 10104
*Rap group*

**Bed and Breakfast**
% Live Music and Ent.
Rothenbaumchaussee 209
Hamburg 20149
Germany
*Music group*

**The Bee Gees**
20505 US Hwy. 19 North, #12-290
Clearwater, FL 33764
Web: http://www.beegees.net
E-mail: beegees@beegees.net

**Bellamy Brothers**
PO Box #801
San Antonio, FL 33576
Or
13917 Restless Lane
Dade City, FL 33525

**Bellini**
Schulterblatt 58
Hamburg 20357
Germany
*Music group*

**Ben Folds Five**
PO Box 1028
Chapel Hill, NC 27514
Website: http://www.bffweb.com
E-mail: bffmail@aol.com
*Music group*

**Berg, Matraca**
Susan Hackney
2100 West End Ave., #1000
Nashville, TN 37203
*Country music duo*

**Big Mountain**
% Giant Records
8900 Wilshire Blvd., #200
Beverly Hills, CA 9021
*Music group*

**Black Crowes, The**
888 7th Ave., #602
New York, NY 10107
*Music group*

**Black Oak Arkansas**
1487 Red Run Fox
Liburn, GA 30247
*Music group*

**Blackhawk**
1018 17th Ave. S., #12
Nashville, TN 37212
*Country music group*

**Blasters, The**
555 Chorro St., #A-1
San Luis Obispo, CA 93401
*Rock band*

**Blind Melon**
9229 Sunset Blvd., #607
Los Angeles, CA 90069
*Alternative band*

**Blood, Sweat and Tears**
43 Washington St.
Groveland, MA 01834
*Music group*

**Blow Monkeys**
370 City Rd.
London EC1V2QA
England
*Music group*

**Blue System**
Metzendorfer Weg
21224 Rosengarten
Germany
*Music group*

**Blues Traveler**
PO Box 1128
New York, NY 10101
Website: http://
www.bluestraveler.com
E-mail: blackcatz@earthlink.net
*Rock band*

**Blur**
20 Manchester Sq.
London W1A 1ES
England
*Music group*

**Bon Jovi**
248 W. 17th St., #502
New York, NY 10107
*Rock group*

**Bone Thugs and Harmony**
8942 Wilshire Blvd.
Beverly Hills, CA 90211
*Music group*

**Book of Love**
12 Charles St., #5A
New York, NY 10019
*Music group*

**Booker T and the MGs**
59 Parsons St.
Newtonville, MA 02160
*Music group*

**Boston**
9200 Sunset Blvd., #530
Los Angeles, CA 90069
*Music group*

**Boston Modern Orchestra Project**
1108 Boylston St., Suite 303
Boston, MA 02115
Website: http://www.bmop.org/
E-mail: bmop@bmop.org
Gil Rose, Music Director

**Boston Symphony Orchestra/
Boston Pops Orchestra**
Symphony Hall
301 Massachusetts Ave.
Boston, MA 02115
Website: http://www.bso.org/
Seiji Ozawa, Music Director

**Boxtops, The**
2011 Ferry Ave., #U-19
Camden, NJ 08104
*Music group*

**Boy Howdy**
% Club Howdy
PO Box 570784
Tarzana, CA 91357-0784
*Country music group*

**Boyz, The**
% Tripple-M-Musik
Postfach 38 01 49
Berlin 14111
Germany
*Music group*

**Boyz II Men**
% WMA
1325 Ave. of the Americas
New York, NY 10019
*Vocal group*

**Boyzone**
9 Whitefriars Aungier St.
Dublin 2
Ireland
*Music group*

**Brands X**
17171 Roscoe Blvd., #104
Northridge, CA 91325
*Music group*

**Breeders, The**
3575 Cahuenga Blvd. W., #450
Los Angeles, CA 90068
*Music group*

**BR5-49**
9830 Wilshire Blvd.
Beverly Hills, CA 90212
*Music group*

**Broadcast Music, Inc. ("BMI")**
London
84 Harley House
Marylebone Rd.
London NW1 5HN
England
Website: http://www.bmi.com/
*Music licensing organization*

**Broadcast Music, Inc. ("BMI")**
8730 Sunset Blvd., 3rd Floor
West Los Angeles, CA 90046
Website: http://www.bmi.com/
E-mail: infotech@bmi.com
Robert Barone, Vice President,
Operations and Information
Technology
*Music licensing organization*

**Broadcast Music, Inc. ("BMI")**
Nashville
10 Music Square East
Nashville, TN 37203
Website: http://www.bmi.com/
*Music licensing organization*

**Broadcast Music, Inc. ("BMI")**
New York
320 West 57th St.
New York, NY 10019
Website: http://www.bmi.com/
*Music licensing organization*

**Brooklyn Bridge**
PO Box 63
Cliffwood, NJ 07721
*Music group*

**Brooks and Dunn**
PO Box 120669
Nashville, TN 37212
*Music group*

**Brothers Four, The**
300 Vine St., #3 14
Seattle, WA 98121
*Music group*

**Buckinghams, The**
620 16th Ave.
So. Hopkins, MN 55343
*Music group*

**Buggles, The**
22 St. Peters Sq.
London W69 NW
England
*Music group*

**Bush**
285 W. Broadway, #230
New York, NY 10013
*Music group*

**The Byrds**
PO Box 106
Rochdale, ON16 4HW
England
*Music group*

**C&C Music Factory**
250 W. 57th St., #821
New York, NY 10107
*Music group*

**Cactus Brothers**
PO Box 120316
Nashville, TN 37212
*Country music group*

**Cadillacs, The**
PO Box 84067
Santa Cruz, CA 95061
*Music group*

**Canned Heat**
PO Box 3773
San Rafael, CA 94912
*Music group*

**Canyon**
Encore Entertainment
PO Box 1259
Dallas, TX 75065
*Country music group*

**Captain and Tennille**
17530 Ventura Blvd., #108
Encino, CA 91316
*Singing duo*

**Cheap Trick**
3805 Country Rd.
Middleton, WI 53262
*Music group*

**Cherry Poppin Daddies**
PO Box 10494
Eugene, OR 97440
*Music group*

**Chicago**
8900 Wilshire Blvd., #300
Beverly Hills, CA 90211
*Music group*

**Chiffons, The**
1650 Broadway, #508
New York, NY 10019
*Music group*

**Chordettes, The**
150 E. Olive Ave., #109
Burbank, CA 91502
*Music group*

**Chuck Wagon Gang**
PO Box 140571
Nashville, TN 37214
*Music group*

**Chumbawamba**
43 Brook Green
London W6 7EF
England
*Music group*

**Clash, The**
268 Camden Rd.
London NW1
England
*Music group*

**Coasters, The**
2756 N. Green Valley Pkwy., #449
Las Vegas, NV 89014
*Music group*

**Commodores, The**
1920 Benson Ave.
St. Paul, MN 55116
*Music group*

**Confederate Railroad**
118 16th Ave. S., #201
Nashville, TN 37203
*Country music group*

**Connells, The**
901 18th Ave. S.
Nashville, TN 37212
*Music group*

**Counting Crows**
947 N. La Cienega Blvd., #G
Los Angeles, CA 90069
*Music group*

**Cowsills, The**
22647 Ventura Blvd., #416
Woodland Hills, CA 91364
*Music group*

**Cox Family, The**
PO Box 787
Cotton Valley, LA 71018
*Country group*

**Cranberries, The**
9255 Sunset Blvd., #200
Los Angeles, CA 90069
*Music group*

**Crash Test Dummies**
1505 W. 2nd St., #200
Vancouver
BC V6H3Y4
Canada
*Music group*

**Creamengine**
% William A. McGrath III
230 Westmar Dr.
Rochester, NY 14624
*Music group*

**Creedence Clearwater Revival**
40 W. 57th St.
New York, NY 10019
*Music group*

**Cult Jam**
PO Box 284
Brooklyn, NY 11203
*Music group*

**Culture Club**
63 Grosvenor St.
London W1X 9DA
England
*Music group*

**Cumberland Gap, The**
159 Madison Ave., #2G
New York, NY 10016
*Music group*

**Cure, The**
% Levine and Schneider PR
8730 Sunset Blvd., #600
Los Angeles, CA 90069
*Music group*

**Cypress Hill**
151 El Camino Dr.
Beverly Hills, CA 90212
*Music group*

**Dead Or Alive**
370 City Rd.
GB-London EC1 V8N4
England
*Music group*

**Deep Purple**
Box 254
Sheffield S61DF
England
*Music group*

**Def Leppard**
72 Chancellor's Rd.
London W69 QB
England
*Music group*

**Del Rubio Sisters, The**
PO Box 6923
San Pedro, CA 90734
*Music group*

**Depeche Mode**
PO Box 1281
London N1 9UX
England
*Music group*

**Devo**
PO Box 6868
Burbank, CA 91410
*Music group*

**Diamond Rio**
33 Music Square W., #110
Nashville, TN 37203
Website: http://
www.diamondrio.com
*Country music group*

**Dire Straits**
72 Chancellor's Rd.
London W6 9RS
England
*Music group*

**Dirt Band**
PO Box 1915
Aspen, CO 81611
*Music group*

**Dixiana**
PO Box 3569
Greenville, SC 29608
*Country music group*

**Dixie Chicks**
68 Lindsley Ave.
Nashville, TN 37210
*Country music group*

**Dixie Cups, The**
7200 Franc Ave., #300
Edina, MN 55435
*Music group*

**Dixieland Rhythym Kings, The**
PO Box 12403
Atlanta, GA 30355
*Music group*

**Doobie Brothers**
15140 Sonoma Hwy.
Glen Ellen, CA 95442
*Music group*

**Doors, The**
8033 Sunset Blvd., #76
Los Angeles, CA 90046
*Music group*

**Dr. Hook**
PO Box 398
Flagler Beach, FL 32136
*Music group*

**D:Ream**
% FXU
"Pumphouse"
71 Fairfield Rd.
GB-London E3 2QA
England
*Music group*

**Dukes of Dixieland**
PO Box 56757
New Orleans, LA 70156
*Music group*

**Duran Duran**
9255 Sunset Blvd., #200
Los Angeles, CA 90069
*Music group*

**Eagles, The**
9200 Sunset Blvd., #1000
Los Angeles, CA 90069
*Music group*

**Earth, Wind and Fire**
9169 Sunset Blvd.
Los Angeles, CA 90069
*Music group*

**Electric Light Orchestra**
297-101 Kinderkamack Rd., #128
Oradell, NJ 07649
*Music group*

**Ellis Brothers**
PO Box 50221
Nashville, TN 37203
*Music group*

**Emerson, Lake and Palmer**
370 City Rd.
Islingon
London EC1V 2QA
England
*Music group*

**En Vogue**
9255 Sunset Blvd., #200
Los Angeles, CA 90069
*Music group*

**Eurythmics**
Box 245
London N8 9QG
England
*Music group*

**Evangeline**
Lafayette Square Station
PO Box 2700
New Orleans, LA 70176
Or
Music Square East
Nashville, TN 37203
*Country music group*

**Everly Brothers**
PO Box 56
Dunmore, KY 42339
*Music duo*

**Faith No More**
5550 Wilshire Blvd., #202
Los Angeles, CA 90036
*Music group*

**Faithless**
% Intercord
Aixheimer Str. 26
70619 Stuttgart
Germany
*Music group*

**Fat Boy**
250 W. 57th St., #1723
New York, NY 10107
*Music group*

**Feelgood, Dr.**
3 E. 54th St.
New York, NY 10022
Website: http://www.drfeelgood.de/
index.htm
*Music group*

**Fifth Dimension**
1900 Ave. of the Stars, #1640
Los Angeles, CA 90067
*Music group*

**Fixx, The**
6255 Sunset Blvd., 2nd Floor
Los Angeles, CA 90028
*Music group*

**Flaming Lips, The**
PO Box 75995
Oklahoma City, OK 73147
*Music group*

**Fleetwood Mac**
4905 S. Atlantic Ave.
Daytona Beach, FL 32127
*Music group*

**Foo Fighters**
370 City Rd.
Islington
London EC1 V2QA
England
*Music group*

**Foreigner**
9830 Wilshire Blvd.
Beverly Hills, CA 90212
*Music group*

**Forester Sisters**
PO Box 1456
Trenton, GA 30752
*Country music group*

**Four Aces, The**
11761 E. Speedway Blvd.
Tucson, AZ 85748
*Music group*

**Four Freshman, The**
PO Box 93534
Las Vegas, NV 89193
*Music group*

**Four Lads, The**
11761 E. Speedway Blvd.
Tucson, AZ 85748
*Music group*

**Four Preps, The**
15760 Ventura Blvd., #1206
Encino, CA 91436
*Music group*

**Four Seasons, The**
PO Box 262
Carteret, NJ 07008
*Music group*

**Four Tops**
40 W. 57th St.
New York, NY 10019
*Music group*

**Fox Brothers**
Rt. 6
Bending Chestnut
Franklin, TN 37064
*Country music group*

**Freddie and the Dreamers**
9 Ridge Rd.
Emerson, NJ 07630
*Music group*

**Gatlin Brothers**
207 Westpoint Rd., #202
Kansas City, MO 64111
*Country music group*

**Genesis**
9200 Sunset Blvd., #900
Los Angeles, CA 90069
*Music group*

**Gerry and the Pacemakers**
6 Ridge Rd.
Emerson, NJ 07630
*Music group*

**Gibson Miller Band**
% Sherry Halton
PO Box 120964
Nashville, TN 37212
*Country music group*

**Gin Blossoms**
151 El Camino Dr.
Beverly Hills, CA 90212
*Music group*

**Gipsy Kings**
1460 4th St., #205
Santa Monica, CA 90401
*Music group*

**Girls Against Boys**
PO Box 020426
Brooklyn, NY 11202
*Music group*

**Goldens, The**
PO Box 1795
Hendersonville, TN 37077
*Country music group*

**Goo Goo Dolls**
129 Park St.
London W1Y 3SA
England
*Music group*

**Grand Funk Railraod**
1229 17th Ave. South
Nashville, TN 37212
*Music group*

**Grateful Dead**
PO Box 1073-C
San Rafael, CA 94915
*Music group*

**Great Plains**
PO Box 2411
Murfreesboro, TN 37133
*Country music group*

**Green Day**
5337 College Ave., #555
Oakland, CA 94618
*Music group*

**Guess Who**
31 Hemlock Pl.
Winnepeg, Manitoba
R2H 1LB
Canada
*Music group*

**Guns N' Roses**
83 Riverside Dr.
New York, NY 10024
*Music group*

**Hall and Oates**
9830 Wilshire Blvd.
Beverly Hills, CA 90212
*Music group*

**Hanson Brothers**
1045 W. 78th St.
Tulsa, OK 74132
*Pop group Brothers*
*Clarke Isaac Hanson*
*Birthday: 11/17/80*
*Jordan Taylor Hanson*
*Birthday: 3/14/83*
*Zachary Walker Hanson*
*Birthday: 10/22/85*

**Freddie Hart and Heartbeats**
% Tessier March Talent, Inc.
505 Canton Pass
Madison, TN 37115
*Country music group*

**Heart**
9220 Sunset Blvd., #900
Los Angeles, CA 90069
*Music group*

**Herman's Hermits**
11761 E. Speedway Blvd.
Tucson, AZ 85748
*Music group*

**Ty Herndon and Friends**
% Leigh Ritsema
PO Box 120658
Nashville, TN 37212
*Country music group*

**Highway 101**
PO Box 1547
Goodlettsville, TN 37050
*Country music group*

**Hiroshima**
1460 4th St., #205
Santa Monica, CA 90401
*Music group*

**Hole**
955 S. Carrillo Dr., #200
Los Angeles, CA 90048
*Music group*

**Hootie and the Blowfish**
PO Box 5656
Columbia, SC 29250
*Music group*

**House of Pain**
151 El Camino Dr.
Beverly Hills, CA 90212
*Music group*

**Hudson Brothers**
151 El Camino Dr.
Beverly Hills, CA 90212
*Music group*

**Indigo Girls**
315 Ponce De Leon Ave., #755
Decatur, GA 30030
*Music group*

**Ink Spots, The**
5100 DuPont Blvd., #10A
Ft. Lauderdale, FL 33308
*Music group*

**INXS**
8 Hayes St., #1
Neutray Bay NSW 20891
Australia
*Music group*

**Irish Rovers, The**
179 John St., #400
Toronto
Ontario M5T 1X4
Canada

**Iron Butterfly**
6400 Pleasant Park Dr.
Chanhassen, MN 55317
*Music group*

**Iron Maiden**
1775 Broadway, #433
New York, NY 10019
*Music group*

**Isley Brothers**
42209 Montieth Dr.
Los Angeles, CA 90043
*Music group*

**Jan and Dean**
1720 N. Ross St.
Santa Ana, CA 92706
*Music duo*

**Jane's Addiction**
532 Colorado Ave.
Santa Monica, CA 90401
*Music group*

**Jay and the Americans**
1045 Pomme De Pin Dr.
New Port Richey, FL 34655
*Music group*

**Jazzy Jeff and The Fresh Prince**
298 Elizabeth St.
New York, NY 10012
*Music group*

**Jefferson Starship**
PO Box 1821
Ojai, CA 93024
*Music group*

**Jethro Tull**
43 Brook Green
London W6 7EF
England
*Music group*

**Jim and Jesse**
PO Box 27
Gallatin, TN 37066
*Country duo*

**Jordanaires, The**
1300 Division St., #205
Nashville, TN 37203
*Singing group*

**Journey**
63 Main St.
Cold Springs, NY 10516
*Music group*

**Judas Priest**
3 E. 54th St., #1400
New York, NY 10022
Website: http://
www.judaspriest.com/
*Music group*

**Kentucky Headhunters**
209 10th Ave. So., #322
Nashville, TN 37203
*Musical group*

**Kingsman, The**
1720 N. Ross Ave.
Santa Ana, CA 92706
*Music group*

**Kingston Trio, The**
941-0 S. 46th St.
Phoenix, AZ 85044
*Music group*

**Kinks, The**
29 Ruston Mews
London W11 1RB
England
*Music group*

**Kiss**
8730 Sunset Blvd., #175
Los Angeles, CA 90069
*Music group*

**Kool and the Gang**
89 Fifth Ave., #700
New York, NY 10003
*Music group*

**Korn**
151 E. El Camino Dr.
Beverly Hills, CA 90212
*Music group*

**Kris Kross**
9380 SW 72nd St., #B220
Miami, FL 33173
*Music duo*

**Limelights, The**
11761 E. Speedway Blvd.
Tucson, AZ 85748
*Music group*

**Limp Bizkit**
% Interscope
10900 Wilshire Blvd.
Los Angeles, CA 90024
*Music group*

**Little Texas**
PO Box 709
Corsicana, TX 75151
*Music group*

**Lonestar**
PO Box 128467
Nashville, TN 37212
*Musical group*

**Los Lobos**
2 Penn Plaza, #2600
New York, NY 10121
*Music group*

**Lynyrd Skynyrd**
6025 The Corner's Parkway, #202
Norcross, GA 30092
*Music group*

**Mamas and The Papas**
PO Box 12821
Ojai, CA 93024
*Music group*

**Manhattan Transfer**
8942 Wilshire Blvd.
Beverly Hills, CA 90211
*Music group*

**Manheim Steamroller**
9120 Mormon Bridge Rd.
Omaha, NE 68152
*Music group*

**Marcy Brothers**
PO Box 2502
Oroville, CA 95965
*Music group*

**Matchbox 20**
9830 Wilshire Blvd.
Beverly Hills, CA 90212
*Music group*

**Dave Matthews Band**
PO Box 1911
Charlottesville, VA 22903
*Music group*

**Mavericks, The**
PO Box 3329
Nashville, TN 37202
*Music group*

**McBride and The Ride**
PO Box 17617
Nashville, TN 37217
*Music group*

**Members of Mayday**
% Low Spirit Recordings
Giesebrechtstr. 16
Berlin 10629
Germany
*Music group*

**Men At Work**
1775 Broadway, #433
New York, NY 10019
*Music group*

**Menudo**
2895 Biscayne Blvd., #455
Miami, FL 33137
*Music group*

**Metallica**
729 7th Ave., #1400
New York, NY 10019
Website: http://www.Metallica.com/
E-mail: email@metallica.com
*Heavy metal group*

**Miami Sound Machine**
6205 Bird Rd.
Miami, FL 33155
*Music group*

**Miller, Glenn Orchestra**
2250 Lucien Way, #100
Maitland, FL 32751

**Mister Mr.**
PO Box 69343
Los Angeles, CA 90069
*Music group*

**Modernaires, The**
11761 E. Speedway Blvd.
Tucson, AZ 85748
*Music group*

**Molly and the Heymakers**
PO Box 1160
Hayward, WI 54843
*Music group*

**Monkees, The**
8369A Sausalito Ave.
West Hills, CA 91304
*Music group*

**Motley Crue**
9255 Sunset Blvd., #200
Los Angeles, CA 90069
*Music group*

**'N Sync**
7616 Soundland Blvd., #115
Orlando, FL 32809
Or
% Wright Stuff Mgmt.
7380 St. Lake Road, #350
Orlando, FL 32819
*Music group*

**New Edition**
151 El Camino Dr.
Beverly Hills, CA 90212
*Music group*

**New Grass Revival**
PO Box 1288037
Nashville, TN 37212
*Music group*

**New Radicals**
645 Quail Ridge Rd.
Aledo, TX 76008
*Music group*

**New Rascals, The**
PO Box 1821
Ojai, CA 93023
*Music group*

**New Riders of the Purple Sage**
PO Box 3773
San Rafael, CA 94912
*Music group*

**Nine Inch Nails**
83 Riverside Dr.
New York, NY 10019
*Music group*

**Nirvana**
151 El Camino Dr.
Beverly Hills, CA 90212
*Music group*

**Nitty Gritty Dirt Band**
1227 17th Ave. S.
Nashville, TN 37212
*Music group*

**Nixons, The**
% Rainmaker Artists
PO Box 720195
Dallas, TX 75372
*Music group*

**No Doubt**
% Interscope Records
10900 Wilshire Blvd.
Los Angeles, CA 90024
*Music group*

**Oak Ridge Boys**
2501 N. Blackwelder
Oklahoma City, OK 73106
*Music group*

**Oasis**
54 Linhope St.
London NW1 6HL
England
*Music group*

**OMC**
% Polydor Records
PO Box 617
Auckland
New Zealand
*Music group*

**Osborne Brothers**
2801 Columbia Pl.
Nashville, TN 37204
*Musical group*

**Osbourne, Jeffrey**
1325 Ave. of the Americas
New York, NY 10019
*Singer*

**Palomino Road**
818 18th Ave. S.
Nashville, TN 37203
*Music group*

**Pearl Jam**
417 Denny Way, #200
Seattle, WA 98109
*Rock group*

**Pearl River**
PO Box 150803
Nashville, TN 37215
*Music group*

**Penguins, The**
708 W. 137th St.
Gardena, CA 90247
*Music group*

**Perfect Stranger**
PO Box 330
Carthage, TX 75633
*Music group*

**Persuaders, The**
225 W. 57th St., #500
New York, NY 10019
*Music group*

**Pet Shop Boys**
27A Pembridge Way, #8
London WII 3EP
England

**Pinkard and Bowden**
% Network, Inc.
1101 18th Ave. So.
Nashville, TN 37212
*Musical duo*

**Pirates of the Mississippi**
PO Box 17087
Nashville, TN 37217
*Country music group*

**Pretenders, The**
28 Kensington Church St.
London W8 4EP
England
*Rock band*

**Public Enemy**
298 Elizabeth St.
New York, NY 10012
*Rap group*

**Quiet Riot**
PO Box 24455
New Orleans, LA 70184
*Music group*

**Red Hot Chilli Peppers**
11116 Aqua Vista, #39
North Hollywood, CA 91693
*Music group*

**Rednex**
% ZYX Music
Benzstraße
Industriegebiet
Merenberg D-35797
Germany
*Music group*

**Reef**
% Sony Music
1 Red Place
London W1Y 3RE
England
*Music group*

**R.E.M.**
170 College Ave.
Athens, GA 30601
*Rock band*

**The Remingtons**
% 3 Amigos
25 Paulson Dr.
Burlington, MA 01803
*Music group*

**Restless Heart**
PO Box 156
Littlestown, PA 17340
Or
% Fitzgerald Hartley Co.
1908 Wedgewood Ave.
Nashville, TN 37212
*Music group*

**Riders in the Sky**
38 Music Square E., #300
Nashville, TN 37203
*Music group*

**RMB**
% Motor Music
Holzdamm 57
Hamburg D-20099
Germany
*Music group*

**Rockers, The**
PO Box 3859
Stamford, CT 06905
*Music group*

**Rolling Stones, The**
110 W. 57th St., #300
New York, NY 10019
*Rock group*

**Roxette**
% EMI Svenska AB
Box 1289
17125 Solna
Sweden
*Music group*

**Salt'n'Pepa**
250 W. 57th St., #821
New York, NY 10107
*Music group*

**Sash**
% Mighty Records/Polydor
Glockengießerwall 3
20095 Hamburg
Germany
*Music group*

**Sawyer Brown**
5200 Old Harding Rd.
Franklin, TN 37064
*Rock band*

**Sex Pistols, The**
100 Wilshire Blvd., #1830
Santa Monica, CA 90401
*Music group*

**Shenandoah**
1028-B 18th Ave. So.
Nashville, TN 37212
*Music group*

**Simple Minds**
% Schoolhouse Mgmt.
63 Frederic St.
GB-Edinburgh EH1 1LH
England
*Music group*

**Simply Red**
48 Princess St.
GB-Manchester M1 6HR
England
*Music group*

**Sista Sledge**
236 West 26th St., Suite #702
New York, NY 10001
*Music group*

**Sisters with Voices**
35 Hart St.
Brooklyn, NY 11206
*Music group*

**Six Shooter**
PO Box 53
Portland, TN 37148
*Music group*

**Smashing Pumpkins**
9830 Wilshire Blvd.
Beverly Hills, CA 90212
*Music group*

**Soul Asylum**
955 S. Carrill Dr., #300
Los Angeles, CA 90048
*Music group*

**Soundgarden**
% Curtis Mgmt.
207 1/2 First Ave., S #300
Seattle, WA 98104
*Music group*

**Sparks**
106 N. Buffalo St., #200
Warsaw, IN 46580
*Music group*

**Spice Girls**
35–37 Parkgate Road Unit 32
Ransomes Dock
London SW11 4NP
England
*Singing group*

**Spinal Tap**
4268 Hazeltine Ave.
Sherman Oaks, CA 91423
*Music group*

**Spyro Gyra**
926 Horseshoe Rd.
Suffern, NY 10301
*Music group*

**Squirrel Nut Zippers**
9056 Santa Monica Blvd., #203
Los Angeles, CA 90069
*Music group*

**Statler Brothers**
PO Box 492
Hernando, MS 68632
*Music group*

**Stray Cats**
113 Wardour St.
GB-London W1
England
*Music group*

**Supertramp**
16530 Ventura Blvd., #201
Encino, CA 91436
*Music group*

**Survivor**
9850 Sandlefoot Blvd., #458
Boca Raton, FL 33428
*Music group*

**Sweethearts of the Rodeo**
5101 Overton Rd.
Nashville, TN 37220
*Musical group*

**Swing Out Sister**
132 Liverpool Rd.
Islington
GB-London N1
England
*Music group*

**Talk Talk**
121 A Revelstone N.
Wimbledon Pl.
GB-London W15
England
*Music group*

**Tangerine Dream**
PO Box 29242
Oakland, CA 94604
*Music group*

**Tears for Fears**
2100 Colorado Ave.
Santa Monica, CA 90404
*Rock band*

**Texas Tornados**
PO Box 530
Bellaire, OH 43906
*Music group*

**Tom Petty and the Heartbreakers**
PO Box 260159
Encino, CA 91426
*Music group*

**Tractors**
PO Box 5034
Tulsa, OK 74150
*Music group*

**Truck Stop**
% Lucius B. Rechling
Quellental 14
Hamburg D-22609
Germany
*Country music group*

**Twister Alley**
Rte. 2, Box 138
Lake City, AR 72437
*Musical group*

**U2**
119 Rockland Center, #350
Nanuet, NY 10954
*Rock band*

**U96**
Bernstorffstr. 123
Hamburg D-22767
Germany
*Rock group*

**UB40**
533-579 Harrow Rd.
London W10 4RN
England
*Music group*

**UFO**
10 Sutherland
GB-London W9 24Q
England
*Music group*

**Van Halen**
10100 Santa Monica Blvd., Suite #2460
Los Angeles, CA 90067
*Rock group*

**Vangelis**
195 Queensgate
GB-London W1
England
*Music group*

**Village People**
165 W. 46th St., #13008
New York, NY 10036
*Music group*

**Wallflowers, The**
9200 Wilshire Blvd.#1000
Los Angeles, CA 90069
*Music group*

**Wet Wet Wet**
% Precius Organisation
Pet Sound Studio
24 Gairbraid Ave., #6-B
Maryhill
GB-Glasgow G20 1XX
England
*Music group*

**Whites, The**
15 Music Square West
Nashville, TN 37203
*Music group*

**Wild Rose**
PO Box 121705
Nashville, TN 37212
*Music group*

**Williams and Ree**
24 Music Square West
Nashville, TN 37203
*Music group*

**Wu-Tang Clan**
% BMG Music
1540 Broadway, #9-FL
New York, NY 10039
*Music group*

**X-Perience**
% WEA Records
Postfach 761260
Hamburg D-22062
Germany
*Music group*

**Yell4You**
% Nady
Postfach 303
Lauffen/N. D-74345
Germany
*Music group*

**Yello**
% Dieter Meier
Aurastraße 78
Zürich CH-8031
Switzerland
*Music group*

**Yellowjackets**
9220 Sunset Blvd., #320
Los Angeles, CA 90069
*Music group*

**Yes**
9 Hillgate St.
GB-London W8 7SP
England
*Music group*

**Yoakam, Dwight**
1250 6th St., #401
Santa Monica, CA 90401
*Country music singer*

**Zaca Creek**
PO Box 237
Santa Ynez, CA 93460
*Music group*

**ZZ Top**
PO Box 163690
Austin, TX 78716

# SPORTS FANS

---

## MAJOR LEAGUE BASEBALL ADDRESSES

### Office of the Commissioner
300 Park Ave., 17th Floor
New York, NY 10022
e-mail: MLB@BAT

### American League
350 Park Ave., 18th Floor
New York, NY 10022

### National League
350 Park Ave., 18th Floor
New York, NY 10022

### Anaheim Angels
Office: 2000 Gene Autry Way
Anaheim, CA 92806
Mailing address: PO Box 2000
Anaheim, CA 92803
Website: http://
www.angelsbaseball.com/

### Baltimore Orioles
333 W. Camden St.
Baltimore, MD 21201
Website: http://
www.theorioles.com/

### Boston Red Sox
Fenway Park
4 Yawkey Way
Boston, MA 02215
Website: http://www.redsox.com/

### Chicago White Sox
333 W. 35th St.
Chicago, IL 60616
Website: http://www.chisox.com/

### Cleveland Indians
Jacobs Field
2401 Ontario St.
Cleveland, OH 44115
Website: http://www.indians.com/

### Detroit Tigers
Tiger Stadium
2121 Trumbull Ave.
Detroit, MI 48216
Website: http://
www.detroittigers.com/

### Kansas City Royals
Office: One Royal Way
Kansas City, MO 64129
Mailing: PO Box 419969
Kansas City, MO 64141
Website: http://www.kcroyals.com/

**Minnesota Twins**
34 Kirby Puckett Pl.
Minneapolis, MN 55415
Website: http://www.wcco.com/
sports/twins/

**New York Yankees**
Yankee Stadium
161st St. and River Ave.
Bronx, NY 10451
Website: http://www.yankees.com/

**Oakland Athletics**
7677 Oakport St., Suite #200
Oakland, CA 94621
Website: http://
www.oaklandathletics.com/

**Seattle Mariners**
Office: 83 S. King St.
Seattle, WA 98104
Mailing: PO Box 4100
Seattle, WA 98104
Website: http://www.mariners.org/

**Tampa Bay Devil Rays**
Tropicana Field
One Tropicana Dr.
St. Petersburg, FL 33705
Website: http://www.devilray.com

**Texas Rangers**
Office: 1000 Ballpark Way
Arlington, TX 76011
Mailing: PO Box 90111
Arlington, TX 76004
Website: http://
www.texasrangers.com/

**Toronto Blue Jays**
One Blue Jays Way
Suite 3200, Skydome
Toronto, Ontario M5V 1J1
Canada
Website: http://www.bluejays.ca/

**NATIONAL LEAGUE**

**Arizona Diamondbacks**
Office: 401 East Jefferson St.
Phoenix, AZ 85004
Mailing: PO Box 2095
Phoenix, AZ 85001
Website: http://
www.azdiamondbacks.com/

**Atlanta Braves**
Office: 755 Hank Aaron Dr.
Atlanta, GA 30315
Mailing: PO Box 4064
Atlanta, GA 30302
Website: http://
www.atlantabraves.com/

**Chicago Cubs**
Wrigley Field
1060 West Addison St.
Chicago, IL 60613
Website: http://www.cubs.com/

**Cincinnati Reds**
100 Cinergy Field
Cincinnati, OH 45202
Website: http://
www.cincinnatireds.com/

**Colorado Rockies**
2001 Blake St.
Denver, CO 80205
Website: http://
www.coloradorockies.com/

**Florida Marlins**
Pro Player Stadium
2267 NW 199th St.
Miami, FL 33056
Website: http://
www.flamarlins.com/

**Houston Astros**
Office: 8400 Kirby Dr.
Houston, TX 77054
Mailing: PO Box 288
Houston, TX 77001
Website: http://www.astros.com/

**Los Angeles Dodgers**
1000 Elysian Park Ave.
Los Angeles, CA 90012
Website: http://www.dodgers.com/

**Milwaukee Brewers**
Stadium
201 S 46th St.
Milwaukee, WI 53214
Mailing: PO Box 3099
Milwaukee, WI 53201
Website: http://
www.milwaukeebrewers.com

**Montreal Expos**
Office: 4549
Pierre-de-Courbertin Ave.
Montreal, Quebec H1V 3N7
Mailing: PO Box 500, Station M
Montreal, Quebec H1V 3P2
Canada
Website: http://
www.montrealexpos.com/

**New York Mets**
Shea Stadium
123-01 Roosevelt Ave.
Flushing, NY 11368

**Philadelphia Phillies**
Veterans Stadium
3501 S. Broad St.
Philadelphia, PA 19148
Mailing: PO Box 7575
Philadelphia, PA 19101
Website: http://www.phillies.com

**Pittsburgh Pirates**
600 Stadium Circle
Pittsburgh, PA 15212
Mailing: PO Box 7000
Pittsburgh, PA 15212
Website: http://www.pirateball.com/

**St. Louis Cardinals**
250 Stadium Plaza
St. Louis, MO 63102
Website: http://
www.stlcardinals.com/

**San Diego Padres**
Office: Jack Murphy Stadium
8880 Rio San Diego Dr., Suite
#400
San Diego, CA 92108
Mailing: PO Box 2000
San Diego, CA 92112
Website: http://www.padres.org/

**San Francisco Giants**
3Com Park at Candlestick Point
San Francisco, CA 94124
Website: http://www.sfgiants.com/

## BASEBALL TEAM SPRING TRAINING ADDRESSES

## AMERICAN LEAGUE

**Anaheim Angels**
Tempe Diable Stadium
2200 West Alameda
Tempe, AZ 85282

**Baltimore Orioles**
Fort Lauderdale Stadium
5301 Northwest 12th Ave.
Ft. Lauderdale, FL 33309

**Boston Red Sox**
City of Palm Park
2201 Edison Ave.
Fort Myers, FL 33901

**Chicago White Sox**
Tucson Electric Park
2500 East Ao Way
Tucson, AZ 85713

**Cleveland Indians**
Chain of Lakes Park
Winter Haven, FL 33880

**Detroit Tigers**
2125 North Lake Ave.
Lakeland, FL 33805

**Kansas City Royals**
Baseball City Stadium
300 Stadium Way
Davenport, FL 33837

**Minnesota Twins**
Hammond Stadium
14100 Six Mile Cypress Pkwy.
Fort Myers, FL 33912

**New York Yankees**
3802 W. Martin Luther King Blvd.
Tampa, FL 33614

**Oakland Athletics**
Phoenix Municipal Stadium
5999 East Van Buren St.
Phoenix, AZ 85008

**Seattle Mariners**
Peoria Sports Complex
PO Box 999
Peoria, AZ 85380–0999

**Tampa Bay Devil Rays**
Al Lang Stadium
180 Second Ave. SE
St. Petersburg, FL 33701

**Texas Rangers**
Rangers Complex
2300 El Jobean Rd.
Port Charlotte, FL 33948

**Toronto Blue Jays**
PO Box 957
Dunedin, FL 34697

## NATIONAL LEAGUE

**Arizona Diamondbacks**
Tucson Electric Park
2500 East Ao Way
Tucson, AZ 85713

**Atlanta Braves**
700 S. Victory Way
Kissimmee, FL 34744

**Chicago Cubs**
HoHoKam Park
1235 North Center St.
Mesa, AZ 85201

**Cincinnati Reds**
12th St. and Tuttle Ave.
Sarasota, FL 34237

**Colorado Rockies**
Hi Corbett Field
3400 E. Camino
Campestre
Tucson, AZ 85716

**Florida Marlins**
Space Coast Stadium
5800 Stadium Pkwy.
Melbourne, FL 32940

**Houston Astros**
PO Box 422229
Kissimmee, FL 34742-2229

**Los Angeles Dodgers**
Holman Stadium at Dodgertown
PO Box 2887
Vero Beach, FL 32961

**Milwaukee Brewers**
Maryvale Baseball Park
3600 North 51st Ave.
Phoenix, AZ 85031

**Montreal Expos**
PO Box 8976
Jupiter, FL 33468

**New York Mets**
525 Northwest Peacock Blvd.
Port St. Lucie, FL 34986

**Philadelphia Phillies**
PO Box 10336
Clearwater, FL 34617

**Pittsburgh Pirates**
Pirate City
PO Box 1359
Bradenton, FL 34206

**St. Louis Cardinals**
PO Box 8929
Jupiter, FL 33468

**San Diego Padres**
Peoria Sports Complex
16101 N. 83rd Ave.
Peoria, AZ 85382

**San Francisco Giants**
Scottsdale Stadium
7408 E. Osborn Rd.
Scottsdale, AZ 85251

**NATIONAL BASKETBALL
ASSOCIATION TEAMS**

**National Basketball Assoc.**
Olympic Tower
645 Fifth Ave.
New York, NY 10022
Official Website: http://
www.nba.com/

**Atlanta Hawks**
One CNN Center
Suite 405, South Tower
Atlanta, GA 30303

**Boston Celtics**
151 Merrimac St., 4th Floor
Boston, MA 02114

**Charlotte Hornets**
100 Hive Dr.
Charlotte, NC 28217

**Chicago Bulls**
1901 West Madison
Chicago, IL 60612

**Cleveland Cavaliers**
Gund Arena
One Center Court
Cleveland, OH 44115

**Dallas Mavericks**
Reunion Arena
777 Sports St.
Dallas, TX 75207

**Denver Nuggets**
1635 Clay St.
Denver, CO 80204

**Detroit Pistons**
The Palace of Auburn Hills
Two Championship Dr.
Auburn Hills, MI 48326

**Golden State Warriors**
Oakland Coliseum Arena
7000 Coliseum Way
Oakland, CA 94621

**Houston Rockets**
10 Greenway Plaza
Houston, TX 77046

**Indiana Pacers**
One Conseco Court
125 S. Pennsylvania St.
Indianapolis, IN 46204

**Los Angeles Clippers**
Staples Center
1111 S. Figueroa St.
Los Angeles, CA 90015

**Los Angeles Lakers**
Staples Center
1111 S. Figueroa St.
Los Angeles, CA 90015

**Miami Heat**
SunTrust International Center
One Southeast Third Ave., Suite
#2300
Miami, FL 33131

**Milwaukee Bucks**
1001 North Fourth St.
Milwaukee, WI 53203

## WOMEN'S NATIONAL BASKETBALL ASSOCIATION TEAMS

### EASTERN CONFERENCE

**Charlotte Sting**
3308 Oak Lake Blvd., Suite B
Charlotte, NC 28208

**Cleveland Rockers**
Gund Arena
1 Center Court
Cleveland, OH 44115

**Detroit Shock**
The Palace of Auburn Hills
Two Championship Dr.
Auburn Hills, MI 48326

**Indiana Fever**
Conselo Fieldhouse
One Conselo Court
125 S. Pennsylvania St.
Indianapolis, IN 46204

**Miami Sol**
Sun Trust International Center,
Suite 2300
One Southeast 3rd Avenue
Miami, FL 33131

**Orlando Miracle**
Two Magic Place
8701 Maitland Summit Blvd.
Orlando, FL 32810

**New York Liberty**
Madison Square Garden
Two Pennsylvania Plaza, 14th
Floor
New York, NY 10121

**Phoenix Mercury**
America West Arena
201 East Jefferson
Phoenix, AZ 85004

**Sacramento Monarchs**
One Sports Pkwy.
Sacramento, CA 95834

**Utah Starzz**
Delta Center
301 West South Temple
Salt Lake City, UT 84101

**Washington Mystics**
MCI Center
601 F Street NW
Washington DC 20004

## WESTERN CONFERENCE

**Houston Comets**
Two Greenway Plaza, Ste. 400
Houston, TX 77046

**Los Angeles Sparks**
Great Western Forum
555 N. Nash St.
El Segundo, CA 90245

**Minnesota Lynx**
600 First Avenue North
Minneapolis, MN 55403

**Phoenix Mercury**
America West Arena
201 E. Jefferson St.
Phoenix, AZ 85004

**Portland Fire**
One Center Court
Suite 150
Portland, OR 97227

**Sacramento Monarchs**
One Sports Pkwy.
Sacramento, CA 95834

**Seattle Storm**
351 Elliott Ave. W., Suite 500
Seattle, WA 98119

**Utah Starzz**
Delta Center
301 W. South Temple
Salt Lake City, 84101

## AMERICAN BASKETBALL LEAGUE TEAMS

**American Basketball League**
1900 Embarcadero Rd., Suite #110
Palo Alto, CA 94303
Website: http://www.ableague.com/
E-mail: hoops@ableague.com

**Atlanta Glory**
2100 Powers Ferry Rd., Suite #400
Atlanta, GA 30339
Website: http://
www.atlantaglory.com
E-mail: info@atlantaglory.com

**Colorado Xplosion**
800 Grant St., Suite #410
Denver CO 80203
Website: http://www.xplosion.com
E-mail: info@xplosion.com

**Columbus Quest**
7451 State Route 161
Dublin, OH 43016
Website: http://
www.columbusquest.com

**Long Beach Stingrays**
One World Trade Center, Suite #202
Long Beach, CA 90831
Website: http://
www.lbstingrays.com

**New England Blizzard**
179 Allyn St., Suite # 403
Hartford, CT 06103
Website: http://www.neblizzard.com
E-mail: info@neblizzard.com

**Portland Power**
439 North Broadway
Portland, OR 97227
Website: http://
www.portlandpower.com

**Philadelphia Rage**
123 Chestnut St., 4th Floor
Philadelphia, PA 19106
Website: http://
www.phillyrage.com/

**San Jose Lasers**
1530 Parkmoor Ave., Suite #A
San Jose, CA 95128
Website: http://www.sjlasers.com

**Seattle Reign**
400 Mercer St., Suite #408
Seattle, WA 98109
Website: http://
www.seattlereign.com
E-mail: reign@seattlereign.com

**CONTINENTAL BASKETBALL ASSOCIATION TEAMS**

**Continental Basketball Assoc.**
Two Arizona Center
400 N. 5th St., Suite #1425
Phoenix, AZ 85004
Website: http://
www.cbahoops.com/
E-mail: cbagc@netcom.com

**Connecticut Pride**
#21 Waterville R.
Avon, CT 06001

**Fort Wayne Fury**
1010 Memorial Way, Suite #210
Fort Wayne, IN 46805

**Grand Rapids Hoops**
190 Monroe NW, Room 222
Grand Rapids, MI 49503

**Idaho Stampede**
90 South Cole Rd.
Franklin Business Park
Boise, ID 83709

**La Crosse Bobcats**
200 Main St., Suite #200
PO Box 1717
La Crosse, WI 54602

**Quad City Thunder**
7800 14th St. West
Rock Island, IL 61201

**Rockford Lightning**
3660 Publisher's Dr.
Rockford, IL 61109

**Sioux Falls Skyforce**
330 N. Main Ave., #101
Sioux Falls, SD 57102

**Yakima Sun Kings**
PO Box 2626
Yakima, WA 98907

## NATIONAL FOOTBALL LEAGUE TEAMS

**National Football League**
410 Park Ave.
New York, NY 10022
Website: http://www.nfl.com

**Arizona Cardinals**
PO Box 888
Phoenix, AZ 85001-0888

**Atlanta Falcons**
2745 Burnette Rd.
Suwanee, GA 30174

**Baltimore Ravens**
11001 Owings Mills Blvd.
Owings Mills, MD 21117

**Buffalo Bills**
One Bills Dr.
Orchard Park, NY 14127

**Carolina Panthers**
227 West Trade St., Suite #1600
Charlotte, NC 28202

**Chicago Bears**
250 North Washington Rd.
Lake Forest, IL 60045

**Cincinnati Bengals**
200 Riverfront Stadium
Cincinnati, OH 45202

**Dallas Cowboys**
One Cowboys Pkwy.
Irving, TX 75063

**Denver Broncos**
13655 Broncos Pkwy.
Englewood, CO 80112

**Detroit Lions**
Pontiac Silverdome
1200 Featherstone Rd.
Pontiac, MI 48342

**Green Bay Packers**
1265 Lombardi Ave.
Green Bay, WI 54304

**Houston Oilers**
6910 Fannin St.
Houston, TX 77030

**Indianapolis Colts**
PO Box 535000
Indianapolis, IN 46253

**Jacksonville Jaguars**
One Stadium Pl.
Jacksonville, FL 32202

**Kansas City Chiefs**
One Arrowhead Dr.
Kansas City, MO 64129

**Miami Dolphins**
2269 N.W. 199th St.
Miami, FL 33056

**Minnesota Vikings**
9520 Viking Dr.
Eden Prairie, MN 55344

**New England Patriots**
60 Washington St.
Foxboro, MA 02035
Website: http://www.patriots.com/

**New Orleans Saints**
6928 Saints Dr.
Metairie, LA 70003

**New York Giants**
Giants Stadium
East Rutherford, NJ 07073

**New York Jets**
1000 Fulton Ave.
Hempstead, NY 11550

**Oakland Raiders**
332 Center St.
El Segundo, CA 90245

**Philadelphia Eagles**
3501 South Broad St.
Philadelphia, PA 19148

**Pittsburgh Steelers**
300 Stadium Circle
Pittsburgh, PA 15212

**St. Louis Rams**
100 North Broadway
St. Louis, MO 63102

**San Diego Chargers**
PO Box 609609
San Diego, CA 92160

**San Francisco 49ers**
4949 Centennial Blvd.
Santa Clara, CA 95054

**Seattle Seahawks**
11220 N.E. 53rd St.
Kirkland, WA 98033

**Tampa Bay Buccaneers**
One Buccaneer Pl.
Tampa, FL 33607

**Washington Redskins**
21300 Redskin Park Dr.
Ashburn, VA 22011

**NATIONAL HOCKEY LEAGUE TEAMS**

**National Hockey League**
1251 Ave. of the Americas
New York, NY 10020
Website: http://www.nhl.com/

**National Hockey League**
Montreal Office
1800 McGill College Ave., Suite #2600
Montreal, Quebec H3A 3J6
Canada

**National Hockey League**
Toronto Office
75 International Blvd., Suite #300
Rexdale, Ontario M9W 6L9
Canada

**The Mighty Ducks of Anaheim**
2695 E. Katella Ave.
PO Box 61077
Anaheim, CA 92803

**Atlanta Thrashers Hockey Club**
Atlanta, GA 30348-5366

**Boston Bruins**
Fleet Center
Boston, MA 02114

**Buffalo Sabres**
Marine Midland Arena
One Seymour Knox III Plaza
Buffalo, NY 14203

**Calgary Flames**
Canadian Airlines Saddledome
PO Box 1540, Station M
Calgary, AB T2P 3B9
Canada

**Chicago Blackhawks**
United Center
1901 W. Madison St.
Chicago, IL 60612

**Colorado Avalanche**
McNichols Sports Arena
1635 Clay St.
Denver, CO 80204

**Columbus Blue Jackets**
Nationwide Arena
200 W. Nationwide Blvd.
Suite Level, 3rd Floor
Columbus, OH 43215

**Dallas Stars**
Star Center
211 Cowboys Pkwy.
Irving, TX 75063

**Detroit Red Wings**
Joe Louis Arena
600 Civic Center
Detroit, MI 48226

**Edmonton Oilers**
11230-110 Ave.
Edmonton, AB T5G 3G8
Canada

**Florida Panthers**
100 N.E. 3rd Ave., 10th Floor
Ft. Lauderdale, FL 33301

**Carolina Hurricanes**
5000 Aerial Center, Suite #1000
Morrisville, NC 27560

**Los Angeles Kings**
Staples Center
1111 S. Figueroa St.
Los Angeles, CA 90015

**Montreal Canadiens**
Molson Centre
1260, rue de la Gauchetiere
Ouest
Monteal, Quebec H3B 5E8
Canada

**Nashville Predators**
Gaylord Entertainment Center
501 Broadway
Nashville, TN 37203

**New Jersey Devils**
Continental Airlines Arena
PO Box 504
East Rutherford, NJ 07073

**New York Islanders**
Nassau Coliseum
Uniondale, NY 11553

**New York Rangers**
Madison Square Garden
4 Pennsylvania Plaza
New York, NY 10001

**Ottawa Senators**
Corel Center
1000 Palladium Dr.
Kanata, ON K2V 1A5
Canada

**Philadelphia Flyers**
CoreStates Center
1 CoreStates Complex
Philadelphia, PA 19148

**Phoenix Coyotes**
One Renaissance Square
2 North Central, Suite #1930
Phoenix, AZ 85004

**Pittsburgh Penguins**
Civic Arena
Gate 9
Pittsburgh, PA 15219

**St. Louis Blues**
Kiel Center
1401 Clark Ave.
St. Louis, MO 63103

**San Jose Sharks**
San Jose Arena
525 W. Santa Clara St.
San Jose, CA 95113

**Tampa Bay Lightning**
Ice Palace
401 Channelside Dr.
Tampa, FL 33602

**Toronto Maple Leafs**
Maple Leaf Gardens
60 Carlton St.
Toronto, Ontario M5B 1L1
Canada

**Vancouver Canucks**
General Motors Pl.
800 Griffiths Way
Vancouver, BC V6B 6G1
Canada

**Washington Capitals**
US Airways Arena
Landover, MD 20785

## AMERICAN HOCKEY LEAGUE TEAM

**American Hockey League**
425 Union St.
West Springfield, MA 01089
Website: http://www.canoe.ca/AHL/

**Adirondack Red Wings**
1 Civic Center Plaza
Glens Falls, NY 12801

**Albany River Rats**
Knickerbocker Arena
51 South Pearl St.
Albany, NY 12207

**Beast of New Haven**
275 Orange St.
New Haven, CT 06510

**Cincinnati Mighty Ducks**
2250 Seymour Ave.
Cincinnati, OH 45212

**Fredericton Canadiens**
Aitken University Centre
PO Box HABS
Fredericton, NB E3B 4Y2
Canada

**Hamilton Bulldogs**
85 York Blvd.
Hamilton, Ontario L8R 3L4
Canada

**Hartford Wolf Pack**
196 Trumbull St., 3rd Floor
Hartford, CT 06103

**Hershey Bears**
PO Box 866
Hershey, PA 17033

**Kentucky Thoroughblades**
410 West Vine St.
Lexington, KY 40507

**Philadelphia Phantoms**
The CoreStates Spectrum
1 CoreStates Complex
Philadelphia, PA 19148

**Portland Pirates**
Cumberland County Civic Center
85 Free St.
Portland, ME 04101

**Providence Bruins**
Providence Civic Center
1 LaSalle Square
Providence, RI 02903

**Rochester Americans**
50 South Ave.
Rochester, NY 14604

**Saint John Flames**
PO Box 4040, Station B
Saint John, NB E2M 5E6
Canada

**Springfield Falcons**
PO Box 3190
Springfield, MA 01101

**St. John's Maple Leafs**
6 Logy Bay Rd.
St. John's, Newfoundland A1A 1J3
Canada

**Syracuse Crunch**
Onondaga County War Memorial
800 South State St.
Syracuse, NY 13202

**Worcester Ice Cats**
303 Main St.
Worcester, MA 01608

## CENTRAL HOCKEY LEAGUE TEAMS

**Central Hockey League**
5840 S. Memorial Dr., Suite #302
Tulsa, OK 74145

**Columbus Cottonmouths**
PO Box 1886
Columbus, GA 31902-1886

**Fayetteville Force**
121 E. Mountain Dr., Room #22B
Fayetteville, NC 28306
Website: http://
www.fayettevilleforce.com

**Fort Worth Fire**
University Centre
1300 S. University, Suite #515
Fort Worth, TX 76107
Website: http://www.fwfire.com/

**Huntsville Channel Cats**
Von Braun Center
700 Monroe St.
Huntsville, AL 35801
Website: http://
www.channelcats.com

**Macon Whoopee**
Macon Centreplex
200 Coliseum Dr.
Macon, GA 31201
Website: http://
www.maconwhoopee.com

**Memphis RiverKings**
Mid-South Coliseum
The Fairgrounds
Memphis, TN 38104

**Nashville Ice Flyers**
PO Box 190595
Nashville, TN 37219

**Oklahoma City Blazers**
119 N. Robinson, Suite #230
Oklahoma City, OK 73102
Website: http://
www.okcblazers.com/

**Tulsa Oilers**
613 S. Mingo
Tulsa, OK 74133

**Wichita Thunder**
505 West Maple, Suite #100
Wichita, KS 67213

## EAST COAST HOCKEY LEAGUE TEAMS

**East Coast Hockey League**
125 Village Blvd., Suite #210
Princeton, NJ 08540
Website: http://www.echl.org/

**Columbus Chill**
7001 Dublin Park Dr.
Dublin, OH 43016

**Dayton Bombers**
Ervin J. Nutter Center
3640 Colonel Glenn Hwy., Suite #417
Dayton, OH 45435

**Huntington Blizzard**
763 Third Ave.
Huntington, WV 25701

**Johnstown Chiefs**
326 Napoleon St.
Johnstown, PA 15901

**Louisville RiverFrogs**
PO Box 36407
Louisville, KY 40233

**Peoria Rivermen**
201 SW Jefferson
Peoria, IL 61602

**Toledo Storm**
One Main St.
Toledo, OH 43605

**Wheeling Nailers**
PO Box 6563
Wheeling, WV 26003-0815

**Baton Rouge Kingfish**
PO Box 2142
Baton Rouge, LA 70821

**Birmingham Bulls**
PO Box 1506
Birmingham, AL 35201

**Jacksonville Lizard Kings**
5569-7 Bowden Rd.
Jacksonville, FL 32216

**Louisiana IceGators**
444 Cajundome Blvd.
Lafayette, LA 70506

**Mississippi Sea Wolves**
2350 Beach Blvd.
Biloxi, MS 39531

**Mobile Mysticks**
PO Box 263
Mobile, AL 36601

**Pensacola Ice Pilots**
Civic Center/201 E. Gregory St.—Rear
Pensacola, FL 32501

**Tallahassee Tiger Sharks**
505 W. Pensacola St., Suite #1
Tallahassee, FL 32301

**Charlotte Checkers**
2700 E. Independence Blvd.
Charlotte, NC 28205

**Hampton Roads Admirals**
PO Box 299
Norfolk, VA 23501

**Knoxville Cherokees**
500 East Church St.
Knoxville, TN 37915

**Raleigh IceCaps**
4000 West Chase Blvd., Suite #110
Raleigh, NC 27607

**Richmond Renegades**
601 East Leigh St.
Richmond, VA 23219

**Roanoke Express**
4502 Starkey Rd. SW, Suite #211
Roanoke, VA 24014

**South Carolina Stingrays**
3107 Firestone Rd.
North Charleston, SC 29418

**WESTERN PROFESSIONAL
HOCKEY LEAGUE TEAMS**

**Western Professional Hockey
League**
14040 North Cave Creek Rd.,
Suite #100
Phoenix, AZ
Website: http://
www.wphlhockey.com
E-mail: wphl@snetzone.com

**Amarillo Rattlers**
320 South Polk St., Suite #800
Amarillo, TX 79101
Website http://www.wphl-
rattlers.com

**Austin Ice Bats**
7311 Decker Lane
Austin, TX 78724

**Central Texas Stampede**
600 Forest Dr.
Belton, TX 76513

**El Paso Buzzards**
4100 East Paisano Dr.
El Paso, TX 79905

**Fort Worth Bramahs**
PO Box 470606
Fort Worth, TX 76147

**Lake Charles Ice Pirates**
900 Lakeshore Dr., 2nd Floor
Lake Charles, LA 70602

**Monroe Moccasins**
2102 Louisville Ave.
Monroe, LA 71201

**New Mexico Scorpions**
1101 Cardenas Plaza, Suite #201
Albuquerque, NM 87110

**Odessa Jackalopes**
PO Box 51187
Midland, TX 79710

**San Angelo Outlaws**
3260 Sherwood Way
San Angelo, TX 76901

**Shreveport Mudbugs**
3701 Hudson St., 2nd Floor
Shreveport, LA 71109

**Waco Wizards**
2040 North Valley Mills Dr.
Waco, TX 76710

**MAJOR LEAGUE SOCCER TEAMS**

**Major League Soccer**
110 East 42nd St. 10th Floor
New York, NY 10017
Website: http://www.mlsnet.com

**Chicago Fire**
311 West Superior, Suite #444
Chicago, IL 60610
Website: http://www.chicago-
fire.com

**Colorado Rapids**
555 17th St. Suite #3350
Denver, CO 80202
Website: http://
www.coloradorapids.com
E-mail: Rapids@mlsnet.com

**Columbus Crew**
77 East Nationwide Blvd.
Columbus, OH 43215
Website: http://www.thecrew.com/
E-mail: crew2739@aol.com

**Dallas Burn**
2602 McKinney, Suite #200
Dallas, TX 75204
Website: http://
www.burnsoccer.com
E-mail: mail@burnsoccer.com

**DC United**
13832 Redskin Dr.
Herndon, VA 22071
Website: http://www.dcunited.com
E-mail: united-fan@mlsnet.com

**Kansas City Wizards**
706 Broadway St., Suite #100
Kansas City, MO 64105
Website: http://
www.kcwizards.com/
E-mail: ctaylor@mlsnet.com

**Los Angeles Galaxy**
1640 S. Sepulveda Blvd., Suite
#114
Los Angeles, CA 90025

**Miami Fusion**
2200 Commercial Blvd., Suite
#104
Ft. Lauderdale, FL 33309
Website: http://
www.miamifusion.com

**New England Revolution**
Foxboro Stadium
60 Washington St., Route 1
Foxboro, MA 02035
Website: http://
www.nerevolution.com/

**NY/NJ MetroStars**
One Harmon Plaza, 8th Floor
Secaucus, NJ 07094
Website: http://
www.metrostars.com/
E-mail: MetroFan@mlsnet.com

**San Jose Clash**
1265 El Camino Real, 2nd Floor
Santa Clara, CA 95050
Website: http://www.clash.com/
E-mail: clash@clash.com

**Tampa Bay Mutiny**
1408 Westshore Blvd, Suite #1004
Tampa, FL 33607
Website: http://
www.tampabaymutiny.com/
E-mail: mutinymail@mlsnet.com

## NATIONAL PROFESSIONAL SOCCER LEAGUE TEAMS

**National Professional Soccer League**
115 Dewalt Ave. NW, Fifth Floor
Canton, OH 44702
E-mail: NPSL1@aol.com

**Baltimore Spirit**
201 West Baltimore St.
Baltimore, MD 21201
Website: http://
www.baltimorespirit.com
E-mail:
spiritsoccer@baltimorespirit.com

**Buffalo Blizzard**
Marine Midland Arena
One Seymour Knox III Plaza
Buffalo, NY 14203
Website: http://
www.buffaloblizzard.com

**Cincinnati Silverbacks**
537 E. Pete Rose Way, 2nd Floor
Cincinnati, OH 45202

**Cleveland Crunch**
34200 Solon Rd.
Solon, OH 44139

**Detroit Rockers**
600 Civic Center Dr.
Detroit, MI 48226
E-mail: rockersoc@aol.com

**Edmonton Drillers**
11230 110th St.
Edmonton, AB T5G 3G8
Canada
Website: http://
www.edmontondrillers.com
E-mail: drillers@compusmart.ab.ca

**Harrisburg Heat**
PO Box 60123
Harrisburg, PA 17106
Website: http://
www.heatsoccer.com/
E-mail: heatsoccer@aol.com

**Kansas City Attack**
1800 Genessee
Kansas City, MO 64102

**Milwaukee Wave**
10201 N. Port Washington Rd.,
Suite #200
Mequon, WI 53092
Website: http://
www.wavesoccer.com

**Montreal Impact**
8000 Langelier, Suite. #104
St. Leonard, QUE H1P 3K2
Canada
Website: http://
www.impactmtl.com
E-mail: Info@impact.usisl.com

**Philadelphia Kixx**
CoreStates Spectrum
1 CoreStates Complex
Philadelphia, PA 19148-9727
Website: http://kixx.phillynews.com
E-mail: kixxsoccer@aol.com

**St. Louis Ambush**
7547 Ravensridge
St. Louis, MO 63119

**Wichita Wings**
500 South Broadway
Wichita, KS 67202
Website: http://www.wichita-
wings.com

## THE A-LEAGUE HOCKEY TEAMS

**The A-League**
14497 N. Dale Mabry, Suite #211
Tampa, FL 33618

**Atlanta Ruckus**
1131 Alpharetta St.
Roswell, GA 30075

**California Jaguars**
12 Clay St.
Salinas, CA 93901

**Carolina Dynamo**
3517 W. Wendover Ave.
Greensboro, NC 27407

**Charleston Battery**
4401 Belle Oaks Dr., Suite #450
Charleston, SC 29405

**Colorado Foxes**
6200 Dahlia St.
Commerce City, CO 80022

**Connecticut Wolves**
PO Box 3196
Veterans Memorial Stadium
New Britain, CT 06050-3196

**El Paso Patriots**
6941 Industrial
El Paso, TX 79915

**Hershey Wildcats**
100 W. Hersheypark Dr.
Hershey, PA 17033

**Jacksonville Cyclones**
9428 Bay Meadows Rd., Suite
#175
Jacksonville, FL 32256

**Long Island Rough Riders**
1670 Old Country Rd., Suite #227
Plainview, NY 11803

**Milwaukee Rampage**
Uihlein Soccer Park
7101 West Good Hope Rd.
Milwaukee, WI 53223

**Minnesota Thunder**
1700 105th Ave. NE
Elaine, MN 55449

**Montreal Impact**
8000 Langelier, Suite #104
St. Leonard, Quebec H1P 3K2
Canada

**Nashville Metros**
7115 South Spring Dr.
Franklin, TN 37067-1616

**New Orleans Riverboat Gamblers**
5690 Eastover Dr.
New Orleans, LA 70128

**Orange County Zodiac**
% Unicor
14210 Quail Ridge Dr.
Riverside, CA 92503

**Orlando Sundogs**
One Citrus Bowl Place
Orlando, FL 32805

**Raleigh Flyers**
130 Wind Chime Ct.
Raleigh, NC 27615

**Richmond Kickers**
2320 West Main St.
Richmond, VA 23220

**Rochester Raging Rhinos**
333 N. Plymouth Ave.
Rochester, NY 14608

**Seattle Sounders**
10838 Main St.
Bellevue, WA 98004

**Toronto Lynx**
% HIT Pro Soccer, Inc.
55 University Ave., Suite #506
Toronto, Ontario M5J 2H7
Canada

**Vancouver 86ers**
1126 Douglas Rd.
Burnaby, BC V5C 4Z6
Canada

**Worcester Wildfire**
500 Main St., Suite #515
Worcester, MA 01608

# ON THE TUBE AND SCREEN

**ABC Entertainment**
2040 Ave. of the Stars
Century City, CA 90067
Or
77 West 66th St., 9th Floor
New York, NY 10023
Robert F. Callahan, President, ABC
Broadcast Group
*Major television network*

**Ablaze Ent., Inc.**
1040 N. Las Palmas Ave.,
Bldg. 30
Los Angeles, CA 90038
*Entertainment agency*

**Above the Line Agency**
9200 Sunset Blvd., #401
Los Angeles, CA 90069
Rima Greer, Agent
*Agency that handles directors,
clients include Irvin Kershner, Ryan
Rowe, John Hopkins, and others*

**Academy of Motion Pictures Arts
and Sciences (AMPAS)**
8949 Wilshire Blvd.
Beverly Hills, CA 90210
Bruce Davis, Executive Director
Website: www.ocar.org
E-mail: ampas@oscar.org
*Film organization, awards the
Oscars*

**Academy of Television Arts and
Sciences (ATAS)**
5220 Lankershim Blvd.
North Hollywood, CA 91601
Or
111 West 57th St., Suite #1050
New York, NY 10019
Website: http://
www.emmyonline.org/
*TV organization, awards the Emmy*

**Actor's Equity Association**
165 W. 46th St.
New York, NY 10036
Website: http://
www.actorsequity.org/
Patrick Quinn, President
*Stage actor's union*

**Adler, Margot**
% National Public Radio
2025 M St. N.W.
Washington, DC 20036
*News correspondent*

**The Agency**
1800 Ave. of the Stars
Los Angeles, CA 90067
*Agency that handles directors,*
*agents include Emile Gladstone,*
*Jerry Zeitman, Walter Van Dyke,*
*Walter Morgan and Nick Mechanic.*

**Agency for the Performing Arts**
9200 Sunset Blvd., #900
Los Angeles, CA 90069
*Entertainment agency*

**Agency for the Performing Arts**
888 7th Ave.
New York, NY 10106
*Entertainment agency*

**Ailes, Roger**
440 Park Ave. South
New York, NY 10016
*Producer, director*

**Alexander, Shana**
156 Fifth Ave., #617
New York, NY 10010
*News correspondent*

**Ally McBeal**
Manhattan Beach Studios
1600 Rosecrans Ave.
Building 4A, 3rd Floor
Attn: *Ally McBeal*
Manhattan Beach, CA 90266

**Amanpour, Christiane**
2 Stephen St., #100
London W1P 2PL
England
*Broadcast journalist*

**American Cinematographer**
PO Box 2230
Hollywood, CA 90078
Website: http://
www.cinematographer.com/
magazine/
Jim McCullaugh, Publisher
E-mail: Jim@theasc.com
*Magazine for cinematographers*
*and editors*

**American Movie Classics**
150 Crossways Park West
Woodbury, NY 11797

**America's Most Wanted: America**
**Fights Back**
PO Box Crime TV
Washington, DC 20016
Website: http://www.amw.com
E-mail: feedback@amw.com

**Amos, Deborah**
% National Public Radio
2025 M St. N.W.
Washington, DC 20036
*News correspondent*

**Anderson, Terry**
50 Rockefeller Plaza
New York, NY 10020
*News correspondent*

**Angle, Jim**
% National Public Radio
2025 M St. N.W.
Washington, DC 20036
*News correspondent*

**Arts and Entertainment**
235 East 45th St.
New York, NY 10017
*Cable network*

**Backstage West**
779 Broadway
New York, NY 10003
Magazine for actors
Website: http://
www.backstage.com/
E-mail: backstage@backstage.com
Steve Elish, Publisher
E-mail: Selish@backstage.com

**Baywatch Hawaii**
The Baywatch Production Co.
510 18th Ave.
Honolulu, HI 96816
Website: http://
www.baywatch.com/
baywatchhawaii/start2.htm
*TV series*

**Believe It or Not!**
16027 Ventura Blvd., Suite 340
Encino, CA 91436
*Television show*

**Beyond Belief: Fact or Fiction**
Maybe Productions
2920 W. Olive Ave., #206
Attn: *Beyond Belief*
Burbank, CA 91505

**Black Entertainment Television**
1232 31st St. NW
Washington, DC 20007

**Boot Camp**
PO Box 900
Attn: Boot Camp
Beverly Hills, CA 90213

**Boston Public**
Manhattan Beach Studios
1600 Rosecrans Ave.
Building 4A, 3rd Floor
Attn: *Boston Public*
Manhattan Beach, CA 90266

**Bravo**
150 Crossways Park West
Woodbury, NY 11797
*Cable network*

**Cable Network News**
One CNN Center
PO Box 105366
Atlanta, GA 30348
*Cable network*

**CBS**
7800 Beverly Blvd.
Los Angeles, CA 90036
Or
51 W. 52 St.
New York, NY 10019
Website: http://ww.cbs.com
E-mail: marketing@cbs.com
Leslie Moonves, President and
CEO
*Television network*

**Chung, Connie**
1 W. 72nd St.
New York, NY 10023
*Newscaster*
*Birthday: 8/20/46*

**Cinemax**
1100 Ave. of the Americas
New York, NY 10036
*Cable network*

**CNBC**
2200 Fletcher Ave.
Fort Lee, NJ 07024
*Cable network*

**Comedy Central**
1775 Broadway
New York, NY 10019
*Cable network*

**Cops**
% John Langley Productions
2225 Colorado Blvd.
Attn: Maria Jordan
Santa Monica, CA 90404

**Court TV**
600 Third Ave., 2nd Floor
New York, NY 10016
*Cable network*

**Creative Authors Agency**
12212 Paradise Village Pkwy.
South, #403-C
Phoenix, AZ 85032
*Writer's agent*

**C-SPAN**
400 North Capital St. NW, Suite
#650
Washington, DC 20001
*Cable network*

**Csupo, Gabor**
6353 Sunset Blvd.
Hollywood, CA 90028
Website: http://
www.klaskycsupo.com
E-mail:
recruitment@klaskycsupo.com
*Creator of Rugrats*

**Dark Angel**
PO Box 900
Attn: *Dark Angel*
Beverly Hills, CA 90213

**Dateline NBC**
30 Rockefeller Plaza
New York, NY 10112
E-mail: dateline@news.nbc.com
*TV series*

**Discovery Channel, The**
7700 Wisconsin Ave.
Bethesda, MD 20814
*Cable network*

**Disney Channel, The**
3800 West Alameda Ave.
Burbank, CA 91505
*Cable network*

**Dramalogue**
PO Box 38771
Hollywood, CA 90038
*Newspaper for actors*

**E!**
5670 Wilshire Blvd.
Los Angeles, NY 90036
*Cable network*

**Encore**
5445 DTC Pkwy., Suite #600
Englewood, CO 80111
*Cable network*

**ESPN**
ESPN Plaza
935 Middle St.
Bristol, CT 06010
*Cable network*

**Family Guy**
4705 Laurel Canyon Blvd.,
3rd Floor
Attn: *Family Guy*
Valley Village, CA 91607

**FLIX**
1633 Broadway
New York, NY 10019
*Cable network*

**Fox**
211 Ave. of the Americas
New York, NY 10036
K. Rupert Murdoch, Chairman and
CEO
Peter Chernin, President and Co-
COO
*Television network*

**Fox Family Channel**
2877 Guardian Lane
PO Box 2050
Virginia Beach, VA 23450
*Cable network*

**Fox Kids**
PO Box 900
Beverly Hills, CA 90213-0900
Website: http://www.foxkids.com

**Fox News Channel**
Website: http://www.foxnews.com

**Fox Sports**
PO Box 900
Beverly Hills, CA 90213-0900
Website: http//www.foxsports.com

*Freakylinks*
PO Box 900
Attn: *Freakylinks*
Beverly Hills, CA 90213
Website: http://
www.FreakyLinks.com

*Friends*
% Warner Bros.
400 Warner Blvd.
Burbank, CA 91522
*TV series*

*Futurama*
PO Box 900
Attn: *Futurama*
Beverly Hills, CA 90213

*fX*
PO Box 900
Beverly Hills, NY 90213
*Cable network*

**FXM: Movies from Fox**
PO Box 900
Beverly Hills, CA 90213
*Cable network*

**Galavision**
605 Third Ave., 12th Floor
New York, NY 10158
*Cable network*

**Game Show Network**
510202 W. Washington Blvd.
Culver City, CA 90232
Michael Fleming, President
E-mail: michael.
fleming@spe.sony.com

**Golf Channel, The**
7580 Commerce Dr.
Orlando, FL 32819
*Cable network*

**Grace Company, The**
829 Langdon Ct.
Rochester Hills, MI 48307
*Entertainment agency*

*Great Detective Stories*
PO Box 900
Attn: *Great Detective Stories*
Beverly Hills, CA 90213

*Grounded for Life*
PO Box 900
Attn: *Grounded for Life*
Beverly Hills, CA 90213

**Guinness World Records: Primetime**
LMNO Productions
PO Box 4361
Attn: *Guinness World Records: Primetime*
Hollywood, CA 90028
Website: http://
www.Guinnessrecords.com

**Headline News**
One CNN Center
PO Box 105366
Atlanta, GA 30348
*Cable network*

**HBO**
1100 Ave. of the Americas
New York, NY 10036
*Cable network*

**Hee Haw**
PO Box 140400
Nashville, TN 38214
*Television show*

**Herman, Richard Talent Agency**
124 Lasky Dr., 2nd Floor
Beverly Hills, CA 90212
*Talent agency*

**History Channel, The**
235 East 45th St.
New York, NY 10017
*Cable network*

**Hollywood Reporter**
5055 Wilshire Blvd., 6th Floor
Los Angeles, CA 90036
Website: http://
www.hollywoodreporter.com/
George Christy, columnist
*Trade newspaper for movie and television professionals*

**Home and Garden TV**
9701 Madison Ave.
Knoxville, TN 37932
*Cable network*

**Home Shopping Network**
1529 US Route 19 South
Clearwater, FL 33546
*Cable network*

**In Search Of**
PO Box 900
Attn: *In Search Of*
Beverly Hills, CA 90213-0900

**Just Kidding**
PO Box 900
Attn: *Just Kidding*
Beverly Hills, CA 90213

**Kick Entertainment**
1934 East 123rd St.
Cleveland, OH 44106
*Entertainment agency*

**King of the Hill**
PO Box 900
Attn: *King of the Hill*
Beverly Hills, CA 90213

**Krypton Factor**
PO Box 900
Attn: *Krypton Factor*
Beverly Hills, CA 90213

**Learning Channel, The**
7700 Wisconsin Ave.
Bethesda, MD 20814
*Cable network*

**Lifetime**
309 West 49th St.
New York, NY 10019
*Cable network*

**Lone Gunmen, The**
PO Box 900
Attn: *The Lone Gunmen*
Beverly Hills, CA 90213-0900

**Love Cruise**
PO Box 900
Attn: *Love Cruise*
Beverly Hills, CA 90213

**MADtv**
5842 Sunset Blvd., Bldg. 11, Suite
#203
Attn: *MADtv*
Hollywood, CA 90028
*Television series*

**Malcolm in the Middle**
4024 Radford Ave.
Office: S
Attn: *Malcolm in the Middle*
Studio City, CA 91604

**Mighty Morphin Power Rangers**
26020-A Ave. Hall
Valencia, CA 91355
*TV series*

**Million Dollar Mysteries**
PO Box 900
Attn: *Million Dollar Mysteries*
Beverly Hills, CA 90213

**Movie Channel, The**
1633 Broadway
New York, NY 10019
*Cable network*

**MSNBC**
2200 Fletcher Ave.
Fort Lee, NJ 07024
*Cable network*

**MTV**
1515 Broadway
New York, NY 10036
*Cable network*

**Nashville Network, The**
2806 Opryland Dr.
Nashville, TN 37214
*Cable network*

**Nickelodeon**
1515 Broadway
New York, NY 10036
*Cable network*

**Night Visions**
PO Box 900
Attn: *Night Visions*
Beverly Hills, CA 90213-0900

**Normal Ohio (starring John Goodman)**
4024 Radford Ave.
Building 1, Suite #111
Attn: *Normal Ohio* show
Studio City, CA 91604

**Party of Five**
High Productions
10202 W. Washington Blvd.
Gable Bldg., Room 210
Attn: *Party of Five*
Culver City, CA 90232

**Phillips, Stone**
30 Rockefeller Plaza
New York, NY 10122
*News correspondent*

**PBS**
1320 Braddock Place
Alexandria, VA 22314
*Broadcast network*

**Police Videos**
PO Box 900
Attn: *Police Videos*
Beverly Hills, CA 90213

**QVC**
1365 Enterprise Dr.
West Chester, PA 19380
*Cable network*

**Rather, Dan**
524 W. 57th St.
New York, NY 10019
*Anchor, correspondent, editor*
*Birthday: 10/31/31*

**Roker, Al**
E-mail at: mailbag@roker.com
Today Show *weatherman*

**Rose, Charlie**
524 W. 57th St.
New York, NY 10019
*Television host, journalist*

**Sci-Fi Channel, The**
1230 Ave. of the Americas
New York, NY 10020
*Cable network*

**Schimmel**
PO Box 900
Attn: *Schimmel*
Beverly Hills, CA 90213

**Sesame Street**
1 Lincoln Plaza
New York, NY 10022
*Television show*

**Siegan and Weisman, Ltd.**
29 S. La Salle
Chicago, IL 60603
*Entertainment agency*

**Simpsons, The**
PO Box 900
Attn: *The Simpsons*
Beverly Hills, CA 90213

**Showtime**
1633 Broadway
New York, NY 10019
*Cable network*

**Shriver, Maria**
3110 Main St., #300
Santa Monica, CA 90405
*Broadcast journalist, wife of Arnold Schwarzenneger*
*Birthday: 11/6/55*

**Starz**
5445 DTC Pkwy., Suite #600
Englewood, CO 80111
*Cable network*

**Street, The**
PO Box 900
Attn: *The Street*
Beverly Hills, CA 90213

**Telemundo**
2290 West 8th Ave.
Hialeah, FL 33010
*Cable network*

**Temptation**
PO Box 900
Attn: *Temptation*
Beverly Hills, CA 90213

**That '70s Show**
4024 Radford Ave.
Building 1, Suite #111
Attn: *That '70s Show*
Studio City, CA 91604
Website: http://
www.that70sshow.com

**Theismann, Joe**
% ESPN
ESPN Plaza
Bristol, CT 06010
*Sportscaster*

**Tick, The**
PO Box 900
Attn: *The Tick*
Beverly Hills, CA 90213-0900

**Titus**
PO Box 900
Attn: *Titus*
Beverly Hills, CA 90213

**Today Show**
30 Rockefeller Plaza, Rm. 374E
New York, NY 10112
E-mail: today@nbc.com

**Total Acting Experience, A**
20501 Ventura Blvd., #399
Woodland Hills, CA 91364
*Entertainment agency*

**Turner Classic Movies**
One CNN Center
PO Box 105366
Atlanta, GA 30348
*Cable network*

**Turner Network Television**
One CNN Center
PO Box 105366
Atlanta, GA 30348
*Cable network*

**20th Century Fox (Theatricals)**
PO Box 900
Beverly Hills, CA 90213-0900
Website: http://
www.foxmovies.com

**20th Century Fox Home Video**
PO Box 900
Beverly Hills, CA 90213-0900
Website: http://www.foxhome.com

**20th Television (Production Company)**
PO Box 900
Beverly Hills, CA 90213-0900
Website: http://www.foxhome.com

**TV Food Network**
1177 Ave. of the Americas
New York, NY 10036
*Cable network*

**Univision**
605 Third Ave., 12th Floor
New York, NY 10158
*Cable network*

**UPN**
5555 Melrose Ave.
Marathon 1200
Los Angeles, CA 90038
*Broadcast network*

**USA Network**
1230 Ave. of the Americas
New York, NY 10020
*Cable network*

**VH-1**
1515 Broadway
New York, NY 10036
*Cable network*

**Wanted**
PO Box 900
Attn: *Wanted*
Beverly Hills, CA 90213

**WB**
4000 Warner Blvd., Bldg. 34R
Burbank, CA 91522
*Broadcast network*

**The Weather Channel**
2600 Cumberland Pkwy.
New York, NY 30339
*Cable network*

**WGN**
One Technology Plaza
7140 South Lewis Ave.
Tulsa, OK 74136-5422
*Cable network*

**Winokur Agency, The**
5575 North Umberland St.
Pittsburgh, PA 15217
*Entertainment agency*

**Ann Wright Representatives**
165 West 46th St., #1105
New York, NY 10036-2501
*Entertainment agency*

**Writers and Artists Agency**
19 West 44th St., #1000
New York, NY 10036
*Entertainment agency*

**WTBS**
One CNN Center
PO Box 105366
Atlanta, GA 30348
*Cable network*

**The X-Files**
% Studio Fan Mail
1122 S. Robertson Blvd., #15
Los Angeles, CA 90035
Or
10201 W. Pico Blvd., Bldg. 41,
Suite #100
Attn: *The X-Files*
Los Angeles, CA 90035
*TV series*

# GET BUSY!

**AARP (American Association for Retired Persons)**
601 E Street NW
Washington, DC 20049
Website: http://www.aarp.org/
E-mail: member@aarp.org
Joseph S. Perkins, President
*Association for senior citizens.*

**ACCESS: A Security Information Service**
1511 K Street NW #643
Washington, DC 20065
E-mail: access@4access.org

**Accuracy in Media, Inc.**
4455 Connecticut Ave.#.330
Washington, DC 20008
Chairman: Reed Irvine
Website: http://www.aim.org/
*Group concerned with fairness, balance, and accuracy in news reporting.*

**Action on Smoking and Health (ASH)**
2013 H Street NW
Washington, DC 20006
Website: http://ash.org/
John F. Banzhaf III, executive director
*ASH is the nation's oldest and largest antismoking organization, and the only one that regularly takes legal action to fight smoking and protect the rights of nonsmokers.*

**Actors and Others for Animals**
11523 Burbank Boulevard
North Hollywood, CA 91601
Website: http://www.actorsandothers.com/
Email: info@actorsandothers.com
Cathy Singleton, executive director
*Protection group for the welfare of animals.*

**Ad Council**
261 Madison Ave., 11th floor
New York, NY 10016
Website: http://www.adcouncil.org/
Peggy Conlon, president
E-mail: editor@marketingclick.com
*Nonprofit volunteer organization that conducts public service advertising.*

**Advocacy Institute**
1629 K Street, NW, Suite 200
Washington, DC 20006
E-mail: info@advocacy.org
Website: http://www.advocacy.org/
*Dedicated to strengthening the capacity of public interest / social and economic justice advocates to influence and change public policy.*

**Advocates for Highway and Auto Safety**
750 First Street NE #901
Washington, DC 20002
Website: http://www.saferoads.org/
Joan Claybrook, consumer co-chair
*Dedicated to traffic safety.*

**Advocates for Self-Government**
1202 N. Tennessee St., Suite 202
Cartersville, GA 30120
Marshall Fritz, founder
Website: http://www.self-gov.org/
E-mail: Advocates@self-gov.org
*Encourages people to encounter, evaluate and embrace the ideas of liberty, and improve communications.*

**Advocates for Youth**
1025 Vermont Avenue NW, #200
Washington, DC 20005
Website: http://
www.advocatesforyouth.org/
E-mail: mailto:
info@advocatesforyouth.org
James Wagoner, president
*Creates programs and promotes policies that help young people make informed and responsible decisions about their sexual and reproductive health.*

**The Africa Fund**
50 Broad Street, Suite 711
New York NY 10004
Website: http://
africafund.prairienet.org/
E-mail: africafund@igc.org
*Works for a positive U.S. policy toward Africa and supports human rights, democracy, and development.*

**Africa American Institute**
The Africa-American Institute
Chanin Building
380 Lexington Avenue
New York, NY 10168
Or
1625 Massachusetts Avenue NW,
Suite 400
Washington, DC 20036
Website: http://www.aaionline.org/
Roger Wilkins, chairman
*A nonprofit, multiracial, multiethnic organization whose mission is to promote African development, primarily through education and training.*

**Alliance for Aging Research**
2021 K Street NW, #305
Washington, DC 20006
Website: http://
www.agingresearch.org
John L. Steffens, national chairman
*Organization promoting medical
research on aging.*

**Alliance for Justice**
2000 P Street, NW, Suite 712
Washington, DC 20036
Website: http://www.afj.org/
E-mail: alliance@afj.org
*National association of
environmental, civil rights, mental
health, women's, children's, and
consumer advocacy organizations.*

**Alliance to Save Energy**
1200 18th Street, NW, Suite 900
Washington, DC 20036
Website: http://www.ase.org/
Senator Jeff Bingaman (D-NM),
chairman of the board
*A nonprofit coalition of business,
government, environmental, and
consumer leaders promoting
efficient use of energy.*

**American Civil Liberties Union
(ACLU)**
125 Broad Street
New York, NY 10004
Website: http://www.aclu.org/
Email: aclu@aclu.org
Ira Glasser, executive director
*Advocate of individual rights.*

**American Conservative Union
(ACU)**
1007 Cameron Street
Alexandria, VA 22314
Website: http://
www.conservative.org/
E-mail: acu@conservative.org
David A. Keene, chairman
Thomas R. Katina, executive
director
*The nation's oldest conservative
lobbying organization, ACU's
purpose is to effectively
communicate and advance the
goals and principles of
conservatism.*

**American Council for Capital
Formation**
1750 K Street NW, #400
Washington, DC 20006
Website: http://www.accf.org/
Email: awilkes@mindspring.com
Dr. Charles E. Walker, chairman
and founder.
*A nonprofit, nonpartisan
organization dedicated to the
advocacy of tax and environmental
policies that encourage saving and
investment.*

**American Council on Education**
One Dupont Circle, #800
Washington, DC 20036
Website: http://www.ACENET.edu/
Stanley O. Ikenberry, president
*ACE is dedicated to the belief that
equal education opportunity and a
strong higher education system are
essential cornerstones of a
democratic society.*

**American Council on Science & Health**
1995 Broadway, 16th Fl.
New York, NY, 10023
Website: http://www.asch.org/
E-mail: whelan@acsh.org
Elizabeth M. Whelan, Sc.D.,
M.P.H., president
A. Alan Moghissi, Ph.D., chairman
of the board
*A consumer education consortium
concerned with issues related to
food, nutrition, chemicals,
pharmaceuticals, lifestyle, the
environment and health, ACSH is
an independent, nonprofit, tax-
exempt organization.*

**American Dietetic Association**
216 West Jackson Blvd.
Chicago, Illinois 60606
Website: http://www.eatright.org/
Email: infocenter@eatright.org.
Polly Fitz, chairman

**American Enterprise Institute for
Public Policy Research**
1150 17th St. NW
Washington, DC 20036
Website: http://www.aei.org/
Email: info@aei.org
Christopher C. DeMuth, president
*Dedicated to preserving and
strengthening the foundations of
freedom—limited government,
private enterprise, vital cultural and
political institutions, and a strong
foreign policy and national defense—
through scholarly research, open
debate, and publications.*

**American Farm Bureau Federation**
225 Touhy Ave.
Park Ridge, IL 60068
Or
600 Maryland Ave. SW, #800
Washington, DC 20024
Website: http://www.fb.com/
E-mail: bstallman@fb.org
Bob Stallman, president
*As the national voice of agriculture.
AFBF's mission is to work
cooperatively with the member
state farm bureaus to promote the
image, political influence, quality of
life, and profitability of the nation's
farm and ranch families.*

**American Federation of
Government Employees**
80 F Street NW
Washington, DC 20001
Website: http://www.afge.org/
splash/splash.htm
Bobby L. Harnage, national
president
*The largest federal employee union
representing some 600,000 federal
and D.C. government workers
nationwide.*

**American Federation of State,
County and Municipal Employees
(AFSCME)**
1625 L Street NW
Washington, DC 20036
Website: http://www.afscme.org/
E-mail: webmaster@afscme.org
Gerald W. McEntee, international
president
*AFSCME is the nation's largest
public employee and health care
workers union.*

**American Federation of Teachers (AFT)**
555 New Jersey Ave. NW
Washington, DC 20001
Website: http://www.aft.org/
E-mail: online@aft.org
Sandy Feldman, president

**American Foreign Policy Council**
1521 16th Street NW
Washington, DC 20036
Website: http://www.afpc.org/
Sandy Bostian, program director
*A nonprofit organization dedicated to bringing information to those who make or influence the foreign policy of the United States and to assisting world leaders, particularly in the former USSR, with building democracies and market economies.*

**American Jewish Congress**
2027 Massachusetts Ave. NW
Washington, DC 20036
Website: http://www.ajcongress.org/
E-mail: washrep@ajcongress.org
Jack Rosen, president
*Considered the legal voice of the American Jewish community.*

**American League of Lobbyists**
PO Box 30005
Alexandria, VA 22310
Website: http://www.alldc.org/
E-mail: info@alldc.org
Kenneth E. Feltman, president
*A national organization founded in 1979 dedicated to serving government relations and public affairs professionals.*

**American Legislative Exchange Council**
910 17th Street NW, 5th Floor
Washington, D.C. 20006
Website: http://www.alec.org/main.cfm
Email. info@alec.org
Email: dparde@alec.org
Duane Parde, executive director
*The nation's largest bipartisan, individual membership association of state legislators, with nearly 2,400 members across America.*

**American Library Association**
50 E. Huron Street
Chicago, Illinois 60611
Website: http://www.ala.org/
Email: ala@ala.org
Email: sarahl@nslsilus.org
Sarah Long, president
*The oldest, largest and most influential library association in the world. For more than a century, it has been a leader in defending intellectual freedom and promoting the highest quality library and information services.*

**American Medical Association (AMA)**
515 N. State Street
Chicago, Illinois 60610
Website: http://www.ama-assn.org
Percy Wootton, M.D., president
*Dedicated to promoting the art and science of medicine and the betterment of public health.*

**American Postal Workers Union**
1300 L Street NW
Washington, DC 20005
Website: http://www.apwu.org/
Moe Biller, president
*The largest postal union representing 366,000 union members in the United States.*

**American Public Health Association**
800 I. Street NW
Washington, DC 20001
Website: http://www.apha.org/
E-mail: comments@apha.org
Mohammad N. Akhter, M.D.,
MPH, executive director
*The oldest and largest organization of public health professionals in the world, representing more than 50,000 members from over 50 occupations of public health.*

**American Rivers**
1025 Vermont Ave. #720
Washington, D.C. 20005
Website: http://www.amrivers.org/
E-mail: amrivers@amrivers.org
Rebecca R. Wodder, president
Amy Butler, associate director of foundation relations
*National river-conservation organization whose mission is to protect and restore America's river systems and to foster a river stewardship ethic.*

**American Security Council**
1155 15th St. NW, #1101
Washington, D.C. 20005

**American Tort Reform Association**
1850 M Street NW, Suite 1095
Washington, D.C. 20036
Website: http://www.atra.org/
E-mail: sjoyce@atra.org
Sherman Joyce, president
*Founded in 1986, it is a broad based, bipartisan coalition of more than 300 businesses, corporations, municipalities, associations, and professional firms who support civil justice reform*

**The Association of Trial Lawyers of America**
1050 31st Street NW
Washington, DC 20007
Website: http://www.atla.org/
E-mail: help@atlahq.org.
*Promotes justice and fairness for injured persons, safeguards victims' rights—particularly the right to trial by jury.*

**American Veterinary Medical Association**
1931 North Meacham Road—Suite 100
Schaumburg, IL 60173
Website: http://www.avma.org/
E-mail: help@atlahq.org
Dr. Joseph Kinnarney, vice president
*The objective of the association is to advance the science and art of veterinary medicine, including its relationship to public health, biological science, and agriculture.*

**American-Arab Anti-Discrimination Committee (ADC)**
4201 Connecticut Ave. NW, #500
Washington, DC 20008
Website: http://www.adc.org/
E-mail: adc@adc.org
Email: hmaksoud@adc.org
Hala Maksoud, president
*Civil rights organization committed to defending the rights of people of Arab descent and promoting their rich cultural heritage.*

**Americans for Democratic Action (ADA)**
1625 K Street NW, #210
Washington, DC 20006
Website: http://adaction.org/
E-mail: adaction@Ix.netcom.com
*The nation's oldest independent liberal political organization, it pioneered the development and promotion of a national liberal agenda of public policy formulation and action.*

**Americans for Indian Opportunity**
681 Juniper Hill Road
Bernalillo, NM 87004
Website: http://Indiannet.indian.com/aio.html
Email: *lharris@unm.edu*

**American Society Of Cinematographers (ASC)**
PO Box 2230
Hollywood, CA 90078
Website: http://www.cinematographer.com/
Email: editor@theasc.com
Stephen Pizzello, editor

**Amnesty International, USA**
322 8th Avenue
New York, NY 10001
Website: http://www.amnesty-usa.org/
E-mail: aimember@aiusa.org
*Founded in 1961, Amnesty International is a grassroots activist organization whose one-million strong members are dedicated to freeing prisoners of conscience, to gaining fair trials for political prisoners, to ending torture, political killings and "disappearances," and to abolishing the death penalty throughout the world. Amnesty International USA (AIUSA) is the U.S. section of this international human rights movement.*

**Anti-Defamation League (ADL)**
823 United Nations Plaza
New York, NY 10017
Website: http://www.adl.org/
E-mail: webmaster@adl.org
Abraham H. Foxman, national director
*Fights anti-Semitism through programs and services that counteract hatred, prejudice, and bigotry.*

**Asian American Journalists Association**
1182 Market Street, Suite 320
San Francisco, CA 94102
Website: http://www.aaja.org/
E-mail: National@aaja.org
Rene Astuidillo, executive director
*Seeks to increase employment of Asian American print and broadcast journalists. Assists high school and college students pursuing journalism careers. Encourages fair, sensitive and accurate news coverage of Asian American issues, and provides support for Asian American journalists.*

**Associated Builders and Contractors**
1300 N. 17th Street, 8th Floor
Roslyn, VA 22209
Website: http://www.abc.org
Robert P. Hepner, Executive vice president
*A national trade association representing over 21,000 contractors, subcontractors, material suppliers and related firms from across the country and from all specialties in the construction industry.*

**Association for Community Based Education**
1805 Florida Ave. NW
Washington, DC 20009
*The ACBE's membership is comprised of community activist organizations, including many that operate literacy projects.*

**Association for the Advancement of Mexican Americans**
204 Clifton
Houston, TX 77083
Website: http://www.neosoft.com/
~aama/
Email: aama@neosoft.com
Matt Miller, president
*Committed to advancing at-risk and disadvantaged youth and families with an array of innovative programs of excellence that provide alternative education, social services, and community development.*

**Association of Independent Commercial Producers (AICP)**
11 East 22nd St, 4th Fl.
New York, NY 10010
Website: http://www.aicp.com/
Email: mattm@aicp.com
Matt Miller, president
*Represents commercial production companies.*

**Ayn Rand Institute**
The Center for the Advancement of Objectivism
4640 Admiralty Way, Suite 406
Marina del Rey, CA 90292
Website: http://www.aynrand.org/
Email: mail@aynrand.org
Leonard Peikoff, founder
*Seeks to promote and expound Rand's philosophy (Objectivism) with various resources and activities.*

**Bread for the World/BFW Institute**
1100 Wayne Ave., #1000
Silver Spring, MD 20910
Website: http://www.bread.org/
*Citizens' movement seeking "justice" for the world's hungry people by lobbying our nation's decision makers.*

**Brechner Center for Freedom of Information**
PO Box 118400
3208 Weimer Hall
University of Florida
Gainesville, FL 32611
Website: http://www.jou.ufl.edu/
brechner/brochure.htm
E-mail: bchamber@jou.ufl.edu
Sandra F. Chanve, Director
*A unit of the College of Journalism and Communications at the University of Florida relied upon by media organizations nationwide for information about media law developments in Florida.*

**Business-Industry Political Action Committee (BIPAC)**
888 Sixteenth St. NW
Washington, DC 20006
Website: http://www.bipac.org/
E-mail: info@bipac.org
*An independent, bipartisan organization, founded in 1963. Through its Political Action Fund, BIPAC works to elect pro-business candidates to Congress. BIPAC's Business Institute for Political Analysis carries out extensive programs of political analysis, research, and communication on campaigns and elections and fosters business participation in the political process.*

## Campaign for an Effective Crime Policy
514 Tenth St., NW
Washington, DC 20004
Website: http://www.crimepolicy.org
E-mail: staf@crimepolicy.org
*Launched in 1992 by a group of criminal justice leaders, the Campaign for an Effective Crime Policy is an organization of progressive criminal justice professionals, academics, and community leaders working together to build safer neighborhoods and reduce crime through policies based on sound information and research—not sound bites and political rhetoric.*

## Campaign for U.N. Reform
420 7th St. SE, Suite C
Washington, DC 20003
Website: http://www.cunr.org/
E-mail: CUNR@cunr.org

## CARE
151 Ellis St.
Atlanta, GA 30303
Website: http://www.care.org/
E-mail: Doherty@care.org or info@care.org
*CARE's programs seek to help poor families obtain a basic level of livelihood security. CARE seeks a world of tolerance and social justice, where people have overcome poverty and live in dignity and security.*

## The Carter Center
453 Freedom Pkwy.
Atlanta, GA 30307
Website: http://www.cartercenter.org/home.html
John Hardman, M.D., Executive Director
*In partnership with Emory University, it is guided by a fundamental commitment to human rights, wages peace by bringing warring parties to the negotiating table, monitoring elections, safeguarding human rights, and building strong democracies through economic development.*

## Cato Institute
1000 Massachusetts Ave. NW
Washington, DC 20001
Website: http://www.cato.org/
E-mail: cato@cato.org
Edward H. Crane, President and CEO
*Promoting public policy based on limited government, free markets, individual liberty, and peace.*

## Center for Defense Information
1779 Massachusetts Ave., N.W.
Washington DC 20036
Website: http://www.cdi.org
E-mail: info@cdi.org
Eugene J. Carroll Jr., USN (Ret.)
Deputy Director: Rear Admiral
*A private, nongovernmental, research organization. Its directors and staff believe that strong social, economic, political and military components and a healthy environment contribute equally to the nation's security.*

**Center for Democracy and Technology**
1634 I St. NW, Suite #1100
Washington, DC 20006
Website: http://www.cdt.org/
E-mail: webmaster@cdt.org
E-mail: jberman@cdt.org
Jerry Berman, Executive Director
*A nonprofit public interest organization based in Washington, D.C. CDT works for public policies that advance civil liberties and democratic values in new computer and communications technologies.*

**Center for Democratic Renewal and Education, Inc.**
PO Box 50469
Atlanta, GA 30302
E-mail: cdr@igc.apc.org
*Founded in 1979 as the National Anti-Klan Network, the Center for Democratic Renewal and Education is a multi-racial organization that advances the vision of a democratic, diverse, and just society free of racism and bigotry. It helps communities combat groups, movements, and government practices that promote hatred and bigotry and is committed to public policies based on equity and justice.*

**Center for Ethics, Capital Markets, Political Economy**
PO Box 1845 University Station
Charlottesville, VA 22903
Website: http://
www.iath.virginia.edu/cecmpe/
E-mail: cecmpe@
jefferson.village.virginia.edu
E. N. Weaver Jr., M.D., Sr. Amata
Miller, OP, Ph.D., John D.
Feldmann, Directors
*A nonprofit organization established in 1994 to provide a discussion forum and information resource for persons who believe that moral concerns should be taken into account in economic and political thinking.*

**Center for Governmental Studies**
California Commission on
Campaign Financing
10951 W. Pico Blvd., #206
Los Angeles, CA 90064
Webpage: http://www.cgs.org/
E-mail: center@cgs.org
*Its goal is to enhance the quality and quantity of governmental information available to citizens through the use of modern communications technologies and to expand the opportunities of citizens to participate in the elective and governmental processes.*

**Center for Law and Social Policy**
1616 P St. NW, #150
Washington, DC 20036
Website: http://www.cgs.org/
E-mail: info@clasp.org
*Education, policy research, and advocacy organization seeking to improve the economic conditions of low-income families and secure access to our civil justice system for the poor.*

**Center for Policy Alternatives**
1875 Connecticut Ave. NW, #710
Washington, DC 20009
Website: http://www.cfpa.org/
Linda Tarr-Whelan, President and
Chair
*A nonprofit, nonpartisan public
policy and leadership development
center devoted to community-
based solutions that strengthen
families and communities.*

**Center for Research on Women**
Wellesley College
106 Central St.
Wellesley, MA 02181-8259
Website: http://www.wellesley.edu/
WCW/crwsub.html
Pamela Baker-Webber
E-mail: pbaker@wellesley.edu
*An interdisciplinary community of
scholars are engaged in research,
programs, and publications which
examine the lives of women, men,
and children in a changing world.*

**Center for Responsive Politics**
1101 14th St., NW Suite #1030
Washington, DC 20005
Website: http://
www.opensecrets.org/
E-mail: info@crp.org
Paul Hoff, Chairman
*A nonprofit, nonpartisan
organization that specializes in the
study of Congress and particularly
the role that money plays in its
elections and actions.*

**Center for Science in the Public
Interest**
1875 Connecticut Ave. NW, #300
Washington, DC 20009
Website: http://www.cspinet.org/
E-mail: cspi@cspinet.org
Michael F. Jacobson, Executive
Director
*A nonprofit education and
advocacy organization that focuses
on improving the safety and
nutritional quality of our food
supply.*

**Center for Strategic and
Budgetary Assessments**
1730 Rhode Island Ave., NW, Suite
#912
Washington, DC 20036
Website:http://www.csbaonline.org/
E-mail: info@csbaonline.org
James G. Roche, Chair
*An independent research institute
established to promote innovative
thinking about defense planning
and investment for the 21st
century.*

**Center for the New West**
600 World Trade Center
1625 Broadway, #600
Denver, CO 80202
Website: http://www.newwest.org/
Kara Steele, Executive Director
E-mail: ksteele@newwest.org
*Policy research institute focusing
on trade, technology, education,
and the enterprise economy.*

**Center for the Study of Popular Culture**
PO Box 67398
Los Angeles, CA 90067
Website: http://www.cspc.org/
E-mail: info@cspc.org
Peter Collier and David Horowitz, founders
*They are nationally known writers, editors and political commentators whose intellectual development has evolved from early, influential support for the New Left and Black Panther movements to the forefront of neoconservatism.*

**Center for Voting and Democracy**
6930 Carroll Ave., Suite #901
Takoma Park, MD 20912
Website: http://www.igc.apc.org/cvd/
E-mail: FairVote@compuserve.com
Robert Richie, Executive Director
John B. Anderson, President
*Nonprofit organization based in Washington, D.C. The Center educates the public about the impact of different voting systems on voter turnout, representation, accountability, and the influence of money in elections.*

**Center for Women's Policy Studies**
1211 Connecticut Ave., N.W., Suite #312
Washington, DC 20036
Website: http://www.centerwomenpolicy.org/
E-mail: tchin@centerwomenpolicy.org
Kathleen Stoll, Policy Analyst
*A national nonprofit, multiethnic, and multicultural feminist policy research and advocacy institution. The Center addresses cutting-edge issues that have significant future implications for women.*

**Center on Budget and Policy Priorities**
820 First St. N.E., Suite #510
Washington, DC 20002
Website: http://www.cbpp.org/
E-mail: bazie@cbpp.org
Robert Greenstein, Founder and Executive Director
*Conducts research and analysis on a range of government policies and programs, with an emphasis on those affecting low- and moderate-income people.*

**Child Welfare League of America**
440 1st St. NW, #310
Washington, DC 20001
Website: http://www.cwla.org/
E-mail: webweaver@cwla.org
Richard H. Fleming, President
*Membership association of public and private nonprofit agencies that serve and advocate for abused, neglected, and otherwise vulnerable children.*

**Citizen Action**
1750 Rhode Island Ave. NW, #403
Washington, DC 20036
Website: http://www.fas.org/pub/gen/ggg/citizen.html
*A nationwide consumer and environmental organization that addresses issues on behalf of its members.*

**Citizens Against Government Waste**
1301 Connecticut Ave. NW, #400
Washington, DC 20036
Website: http://www.cagw.org/
E-mail: webmaster@cagw
Thomas A. Schatz, President
*A private, nonpartisan, nonprofit organization dedicated to educating Americans about the waste, mismanagement, and inefficiency in the federal government.*

## Citizens Committee for the Right to Keep and Bear Arms
600 Pennsylvania Ave. SE, #205
Washington, DC 20003
Website: http://www.ccrkba.org/
E-mail: info@ccrkba.org
Alan Gottlieb, President
*Organizat ion dedicated to preserving and protecting the Second Amendment.*

## Citizens for a Sound Economy
1250 H St. NW, #700
Washington, DC 20005-3908
Website: http://www.cse.org/cse
Paul Beckner, President
*Fights for lower taxes and less regulation.*

## Citizens for Tax Justice
1311 L St. NW, #400
Washington, DC 20005
Website: http://www.ctj.org/
E-mail: mattg@ctj.org/
Robert S. McIntyre, Director
*A nonpartisan research and advocacy organization working for a fair, progressive tax system.*

## Citizen Information Center
380 A Ave., PO Box 369
Lake Oswego, OR 97034
Website: http://
www.ci.oswego.or.us/citizen/
citizen.htm
E-mail:
webmistress@ci.oswego.or.us
*Organization which helps citizens of Lake Oswego, Oregon, solve city-related problems.*

## Citizens' Commission on Civil Rights
2000 M St. NW, #400
Washington, DC 20036
Website: http://www.cccr.org/
E-mail: citizens@cccr.org
Corrine M. Yu, Director and Counsel
*Established to monitor civil rights policies and practices of the federal government and seek ways to accelerate progress in the area of civil rights.*

## Clean Air Trust
1625 K St. NW, #725
Washington, DC 20006
Website: http://
www.cleanairtrust.org/
E-mail: frank@cleanairtrust.org
The Hon. Robert T. Stafford,
Honorary Co-Chairman
*Environmental organization*

## Clean Water Action
4455 Connecticut Ave. N.W., Suite #A300
Washington, DC 20008
Website: http://
www.cleanwateraction.org/
E-mail: cwa@cleanwater.org
David Zwick, President
*Organizes strong grassroots groups, coalitions, and campaigns to protect our environment, health, economic well-being, and community quality of life.*

## Coalition on Human Needs (CHN)
1700 K St., NW, Suite #1150
Washington, DC 20006
Website: http://www.chn.org/
Stuart P. Campbell, Executive Director
*An alliance of over 100 national organizations working together to promote public policies which address the needs of low-income and other vulnerable populations.*

## Coalition to Stop Gun Violence
1000 16th St., N.W., Suite #603
Washington, DC 20036
Website: http://www.gunfree.org/
Michael Beard, President
*Gun ban organization*

## Commission on Presidential Debates
1200 New Hampshire N.W., Box 445
Washington, DC 20036
Website: http://www.debates.org/
Frank J. Fahrenkopf Jr. and Paul G. Kirk Jr., co-chairmen
*Established in 1987 to ensure that debates, as a permanent part of every general election, provide the best possible information to viewers and listeners. Its primary purpose is to sponsor and produce debates for the United States presidential and vice presidential candidates and to undertake research and educational activities relating to the debates.*

## Committee for a Responsible Federal Budget
220 1/2 E St. NE
Washington, DC 20002
Website: http://www.network-democracy.org/social-security/bb/whc/crfb.html
E-mail: crfb@aol.com
Bill Frenzel and Timothy Penny, co-chairmen
*A bipartisan, nonprofit educational organization committed to educating the public regarding the budget process and particular issues that have significant fiscal policy impact.*

## Committee for Study of the American Electorate
421 New Jersey Ave. SE
Washington, DC 20003
Website: http://tap.epn.org/csae/
Maurice Rosenblatt, President
*A Washington-based, nonpartisan, nonprofit, tax exempt research institution with a primary focus on issues surrounding citizen engagement in politics.*

## Committee to Advocate Texas Sovereignty (CATS)
5303 Allum Rd.
Houston, TX 77045
Website: http://www.texassovereignty.org/intro.html
E-mail: JDavidson@cbjd.net
Jim Davidson, co-founder
*Organization that believes Texas should be sovereign and independent of the United States.*

## Common Cause
1250 Connecticut Ave., NW
Washington, DC 20036
Website: http://www.commoncause.org/
John Gardner, Founder
*A nonprofit, nonpartisan citizen's lobbying organization promoting open, honest, and accountable government.*

## Community Nutrition Institute
910 17th St. NW, #413
Washington, DC 20006
Website: http://www.unidial.com/~cni/
Rodney E. Leonard, Executive Director and Founder
E-mail: relcni@ecenet.com
*A leading advocate for consumer protection food program development and management and sound federal diet and health policies.*

**Compassion in Dying**
PMB 415, 6312 SW Capitol Hwy.
Portland, OR 97201
Website: http://
www.CompassionInDying.org
E-mail:
info@compassionindying.org
Barbara Coombs Lee, PA, FNP, JD,
Executive Director
*An organization which believes in
the right to die with dignity.*

**Competitive Enterprise Institute**
1001 Connecticut Ave. NW, #1250
Washington, DC 20036
Website: http://www.cei.org/
E-mail: eduke@cei.org
E-mail: info@cei.org
Emily Duke, Director of
Development
*A pro-market, public policy group
committed to advancing the
principles of free enterprise and
limited government.*

**Computer Professionals for Social
Responsibility**
PO Box 717
Palo Alto, CA 94302
Website: http://www.cpsr.org/
E-mail: cpsr@cpsr.org or
webmaster@cpsr.org
*A public-interest alliance of
computer scientists and others
concerned about the impact of
computer technology on society.*

**Concerned Women for America**
1015 Fifteenth St., N.W. Suite
#1100
Washington, DC 20005
Website: http://www.cwfa.org/
Beverly LaHaye, Chairman and
Founder
*A national politically active
women's organization promoting
Christian values and morality in
family life and public policy.*

**Concord Coalition**
1819 H St., NW, Suite #800
Washington, DC 20006
Website: http://
www.concordcoalition.org/
E-mail:
concord@concordcoalition.org
*A nonprofit, charitable
organization. Nearly 200,000
citizens nationwide have joined
Concord's movement for a strong
economic future for all generations.
They are changing the political
calculus by standing up for the
general interest—for an end to
federal budget deficits, for
equitable Social Security and
Medicare reform, for stronger long-
term economic growth and for a
higher standard of living for future
generations of Americans.*

**Congressional Accountability
Project**
Connecticut Ave. NW, Suite #3A
Washington, DC 20009
Website: http://www.essential.org/
orgs/CAP/CAP.html
E-mail: cap@essential.org
Gary Ruskin, Director
*Congressional watchdog
organization*

**Congressional Budget Office**
U.S. Congress
2nd and D Streets SW
Washington, DC 20515
Website: http://www.cbo.gov/
Daniel L. Crippen, Director
*Created by the Congressional
Budget and Impoundment Control
Act of 1974. CBO's mission is to
provide the Congress with
objective, timely, nonpartisan
analyses needed for economic and
budget decisions and with the
information and estimates required
for the Congressional budget
process.*

**Congressional Quarterly, Inc.**
1414 22nd St. NW
Washington, DC 20037
Website: http://www.cq.com/
E-mail: mailto:webmaster@cq.com
Andrew Barnes, Chairman
*Congressional Quarterly is a world-
class provider of information on
government, politics, and public
policy.*

**Conservative Caucus**
450 Maple Ave. East
Vienna, VA 22180
Website: http://
www.conservativeusa.org
E-mail:
webmaster@conservativeusa.org
Howard Phillips, Founder and
Chairman
*Dedicated to educating citizens
about how we must take action to
restore America to its
Constitutionally limited
government.*

**Constitution Society, The**
1731 Howe Ave., #370
Sacramento, CA 95825
Or
6900 San Pedro, #147-230
San Antonio, TX 78216
Website: http://
www.constitution.org/
*A private nonprofit organization
dedicated to research and public
education on the principles of
constitutional republican
government. It publishes
documentation, engages in
litigation, and organizes local
citizens groups to work for reform.
This organization was founded in
response to the growing concern
that noncompliance with the U.S.
Constitution and most state
constitutions is creating a crisis of
legitimacy that threatens freedom
and civil rights.*

**Consumer Energy Council of
America Research Foundation**
2000 L St. NW, #802
Washington, DC 20036
Website: http://www.cecarf.org
*CECA is committed to constructive
involvement of government and
private organizations in broad
educational initiatives and in the
creation of self-sustaining and
socially responsible markets for
essential services.*

**Consumer Federation of America**
1424 16th St. NW, #604
Washington, DC 20036
Website: http://
www.stateandlocal.org/
*Founded in 1972 as a private,
nonprofit, 501(c)(3) research and
education organization to
complement the work of
Consumer Federation of America,
the Foundation has a threefold
mission: to assist state and local
organizations, to provide
information to the public on
consumer issues, and to conduct
consumer research projects.*

**Consumers Union**
101 Truman Ave.
Yonkers, NY 10703
Website: http://
www.consumersunion.org/
Naomi Meyer, Fellow for
Economic Justice
*Its mission has been to test
products, inform the public, and
protect consumers.*

**Council of State Governments**
2760 Research Park Dr.
PO Box 11910
Lexington, KY 40578
Website: http://www.csg.org
E-mail: info@csg.org
Paul Patton, President Governor
*Founded on the premise that the
states are the best sources of
insight and innovation, CSG
provides a network for identifying
and sharing ideas with state
leaders.*

**Council on Competitiveness**
1500 K St. N.W., Suite #850
Washington, DC 20005
Website: http://www.compete.org/
John Yochelson, President
*Shapes the national debate on
competitiveness by concentrating
on a few critical issues. These
issues include technological
innovation, workforce
development, and the
benchmarking of U.S. economic
performance against other
countries.*

**Council on Foreign Relations**
The Harold Pratt House
58 East 68th St.
New York, NY 10021
Website: http://www.cfr.org
E-mail: ppappachan@cfr.org
Peter G. Peterson, Chairman of the
Board
*Founded in 1921 by businessmen,
bankers and lawyers determined to
keep the United States engaged in
the world. Today, the Council is
composed of men and women
from all walks of international life
and from all parts of America,
dedicated to the belief that the
nation's peace and prosperity are
firmly linked to that of the rest of
the world.*

**Dana**
4500 Dorr St., PO Box 1000
Toledo, OH 43697
Website: http://www.dana.com
Joseph M. Magliochetti, Chairman,
President, and CEO
*Motor vehicles and parts.*

## Death with Dignity Education Center

1818 N St., NW Suite #450
Washington, DC 20036
Website: http://
www.deathwithdignity.org/
E-mail:
admin@deathwithdignity.org
Estelle Rogers, Executive Director
*Promotes a comprehensive, humane, responsive system of care for terminally ill patients.*

## Defenders of Wildlife

1101 14th St. NW, #1400
Washington, DC 20005
Website: http://www.defenders.org/
E-mail: webmaster@defenders.org
Alan R. Pilkington, Chairman Board of Directors
*Dedicated to the protection of all native wild animals and plants in their natural communities.*

## Democratic Congressional Campaign Committee

430 S. Capitol St. SE
Washington, DC 20003
Website: http://www.dccc.org/
Patrick Kennedy, Chairman
*Devoted to electing a Democratic majority in the House of Representatives.*

## Democratic Freedom Caucus

PO Box 9466
Baltimore, MD 21228
Website: http://www.progress.org/dfc/
E-mail: romike@crosslink.net
*A "progressive libertarian" group within the Democratic Party.*

## Democratic National Committee

430 S. Capitol St. SE
Washington, DC 20003
Website: http://www.democrats.org/index.html
Joe Andrew, National Chair
*The national party organization for the Democratic Party of the United States*

## Democratic Senatorial Campaign Committee

430 S. Capitol St. SE
Washington, DC 20003
Website: http://www.dscc.org/
E-mail: info@dscc.org
Senator Robert Torricelli, Chairman
*A national party committee formed by the Democratic members of the U.S. Senate to raise funds for Democratic U.S. Senate candidates throughout the country.*

## Drug Policy Foundation

925 Ninth Ave.
New York, NY 10019
Website: http://www.drugpolicy.org/
E-mail: webfeedback@dpf.org
E-mail: enadelmann@sorosny.org
Ethan Nadelmann, Director
*An independent, nonprofit organization with over 20,000 members that publicizes alternatives to current drug strategies. DPF believes that the drug war is not working.*

**Eagle Forum**
316 Pennsylvania Ave., Suite #203
Washington, DC 20003
Website: http://
www.eagleforum.org/
E-mail: eagle@eagleforum.org
Phyllis Schlafly, President
*Stands for the fundamental right of
parents to guide the education of
their own children.*

**Eagleton Institute on Politics**
Rutgers University
191 Ryders Lane
New Brunswick, NJ 08901
Website: http://
www.rci.rutgers.edu/~eagleton/
E-mail: eagleton@rci.rutgers.edu
E-mail: rmandel@rci.rutgers.edu
Ruth B. Mandel, Director
*Develops new knowledge and
understanding of emerging topics
and themes in American politics
and government in order to
encourage more responsive and
effective leadership.*

**East-West Center**
1601 East-West Rd.
Honolulu, HI 96848
Website: http://
www.ewc.hawaii.edu/
E-mail:
ewcinfo@EastWestCenter.org
Daniel Berman, President, East-
West Center Association
*The East-West Center is an
internationally recognized
education and research
organization established by the
U.S. Congress to strengthen
understanding and relations
between the United States and the
countries of the Asia Pacific region.*

**Economic Policy Institute**
1660 L St. NW, Suite 1200
Washington, DC 20036
Website: http://www.epinet.org/
E-mail: epi@epinet.org
E-mail: jfaux@epinet.org
Jeff Faux, President
*A nonprofit, nonpartisan think tank
that seeks to broaden the public
debate about strategies to achieve
a prosperous and fair economy.*

**Electronic Frontier Foundation**
1550 Bryant, #725
San Francisco, CA 94117
Website: http://www.eff.org
E-mail: eff@eff.org or info@eff.org
E-mail: ssteele@eff.org
Shari Steele, Executive Director and
President
*A nonprofit, nonpartisan
organization working in the public
interest to protect fundamental civil
liberties, including privacy and
freedom of expression in the arena
of computers and the Internet.*

**Empower America**
1701 Pennsylvania Ave. N.W.,
Suite 900
Washington, DC 20006
Website: http://www.empower.org/
E-mail: jeffk@empower.org
William J. Bennett, Co-Director
E-mail: empower1@empower.org
Jack Kemp, Co-Director
E-mail: jfkemp@empower.org
Josette Shiner, President
*Encourages public policy solutions
that maximize free markets and
individual responsibility.*

**Environmental. Defense Fund**
257 Park Ave. South
New York, NY 10010
Website: http://www.edf.org/
E-mail:
Contact@
environmentaldefense.org
Fred Krupp, Executive Director
*Representing 300,000 members,*
*combines science, economics and*
*law to find economically*
*sustainable solutions to*
*environmental problems.*

**Environmental Health Center—
Dallas**
8345 Walnut Hill Lane, Suite #220
Dallas, TX 75231
Website: http://www.ehcd.com/
E-mail: cg@ehcd.com
*Diagnosis/treatment for individuals*
*with allergy and environmental-*
*related illnesses.*

**Environmental Law Institute**
1616 P St. NW, #200
Washington, DC 20036
Website: http://www.eli.org/
J. William Futrell, President
*Working to advance environmental*
*protection by improving law, policy*
*and management.*

**Ethics and Public Policy Center**
1015 15th St. NW, #900
Washington, DC 20005
Website: http://www.eppc.org/
E-mail: ethics@eppc.org
Elliott Abrams, President
*Studies the interconnections*
*between religious faith, political*
*practice, and social values.*

**Euthanasia Research and
Guidance Organization (ERGO!)**
24829 Norris Lane
Junction City, OR 97448
Website: http://www.FinalExit.org
E-mail: ergo@efn.org
Derek Humphry, Founder and
President
*Organization that believes in the*
*right to die.*

**F.E.A.R. Foundation**
PO Box 33985
Washington, DC 20033
Website: http://www.fear.org/
E-mail: powerhit@fli.net
Robert Bauman, Member Board of
Directors
*Forfeiture Endangers American*
*Rights is a national nonprofit*
*organization dedicated to reform of*
*federal and state asset forfeiture*
*laws to restore due process and*
*protect the property rights of*
*innocent citizens.*

**Federal Bureau of Investigation
(FBI)**
J. Edgar Hoover Building
935 Pennsylvania Ave., N.W.
Washington, DC 20535
Website: http://www.fbi.gov
Louis J. Freeh, Director of the FBI

**Federal Election Commission
(FEC)**
999 E St. NW
Washington, DC 20463
Website: http://www.fec.gov/
E-mail: webmaster@fec.gov
Lynne A. McFarland, Inspector
General
*Administers and enforces the*
*Federal Election Campaign Act*
*(FECA).*

**The Federalist Society**
1015 18th St. NW, Suite #425
Washington, DC 20036
Website: http://www.fed-soc.org/
E-mail: fedsoc@radix.net
Steven G. Calabresi, National Co-Chairman
David M. McIntosh, National Co-Chairman
Eugene B. Meyer, Executive Director
E-mail: ebmeyer@fed-soc.org
*A group of conservatives and libertarians interested in the current state of the legal order. It is founded on the principles that the state exists to preserve freedom, that the separation of governmental powers is central to our Constitution, and that it is emphatically the province and duty of the judiciary to say what the law is, not what it should be. The Society seeks both to promote an awareness of these principles and to further their application through its activities.*

**Federation for American Immigration Reform**
1666 Connecticut Ave. NW, #400
Washington, DC 20009
Website: http://www.fairus.org/
E-mail: info@fairus.org
Sharon Barnes, Chairman, Board of Directors
*A national, membership-based, educational organization with 70,000 members across the country working to help the American public convince Congress that our nation's immigration laws must be reformed.*

**Fleming**
6301 Waterford Blvd.
Oklahoma City, OK 73126
Website: http://www.fleming.com
Marks S. Hansen, chairman and CEO
*Wholesalers, food products*

**Food Research and Action Center**
1875 Connecticut Ave. NW, #540
Washington, DC 20009
Website: http://www.frac.org/
E-mail: webmaster@frac.org
Matthew E. Melmed, Chair, Board of Directors
*Working to improve public policies to eradicate hunger and undernutrition in the United States.*

**Ford Foundation**
320 East 43rd St.
New York, NY 10017
Website: http://www.fordfound.org
Paul A. Allaire, Chairman, Board of Trustees
*Grant organization that supports activities that "strengthen democratic values, reduce poverty and injustice, promote international cooperation, and advance human achievement."*

**Foundation for Biomedical Research**
818 Connecticut Ave. NW, #303
Washington, DC 20006
Website: http://www.fbresearch.org/
E-mail: info@fbresearch.org
Frankie Trull, President
*A nonprofit organization that focuses on the proper use of animals in medical research.*

**Foundation for Economic Education (FEE)**
30 S. Broadway
Irvington-on-Hudson, NY 10533
Website: http://www.fee.org/
E-mail: freeman@fee.org
Dr. Donald J. Boudreaux, President
*Nonpolitical, educational champion of private property, the free-market, and limited government.*

**Freedom Forum**
1101 Wilson Blvd.
Arlington, VA 22209
Website: http://
www.freedomforum.org/
E-mail: news@freedomforum.org
Charles L. Overby, Chairman and CEO
*A nonpartisan, international foundation dedicated to free press, free speech, and free spirit for all people. Its mission is to help the public and the news media understand one another better.*

**Freedom Forum Media Studies Center**
580 Madison Ave., 42nd Floor
New York, NY 10022
Website: http://
www.freedomforum.org/
whoweare/media.asp
E-mail: mfitzsi@mediastudies.org
Robert H. Giles, Director
*The Media Studies Center is the nation's premier media think tank devoted to improving understanding of media issues by the press and the public.*

**Friends Committee on National Legislation**
245 2nd St. NE
Washington, DC 20002
Website: www.fcnl.org
E-mail: fcnl@fcnl.org
Joe Volk, Executive Secretary
*A nationwide network of thousands of Quakers Lobby bringing the testimonies of Friends to bear on a wide range of national legislation regarding peace and social justice issues.*

**Friends of the Earth**
1025 Vermont Ave. NW
Washington, DC 20005
Website: http://www.foe.org
E-mail: foe@foe.org
Charles Secrett, Executive Director
*The largest international network of environmental groups in the world, represented in 52 countries.*

**Fuel Cells 2000**
1625 K St. NW, Suite #725
Washington, DC 20006
Website: http://www.fuelcells.org/
E-mail: webmaster@fuelcells.org
Bernadette Geyer, Director
*A private, nonprofit, educational organization providing information to policy makers, the media, and the public and supporting the early utilization of fuel cells by such means as pilot projects and government purchases.*

**Fully Informed Jury Association (FIJA)**
PO Box 59
Helmville, MT 59843
Website: http://www.fija.org/
E-mail: WebForeman@fija.org
*A nonprofit association dedicated to education of all Americans about their rights, powers, and responsibilities as trial jurors. FIJA seeks to restore the traditional trial by jury and protect it from further incursions. FIJA believes that the jury is not only a dispenser of justice for the accused, but also crucial check and balance in our system of government. The power of the jury to judge not only the evidence, but also the merits of the law itself is central to its proper functioning as a judicial and political institution.*

**Fund for Animals**
200 W. 57th St.
New York, NY 10019
Website: http://www.fund.org/home/
E-mail: fundinfo@fund.org
Cleveland Amory, Founder and President
Michael Markarian, Executive Vice President
E-mail: mmarkarian@fund.org
*Animal activist organization*

**Future of Freedom Foundation**
11350 Random Hills Rd., Suite #800
Fairfax, VA 22030
Website: http://www.fff.org
E-mail: freedom@fff.org
Jacob G. Hornberger, President
*Advances the libertarian philosophy by providing an uncompromising moral and economic case for individual liberty, free markets, private property, and limited government.*

**International Ghost Hunters Society**
12885 SW North Rim Rd.
Crooked River Ranch, OR 97760
Website: http://www.ghostweb.com/
E-mail: ghostweb@ghostweb.com
Rev. Dave Oester and Rev. Sharon Gill, Ghost Hunters
*A worldwide paranormal research organization dedicated to the study of ghosts and poltergeists phenomena known as the spirits of the dead.*

**Gray Panthers**
733 15th St., NW Suite #437
Washington, DC 20005
Website: http://www.graypanthers.org/
E-mail: info@graypanthers.org
*Founded in 1970 by social activist Maggie Kuhn, Gray Panthers believe that all Americans should benefit from our country's abundance.*

**Greenpeace**
702 H St. NW
Washington, DC 20001
Website: http://www.greenpeaceusa.org/
E-mail: info@wdc.greenpeace.org
E-mail: Craig.Culp@wdc.greenpeace.org
Craig Culp, Greenpeace Media Coordinator
*Worldwide environmental group*

**The Greens/Green Party USA**
PO Box 1134
Lawrence, MA 01842
Website: http://www.greenparty.org/page3.html
E-mail: andyg@greens.org
Tamara Trejo, Clearinghouse Coordinator
*Environmental political party*

**Gun Owners of America**
8001 Forbes Pl., Suite #102
Springfield, VA 22151
Website: http://
www.gunowners.org/
E-mail: goamail@gunowners.org
Larry Pratt, Executive Director
*Group devoted to protecting the Second Amendment*

**Handgun Control, Inc.**
1225 I St. NW, Suite #1100
Washington, DC 20005
Website: http://
www.handguncontrol.org/
Sarah Brady, Chariman
*Gun control organization*

**The H. John Heinz III Center for Science, Economics and the Environment**
1001 Pennsylvania Ave., NW Suite #735 South
Washington, DC 20004
Website: http://www.heinzctr.org/
E-mail: info@heinzctr.org
G. William Miller, Chairman, Board of Trustees
*A nonprofit organization devoted to collaborative research on environmental problems. Its mission is to create and disseminate nonpartisan policy options for solving environmental problems.*

**Hemlock Society USA**
PO Box 101810
Denver, CO 80250
Website: http://www.hemlock.org/
hemlock/
E-mail: hemlock@privatei.com
Faye Girsh, President
*A right-to-die organization*

**High Frontier, Inc.**
2800 Shirlington Rd., #405A
Arlington, VA 22206
Website: http://
www.highfrontier.org/
E-mail: hifront@erols.com
Ambassador Henry F. (Hank) Cooper, Chairman of the Board
*Its mission is "to ensure the nation is protected against ballistic missile attack."*

**Hoover Institution**
Stanford University
Palo Alto, CA 94305
Website: http://www.hoover.org/
Peyton M. Lake, Chairman
Peter B. Bedford, Vice Chairman
*The principles of individual, economic, and political freedom; private enterprise and representative government were fundamental to the vision of the Institution's founder. By collecting knowledge, generating ideas and disseminating both, the Institution seeks to secure and safeguard peace, improve the human condition, and limit government intrusion into the lives of individuals.*

**Hudson Institute**
Indianapolis Headquarters
Herman Kahn Center
5395 Emerson Way
Indianapolis, Indiana 46226
John Clark, Ph.D., Senior Research Fellow and Director, Center for Central European and Eurasian Studies

**Hudson Institute**
Washington, D.C. Office
1015 18th St., N.W. Suite #300
Washington, DC 20036
Website: http://www.hudson.org/
Robert Dujarric, Research Fellow
National Security Issues
*A private, not-for-profit research
organization founded in 1961 by
the late Herman Kahn. It analyzes
and makes recommendations
about public policy for business
and government executives and for
the public at large.*

**Human Rights Campaign**
1101 14th St. NW, #200
Washington, DC 20005
Website: http://www.hrcusa.org/
E-mail: hrc@hrc.org
Catherine Reno Brouillet, Director
E-mail:
HRCptown@mindspring.com
*The largest full-time lobbying team
in the nation devoted to issues of
fairness for lesbian and gay
Americans.*

**Information Infrastructure Project**
Science, Technology and Public
Policy Program
John F. Kennedy School of
Government
Harvard University
79 John F. Kennedy St.
Cambridge, MA 02138

**Institute for Contemporary
Studies**
Latham Square
1611 Telegraph Ave., Suite #902
Oakland, CA 94612
Website: http://www.icspress.com
Robert B. Hawkins, Jr., President
and CEO
*A nonprofit, nonpartisan policy
research institute promoting self-
governance and entrepreneurial
ways of life.*

**Institute for Food and
Development Policy**
398 60th St.
Oakland, CA 94618
Website: http://www.foodfirst.org/
E-mail: foodfirst@igc.apc.org
Peter Rosset, Ph.D., Executive
Director
*Purpose is to eliminate the
injustices that cause hunger.*

**Institute for Humane Studies
(IHS)**
at George Mason University
3401 N. Fairfax Dr.
Arlington, VA 22201
Website: http://osf1.gmu.edu/~ihs/
E-mail: ihs@gmu.edu
Damon Chetson, Program Director
Paul Edwards, Vice President of
Academic Affairs
*A unique organization that assists
undergraduate and graduate
students who have a special
interest in individual liberty.*

**Institute for International
Economics**
11 DuPont Circle NW, #620
Washington, DC 20036
Website: http://www.iie.com/
E-mail: bcoulton@iie.com
C. Fred Bergsten, Director
E-mail: alreeves@iie.com or
anelson@iie.com
*A private, nonprofit, nonpartisan
research institution devoted to the
study of international economic
policy.*

**Institute for Policy Studies**
733 15th St. NW, Suite #1020
Washington, DC 20005
Website: http://www.ips-dc.org/
E-mail: scott@hotsalsa.org
Richard J. Barnet, Co-Founder,
former Co-Director, and current
Fellow
E-mail: arbarnet@dwu.edu
*Nonprofit, nonpartisan research
and public education organization
dedicated to educating the public
on the need and the means for an
orderly transfer of military
resources to civilian use.*

**International Society for
Individual Liberty (ISIL)**
836-B Southampton Rd., #299
Benicia, CA 94510
Website: http://
www.seventhquest.net/isil.org/
E-mail: isil@isil.org
Mary Lou Gutscher, ISIL 2000
Conference Coordinator
*An association of individuals and
organizations with members in
over 80 countries dedicated to
building a free and peaceful world,
respect for individual rights and
liberties, and an open and
competitive economic system
based on voluntary exchange and
free trade.*

**Institute for Women's Policy
Research**
1707 L St., NW, Suite #750
Washington, DC 20036
Website: http://www.iwpr.org/
E-mail: iwpr@iwpr.org
Heidi Hartmann, Ph.D., Director
and President
E-mail: hartmann@iwpr.org
*An independent, nonprofit,
scientific research organization
incorporated in the District of
Columbia, established in 1987 to
rectify the limited availability of
policy relevant research on
women's lives and to inform and
stimulate debate on issues of
critical importance for women.*

**International Society for
Technology in Education (ISTE)**
480 Charnelton St.
Eugene, OR 97401
Website: http://www.iste.org/
E-mail: iste@iste.org
Dr. David Moursund, Executive
Director for Research and
Development
*The largest teacher-based,
nonprofit organization in the field
of educational technology. Its
mission is to help K–12 classroom
teachers and administrators share
effective methods for enhancing
student learning through the use of
new classroom technologies.*

**International Women's Health Coalition**
24 E. 21st St.
New York, NY 10010
Website: http://www.iwhc.org/
E-mail: mailto:info@iwhc.org
Adrienne Germain, President
*A nonprofit organization based in New York City that works with individuals and groups in Africa, Asia, and Latin America to promote women's reproductive and sexual health and rights.*

**Investigative Reporters and Editors (IRE)**
UMC School of Journalism/26A
University of Missouri
Columbia, MO 65211
Website: http://www.ire.org
E-mail: jourire@muccmail.missouri.edu
Rosemary Armao, Executive Director
E-mail: r2croak@aol.com
*A grassroots nonprofit organization dedicated to improving the quality of investigative reporting within the field of journalism.*

**Izaak Walton League of America**
707 Conservation Lane
Gaithersburg, MD 20878
Website: http://www.iwla.org/
E-mail: general@iwla.org
Paul Hansen, Executive Director
*One of the oldest conservation organizations in the United States.*

**Japanese American Citizens League (JACL)**
1765 Sutter St.
San Francisco, CA 94065
Website: http://www.jacl.org/
E-mail: jacl@jacl.org
S. Floyd Mori, National President
E-mail: president@jacl.org
*It was founded in 1929 to fight discrimination against people of Japanese ancestry. It is the largest and one of the oldest Asian-American organizations in the United States.*

**Jefferson Center Citizens Jury**
1111 Third Ave. S., #364
Minneapolis, MN 55404
Website: http://www.jefferson-center.org/citizens_jury.htm
E-mail: mail@jefferson-center.org
*A comprehensive tool that allows decision makers to hear thoughtful citizen input and the people's authentic voice.*

**Jewish Defense League**
PO Box 480370
Los Angeles, CA 90048
Website: http://www.jdl.org
E-mail: jdljdl@aol.com
Irv Rubin, National Chairman
*Organization that sees the need for a movement that is dedicated specifically to Jewish problems and that allocates its time, resources, energies, and funds to Jews.*

**Jews for the Preservation of Firearms Ownership**
PO Box 270143
Hartford, WI 53027
Website: http://www.jpfo.org/
E-mail: Against-Genocide@JPFO.org
Aaron Zelman, Executive Director
*Membership in Jews for the Preservation of Firearms Ownership (JPFO) is open to all law abiding firearms owners who believe that ownership of firearms is a civil right, not a privilege, as a drivers license is.*

**The John Birch Society, Inc.**
PO Box 8040
Appleton, WI 54913
Website: http://www.jbs.org/
E-mail: jbs@jbs.org
Thomas R. Eddlem, Research Director
E-mail: teddlem@jbs.org
*Organization devoted to the free market system, competitive capitalism, and private enterprise.*

**John D. and Catherine T. MacArthur Foundation**
140 S. Dearborn St., Suite #100
Chicago, IL 60603
Website: http://www.macfdn.org/
E-mail: 4answers@macfdn.org
John E. Corbally, Chairman of the Board
*This foundation gives "genius grants"—no-strings money awarded to people with exceptional creative ability.*

**John Locke Foundation, The**
200 West Morgan St., Suite #200
Raleigh, NC 27601
Website: http://www.johnlocke.org/
E-mail: info@johnlocke.org
Bruce M. Babcock, Board of Directors
Marilyn Avila, Admimistrative Director
E-mail: mavila@johnlocke.org
*A nonprofit, nonpartisan policy institute based in Raleigh, North Carolina. Its purpose is to conduct research, disseminate information, and advance public understanding of society based on the principles of individual liberty, the voluntary exchanges of a free market economy, and limited government.*

**John Simon Guggenheim Memorial Foundation**
90 Park Ave.
New York, NY 10016
Website: http://www.gf.org
E-mail: fellowships@gf.org
Joseph A. Rice, Chairman of the Board
*A grant foundation for arts and sciences and the humanities, except for performers. They will fund a choreographer, but not a dancer.*

**Joint Center for Political and Economic Studies**
1090 Vermont Ave. NW, #1100
Washington, DC 20005
Website: http://www.jointctr.org/
Eddie N. Williams, President
Barry K. Campbell, Executive Vice President
*A nonprofit institution conducting research on political, economic, and social policy issues of concern to African Americans.*

**Joseph and Edna Josephson Institute of Ethics**
4640 Admiralty Way, #1001
Marina del Rey, CA 90292
Website: http://
www.josephsoninstitute.org/
E-mail: ji@jiethics.org
Michael S. Josephson, Founder
and President
*A public-benefit, nonpartisan, nonprofit membership organization founded by Michael Josephson in honor of his parents to improve the ethical quality of society by advocating principled reasoning and ethical decision making.*

**League of Conservation Voters**
1920 L Street, NW, Suite. #800
Washington, DC 20036
Website: http://www.lcv.org
E-mail: lcv@lcv.org
Deb Callahan, President
*Works to create a Congress more responsive to your environmental concerns.*

**League of United Latin American Citizens (LULAC)**
2000 L St. NW, Suite #610
Washington, DC 20036
Website: http://www.lulac.org/
Enrique "Rick" Dovalina, LULAC
National President
E-mail: RickDovalina@LULAC.org
Brent Wilkes, LULAC National
Executive Director
E-mail: BWilkes@LULAC.org
*Works to bring about positive social and economic changes for Hispanic Americans.*

**League of Women Voters of the United States**
1730 M St. NW
Washington, DC 20036
Website: http://www.lwv.org/
Carolyn Jefferson-Jenkins, Ph.D.,
President
*A multi-issue organization whose mission is to encourage the informed and active participation of citizens in government and to influence public policy through education and advocacy.*

**Libertarian Party**
2600 Virginia Ave. NW, #100
Washington, DC 20037
Website: http://www.lp.org/
Steve Dasbach, National Director
E-mail: Steve.Dasbach@hq.lp.org
Ron Crickenberger, Political
Director
E-mail:
Ron.Crickenberger@hq.LP.org
*Holds that all individuals have the right to exercise sole dominion over their own lives and have the right to live in whatever manner they choose, so long as they do not forcibly interfere with the equal right of others to live in whatever manner they choose.*

**Low Income Housing Information Service**
1012 14th St., #1200
Washington, DC 20005
Website: http://www.nlihc.org/
index.htm
E-mail: info@nlihc.org
Sheila Crowley, President
E-mail: sheila@nlihc.org
*The only national organization dedicated solely to ending America's affordable housing crisis.*

**Manhattan Institute**
52 Vanderbilt Ave.
New York, NY 10017
Website: http://www.manhattan-
institute.org/
E-mail: barreiro@manhattan-
institute.org
Lawrence Mone, President
*A think tank whose mission is to
develop and disseminate new
ideas that foster greater economic
choice and individual
responsibility.*

**Manpower Demonstration
Research Corporation**
19th Floor
16 East 34 St.
New York, NY 10016
Website: http://www.mdrc.org/
E-mail: information@mdrc.org
Judith M. Gueron, President
*A nonprofit, nonpartisan research
organization that develops and
evaluates innovative approaches to
moving people from welfare to
work, building a stronger work
force through training, revitalizing
low-income communities, and
improving education for at-risk
youth.*

**Media Access Project**
950 18th St. NW, Suite #220
Washington, DC 20006
Andrew Jay Schwartzman,
President and CEO
Website: http://
www.mediaaccess.org/index.html
*A twenty-four-year-old nonprofit,
public interest law firm which
promotes the public's First
Amendment right to hear and be
heard on the electronic media of
today and tomorrow.*

**Media Research Center**
325 S. Patrick St.
Alexandria, VA 22314
Website: http://
www.mediaresearch.org/
E-mail: mrc@mediaresearch.org
L. Brent Bozell III, Founder and
Chairman
*Founded by L. Brent Bozell III in
1987 with the mission of bringing
political balance to the nation's
news media and responsibility to
the entertainment media, the
Media Research Center (MRC) has
grown into the nation's largest and
most respected conservative media
watchdog organization.*

**Mediascope**
12711 Ventura Blvd., #280
Studio City, CA 91604
Website: http://
www.mediascope.org/mediascope/
index.htm
E-mail: facts@mediascope.org
Hubert D. Jessup, President
*A national, nonprofit public policy
organization founded in 1992 to
promote constructive depictions of
health and social issues in the
media, particularly as they relate to
children and adolescents.*

**Medical Research Modernization
Committee**
3200 Morley Rd.
Shaker Heights, OH 44122
Website:http://www.mrmcmed.org/
E-mail: mrmcmed@aol.com
*Works to modernize medical
research and promote human
health. Concludes that animal
experiments take desperately
needed money but rarely
contribute to human health.*

**Miss America Pageant**
1325 Boardwalk
Atlantic City, NJ 08401
Website: http://www.misamerica.org
Robert Renneisen Jr., President and CEO
Heather French, Miss America 2000
*The Miss America competition has been broadcast live at one time or another by all three of the country's major television networks and remains one of the highest rated annual events on national television today.*

**Miss Teen USA**
% Dara Arbeiter
Rubenstein Public Relations
1345 Ave. of the Americas
New York, NY 10105
Website: http://www.missteenusa.com/home.html
Maureen J. Reidy, President
Jillian Parry, Miss Teen USA® 2000

**Montanans for Property Rights**
PO Box 130399
Coram, MT 59913
Website: http://www.members.spree.com/mfpr/
E-mail: mfpr7@yahoo.com
Russell Crowder, Member Board of Directors
*Defends the rights of Montana property owners*

**National Association for the Advancement of Colored People (NAACP)**
Washington Bureau
4805 Mt. Hope Dr.
Baltimore, MD 21215
Website: http://www.naacp.org/
Kweisi Mfume, President and CEO
*Its primary objective is to ensure the political, educational, social, and economic equality of minority group citizens of the United States.*

**National Academy of Science**
2101 Constitution Ave. NW
Washington, DC 20418
Website: http://www.nas.edu/
E-mail: wwwfdbk@nas.edu
Bruce Alberts, President
*A private, nonprofit society of scholars engaged in scientific and engineering research, dedicated to the furtherance of science and technology and to their use for the general welfare.*

**National Association of Home Builders**
1201 15th St. NW
Washington, DC 20005
Website: http://www.nahb.com/
E-mail: info@nahb.com.
Robert Mitchell, President
*The voice of America's housing industry*

**National Association of Manufacturers**
1331 Pennsylvania Ave. NW, #1500
Washington, DC 20004
Website: http://www.nam.org/
E-mail: manufacturing@nam.org
E-mail: afoscue@nam.org
Amy Foscue, Associate Director
*Was founded in 1895 to advance a pro-growth, pro-manufacturing policy agenda*

**National Association of Professional Pet Sitters (NAPPS)**
1030 15th St. NW, Suite #870
Washington, DC 20005
Website: http://www.petsitters.org/
E-mail: napps@rgminc.com
*Promotes the concept of in-home pet care, to support the professionals engaged in at-home pet care, promote the welfare of animals, and to improve and expand the industry of pet sitting.*

**National Association of Realtors**
700 11th St. NW
Washington, DC 20001
Website: http://nar.realtor.com/
E-mail: infocentral@realtors.org
Steve Cook, Vice President
*It is composed of residential and commercial Realtors®, who are brokers, salespeople, property managers, appraisers, counselors, and others engaged in all aspects of the real estate industry.*

**National Audubon Society**
700 Broadway
New York, NY 10003
Website: http://www.audubon.org/
E-mail: jbianchi@audubon.org
Oakes Ames, Boardmember
Ruth O. Russell, Boardmember
*The mission of the National Audubon Society is to conserve and restore natural ecosystems, focusing on birds and other wildlife for the benefit of humanity and the earth's biological diversity.*

**National Caucus and Center on Black Aged Inc.**
1424 K St. NW, #500
Washington, DC 20005
Website: http://www.ncba-blackaged.org/
E-mail: ncba@aol.com
*A national nonprofit organization dedicated to improving the quality of life for African Americans and low-income elderly.*

**National Center for Law and Deafness**
800 Florida Ave. NE
Washington, DC 20002

**National Center for State Courts**
300 Newport Ave.
Williamsburg, VA 23185
Website: http://www.ncsc.dni.us/
Gerald W. Vandewalle, Chair
E-mail: vandewallej@court.state.nd.us
*An independent, nonprofit organization dedicated to the improvement of justice. It was founded in 1971 at the urging of Chief Justice Warren E. Burger. NCSC accomplishes its mission by providing leadership and service to the state courts.*

**National Center on Institutions and Alternatives (NCIA)**
3125 Mt. Vernon Ave.
Alexandria, VA 22305
Website: http://www.igc.apc.org/ncia/
E-mail: info@ncianet.org
*Its mission is to help create a society in which all persons who come into contact with the human service or correctional systems will be provided an environment of individual care, concern and treatment.*

**National City Corp.**
1900 E. Ninth St.
Cleveland, OH 44114
Website: http://www.national-city.com
David A. Daberko, Chairman and CEO
*Commercial bank*

**National Organization for the Reform of Marijuana Laws (NORML)**
1001 Connecticut Ave. NW, #1010
Washington, DC 20036
Website: http://www.norml.org/
Email: norml@norml.org
R. Keith Stroup, Executive Director (and NORML founder)
*Since its founding in 1970, NORML has been the principal national advocate for legalizing marijuana.*

**National Organization for Women (NOW)**
1000 16th St. NW, #700
Washington, DC 20036
Website: http://www.now.org/
E-mail: now@now.org
Patricia Ireland, President
*It is dedicated to making legal, political, social, and economic change in our society in order to achieve its goal, which is to eliminate sexism.*

**National Republican Congressional Campaign Committee**
320 1st St. SE
Washington, DC 20003
Website: http://www.nrcc.org
Tom Davis, Chairman
*A political committee devoted to increasing the 223-member Republican majority in the U.S. House of Representatives.*

**National Rifle Association**
Website: http://www.nra.org/
E-mail: nra-contact@NRA.org
Tanya K. Metaksa, Executive Director, NRA-ILA
Wayne La Pierre, Executive Vice President
Charlton Heston, President
*The NRA was incorporated in 1871 to provide firearms training and encourage interest in the shooting sports.*

**National Taxpayer's Union**
108 North Alfred St.
Alexandria, VA 22314
Website: http://www.ntu.org/
E-mail: ntu@ntu.org
John Berthoud, President
*The largest grassroots taxpayer organization with more than 300,000 members across all 50 states.*

**National Trust for Historic Preservation**
1785 Massachusetts Ave. NW
Washington, DC 20036
Website: http://www.nthp.org
Richard Moe, President
*The National Trust is dedicated to showing how preservation can play an important role in strengthening a sense of community and improving the quality of life.*

**National Urban League**
500 East 62nd St.
New York, NY 10021
Website: http://www.nul.org/
E-mail: info@nul.org
Jonathan S. Linen, Chairman
*The premier social service and civil rights organization in America.*

**National Wildlife Federation**
8925 Leesburg Pike
Vienna, VA 22184
Website: http://www.nwf.org/
Mark Van Putten, President and
CEO
*NWF focuses its efforts on five core
issue areas (Endangered Habitat,
Water Quality, Land Stewardship,
Wetlands, and Sustainable
Communities), and pursues a
range of educational projects, and
activist, advocacy, and litigation
initiatives within these core areas.*

**Native American Rights Fund**
1506 Broadway
Boulder, CO 80302
Website: http://www.narf.org/
E-mail: pereira@narf.org
John E. Echohawk, Executive
Director
*A nonprofit legal organization
dedicated to the preservation of the
rights and culture of Native
Americans.*

**New Israel Fund**
National Office
1101 14th St. NW, Sixth Floor
Washington, DC 20005
Website: http://www.nif.org/home/
E-mail: info@nif.org
Mary Ann Stein, North American
Chair
*Organization for pluralism and
religious freedom in Israel.*

**Pacific Research Institute for
Public Policy**
755 Sansome St., #450
San Francisco, CA 94111
Website: http://
www.pacificresearch.org/
Sally C. Pipes, President and CEO
*Promotes the principles of
individual freedom and personal
responsibility. The Institute
believes these principles are best
encouraged through policies that
emphasize a free economy, private
initiative, and limited government.*

**Pacific Rocket Society**
Rod and Randa Milliron
PO Box 662
Mojave, CA 93502
Website: http://www.translunar.org/
prs/
*Organization dedicated to the
promotion of rocketry, space
travel, and off-world colonization.*

**Partnership for the Homeless**
305 7th Ave., 13th Floor
New York, NY 10001
Website: http://
www.partnershipforhomeless.org/
E-mail: tpfth@
partnershipforhomeless.org
*Organization that coordinates
shelters and assists homeless and
formerly homeless individuals and
families obtain housing and other
basic needs.*

**People for the American Way**
2000 M St. NW, #400
Washington, DC 20036
Website: http://www.pfaw.org/
E-mail: pfaw@pfaw.org
Ralph G. Neas, President
*Founded by a group of civic and religious leaders who were concerned by the rising tide of intolerance against lesbians and gays sweeping the nation. Produces monthly updates of anti-gay activity around the United States.*

**People for the Ethical Treatment of Animals (PETA)**
501 Front St.
Norfolk, VA 23510
Website: http://www.peta-online.org/
E-mail: info@peta-online.org
Alex Pacheco, Co-Founder
*Believes that animals have the same rights as humans. PETA operates under the simple principle that animals are not ours to eat, wear, experiment on, or use for entertainment.*

**Physicians Committee for Responsible Medicine**
5100 Wisconsin Ave., #404
Washington, DC 20016
Website: http://www.pcrm.org/
E-mail: pcrm@pcrm.org
Neal Barnard, M.D., President
*Promotes preventive medicine through innovative programs, encourages higher standards for ethics and effectiveness in research, and advocates broader access to medical services.*

**Planned Parenthood Federation of America**
810 Seventh Ave.
New York, NY 10019
Website: http://www.plannedparenthood.org/
E-mail: communications@ppfa.org
Gloria Feldt, President
*Offers extensive information on all aspects of sexual and reproductive health.*

**Points of Light Foundation**
400 I St., NW Suite #800
Washington, DC 20005
Website: http://www.pointsoflight.org/
Robert K. Goodwin, President and Chief Executive Officer
E-mail: rgoodwin@pointsoflight.org
*A nonpartisan organization whose mission is to engage more people more effectively in volunteer community service. Offers a hotline for volunteer opportunity information.*

**Population Reference Bureau, Inc.**
1875 Connecticut Ave., NW, Suite #520
Washington, DC 20009
Website: http://www.prb.org/prb/
E-mail: ecarnevale@prb
Michael P. Bentzen, Chairman of the Board
*Dedicated to providing timely and objective information on U.S. and international population trends.*

**Public Service Research Council**
320-D Maple Ave. E
Vienna, VA 22180
Website: http://www.psrf.org/
E-mail: info@psrf.org
David Y. Denholm, President
*Studying the impact of unionism in government on government.*

**Radio-Television News Directors Association (RTNDA)**
1000 Connecticut Ave. NW, #615
Washington, DC 20036
Website: http://www.rtnda.org/
E-mail: rtnda@rtnda.org
Barbara Cochran, RTNDA President
E-mail: barbarac@rtnda.org
*The world's largest professional organization devoted exclusively to electronic journalism. RTNDA represents local and network news executives in broadcasting, cable, and other electronic media in more than 30 countries.*

**The Rainbow/Push Coalition**
930 East 50th St.
Chicago, IL 60615-2702
Reverend Jesse L. Jackson, Sr.
President and CEO
Website: http://www.rainbowpush.org/aboutrpc/index.html
E-mail: info@rainbowpush.org
*A multiracial, multi-issue, international membership organization founded by Rev. Jesse L. Jackson Sr.*

**Reason Foundation**
3415 S. Sepulveda Blvd., #400
Los Angeles, CA 90034
Website: http://www.reason.org/
George Passantino, Public Affairs Director
E-mail: gpassantino@reason.org
*A national research and educational organization that explores and promotes the twin values of rationality and freedom as the basic underpinnings of a good society.*

**Republican Liberty Caucus**
611 Pennsylvania Ave. SE, #370
Washington, DC 20003
Website: http://www.rlc.org/
Clifford Thies, Chairman
E-mail: cthies@su.edu
Thomas D. Walls, Executive Director
E-mail: afn18566@afn.org
*The primary objective of the RLC is to help elect libertarian-leaning Republicans to public office at all levels.*

**Republican National Committee**
310 1st St. SE
Washington, DC 20003
Website: http://www.rnc.org
E-mail: info@rnc.org
Jim Nicholson, Chairman

**Ripon Society**
501 Capitol Court NE, #300
Washington, DC 22000
Website: http://www.riponsoc.org/
The Honorable Bill Frenzel, President
Michael D. Gill, Executive Director
*A moderate Republican research and policy organization dedicated to a commonsense, pragmatic system of governance.*

**Rockefeller Foundation, The**
420 Fifth Ave.
New York, NY 10018
Website: http://www.rockfound.org
Alice Stone Ilchman, Chair
*Grant organization for arts, the humanities, equal opportunity, school reform, and international science-based development.*

**Ronald Reagan Presidential Library**
40 Presidential Dr.
Simi Valley, CA 93065
Website: http://
www.reaganlibrary.net/lobby.html
E-mail: library@reagan.nara.gov
Mark Burson, Executive Director

**Roper Center for Public Opinion Research**
University of Connecticut
U-164 Montieth Bldg.
341 Mansfield Rd., Room 421
Storrs, CT 06269
Website: http://
www.ropercenter.uconn.edu/
Lois Timms-Ferrara, Associate Director
E-mail: lois@opinion.isi.uconn.edu
*The leading nonprofit center for the study of public opinion maintaining the world's largest archive of public opinion data.*

**Saint Patrick's Cathedral**
460 Madison Ave.
New York, NY 10022
Msgr. Anthony Dalla Villa
*The largest Roman Catholic church in the United States.*

**Second Amendment Sisters**
18484 Preston Rd., Suite 102 #141
Dallas, TX 75252
Website: http://www.sas-aim.org/
E-mail: inquire@sas-aim.org
Juli Bednarzyk, Director
*Women's advocacy group dedicated to promoting the human right to self-defense, as recognized by the Second Amendment. Second Amendment Sisters hope to raise awareness for the importance of the Second amendment and the role it plays in protecting our right to self-defense.*

**Shapiro, Joshua and Vera**
VJ Enterprises
Attn: Joshua "Illinois" Shapiro
PO Box 295
Morton Grove, IL 60053
Website: http://www.v-j-enterprises.com/
E-mail: rjoshua@sprintmail.com
*Metaphysical tours to sacred sites, etc.*

**Sierra Club National Office**
85 Second St., Second Floor
San Francisco, CA 94105
Website: http://www.sierraclub.org
E-mail: information@sierraclub.org
*A nonprofit organization that promotes conservation.*

**Smithsonian Institution**
1000 Jefferson Dr. SW
Washington, DC 20560
Website: http://www.si.edu/
E-mail: webmaster@si.edu
Larry Small, Secretary of the Smithsonian Institution
*The Institution is an independent trust of the United States holding more than 140 million artifacts and specimens in its trust for "the increase and diffusion of knowledge."*

**Sojourners**
2401 15th St. NW
Washington, DC 20009
E-mail: sojourners@sojo.net
Ryan Beiler, Web Editor
E-mail: rbeiler@sojo.net
*Christian ministry whose mission is to proclaim and practice the biblical call to integrate spiritual renewal and social justice.*

## Solar Energy Industries Association

1616 H St., NW, 8th Floor
Washington, DC 20006
Website: http://www.seia.org/
E-mail: seiaopps@digex.com
Mike Davis, President
*A national trade association for all solar businesses and enterprises in the fields of photovoltaics, solar electric power, solar thermal power, and solar building products.*

## Soros Foundation Network

Open Society Institute
888 Seventh Ave.
New York, NY 10606
Website: http://www.soros.org
George Soros, Founder
*Grant organization that supports research that promotes an "open society."*

## Special Olympics International

1325 G St. NW, Suite #500
Washington, DC 20005
Website: http://www.specialolympics.org/
Sargent Shriver, Chairman of the Board
*An international program of year-round sports training and athletic competition for more than one million children and adults with mental retardation.*

## Tomas Rivera Policy Institute, The

1050 North Mills Ave.
Pitzer College, Scott Hall
Claremont, CA 91711
Website: http://www.trpi.org/
Harry P. Pachon, President
*Freestanding, nonprofit, policy research organization which has attained a reputation as the nation's "premier Latino think tank."*

## Thomas Jefferson Center for the Protection of Free Expression

400 Peter Jefferson Pl.
Charlottesville, VA 22911
Website: http://www.tjcenter.org/
E-mail: freespeech@tjcenter.org
Robert M. O'Neil, Director
Judith G. Clabes, President and CEO
*A unique organization, devoted solely to the defense of free expression in all its forms. While its charge is sharply focused, the Center's mission is broad. It is as concerned with the musician as with the mass media, with the painter as with the publisher, and as much with the sculptor as the editor.*

## Trends Research Institute

PO Box 660
Rhinebeck, NY 12572-0660
Website: http://www.trendsresearch.com/
E-mail: webmaster@trendsresearch.com
Gerald Celente, Director
E-mail: celente@trendsresearch.com
*Combines unique resources with its own trademarked methodology to help companies profit from trends.*

## Union of Concerned Scientists

2 Brattle Square
Cambridge, MA 02238
Website: http://www.ucsusa.org/
E-mail: ucs@ucsusa.org
Howard Ris, Executive Director
*A nonprofit alliance of scientists and citizens working for a healthy environment and a safe world, UCS researches and promotes clean energy and transportation technologies.*

**United States Martial Arts Association, The**
011 Mariposa Ave.
Citrus Heights, CA 95610
Website: http://www.mararts.org
E-mail: psp4@flash.net
Mr. Charles Matza, Chairman of the Board of Directors

**United We Stand America**
7616 LBJ Freeway, #727
Dallas, TX 75221
Website: http://www.uwsa.com/
E-mail: uw-bill@uwsa.com

**Urban Institute**
2100 M St. NW
Washington, DC 20037
Website: http://www.urban.org
Robert D. Reischauer, President
*A nonprofit economic, social, and policy research organization*

**U.S. Term Limits**
10 G St., N.W., Suite #410
Washington, DC 20002
Website: http://www.termlimits.org/
E-mail: admin@termlimits.org
Howard Rich, President
Jon Lerner, Executive Director
*Organization devoted to setting term limits for elected officials*

**Veterans of Foreign Wars (VFW) Political Action Committee**
406 W. 34th St.
Kansas City, MO 64111
Website: http://www.vfw.org/
E-mail: info@vfw.org
*Organization dedicated to securing the rights and benefits of veterans*

**Vietnam Veterans of America**
8605 Cameron St., Suite #400
Silver Spring, MD 20910
Website: http://www.vva.org/
E-mail: membership@vva.org
George C. Duggins, President
National veterans service organization

**Vince Shute Wildlife Sanctuary**
PO Box 77
Orr, MN 55711
Klari Lee, Co-Founder
*360-acre refuge and black bear sanctuary which experts regard as one of the best places in North America to view wild bears and their behavior*

**Wilderness Society, The**
1615 M St., NW
Washington, DC 20036
Website: http://www.wilderness.org/
Bill Meadows, President
*Devoted primarily to public lands protection and management issues*

**World Future Society**
7910 Woodmont Ave., #450
Bethesda, MD 20814
Website: http://www.wfs.org/
E-mail: schley@wfs.org
Clement Bezold, Executive Director
*A nonprofit educational and scientific organization for people interested in how social and technological developments are shaping the future*

**Zero Population Growth (ZPG)**
1400 16th St. NW, #320
Washington, DC 20036
Website: http://www.zpg.org
Dr. Nafis Sadik, Executive Director
*The nation's largest grassroots organization concerned with the impacts of rapid population growth and wasteful consumption.*

**Zero To Three**
National Center for Clinical Infant Programs
734 15th St. NW, Suite #1000
Washington, DC 20005
Website: http://www.zerotothree.org/
E-mail: webmaster@cyberserv.com
Joy D. Osofsky, Ph.D, Board of Directors
*A national nonprofit dedicated to the healthy development of infants, toddlers, and their families, with information for parents and professionals.*

# IT IS YOUR BUSINESS

**Abbott Laboratories**
100 Abbott Park Rd.
Abbott Park, IL 60064
Website: http://www.abbott.com
Miles D. White, Chairman and CEO
*Drug manufacturer*

**Ace Hardware**
2200 Kensington Ct.
Oak Brook, IL 60523
Website: http://
www.acehardware.com
David F. Hodnik, President and
CEO
*Wholesalers*

**Aetna**
151 Farmington Ave.
Hartford, CT 06156
Website: http://www.aetna.com
William Donaldson, Chairman,
President, and CEO
*Health and life insurance*

**AFLAC**
1932 Wynnton Rd.
Columbus, GA 31999
Website: http://www.aflac.com
Paul S. Amos, CEO
*Life and health insurance*

**AGCO**
4205 River Green Pkwy.
Duluth, GA 30096
Website: http://www.agcocorp.com
Robert J. Ratliff, Chairman
*Distributor of agricultural
equipment*

**Air Products and Chemicals**
7201 Hamilton Blvd.
Allentown, PA 18195
Website: http://
www.airproducts.com
Harold A. Wagner, Chairman and
CEO
*Chemicals*

**Airborne Freight**
3101 Western Ave.
Seattle, WA 98121
Website: http://www.airborne-
express.com
Robert S. Cline, Chairman and
CEO
*Mail, package, freight delivery*

**Albertsons**
250 Parkcenter Blvd.
Boise, ID 83706
Gary G. Michael, Chairman and
CEO
*Food and drug stores*

**Alcoa**
201 Isabella St. at 7th St. Bridge
Pittsburgh, PA 15212
Website: http://www.alcoa.com
Paul H. O'Neill, Chairman
Alain J. P. Belda, President and
CEO
*Metals*

**Allegheny Technologies
Incorporated**
1000 Six PPG Place
Pittsburgh, PA 15222
Thomas A. Corcoran, Chairman,
President, and CEO
*Specialty metals*

**Allegiance**
1430 Waukegan Rd.
McGaw Park, IL 60085
Website: http://www.allegiance.net
Joseph F. Damico, Group
President, EVP, Cardinal Health
*Healthcare*

**Allmerica Financial**
440 Lincoln St.
Worcester, MA 01653
Website: http://www.allmerica.com
John F. O'Brien, President and CEO
Henry St. Cyr, Vice President,
Investor Relations
*P and C insurance*

**Allstate**
Allstate Plaza
2775 Sanders Rd.
Northbrook, IL 60062
Website: http://www.allstate.com
Edward M. Liddy, Chairman,
President, and CEO, Allstate
Corporation and Allstate Insurance
*Insurance*

**Alltel**
1 Allied Dr.
Little Rock, AR 72202
Website: http://www.alltel.com
Joe T. Ford, Chairman and CEO
*Telecommunications*

**Amerada Hess**
1185 Ave. of the Americas
New York, NY 10036
Website: http://www.hew.com
John B. Hess, Chairman and CEO
*Petroleum refining*

**Ameren**
1901 Chouteau Ave.
St. Louis, MO 63103
Website: http://www.ameren.com
Charles W. Mueller, Chairman,
President, and CEO
*Gas and electric utilities*

**American Electric Power**
1 Riverside Plaza
Columbus, OH 43215
Website: http://www.aep.com
E. Linn Draper Jr., Chairman,
President, and CEO
*Gas and electric utilities*

**American Express**
200 Vesey St.
New York, NY 10285
Website: http://
www.americanexpress.com
Harvey Golub, Chairman and CEO
*Diversified financials*

**American Family Insurance Group**
6000 American Pkwy.
Madison, WI 53783
Website: http://www.amfam.com
Dale F. Mathwich, Chairman and
CEO
*Insurance*

**American Financial Group**
1 E. Fourth St.
Cincinnati, OH 45202
Website: http://www.amfnl.com
Carl H. Lindner, CEO
*Insurance*

**American General**
2929 Allen Pkwy.
Houston, TX 77019
Website: http://www.agc.com
Robert M. Devlin, Chairman,
President, and CEO
*Life and health insurance*

**American Home Products**
5 Giralda Farms
Madison, NJ 07940
Website: http://www.ahp.com
John R. Stafford, Chairman,
President, and CEO
*Pharmaceuticals*

**American International Group**
70 Pine St.
New York, NY 10270
Website: http://www.aig.com
C. V. Starr, Chairman and CEO;
Chairman, Transatlantic Holdings;
President, and CEO
Maurice R. "Hank" Greenberg,
Chairman & CEO
*P and C insurance*

**American Standard**
1 Centennial Ave.
Piscataway, NJ 08855
Website: http://
www.americanstandard.com
Frederic M. Poses, Chairman and
CEO
*Industrial and farm equipment*

**AmeriSource Health**
300 Chester Field Pkwy.
Malvern, PA 19355
Website: http://
www.amerisource.com
R. David Yost, President and CEO
*Wholesale pharmaceuticals*

**Ameritech**
2000 West Ameritech Center Dr.
Hoffman Estates, IL 60195
Website: http://
www.ameritech.com
Walt Catlow, CEO
*Telecommunications*

**Amgen, Inc.**
1 Amgen Center Dr.
Thousand Oaks, CA 91320
Website: http://www.amgen.com
George B. Rathmann, Chairman
Emeritus; Chairman, and President
*One of the world's largest
biotechnology companies*

**AMR**
4333 Amon Carter Blvd.
Fort Worth, TX 76155
Website: http://www.amrcorp.com
Donald J. Carty, Chairman,
President, and CEO
*Airline*

**Anheuser-Busch**
1 Busch Place
St. Louis, MO 63118
Website: http://www.anheuser-
busch.com
August A. Busch III, Chairman and
President; Chairman, and CEO
*Beverages*

**Anixter**
4711 Golf Rd.
Skokie, IL 60637
Website: http://www.anixter.com
Samuel Zell, Chairman
Robert W. Grubbs Jr., President
and CEO
*Wholesalers wire and cable*

**Anthem Insurance**
120 Monument Circle
Indianapolis, IN 46204
L. Ben Lytle, Chairman, President,
and CEO
*Health and life insurance*

**Aon**
123 N. Wacker Dr.
Chicago, IL 60606
Website: http://www.aon.com
Patrick G. Ryan, Chairman and
CEO
*Diversified financials*

**Apple Computer**
1 Infinite Loop
Cupertino, CA 95014
Website: http://www.apple.com
Steven P. Jobs, CEO
*Computers, office equipment*

**Applied Materials**
3050 Bowers Ave.
Santa Clara, CA 95054
Website: http://
www.appliedmaterials.com
James C. Morgan, Chairman and
CEO
*Electronics, semiconductors*

**Aramark**
1101 Market St.
Philadelphia, PA 19107
Joseph Neubauer, Chairman and
CEO
*Food and support services,
uniforms, and child care*

**Archer Daniel's Midland**
4666 Faries Pkwy.
Decatur, IL 62526
Website: http://
www.admworld.com
Dwayne O. Andreas, Chairman
Emeritus
Allen Andreas, Chairman and CEO
*One of the world's largest
processors of oilseeds, corn, and
wheat*

**Arrow Electronics**
25 Hub Dr.
Melville, NY 11747
Website: http://www.arrow.com
Stephen P. Kaufman, CEO
*Wholesale electronics*

**AT&T**
32 Ave. of the Americas
New York, NY 10013
Website: http://www.att.com
C. Michael Armstrong, Chairman
and CEO
*Telecommunications company*

**AtomFilms**
80 S. Washington St., Suite #303
Seattle, WA 98014
Website: http://
www.atomfilms.com
E-mail: info@atomfilms.com
Mika Salmi, CEO and Founder
*Web content provider*

**Atomic Pop**
1447 Cloverfield Blvd., Suite #201
Santa Monica, CA 90404
Al Teller, CEO and Founder
E-mail: ateller@atomicpop.com
*E-commerce*

**Autobytel.com**
18872 MacArthur Blvd.
Irvine, CA 92612
Mark Lorimer, President and CEO
Website: http://www.autobytel.com
E-mail: markl@autobytel.com
*E-commerce*

**Avery Dennison**
150 N. Orange Grove Blvd.
Pasadena, CA 91103
Website: http://
www.averydennison.com
Philip M. Neal, Chairman and CEO
*Labels, office supplies*

**Avon**
1345 Ave. of the Americas
New York, NY 10105
Website: http://www.avon.com
Stanley C. Gault, Chairman
*Cosmetics and soaps*

**Baker Hughes**
3900 Essex Lane
PO Box 4740
Houston, TX 77027
Website: http://
www.bakerhughes.com
Joe B. Foster, Chairman, President,
and CEO
*Provides products and services for
the global petroleum market*

**Baltimore Gas and Electric**
PO Box 1475
Baltimore, MD 21203
Website: http://www.bge.com
Christian H. Poindexter, President
and CEO
*Gas and electric utilities*

**Banc One Corp.**
100 E. Broad St.
Columbus, OH 43271
Website: http://www.bankone.com
John B. McCoy, CEO
*Commercial bank*

**Bank of America**
100 N. Tryon St., 18th Floor
Charlotte, NC 28255
Website: http://
www.bankofamerica.com
Hugh L. McColl Jr., Chairman and
CEO
*Commercial bank*

**Bank of New York Company**
48 Wall St.
New York, NY 10286
Website: http://www.bankofny.com
Thomas A. Renyi, Chairman and
CEO, The Bank of New York
Company and The Bank of New
York
*Commercial bank*

## Barnes and Noble
122 Fifth Ave.
New York, NY 10011
Website: http://
www.barnesandnoble.com
Leonard Riggio, Chairman and
CEO; Chairman,
barnesandnoble.com
*Bookseller*

## Baxter International
1 Baxter Pkwy.
Deerfield, IL 60015
Website: http://www.baxter.com
William B. Graham, Chairman
Emeritus
Harry M. Jansen Kraemer Jr.,
Chairman and CEO, Baxter
International, Baxter World Trade
Corporation, and Baxter Healthcare
Corporation
*Scientific, photo, control
equipment, medical systems*

## Bear Stearns
245 Park Ave.
New York, NY 10167
Website: http://
www.bearstearns.com
Alan C. Greenberg, Chairman, Bear
Stearns Companies and Bear,
Stearns and Co.
*Securities*

## Becton Dickinson
1 Becton Dr.
Franklin Lakes, NJ 07417
Website: http://www.bd.com
Clateo Castellini, Chairman
*Scientific, photo, control
equipment, medical systems, bio
systems*

## Bell Atlantic
1095 Sixth Ave.
New York, NY 10036
Website: http://
www.bellatlantic.com
Charles R. Lee, Chairman and Co-
CEO
Ivan G. Seidenberg, President and
Co-CEO
*Telecommunications*

## BellSouth
1155 Peachtree St. N.E.
Atlanta, GA 30309
Website: http://
www.bellsouthcorp.policy.net
F. Duane Ackerman, Chairman and
CEO
*Telecommunications*

## Beneficial
301 N. Walnut St.
Wilmington, DE 19801
Website: http://
www.beneficial.com/
Finn M. W. Caspersen, CEO
*Financial corporation*

## Bergen Brunswick
4000 Metropolitan Dr.
Orange, CA 92868
Website: http://
www.bergenbrunswig.com
Robert E. Martini, Chairman,
Interim President, and Interim CEO
*Pharmaceuticals, healthcare
supplier*

## Berkshire Hathaway
1440 Kiewit Plaza
Omaha, NE 68131
Website:
www.berkshirehathaway.com
Warren E. Buffett, Chairman and
CEO
*(stock) P and C insurance*

**Best Buy**
7075 Flying Cloud Dr.
Eden Prairie, MN 55344
Website: http://www.bestbuy.com
Richard M. Schulze, Chairman and
CEO
*Specialist electronics retailers*

**Best Foods**
International Plaza
700 Sylvan Ave.
Englewood Cliffs, NJ 07632
Website: http://
www.bestfoods.com/index.shtml
Charles R. Shoemate, CEO
*Food producer*

**Bethlehem Steel**
1170 Eighth Ave.
Bethlehem, PA 18016
Website: http://www.bethsteel.com
Curtis H. Barnette, Chairman and
CEO
*Metals*

**Beverly Enterprises**
1000 Beverly Way
Fort Smith, AR 72919
Website: http://
www.beverlynet.com
David R. Banks, Chairman and
CEO
*Healthcare, nursing homes*

**Beverly Hills Hotel, The**
9641 Sunset Blvd.
Beverly Hills, CA 90210
Website: http://
www.thebeverlyhillshotel.com/
home.htm
Email: Concierge@
BeverlyHillsHotel.com or
Reservations@
BeverlyHillsHotel.com
*Famous hotel renowned for its
celebrity clientele and home of the
world famous Polo Lounge. The
hotel was built in 1912 and
magnificently renovated in 1995.*

**B. F. Goodrich**
Four Coliseum Centre
2730 W. Tyvola Rd.
Charlotte, NC 28217
Website: http://
www.bfgoodrich.com/index2.html
David L. Burner, Chairman,
President, and CEO
*Aerospace systems and services
and specialty chemicals*

**Bindley Western**
8909 Purdue Rd.
Indianapolis, IN 46268
Website: http://www.bindley.com
William E. Bindley, Chairman,
President, and CEO
*Wholesale distributors of
pharmaceuticals, health and
beauty care products, and home
healthcare products in the United
States*

**BizRate**
4053 Redwood Ave.
Los Angeles, CA 90066
Website: http://www.bizrate.com
E-mail: farhad@bizrate.com
Farhad Mohit, CEO and President
*E-commerce*

**B. J.'s Wholesale Club**
1 Mercer Rd.
Natick, MA 01760
Website: http://
www.bjswholesale.com
Herbert J. Zarkin, Chairman
John J. Nugent, President and CEO
*Membership food and drug stores*

## Black & Decker
701 E. Joppa Rd.
Towson, MD 21286
Website: http://
www.blackanddecker.com
Nolan D. Archibald, Chairman,
President, and CEO
*Tools, industrial and farm
equipment*

## Boeing
7755 E. Marginal Way S.
Seattle, WA 98108
Website: http://www.boeing.com
Philip M. Condit, Chairman and
CEO
*Aerospace*

## Boise Cascade
1111 W. Jefferson St.
Boise, ID 83702
Website: http://www.bc.com
George J. Harad, Chairman and
CEO; Chairman, Boise Cascade
Office Products
*Forest and paper products, office
supplies*

## Borden
180 E. Broad St.
Columbus, OH 43215
C. Robert Kidder, Chairman
*Specialty chemicals and consumer
adhesives. The company rates as
the #1 producer of household and
school glues (Elmer's) in the United
States, and also makes caulks and
sealants.*

## BP Amoco p.l.c.
Britannic House
1 Finsbury Circus
London EC2M 7BA
United Kingdom
www.bp.com/index.asp
Peter D. Sutherland, Chairman
*Petroleum refining*

## Bristol-Meyers Squibb
345 Park Ave.
New York, NY 10154
Website: http://www.bms.com/
landing/data/index.html
Charles A. Heimbold Jr., Chairman
and CEO
*Pharmaceutical manufacturer*

## Browning Ferris Industries (now a subsidiary of Allied Waste Industries)
757 N. Eldridge Rd.
Houston, TX 77079
Website: http://www.bfi.com
Donald W. Slager, President and
CEO; VP Operations, Allied Waste
Industries
*Waste management*

## Brunswick
1 N. Field Court
Lake Forest, IL 60045
George W. Buckley, Chairman and
CEO
*Transportation equipment*

## Burlington Northern Santa FE
2650 Lou Menk Dr.
Fort Worth, TX 76131
Website: http://www.bnsf.com
Robert D. Krebs, Chairman and
CEO
*Railroads*

## Campbell Soup
Campbell Place
Camden, NJ 08103
Website: http://
www.campbellsoups.com
Dale F. Morrisson, CEO
*Food manufacturer*

**Cardinal Health**
7000 Cardinal Place
Dublin, OH 43017
Website: http://www.cardinal-
health.com
Robert D. Walter, Chairman and
CEO
*Wholesaler*

**Case**
700 State St.
Racine, WI 53404
Website: http://www.casecorp.com
Jean-Pierre Rosso, CEO
*Industrial and farm equipment*

**Caterpillar**
100 N.E. Adams St.
Peoria, IL 61629
Website: http://
www.caterpillar.com
Glen A. Barton, Chairman and CEO
*Industrial and farm equipment*

**Cendant**
9 W. 57th St.
New York, NY 1001
Website: http://www.cendant.com
Henry R. Silverman, Chairman,
President, and CEO
*Advertising, marketing*

**Centex**
2728 North Harwood
Dallas, TX 75201
Website: http://www.centex.com
Laurence E. Hirsch, Chairman and
CEO
*Engineering, construction*

**Chase Manhattan Corp.**
270 Park Ave.
New York, NY 10017
Website: http://www.chase.com
William B. Harrison Jr., Chairman,
President, and CEO, Chase
Manhattan and Chase Bank
*Commercial bank*

**Chateau Marmont**
8221 Sunset Blvd.
Los Angeles, CA 90046
*John Belushi died here in 1982.*

**Chevron**
575 Market St.
San Francisco, CA 94105
Website: http://www.chevron.com
David J. O'Reilly, Chairman and
CEO
*Petroleum refining*

**Chubb**
15 Mountain View Rd.
Warren, NJ 07061
Website: http://www.chubb.com
Dean R. O'Hare, CEO
*(stock) P and C insurance*

**Cigna**
1 Liberty Place
Philadelphia, PA 19192
Website: http://www.cigna.com
Wilson H. Taylor, CEO
*(stock) Life and health insurance*

**Cinergy**
139 E. Fourth St.
Cincinnati, OH 45202
Website: http://www.cinergy.com
Jackson H. Randolph, Chairman
James E. Rogers, VC, President,
and CEO
*Gas and electric utilities*

## Circuit City
9950 Maryland Dr.
Richmond, VA 23233
Website: http://www.circuitcity.com
Richard L. Sharp, President and
CEO
*The #2 U.S. retailer of major
appliances and consumer
electronics*

## Cisco Systems
170 W. Tasman Dr.
San Jose, CA 95134
Website: http://www.cisco.com
John P. Morgridge, Chairman
*Electronics, network
communications*

## Citicorp
153 E. 53rd St.
New York, NY 10043
Website: http://www.citibank.com
Sanford I. Weill, Chairman and
CEO
*Multinational bank*

## CMS Energy
Fairlane Plaza South, Suite #1100
330 Town Center Dr.
Dearborn, MI 48126
Website: http://
www.cmsenergy.com
William T. McCormick Jr., CEO
*Gas and electric utilities*

## CNF Inc.
3240 Hillview Ave.
Palo Alto, CA 94304
Website: http://www.cnf.com
Donald E. Moffitt, CEO
*Trucking*

## Coastal
9 Greenway Plaza
Houston, TX 77046
Website: http://
www.coastalcorp.com
David A. Arledge, Chariman,
President, and CEO
*Petroleum refining*

## Coca-Cola
1 Coca-Cola Plaza
Atlanta, GA 30313
Website: http://www.cocacola.com
Douglas N. Daft, Chairman and
CEO
*Beverages*

## Coca-Cola Enterprises
2500 Windy Ridge Pkwy.
Atlanta, GA 30339
Website: http://www.cokecce.com
Summerfield K. Johnston Jr.,
Chairman and CEO
*Beverages*

## Colgate-Palmolive
300 Park Ave.
New York, NY 10022
Website: http://www.colgate.com
Reuben Mark, CEO
*Soaps, cosmetics*

## Columbia Energy Group
13880 Dulles Corner Ln.
Herndon, VA 20171
Website: http://
www.columbiaenergy.com
Oliver G. Richard III, Chairman,
President, and CEO
*Gas and electric utilities*

**Columbia/HCA Healthcare**
1 Park Plaza
Nashville, TN 37203
Thomas F. Frist Jr., Chairman and
CEO
*Healthcare*

**Comcast**
1500 Market St.
Philadelphia, PA 19102
Website: http://www.comcast.com
Ralph J. Roberts, Chairman
*Telecommunications*

**Comdisco**
6111 N. River Rd.
Rosemont, IL 60018
Website: http://
www.comdisco.com
Nicholas K. Pontikes, President and
CEO
*Computer and data services*

**Comerica**
Comerica Tower at Detroit Center
500
Woodward Ave., MC 3391
Detroit, MI 48226
Website: http://www.comerica.com
Eugene A. Miller, Chairman,
President, and CEO
*Commercial banks*

**Compaq Computer**
20555 State Hwy. 249
Houston, TX 77070
Website: http://www.compaq.com
Michael D. Capellas, President and
CEO
*Computers, office equipment*

**CompUSA**
14951 N. Dallas Pkwy.
Dallas, TX 75240
Website: http://www.compusa.com
Carlos Slim Domit, Chairman
Harold F. Compton, CEO
*Computer retailers*

**Computer Associates
International**
1 Computer Associates Plaza
Islandia, NY 11788
Website: http://www.cai.com
Charles B. Wang, Chairman and
CEO
*Computer software*

**Computer Sciences**
2100 E. Grand Ave.
El Segundo, CA 90245
Website: http://www.csc.com
Van B. Honeycutt, Chairman,
President, and CEO
*Computer and data services*

**ConAgra**
1 ConAgra Dr.
Omaha, NE 68102
Website: http://www.conagra.com
Bruce Rohde, Chairman, President,
and CEO
*Food producer*

**Conseco**
11825 N. Pennsylvania St.
Carmel, IN 46032
Website: http://www.conseco.com
Gary C. Wendt, Chairman and CEO
*(stock) Life, and Health insurance*

**Consolidated Edison**
4 Irving Place
New York, NY 10003
Website: http://www.coned.com
Eugene R. McGrath, Chairman,
President, and CEO
*Gas and electric utilities*

**Consolidated Stores**
300 Phillipi Rd.
Columbus, OH 43228
Website: http://www.cnstores.com
William G. Kelley, CEO
*Specialist retailers, KB Stores,
Big Lot/Odd/Lot Stores*

**Continental Airlines**
1600 Smith St., Dept. HQSEO
Houston, TX 77002
Website http://
www.continental.com
Gordon M. Bethune, Chairman and
CEO
*Airline*

**Cooper Industries**
600 Travis St., Suite #5800
Houston, TX 77002
Website: http://
www.cooperindustries.com
H. John Riley Jr., Chairman,
President, and CEO
*Electronics, electrical equipment*

**CoreStates Financial Corp.**
One First Union Center
301 South College St. Suite #4000
Charlotte, NC 28288
Website: http://
www.corestates.com
G. Alex Bernhardt Sr., Chairman
and CEO
*Commercial bank*

**Corning**
1 Riverfront Plaza
Corning, NY 14831
Website: http://www.corning.com
Roger G. Ackerman, Chairman and
CEO
*Building materials, glass*

**Corporate Express**
1 Environmental Way
Broomfield, CO 80021
Website: http://www.corporate-
express.com
Robert L. King, President and CEO,
North American Operations
*Specialist retailers, office products*

**Costco**
999 Lake Dr.
Issaquah, WA 98027
Website: http://www.costco.com
Jeffrey H. Brotman, Chairman
James D. Sinegal, President and
CEO
*Specialist retailers, warehouse
store*

**CP&L Energy, Inc.**
411 Fayetteville St.
Raleigh, NC 27602
Website: http://www.cplc.com
William Cavanaugh III, Chairman,
President, and CEO
*Gas and electric utilities*

**Crown, Cork and Seal**
1 Crown Way
Philadelphia, PA 19106
Website: http://
www.crowncork.com
William J. Avery, Chariman and
CEO
*Metal products*

**CSX**
James Center
901 E. Cary St.
Richmond, VA 23219
Website: http://www.csx.com
John W. Snow, CEO
*Railroads*

**Culinary Arts Institute of Louisiana**
427 Lafayette St.
Baton Rouge, LA 70802
Website: http://www.caila.com/
Vi Harrington, Founder and Owner
*An associate degree–granting institute located in the deep South. It is unique in that 50 percent of the culinary student's time is spent cooking and running a white-linen, full service restaurant. Because of this, a two-year program can be completed in 15 months. The institute participates in exchange programs with Le Cordon Bleu, in Paris, France, and the University of Hawaii.*

**Culinary Institute of America at Greystone**
2555 Main St.
St. Helena, CA 94574
Website: http://www.ciachef.edu
Roger Riccardi, Managing Director
*Offers continuing education and career development classes for food and wine professionals in highly focused formats. Courses vary in length from three days to a 30-week Baking and Pastry Arts Certification Program, with the average class lasting one week and an average student stay of three weeks.*

**Cummins Engine**
500 Jackson St.
Columbus, IN 47202
Theodore M. Solso, Chairman and CEO
*Industrial and farm equipment*

**CVS**
One CVS Dr.
Woonsocket, RI 02895
Website: http://www.cvs.com/splash.asp
Thomas M. Ryan, Chairman, President, and CEO
*Food and drug stores*

**DaimlerChrysler**
Epplestrasse 225
70546 Stuttgart
Germany
Website: http://www.daimlerchrysler.com
Hilmar Kopper, Chairman, Supervisory Board
*Motor vehicles*

**Darden Restaurants**
5900 Lake Ellenor Dr.
Orlando, FL 32809
Joe R. Lee, Chairman and CEO
*Food services*

**Dean Foods**
600 N. River Rd.
Franklin Park, IL 60131
Website: http://www.deanfoods.com
Howard M. Dean, CEO
*Food producer*

**Deere**
1 John Deere Place
Moline, IL 61265
Website: http://www.deere.com
Hans W. Becherer, Chairman
Robert Lane, President and CEO
*Industrial and farm equipment*

**Dell Computer**
1 Dell Way
Round Rock, TX 78682
Website: http://www.dell.com
Michael S. Dell, CEO
*Computers, office equipment*

**Delta Airlines**
1030 Delta Blvd.
Atlanta, GA 30320
Website: http://www.delta-air.com
Leo F. Mullin, Chairman, President,
and CEO
*Airline*

**Dillards**
1600 Cantrell Rd.
Little Rock, AR 72201
Website: http://www.dillards.com
William Dillard, Chairman
William Dillard II, CEO
*General merchandisers,
department stores*

**Dole Foods**
1365 Oak Crest Dr.
Westlake Village, CA 91361
Website: http://www.dole.com
David H. Murdock, Chairman and
CEO
*Food producer*

**Dominion Resources Black
Warrior Trust**
Bank of America Plaza
901 Main St., 17th Floor
Dallas, TX 75202
Website: http://www.dom.com
Ron E. Hooper, VP and
Administrator
*Gas and electric utilities*

**Domino's Pizza LLC**
30 Frank Lloyd Wright Dr.
PO Box 997
Ann Arbor, MI 48106
Website: http://www.dominos.com
David Brandon, Chairman and
CEO

**Doodie.com**
PO Box 93757
Los Angeles, CA 90093
Website: http://www.doodie.com
E-mail: tommyswan@eartlink.net
Tom Winkler, Creator
*Internet content provider*

**Dover**
280 Park Ave.
New York, NY 10017
Website: http://
www.dovercorporation.com
Thomas L. Reece, Chairman,
President, and CEO
*Industrial and farm equipment*

**Dow Chemical**
2030 Dow Center
Midland, MI 48674
Website: http://www.dow.com
Frank P. Popoff, Chairman
William S. Stavropoulos, President
and CEO
*Chemicals*

**The Dow Chemical Company**
39 Old Ridgebury Rd.
Danbury, CT 06817
Website: http://www.dow.com
William H. Joyce, Chairman,
President, and CEO
*Chemicals*

**Dresser Industries**
10077 Grogans Mill Rd., Suite
#500
The Woodlands, TX 77380
Website: http://www.dresser.com
David Norton, President and CEO
*Industrial and farm equipment*

**DTE Energy**
2000 Second Ave.
Detroit, MI 48226
Website: http://
www.dteenergy.com
Anthony F. Earley Jr., Chairman,
President, CEO, and COO, DTE
Energy and Detroit Edison
*Gas and electric utilities*

**Duke Energy**
422 S. Church St.
Charlotte, NC 28202
Website: http://www.duke-
energy.com
Richard B. Priory, CEO
*Gas and electric utilities*

**Eastman Chemical**
100 N. Eastman Rd.
Kingsport, TN 37660
Website: http://www.eastman.com
Earnest W. Deavenport Jr., CEO
*Chemicals*

**Eastman Kodak**
343 State St.
Rochester, NY 14650
Website: http://www.kodak.com
George M. C. Fisher, CEO
Daniel A. Carp, President, CEO,
and COO
*Scientific, photography equipment,
control equipment*

**Eaton**
Eaton Center
Cleveland, OH 44114
Website: http://www.eaton.com
Alexander M. "Sandy" Cutler,
Chairman, President, and CEO
*Electrical power distribution and
control equipment, truck drivetrain
systems, engine components, and
hydraulic products for the
aerospace, automotive, and
marine industries*

**Edison International**
2244 Walnut Grove Ave.
Rosemead, CA 91770
Website: http://www.edisonx.com
John E. Bryson, Chairman,
President, and CEO
*Gas and electric utilities*

**E. I. du Pont de Nemours**
1007 Market St.
Wilmington, DE 19898
Website: http://www.dupont.com
Charles O. Holliday Jr., Chairman
and CEO
*The largest chemical company in
the United States*

**Eli Lilly**
Lilly Corporate Center
Indianapolis, IN 46285
Website: http://www.lilly.com
Sidney Taurel, Chairman,
President, and CEO
*Pharmaceuticals, makes Prozac,
the world's best-selling
antidepressant*

**El Paso Natural Gas**
1001 Louisiana St.
Houston, TX 77002
William A. Wise, Chairman,
President, and CEO
*Pipelines*

## Electronic Data Systems
5400 Legacy Dr.
Plano, TX 75024
Website: http://www.eds.com
Richard H. Brown, Chairman and
CEO
*Computer and data services*

## EMC
35 Parkwood Dr.
Hopkinton, MA 01748
Website: http://www.emc.com
Richard J. Egan, Chairman
Michael C. Ruettgers, CEO
*Computer peripherals*

## Emerson Electric
8000 W. Florissant Ave.
St. Louis, MO 63136
Website: http://
www.gotoemerson.com
Charles F. Knight, Chairman and
CEO
*Electronics, electrical equipment*

## Energizer Holdings, Inc.
800 Chouteau Ave.
St. Louis, MO 63164
Website: http://www.energizer.com
William P. Stiritz, Chairman
J. Patrick Mulcahy, CEO
*The #2 battery maker in the United
States*

## Engelhard
101 Wood Ave.
Iselin, NJ 08830
Website: http://
www.engelhard.com
Orin R. Smith, Chairman and CEO
*Chemicals*

## Enron
1400 Smith St.
Houston, TX 77002
Website: http://www.enron.com
Kenneth L. Lay, CEO
*The #1 buyer and seller of natural
gas and the top wholesale power
marketer in the United States*

## Entergy
639 Loyola Ave.
New Orleans, LA 70113
Website: http://www.entergy.com
Robert Luft, Chairman
J. Wayne Leonard, CEO
Donald C. Hintz, President
*Gas and electric utilities*

## Entertainment Media Ventures
LLC
828 Moraga Dr., 2nd Floor
Los Angeles, CA 90049
Website: http://
www.emventures.com
E-mail: sandy@emventures.com
Sanford R. Climan, Founder
*Venture capital*

## Estee Lauder
767 Fifth Ave.
New York, NY 10153
Website: http://
www.elcompanies.com
Leonard A. Lauder, CEO
*Soaps, cosmetics*

## Exxon Mobil Corporation
5959 Las Colinas Blvd.
Irving, TX 75039
Website: http://
www.exxon.mobil.com
Lee R. Raymond, Chairman,
President, and CEO

## Fannie Mae
3900 Wisconsin Ave. N.W.
Washington, DC 20016
Website: http://
www.fanniemae.com
E-mail:
webmaster@fanniemae.com.
Franklin D. Raines, Chairman and
CEO
*The world's largest diversified
financial company and the nation's
largest source of home mortagage
funds*

## Farmland Industries
3315 N. Farmland Trffcwy.
Kansas City, MO 64116
Website: http://www.farmland.com
Albert J. Shivley, Chairman
*Food producer*

## FasTV
5670 Wilshire Blvd., Suite #1550
Los Angeles, CA 90036
E-mail: bswegles@fastv.com
Prince Khaled Al-Nehyen, Chaiman
William Wegles, President and COO
*Interactive TV*

## Federal Home Loan Mortgage
8200 Jones Branch Dr.
McLean, VA 22102
Website: http://
www.freddiemac.com
Leland C. Brendsel, Chairman and
CEO
*A stockholder-owned corporation
chartered by Congress in 1970 to
create a continuous flow of funds
to mortgage lenders in support of
homeownership and rental
housing*

## Federated Department Stores
7 W. Seventh St.
Cincinnati, OH 45202
Website: http://www.federated-
fds.com
James M. Zimmerman, Chairman
and CEO
*General merchandisers; Federated
runs Bloomingdale's and Macy's
chains, six regional chains:
Lazarus, The Bon Marche,
Burdines, Stern's, Rich's,
Goldsmith's*

## FedEx
6075 Poplar Ave., Suite #300
Memphis, TN 38119
Website: http://www.fedexcorp.com
Frederick W. Smith, Chairman,
President, and CEO
*Mail, package, freight delivery*

## First Data
5660 New Northside Dr., Suite
#1400
Atlanta, GA 30328
Website: http://
www.firstdatacorp.com
Henry C. "Ric" Duques, Chairman
and CEO
*Computer and data services*

## First Union Corp.
1 First Union Center
Charlotte, NC 28288
Website: http://www.firstunion.com
G. Kennedy "Ken" Thompson, CEO
*Commercial bank*

**FirstEnergy**
76 S. Main St.
Akron, OH 44308
Website: http://
www.firstenergycorp.com
H. Peter Burg, Chairman and CEO
Anthony J. Alexander, President
*Gas and electric utilities*

**Fleet Boston Financial Group**
1 Federal St.
Boston, MA 02110
Website: http://www.fleet.com
Terrence Murray, Chairman and
CEO
*Commercial bank*

**Fleetwood Enterprises**
3125 Myers St.
Riverside, CA 92503
Website: http://
www.fleetwood.com
Glenn F. Kummer, Chairman and
CEO
*Engineering, construction*

**Florida Progress**
1 Progress Plaza
St. Petersburg, FL 33701
Website: http://www.fpc.com
Richard Korpan, Chairman,
President, and CEO
*Gas and electric utilities*

**Fluor**
1 Enterprise Dr.
Aliso Viejo, CA 92656
Website: http://www.fluor.com
Philip J. Carroll Jr., Chairman and
CEO
*Engineering, construction*

**FMC**
200 E. Randolph Dr.
Chicago, IL 60601
Website: http://www.fmc.com
Robert N. Burt, Chairman and CEO
*Chemicals*

**Ford Motor Company**
One American Rd.
Dearborn, MI 48126
Website: http://www.ford.com
William C. Ford Jr., Chairman
Jacques A. Nasser, President and
CEO
*Autos and trucks*

**Fort James Corp.**
1650 Lake Cook Rd.
Deerfield, IL 60015
Website: http://www.fortjames.com
Miles L. Marsh, Chairman and CEO
*Forest and paper products*

**Fortune Brands**
300 Tower Pkwy.
Lincolnshire, IL 60069
Website: http://
www.fortunebrands.com
Norman H. Wesley, Chairman and
CEO
*Leading U.S. producer of distilled
spirits (Jim Beam, DeKuyper,
Ronrico) and golf equipment
(Titleist, Cobra, FootJoy, Pinnacle).
Fortune also makes home
products (Moen faucets, Aristokraft
and Schrock cabinets, and Master
Lock padlocks) as well as office
products (ACCO, Day-Timers,
Swingline).*

**Foster Wheeler**
Perryville Corporate Park
Clinton, NJ 08809
Website: http://www.fwc.com
Richard J. Swift, Chairman,
President, and CEO
*Engineering, construction*

**FPL Group**
700 Universe Blvd.
Juno Beach, FL 33408
Website: http://www.fplgroup.com
James L. Broadhead, Chairman
and CEO
*Gas and electric utilities*

**Fred Meyer, Inc.**
3800 S.E. 22nd Ave.
Portland, OR 97202
Website: http://
www.fredmeyer.com
Ronald W. Burkle, Chairman
*Food and drug stores*

**Gannett**
1100 Wilson Blvd.
Arlington, VA 22234
Website: http://www.gannett.com
John J. Curley, CEO
Douglas H. McCorkindale,
President and CEO
*Publishing, printing*

**GAP**
1 Harrison St.
San Francisco, CA 94105
Website: http://www.gap.com
Donald G. Fisher, Chairman
Millard S. "Mickey" Dre, President
and CEO
*Clothing retailer*

**Gateway**
4545 Towne Centre Ct.
San Diego, CA 92121
Website: http://www.gateway.com
Theodore W. Waitt, Chairman
David J. Robino, Vice Chairman
Jeffrey Weitzen, President and CEO
*Computers, office equipment*

**GenAmerica Corporation**
700 Market St.
St. Louis, MO 63101
Richard A. Liddy, Chairman,
President, and CEO
*Life and health (stock) insurance*

**General Dynamics**
3190 Fairview Park Dr.
Falls Church, VA 22042
Nicholas D. Chabraja, Chairman
and CEO
*Aerospace*

**General Electric**
3135 Easton Turnpike
Fairfield, CT 06431
Website: http://www.ge.com
Mr. John F. "Jack" Welch Jr.,
Chairman and CEO
*Electrical equipment company*

**General Mills**
1 General Mills Blvd.
Minneapolis, MN 55426
Website: http://
www.generalmills.com
Stephen W. Sanger, Chairman and
CEO
*Food producer*

**General Motors**
300 Renaissance Center
Detroit, MI 48265
Website http://www.gm.com
Mr. John F Smith Jr., CEO
*The world's #1 maker of cars and trucks*

**Genuine Parts**
2999 Circle 75 Pkwy.
Atlanta, GA 30339
Website: http://www.genpt.com
Larry L. Prince, Chairman and CEO
*Wholesalers, automobile parts*

**Georgia-Pacific**
133 Peachtree St. N.E.
Atlanta, GA 30303
Website: http://www.gp.com
A. D. Correll, Chairman, President, and CEO
*Forest and paper products*

**Giant Food**
6300 Sheriff Rd.
Landover, MD 20785
Richard Baird, Chairman, President, and CEO
*Food and drug stores*

**Gillette**
Prudential Tower Building
Boston, MA 02199
Michael C. Hawley, Chairman and CEO
Edward F. DeGraan, President and COO
*Metal products*

**Golden West Financial Corp.**
1901 Harrison St.
Oakland, CA 94612
Herbert M. Sandler, Co-Chairman and Co-CEO
Marion Sandler, Co-Chairman and Co-CEO
*Savings institution*

**Goodyear Tire and Rubber**
1144 E. Market St.
Akron, OH 44316
Website: http://www.goodyear.com
Samir G. Gibara, Chairman, President, and CEO
*Rubber and plastic products*

**GoTo.com**
140 West Union St.
Pasadena, CA 91103
Website: http://www.goto.com
E-mail: info@goto.com
Jeffrey Brewer, CEO
*Web portal*

**Graybar Electric**
34 N. Meramec Ave.
St. Louis, MO 63105
Carl L. Hall, President and CEO
*Wholesaler*

**Green Bay Packers, Inc.**
Lombardi Ave.
Green Bay, WI 54304
Robert E. Harlan, President and CEO
Ron Wolf, EVP and General Manager
*A publically owned nonprofit corporation unlike any other football team.*

**Guardian Life Insurance Co. of America**
7 Hanover Sq.
New York, NY 10004
Website: http://www.glic.com
Joseph D. Sargent, President and CEO
*Life and health (mutual) insurance*

**Halliburton**
3600 Lincoln Plaza
Dallas, TX 75201
Website: http://www.halliburton.com
Richard B. Cheney, CEO
David J. Lesar, President and COO
*The world's #1 provider of oil field services*

**Hannaford Bros.**
145 Pleasant Hill Rd.
Scarborough, ME 04074
Website: http://www.hannaford.com
Walter J. Salmon, Chairman
Hugh G. Farrington, President and CEO
*Food and drug stores*

**Harcourt General**
27 Boylston St.
Chestnut Hill, MA 02167
Website: http://www.harcourtgeneral.com
Richard A. Smith, CEO
Brian J. Knez, President and Co-CEO
*General merchandisers*

**Harnischfeger Ind.**
3600 S. Lake Dr.
St. Francis, WI 53235
Website: http://www.harnischfeger.com
Robert B. Hoffman, Chairman
John N. Hanson, VC, CEO, President, and COO
*Industrial and farm equipment*

**Harris**
1025 W. NASA Blvd.
Melbourne, FL 32919
Website: http://www.harris.com
Phillip W. Farmer, Chairman, President, and CEO
*Electronics, electrical equipment*

**Hartford Financial Services**
Hartford Plaza
Hartford, CT 06115
Website: http://www.thehartford.com
Ramani Ayer, CEO
*P and C (stock) insurance*

**Hasbro**
1027 Newport Ave.
Pawtucket, RI 02862
Website: http://www.hasbro.com
Alan G. Hassenfeld, Chairman and CEO
*The #2 toy maker in the United States*

**H. J. Heinz**
600 Grant St.
Pittsburgh, PA 15219
Anthony J. F. O'Reilly, CEO
William R. Johnson, President and CEO
*Food producer*

**Health Care Finance Administration**
7500 Security Blvd.
Baltimore, MD 21244
Website: http://www.hcfa.gov/
E-mail: Question@hcfa.gov
Nancy-Ann Min DeParle, Administrator
*Federal agency that administers the Medicare, Medicaid, and Child Health Insurance Programs*

**Health Insurance Association of America**
555 13th St. NW, #600E
Washington, DC 20004
Website: http://www.hiaa.org/
E-mail: webmaster@hiaa.org
Charles N. Kahn, President
*A national trade association based in Washington, D.C. Its more than 250 members are insurers and managed care companies that serve tens of millions of Americans.*

**Health Net, Inc.**
21600 Oxnard St.
Woodland Hills, CA 91367
www.health.net
Richard W. Hanselman, Chairman
Jay M. Gellert, President and CEO
*Healthcare*

**HealthSouth**
1 HealthSouth Pkwy.
Birmingham, AL 35243
Website: http://
www.healthsouth.com
E-mail: info@healthsouth.net
Richard M. Scrushy, Chairman and CEO
*Healthcare*

**Hershey Foods**
100 Crystal A Dr.
Hershey, PA 17033
Website: http://www.hersheys.com
Kenneth L. Wolfe, Chairman and CEO
*Food producer, chocolate maker. The market leader in the U.S. candy business.*

**Hewlett Packard**
3000 Hanover St.
Palo Alto, CA 94304
Website: http://www.hp.com
Richard A. Hackborn, Chairman
Carleton S. "Carly" Fiorina, CEO and President
*Computers, office equipment*

**H. F. Amhanson**
225 S. Main Ave.
Sioux Falls, SD 57104
Curtis L. Hage, Chairman, President, and CEO
*Savings institution*

**Hilton Hotels**
9336 Civic Center Dr.
Beverly Hills, CA 90210
Website: http://www.hilton.com
Barron Hilton, Chairman
Stephen F. Bollenbach, President and CEO
*Hotels, casinos, resorts*

**Hollywood Stock Exchange**
225 Arizona Ave., #250
Santa Monica, CA 90401
Website: http://www.hsx.com
E-mail: max@hsx.com
Max Keiser, Co-Founder and chairman
*Internet content provider*

**Home Depot**
2455 Paces Ferry Rd. N.W.
Atlanta, GA 30339
Website: http://
www.homedepot.com
Arthur Blank, President and CEO
*Specialist retailers, hardware*

**Homestore.com**
225 W. Hillcrest Dr., Suite #100
Thousand Oaks, CA 91360
Website: http://
www.homestore.com
E-mail:
webmaster@homestore.com
Stuart H. Wolff, Chairman and CEO

**Honeywell**
101 Columbia Rd. PO Box 2245
Morristown, NJ 07962-2245
Website: http://
www.honeywell.com
Michael R. Bonsignore, Chairman
and CEO
*Scientific, photo, control equipment*

**Hormel Foods**
1 Hormel Place
Austin, MN 55912
Website: http://www.hormel.com
Joel W. Johnson, Chairman,
President, and CEO
*Food maker*

**Household Financial**
2700 Sanders Rd.
Prospect Heights, IL 60070
Website: http://
www.household.com
William F. Aldinger III, Chairman
and CEO
*Diversified financials*

**Humana**
500 W. Main St.
Louisville, KY 40201
Website: http://www.humana.com
David A. Jones, Chairman
David A. Jones Jr., VC
Michael B. McCallister, President
and CEO
*Healthcare*

**IBP**
800 Stevens Port Dr.
Dakota Dunes, SD 57049
Website: http://www.ibpinc.com
Robert L. Peterson, Chairman and
CEO
Richard L. Bond, President and
COO
*Food producer*

**Idealab**
130 W. Union St.
Pasadena, CA 91103
Web site: http://www.idealab.com
E-mail: info@idealab.com
Bill Gross, Chairman and Founder
*Venture capital*

**iFilm Network**
400 Pacific Ave., 3rd Floor
San Francisco, CA 94133
Website: http://www.ifilm.net
E-mail: rodger@ifilm.net
Rodger Radereman, Co-Chairman
and Founder
*Online film community*

**Ikon Office Solutions**
70 Valley Stream Pkwy.
Valley Forge, PA 19482
Website: http://www.ikon.com
James J. Forese, Chairman,
President, and CEO
*Wholesalers*

**Illinois Tool Works**
3600 W. Lake Ave.
Glenview, IL 60025
Website: http://www.itwinc.com
W. James Farrell, CEO
*Metal products*

**IMC Global**
2100 Sanders Rd.
Northbrook, IL 60062
Website: http://www.imcglobal.com
Joseph P. Sullivan, Chairman
Douglas A. Pertz, President and
CEO
*Chemicals, fertilizer*

**Ingersoll-Rand**
200 Chestnut Ridge Rd.
Woodcliff Lake, NJ 07675
Website: http://www.ingersoll-
rand.com
Herbert L. Henkel, Chairman,
President, and CEO
*Industrial and farm equipment*

**Ingram Micro**
1600 E. St. Andrew Place
Santa Ana, CA 92705
Website: http://
www.ingrammicro.com
Jerre L. Stead, Chairman
Mr. Kent B. Foster, President and
CEO
*Wholesalers, computer technology
products and service*

**Intel**
2200 Mission College Blvd.
Santa Clara, CA 95052-8119
Website: http://www.intel.com
Gordon E. Moore, Chairman
Emeritus
Andrew S. Grove, Chairman
Craig R. Barrett, President and CEO
*Computer peripherals and chip
maker*

**International Business Machines**
Old Orchard Rd.
Armonk, NY 10504
Website: http://www.ibm.com
Mr. Louis V Gerstner, Chairman
and CEO
*Maker of computer systems*

**International Paper**
2 Manhattanville Rd.
Purchase, NY 10577
Website: http://
www.internationalpaper.com
John T. Dillon, Chairman and CEO
*Forest and paper products*

**Interpublic Group**
1271 Ave. of the Americas
New York, NY 10020
Website: http://
www.interpublic.com
Philip H. Geier Jr., Chairman and
CEO
John J. Dooner Jr., President and
COO
*Advertising, marketing*

**Interstate Bakeries**
12 E. Armour Blvd.
Kansas City, MO 64111
Charles A. Sullivan, CEO
Michael D. Kafoure, President and
COO
*Food producers*

**Intertainer**
10950 Washington Blvd.
Culver City, CA 90232
Website: http://
www.intertainer.com
Richard Baskin, Co-Chairman and
CEO
E-mail: rb@intertainer.com
Jonathan Taplan, Co-Chairman and
CEP
E-mail: tap@intertainer.com
*Web portal*

**ITT Industries**
4 W. Red Oak Lane
White Plains, NY 10604
Website: http://www.ittind.com
D. Travis Engen, Chairman and
CEO
*Pipeline of products includes
pumps, defense systems, and
services, specialty products, and
connectors and switches*

**JC Penney**
6501 Legacy Dr.
Plano, TX 75024
Website: http://www.jcpenney.com
James E. Oesterreicher, Chairman
and CEO
*General merchandisers*

**John Hancock Financial Services**
John Hancock Place
Boston, MA 02117
Website: http://
www.johnhancock.com
Stephen L. Brown, CEO
*Insurance (including variable,
universal, and term life, as well as
group long-term-care), annuities
and mutual funds, financial
products, investment
management, and corporate
services*

**Johnson Controls**
5757 N. Green Bay Ave.
Milwaukee, WI 53209
Website: http://www.jci.com
James H. Keyes, Chairman and
CEO
*Motor vehicles and parts*

**Johnson & Johnson**
1 J&J Plaza
New Brunswick, NJ 08933
Website: http://www.jnj.com
Ralph S. Larsen, Chairman and
CEO
*Pharmaceuticals*

**J. P. Morgan**
60 Wall St.
New York, NY 10260
Website: http://
www.jpmorgan.com
Douglas A. "Sandy" Warner III,
Chairman and CEO
*Commercial bank*

**Kellogg**
1 Kellogg Square
Battle Creek, MI 49016
Website: http://www.kelloggs.com
Arnold G. Langbo, CEO
*Food producer*

**Kelly Services**
999 W. Big Beaver Rd.
Troy, MI 48084
Website: http://
www.kellyservices.com
Terence E. Adderley, Chairman,
President and CEO
Temporary services

**KeyCorp**
127 Public Square
Cleveland, OH 44114
Website: http://www.keybank.com
Robert W. Gillespie, Chairman &
CEO
*Commercial bank*

**Kimberly-Clark**
351 Phelps Dr.
Irving, TX 75038
Website: http://www.kimberly-clark.com
Wayne R. Sanders, Chairman &
CEO
*Forest and paper products*

**Kmart**
3100 W. Big Beaver Rd.
Troy, MI 48084
Website: http://www.kmart.com
Charles C. Conaway, Chairman of
the Board and CEO
*General merchandisers*

**Knight-Ridder**
50 W. San Fernando St.
San Jose, CA 95113
Website: http://www.kri.com
P. Anthony Ridder, Chairman &
CEO
*Publishing, printing*

**Kohl's**
N. 56 W. 17000 Ridgewood Dr.
Menomonee Falls, WI 53051
William S. Kellogg, CEO
*General merchandisers*

**Kroeger**
1014 Vine St.
Cincinnati, OH 45202
Website: http://www.kroger.com
Dave Dillon, President and COO
*Food and drug stores*

**Kroft, Sid & Marty**
7710 Woodrow Wilson Dr.
Los Angeles, CA 90046
*Producers of classic children's
television shows*

**Lear**
21557 Telegraph Rd.
Southfield, MI 48086
Website: http://www.lear.com
Kenneth L. Way, CEO
*Motor vehicles and parts*

**Leggett and Platt**
No. 1 Leggett Rd.
Carthage, MO 64836
Website: http://www.regionalstock.com/
Harry M. Cornell Jr., Chairman
Felix E. Wright, VC, President, and
CEO
*Furniture*

**Lehman Brothers Holdings**
3 World Financial Center
New York, NY 10285
Website: http://www.lehman.com
Richard S. Fuld Jr., Chairman and
CEO
*Securities*

**LG & E**
220 W. Main St.
Louisville, KY 40232
Website: http://www.lgeenergy.com
Roger W. Hale, Chairman and CEO
*Gas and electric utilities*

**Liberty Mutual Insurance Group**
Headquarters:
175 Berkeley St.
Boston, MA 02117
Gary L. Countryman, CEO
*P and C (mutual) insurance*

**Limited**
3 Limited Pkwy.
Columbus, OH 43230
Website: http://www.limited.com
Leslie H. Wexner, CEO
*Specialist retailers*

**Lincoln National**
1500 Market St., Suite 3900
Philadelphia, PA 19012
Website: http://www.lfg.com
Jon A. Boscia, President and CEO
*Life and health (stock) Insurance*

**Litton Industries**
21240 Burbank Blvd.
Woodland Hills, CA 91367
Website: http://www.littoncorp.com
Orion L. Hoch, Chairman Emeritus
Michael R. Brown, Chairman and
CEO
Ronald Sugar, President and COO
*Electronics, electrical equipment*

**Lockheed Martin**
6801 Rockledge Dr.
Bethesda, MD 20817
Website: http://
www.lockheedmartin.com
Robert H. Trice Jr., Vice President,
Corporate Business Development
*Aerospace*

**Loews**
667 Madison Ave.
New York, NY 10021
Website: http://www.loews.com
Laurence A. Tisch, Co-Chairman
Preston R. Tisch, Co-Chairman
James S. Tisch, Office of the
President, President, and CEO
*P and C (stock) insurance*

**Long Island Power Authority**
333 Earle Ovington Blvd.
Uniondale, NY 11553
Website: http://www.lipower.org/
Richard M. Kessel, Chairman
Patrick J. Foye, Deputy Chairman
Howard E. Steinberg, Deputy
Chairman
*Gas and electric utilities*

**Longs Drug Stores**
141 N. Civic Dr.
Walnut Creek, CA 94596
Website: http://www.longs.com
Robert M. Long, Chairman
Steve D. Roath, President and CEO
*Food and drug stores*

**Lowe's**
1605 Curtis Bridge Rd.
Wilkesboro, NC 28697
Website: http://www.lowes.com
Robert L. Tillman, Chairman,
President and CEO
*Specialist retailers*

**LTV**
200 Public Square
Cleveland, OH 44114
Website: http://www.ltvsteel.com
Peter Kelly, Chairman, President,
and CEO
*Metal producer*

**Lucent Technologies**
600 Mountain Ave.
Murray Hill, NJ 07974-0636
Website: http://www.lucent.com
Richard A. McGinn, Chairman and
CEO
*Electronics, electrical equipment*

**LULAC National Education Service Center (League of United Latin American Citizens)**
221 North Kansas, Suite 1200
El Paso, TX 79901
Website: http://www.lulac.org/
E-mail: BWilkes@LULAC.org
Brent Wilkes, LULAC National Executive Director
*Its mission is to advance the economic condition, educational attainment, political influence, health, and civil rights of the Hispanic population of the United States*

**Lutheran Brotherhood**
625 Fourth Ave. S.
Minneapolis, MN 55415
Website: http://www.luthbro.com
Robert P. Gandrud, Chairman
Bruce J. Nicholson, President, CEO, and COO
*Life insurance*

**Lyondell Petrochemical**
William T. Butler, Chairman
Dan F. Smith, President and CEO
Website: http://www.lyondell.com
*Chemicals*

**Manpower**
5301 N. Ironwood Rd.
Milwaukee, WI 53217
Website: http://
www.manpower.com
John R. Walter, Chairman
Jeffrey A. Joerres, President and CEO
*Temporary help*

**Marriott International**
10400 Fernwood Rd.
Bethesda, MD 20817
Website: http://www.marriott.com
J. Willard Marriott Jr., CEO
*Hotels, casinos, resorts*

**Marsh and McLennan**
1166 Ave. of the Americas
New York, NY 10036
Website: http://
www.marshmac.com
Jeffrey W. Greenberg, Chairman, President, and CEO
*Diversified financials*

**Masco**
21001 Van Born Rd.
Taylor, MI 48180
Website: http://www.masco.com
Richard A. Manoogian, Chairman and CEO
*Metal products*

**Mattel**
333 Continental Blvd.
El Segundo, CA 90245
Website: http://www.barbie.com
Robert A. Eckert, Chairman and CEO
*Toys, sporting goods*

**Maxxam**
5847 San Felipe
Houston, TX 77057
Charles E. Hurwitz, CEO
*Metals*

**The May Department Stores Company**
611 Olive St.
St. Louis, MO 63101
Website: http://www.mayco.com
Jerome T. Loeb, Chairman
John L. Dunham, VC and CFO
Richard W. Bennet III, VC
William P. McNamara, VC
Anthony J. Torcasio, VC
*General merchandisers*

**Maytag**
403 W. Fourth St. N.
Newton, IA 50208
Website: http://www.maytagcorp.com
Lloyd D. Ward, Chairman and CEO
*Electronics, electrical equipment*

**MBNA**
1100 N. King St.
Wilmington, DE 19884
Website: http://www.mbnainternational.com
Alfred Lerner, Chairman and CEO
*Commercial bank*

**McDonald's**
McDonald's Plaza
Oak Brook, IL 60523
Website: http://www.mcdonalds.com
Jack M. Greenberg, Chairman and CEO
*Food services*

**McGraw Hill**
1221 Ave. of the Americas
New York, NY 10020
Website: http://www.mcgraw-hill.com
Harold W. "Terry" McGraw III, Chairman, President and CEO
*Publishing, printing*

**McKesson HBOC, Inc.**
McKesson HBOC Plaza,
One Post St.
San Francisco, CA 94104
Website: http://www.mckesson.com
Alan Seelenfreund, Chairman
John H. Hammergren, Co-President and Co-CEO
David L. Mahoney, Co-President and Co-CEO
*Wholesalers*

**Mead**
Courthouse Plaza N.E.
Dayton, OH 45463
Website: http://www.mead.com
Jerome F. Tatar, Chairman, President and CEO
*Forest and paper products*

**Mellon Bank Corporation**
1 Mellon Bank Center
Pittsburgh, PA 15258
Website: http://www.mellon.com
Martin G. McGuinn, Chairman and CEO, Mellon Financial and Mellon Bank
*Commercial banks*

**Mercantile Bank Corporation**
216 N. Division Ave.
Grand Rapids, MI 49503
Gerald R. Johnson Jr., Chairman and CEO
*Banking*

**Merisel**
200 Continental Blvd.
El Segundo, CA 90245
Website: http://www.merisel.com
David G. Sadler, President, CEO, and COO
*Computer wholesalers*

## Merck
1 Merck Dr.
Whitehouse Station, NJ 08889
Website: http://www.merck.com
Raymond V. Gilmartin, Chairman
and CEO
*Pharmaceuticals*

## Merrill Lynch
250 Vesey St.
New York, NY 10281
Website: http://www.ml.com
David H. Komansky, Chairman
and CEO
*Securities*

## Metropolitan Life Insurance
1 Madison Ave.
New York, NY 10010
Robert H. Benmosche, Chairman,
President, and CEO
*Life and Health (stock) Insurance*

## MicroAge
2400 S. MicroAge Way
Tempe, AZ 85282
Website: http://www.microage.com
Jeffrey D. McKeever, Chairman and
CEO
*Computer wholesaler*

## Micron Technology
8000 S. Federal Way
Boise, ID 83707
Website: http://www.micron.com
Steven R. Appleton, Chairman
President and CEO
*Electronics, electrical equipment*

## Microsoft
1 Microsoft Way
Redmond, WA 98052
Website: http://www.microsoft.com
William H. Gates III, Chairman and
Chief Software Architect
Steven A. Ballmer, President and
CEO
*Computer software*

## Minnesota Mining and Manufacturing (3M)
3M Center
St. Paul, MN 55144
Website: http://www.mmm.com
Livio D. DeSimone, Chairman and
CEO
*Scientific, photo, control equipment, scotch tape*

## Monsanto
800 N. Lindbergh Blvd.
St. Louis, MO 63167
Website: http://
www.monsanto.com
Hendrik A. Verfaillie, President and
CEO
*Chemicals*

## Morgan Stanley Dean Witter and Co
1585 Broadway
New York, NY 10036
Website: http://
www.deanwitterdiscover.com
Philip J. Purcell, CEO
*Securities*

## MTV
1515 Broadway
New York, NY 10036
Website: http://www.mtv.com/
E-mail: mtvnews@mtv.com
Tom Freston, Chairman and CEO
Judy McGrath, President, MTV
Group; Chairman, MTVi Group
*Cable TV network*

**Mutual of Omaha Insurance**
Mutual of Omaha Plaza
Omaha, NE 68175
Website: http://
www.mutualofomaha.com
John William Weekly, Chairman
and CEO
*Life and health (mutual) insurance*

**Nash Finch**
7600 France Ave. S.
Edina, MN 55435
Allister P. Graham, Chairman
Ron Marshall, President and CEO
*Wholesalers*

**Nationwide Financial Services, Inc.**
1 Nationwide Plaza
Columbus, OH 43215
E-mail: http://www.boafuture.com
Dimon R. McFerson, CEO
*P and C (stock) insurance*

**Navistar International**
455 N. Cityfront Plaza Dr.
Chicago, IL 60611
Website: http://www.navistar.com
John R. Horne, CEO
*Motor vehicles and parts*

**NCR**
1700 S. Patterson Blvd.
Dayton, OH 45479
Website: http://www.ncr.com/
index.asp
Lars Nyberg, Chairman, Chairman,
President, and CEO
*Computers, office equipment*

**New York Times**
229 W. 43rd St.
New York, NY 10036
Website: http://www.nytimes.com
or http://www.nytco.com
Russell T. Lewis, President and
CEO
*Publishing, printing*

**New York Life Insurance**
51 Madison Ave.
New York, NY 10010
Seymour G. Sternberg, Chairman,
President and CEO
*Life and health (mutual) insurance*

**Newell Rubbermaid Inc.**
29 E. Stephenson St.
Freeport, IL 61032
Website: http://www.newellco.com
John J. McDonough, VC and CEO
*Metal products*

**Niagara Mohawk Holdings, Inc.**
300 Erie Blvd. W.
Syracuse, NY 13202
Website http://www.nimo.com
William E. Davis, CEO
*Gas and electric utilities*

**Nike**
1 Bowerman Dr.
Beaverton, OR 97005
Website: http://www.nike.com/
Philip H. Knight, Chairman,
President, and CEO

**Nintendo of America, Inc.**
4820 150th Ave. NE
Redmond, WA 98052
Website: http://www.nintendo.com
Minoru Arakawa, President
Jacqualee Story, EVP, Business
Affairs

**Nordstrom**
617 Sixth Ave.
Seattle, WA 98101
Website: http://
www.nordstrom.com
Bruce Nordstrom, Chairman
Blake W. Nordstrom, President
*General merchandisers*

**Norfolk Southern**
3 Commercial Place
Norfolk, VA 23510
Website: http://www.nscorp.com
David R. Goode, Chairman,
President, and CEO
*Railroads*

**Northeast Utilities**
174 Brush Hill Ave.
West Springfield, MA 01090
Website: http://www.nu.com
Michael G. Morris, CEO
*Gas and electric utilities*

**Northup Grumman**
1840 Century Park E.
Los Angeles, CA 90067
Website: http://
www.northgrum.com
Kent Kresa, Chairman, President,
and CEO
*Aerospace*

**Northwest Airlines**
5101 Northwest Dr.
St. Paul, MN 55111
Website: http://www.nwa.com
Gary L. Wilson, Chairman
John H. Dasburg, President and
CEO
*Airlines*

**Norwest Venture Capital.**
3600 IDS Center 80 South 8th St.
Minneapolis, MN 55402
Website: http://
www.norwestvc.com
John E. Lindahl, EO and Managing
General Partner
Kevin G. Hall, Venture Partner,
Palo Alto
*Venture capital*

**Northwestern Mutual Life
Insurance**
720 E. Wisconsin Ave.
Milwaukee, WI 53202
Website: http://
www.northwesternmutual.com
James D. Ericson, Chairman and
CEO
*Life and health (mutual) insurance*

**Nuclear Energy Institute**
1776 I St. NW, #400
Washington, DC 20006
Website: http://www.nei.org/
E-mail: media@nei.org
Scott Peterson, Media Relations
*The nuclear energy industry's
Washington-based policy
organization*

**Nuclear Information and Resource
Service**
1424 16th St. NW #601
Washington, DC 20036
Website: http://www.nirs.org/
E-mail: NirsNet@igc.apc.org
Robert Backus, Chair
*Organization concerned with
nuclear power, radioactive waste,
radiation, and sustainable energy
issues.*

**Nucor**
2100 Rexford Rd.
Charlotte, NC 28211
Website: http://www.nucor.com
H. David Aycock, Chairman,
President, and CEO
*Metals*

**Occidental Petroleum**
10889 Wilshire Blvd.
Los Angeles, CA 90024
Website: http://www.oxy.com
Ray R. Irani, Chairman and CEO
*Chemicals*

**Office Depot**
2200 Old Germantown Rd.
Delray Beach, FL 33445
Website: http://
www.officedepot.com/
David I. Fuente, Chairman
Irwin Helford, VC
M. Bruce Nelson, CEO
*Specialist retailers*

**Office Max**
3605 Warrensville Ctr. Rd.
Shaker Heights, OH 44122
Website: http://
www.officemax.com
Michael Feuer, Chairman and CEO
Gary Peterson, President and COO
*Specialist retailers*

**Olsten**
175 Broad Hollow Rd.
Melville, NY 11747
Website: http://www.olsten.com
Frank N. Liguori, CEO
*Temporary help*

**Omnicom**
437 Madison Ave.
New York, NY 10022
Bruce Crawford, Chairman
Fred J. Meyer, VC
John D. Wren, President and CEO
*Advertising, marketing*

**Oracle**
500 Oracle Pkwy.
Redwood City, CA 94065
Website: http://www.oracle.com
Lawrence J. Ellison, Chairman and
CEO
*Computer software*

**Owens Corning**
1 Owens Corning Pkwy.
Toledo, OH 43659
Website: http://
www.owenscorning.com
Glen H. Hiner, Chairman and CEO
*Building materials, glass*

**Owens-Illinois**
1 SeaGate
Toledo, OH 43666
Joseph H. Lemieux, Chairman and
CEO
*Building materials, glass*

**Owens and Minor**
4800 Cox Rd.
Glen Allen, VA 23060
Website: http://www.owens-
minor.com
G. Gilmer Minor III, Chairman and
CEO
*Wholesalers*

**Oxford Health Plans**
48 Monroe Turnpike
Trumbull, CT 06611
Website: http://www.oxhp.com
Norman C. Payson, Chairman and
CEO
*Health care*

**PACCAR**
PACCAR Bldg.
777 106th Ave. NE, PO Box 1518
Bellevue, WA 98009
Website: http://www.paccar.com
Charles M. Pigott, Chairman
Emeritus
Mark C. Pigott, Chairman and CEO
*Motor vehicles and parts*

**Pacific Life Insurance**
700 Newport Center Dr.
Newport Beach, CA 92660
Website: http://www.pacificlife.com
Thomas C. Sutton, Chairman and
CEO
*Life and Health (mutual) insurance*

**PacifiCare Health Systems**
3120 W. Lake Center Dr.
Santa Ana, CA 92704
Website: http://www.pacificare.com
David A. Reed, Chairman
Terry O. Hartshorn, VC
Alan R. Hoops, President and CEO
*Healthcare*

**PacifiCorp**
700 N.E. Multnomah St.
Portland, OR 97232
Website: http://
www.pacificorp.com
Alan Richardson, President and
CEO
*Gas and electric utilities*

**Paine Webber Group**
1285 Ave. of the Americas
New York, NY 10019
Website: http://
www.painewebber.com
Donald B. Marron, Chairman and
CEO
*Securities*

**Parker Hannifin**
6035 Parkland Blvd.
Cleveland, OH 44124
Website: http://www.parker.com
Duane E. Collins, Chairman,
President, and CEO
*Industrial and farm equipment*

**PECO Energy**
2301 Market St.
Philadelphia, PA 19103
Website: http://www.peco.com
Corbin A. McNeill Jr., Chairman,
President, and CEO
*Gas and electric utilities*

**Penn Traffic**
1200 State Fair Blvd.
Syracuse, NY 13221
Peter L. Zirkow, Chairman
Joseph V. Fisher, President and
CEO
*Food and drug stores*

**PepsiCo**
700 Anderson Hill Rd.
Purchase, NY 10577
Website: http://www.pepsico.com
Roger A. Enrico, Chairman and
CEO
*Beverages*

**Peter Kiewit Sons'**
1000 Kiewit Plaza
Omaha, NE 68131
Kenneth E. Stinson, Chairman and
CEO
*Engineering, construction*

**Pfizer**
235 E. 42nd St.
New York, NY 10017
Website: http://www.pfizer.com
William C. Steere Jr., Chairman and
CEO
*Pharmaceuticals*

**PG & E**
1 Market St.
Spear Tower, Suite #2400
San Francisco, CA 94105
Website: http://www.pge.com
Robert D. Glynn Jr., Chairman,
President and CEO
*Gas and electric utilities*

**Pharmacia Corporation**
100 Rt. 206 N.
Peapack, NJ 07977
Website: http://www.pnu.com
Fred Hassan, President and CEO
*Pharmaceuticals*

**Phelps Dodge**
2600 N. Central Ave.
Phoenix, AZ 85004
Website: http://
www.phelpsdodge.com
Douglas C. Yearley, Chairman
J. Steven Whisler, President and
CEO
*Metals*

**Philip Morris U.S.A**
120 Park Ave.
New York, NY 10017-5592
Website: http://
www.philipmorrisusa.com
Michael Szymanczyk, President
and CEO
*Tobacco company*

**Phillips Petroleum**
Phillips Building
Bartlesville, OK 74004
Website: http://
www.phillips66.com
Jim J. Mulva, Chairman and CEO
*Petroleum refining*

**Phoenix Home Life Mutual
Insurance**
1 American Row
Hartford, CT 06115
Robert W. Fiondella, Chairman and
CEO
*Life and Health (stock) insurance*

**Pitney Bowes**
1 Elmcroft Rd.
Stamford, CT 06926
Website: http://
www.pitneybowes.com
Michael J. Critelli, Chairman
*Computers, office equipment*

**Pittston Minerals Group**
448 NE Main St.
Lebanon, VA 24266
Website: http://
www.pittstonminerals.com
Thomas W. Garges, President and
CEO, Pittston Coal Company and
Mineral Ventures
*Mining*

**Pleasant Company**
The American Girl Collection
8400 Fairway Place
PO Box 620190
Middleton, WI 53562
Website: http://
www.americangirl.com/
Pleasant Rowland, Founder,
Chairman, and CEO
*Makers of American Girl dolls*

**The PNC Financial Services
Group, Inc.**
1 PNC Plaza, 249 5th Ave.
Pittsburgh, PA 15222
Website http://www.pncbank.com
Thomas H. O'Brien, Chairman
James E. Rohr, President and CEO
*Commercial bank*

**PPG Industries**
1 PPG Place
Pittsburgh, PA 15272
Website: http://www.ppg.com
Raymond W. LeBoeuf, CEO
*Chemicals*

**PP & L Industries**
2 N. Ninth St.
Allentown, PA 18101
William F. Hecht, Chairman,
President, and CEO
*Gas and electric utilities*

**Praxair**
39 Old Ridgebury Rd.
Danbury, CT 06810
Website: http://www.praxair.com
H. William Lichtenberger,
Chairman
Dennis H. Reilley, President and
CEO
*Chemicals*

**The Principal Financial Group**
711 High St.
Des Moines, IA 50392
Website: http://www.principal.com
David J. Drury, Chairman
J. Barry Griswell, President and
CEO
*Life and health (stock) insurance*

**Procter & Gamble**
1 P&G Plaza
Cincinnati, OH 45202
Website: http://www.pg.com
John E. Pepper, Chairman
Alan G. "A. G." Lafley, President
and CEO
*Soaps, cosmetics*

**The Progressive Corporation**
6300 Wilson Mills Rd.
Mayfield Village, OH 44143
Website: http://
www.progressive.com
Peter B. Lewis, Chairman,
President, and CEO
*P and C (stock) insurance*

**Provident Financial Group, Inc.**
1 E. 4th St.
Cincinnati, OH 45202
Website: http://www.provident-
bank.com
Robert L. Hoverson, Chairman,
President, and CEO
*Commercial bank*

**Prudential Insurance Company of
America**
751 Broad St.
Newark, NJ 07102
Website: http://
www.prudential.com
Arthur F. Ryan, Chairman and CEO
*Life and health insurance (stock)*

**Public Service Enterprise Group**
80 Park Plaza
Newark, NJ 07101
Website: http://www.pseg.com
E. James Ferland, Chairman,
President, and CEO
*Gas and electric utilities*

**Publix Super Markets**
1936 George Jenkins Blvd.
Lakeland, FL 33815
Howard M. Jenkins, Chairman and
CEO
*Food and drug stores*

**The Quaker Oats Company**
Quaker Tower
321 N. Clark St.
Chicago, IL 60610
Website: http://
www.quakeroats.com
Robert S. Morrison, Chairman,
President, and CEO
*Food producer*

**Quantum**
500 McCarthy Blvd.
Milpitas, CA 95035
Website: http://www.quantum.com
Michael A. Brown, Chairman and
CEO
*Computer peripherals*

**Queen Mary Hotel**
PO Box 8
1126 Queens Hwy.
Long Beach, CA 90802
Website: http://
www.queenmary.com
E-mail: queenmry@gte.net
*Former cruise ship turned hotel
and tourist attraction*

**Ralston Purina Company**
Checkerboard Square
St. Louis, MO 63164
Website: http://www.ralston.com
W. Partick McGinnis, President and
CEO
*Food and pet food producer*

**Rand**
1700 Main St.
PO Box 2138
Santa Monica, CA 90407
Website: http://www.rand.org
E-mail: correspondence@rand.org
Paul H. O'Neill, Chairman
*A nonprofit institution that helps
improve policy and decision-
making through research and
analysis*

**Reader's Digest Association**
Reader's Digest Rd.
Pleasantville, NY 10570
Website: http://
www.readersdigest.com
Thomas O. Ryder, Chairman and
CEO
*Publishing, printing*

**Reebok**
100 Technology Center Dr.
Stoughton, MA 02072
Website: http://www.reebok.com
Paul B. Fireman, Chairman,
President and CEO
Angel Martinez, Chief Marketing
Officer
*Apparel*

**Reliance Group Holdings**
Park Avenue Plaza
55 E. 52nd St.
New York, NY 10055
Website: http://rgh.com
Saul P. Steinberg, Chairman
George R. Baker, President and
CEO
*P and C (stock) insurance*

### Reynolds Metals
6601 W. Broad St.
Richmond, VA 23230
Website: http://www.rmc.com
Jeremiah J. Sheehan, Chairman
and CEO
*Metals*

### Rite Aid
30 Hunter Lane
Camp Hill, PA 17011
Website: http://www.riteaid.com
Alex Grass, Honorary Chairman
Robert G. Miller, Chairman and
CEO
Mary Sammons, President and
COO
*Food and drug stores*

### RJR Nabisco
7 Campus Dr.
Parsippany, NJ 07054
Website: http://www.nabisco.com
Steven F. Goldstone, Chairman
James M. Kilts, President and CEO
*Food producer*

### Rockwell International
777 E. Wisconsin Ave., Suite.
#1400
Milwaukee, WI 53202
Website: http://www.rockwell.com
Don H. Davis Jr., Chairman and
CEO
*Electronics, electrical equipment*

### R. R. Donnelley and Sons
77 W. Wacker Dr.
Chicago, IL 60601
Website: http://
www.rrdonnelley.com
William L. Davis, Chairman and
CEO
*Publishing, printing*

### Ryder Systems
3600 N.W. 82nd Ave.
Miami, FL 33166
Website: http://www.ryder.com
M. Anthony Burns, Chairman and
CEO
*Truck leasing*

### Safeco
Safeco Plaza
Seattle, WA 98185
Website: http://www.safeco.com
Roger H. Eigsti, Chairman and CEO
*P and C (stock) insurance*

### Safeway
5918 Stoneridge Mall Rd.
Pleasanton, CA 94588
Website: http://www.safeway.com
Steven A. Burd, Chairman,
President and CEO
*Food and drug stores*

### SBC Communications
175 E. Houston
San Antonio, TX 78205
Website: http://www.sbc.com
Edward E. Whitacre Jr., Chairman
and CEO
*Telecommunications*

### Schering-Plough
1 Giralda Farms
Madison, NJ 07940
Website: http://www.sch-
plough.com
Richard Jay Kogan, Chairman and
CEO
*Pharmaceuticals*

**SCI Systems**
2101 W. Clinton Ave.
Huntsville, AL 35807
Olin B. King, Chairman
A. Eugene Sapp Jr., President and
CEO
*Electronics, electrical equipment*

**Scott, Gini Graham**
Creative Communications and
Research
6114 La Salle Ave., #358
Oakland, CA 94611.
Website: http://www.giniscott.com/
cbkwpb.htm
E-mail:
GiniGrahamScott@giniscott.com
*Gini Graham Scott is the author of
over 30 books, host of the
internationally aired radio show
"Changemakers," a speaker and
seminar leader, and the director of
Changemakers and Creative
Communications and Research.
She specializes in the area of social
issues, criminal justice, and
lifestyles.*

**Sears Roebuck**
3333 Beverly Rd.
Hoffman Estates, IL 60179
Website: http://www.sears.com
Arthur C. Martinez, Chairman,
President, and CEO
*General merchandisers*

**Seagate Technology**
920 Disc Dr.
Scotts Valley, CA 95066
Website: http://www.seagate.com
Gary Filler, Co-Chairman
Lawrence Perlman, Co-Chairman
Stephen J. Luczo, CEO, Chairman,
Seagate Software
William D. Watkins, President and
COO
*Computer peripherals, software*

**Sega of America, Inc.**
Townsend Center, 650 Townsend
St., Suite #650
San Francisco, CA 94103
Website: http://www.sega.com
Peter Moore, President and COO,
Sega of America Dreamcast

**Service Merchandise**
7100 Service Merchandise Dr.
Brentwood, TN 37027
Website: http://
www.servicemerchandise.com
Raymond Zimmerman, Chairman
Sam Cusano, CEO
Charles Septer, President and COO
*Specialist retailers*

**ServiceMaster**
1 ServiceMaster Way
Downers Grove, IL 60515
Website: http://www.svm.com
C. William Pollard, Chairman and
CEO
*Diversified outsourcing services*

**Shaw Industries**
616 E. Walnut Ave.
Dalton, GA 30720
J. C. "Bud" Shaw, Chairman
Emeritus
Robert E. Shaw, Chairman and
CEO
*Textiles*

**Sherwin-Williams**
101 Prospect Ave. N.W.
Cleveland, OH 44115
Website: http://www.sherwin-williams.com
John G. Breen, Chairman
Christopher M. Connor, VC and CEO
*Chemicals*

**Silicon Graphics**
1600 Amphitheatre Pkwy.
Mountain View, CA 94043
Website: http://www.sgi.com
Robert R. Bishop, Chairman and CEO
*Computers, office equipment*

**Smith and Wesson**
2100 Roosevelt Ave.
Springfield, MA 01102
Website: www.smith-wesson.com
Ed Schultz, CEO and President
E-mail: eshultz@smith-wesson.com
*Firearms*

**Smithfield Foods**
200 Commerce St.
Smithfield, VA 23430
Joseph W. Luter III, Chairman, President, and CEO
*Food company*

**Smurfit-Stone Container Corporation**
150 N. Michigan Ave.
Chicago, IL 60601
Website: http://www.smurfit.com
Michael W.J. Smurfit, Chairman
Ray Curran, President and CEO
*The world's top maker of containerboard and corrugated containers and a leading wastepaper recycler*

**Solectron**
777 Gibraltar Dr.
Milpitas, CA 95035
Website: http://www.solectron.com
Koichi Nishimura, Chairman, President, and CEO
*Electronics, electrical equipment*

**Sonoco**
1 N. Second St.
Hartsville, SC 29550
Website: http://www.sonoco.com
Charles W. Coker, Chairman
Harris E. DeLoach Jr., CEO and President
*Forest and paper products*

**Southern Energy, Inc.**
900 Ashwood Pkwy., Suite 500
Atlanta, GA 30338
Website: http://www.southernco.com
A.W. Dahlberg, Chairman and CEO
*Gas and electric utilities*

**Southwest Airlines**
2702 Love Field Dr.
Dallas, TX 75235
Website: http://www.iflyswa.com
Herbert D. Kelleher, Chairman, President, and CEO
*Airlines*

**Sprint**
2330 Shawnee Mission Pkwy.
Westwood, KS 66205
Website: http://www.sprint.com
William T. Esrey, CEO
*Telecommunications*

**Staples**
500 Staples Dr.
Framingham, MA 01702
Website: http://www.staples.com
Thomas G. Stemberg, Chairman
and CEO
*Specialist retailers*

**State Farm Insurance Companie**
1 State Farm Plaza
Bloomington, IL 61710
Edward B. Rust Jr., Chairman and
CEO
*P and C (mutual) Insurance*

**State Street Corp.**
225 Franklin St.
Boston, MA 02110
Website: http://
www.statestreet.com
Marshall N. Carter, Chairman
David A. Spina, CEO
*Commercial bank*

**The St. Paul Companies, Inc.**
385 Washington St.
St. Paul, MN 55102
Website: http://www.stpaul.com
Douglas W. Leatherdale, Chairman
and CEO
*P and C (stock) insurance*

**Sun Microsystems**
901 San Antonio Rd.
Palo Alto, CA 94303
Website: http://www.sun.com
Chairman and CEO, Scott G.
McNealy
*Computers, office equipment*

**Sun Trust Bank**
303 Peachtree St. N.E.
Atlanta, GA 30308
Website: http://www.suntrust.com/
index.html
L. Phillip Humann, Chairman,
President, and CEO
*Commercial bank*

**Supervalu**
11840 Valley View Rd.
Eden Prairie, MN 55344
Website: http://
www.supervalu.com
Michael W. Wright, Chairman and
CEO
*Wholesaler*

**Sysco**
1390 Enclave Pkwy.
Houston, TX 77077
Website: http://www.sysco.com
John F. Woodhouse, Senior
Chairman
Charles H. Cotros, Chairman and
CEO
Richard J. Schnieders, President
and COO
*Food wholesalers*

**Tandy Brands Accessories, Inc.**
90 E. Lamar Blvd., Suite 200
Arlington, TX 76011
Website: http://
www.tandybrands.com
James F. Gaertner, Chairman
J. S. Britt Jenkins, President and
CEO
*Leather goods manufacturer*

**Tech-Data**
5350 Tech Data Dr.
Clearwater, FL 33760
Website: http://www.techdata.com
Edward C. Raymund, Chairman
Emeritus
Steven A. Raymund, Chairman and
CEO
*Wholesalers*

**Temple-Inland**
303 S. Temple Dr.
Diboll, TX 75941
Website: http://
www.templeinland.com
Kenneth M. Jastrow II, Chairman
and CEO
*Forest and paper products*

**Tenet Healthcare**
3820 State St.
Santa Barbara, CA 93105
Website: http://
www.tenethealth.com
Jeffrey C. Barbakow, Chairman and
CEO
*Healthcare*

**Tenneco Automotive, Inc.**
500 North Field Dr.
Lake Forest, IL 60045
Website: http://www.tenneco-
automotive.com/
Mark P. Frissora, Chairman and
CEO
*Motor vehicles and Parts*

**Texaco**
2000 Westchester Ave.
White Plains, NY 10650
Website: http://www.texaco.com
Peter I. Bijur, CEO
*Petroleum refining*

**Texas Instruments**
12500 TI Blvd.
Dallas, TX 75243
Website: http://www.ti.com
Thomas J. Engibous, Chairman,
President, and CEO
*Electronics, semiconductors*

**Textron**
40 Westminster St.
Providence, RI 02903
Website: http://www.textron.com
Lewis B. Campbell, Chairman and
CEO
*Aerospace*

**Thermo Electron**
81 Wyman St.
Waltham, MA 02254
Website: http://www.thermo.com
Richard F. Syron, Chairman,
President, and CEO
*Scientific, photo, control equipment*

**TIAA-CREF (Teachers Insurance
and Annuity Association-College
Retirement Equities Fund)**
730 Third Ave.
New York, NY 10017
John H. Biggs, Chairman,
President, and CEO
*Life and health (mutual) insurance*

**Time Warner**
75 Rockefeller Plaza
New York, NY 10019
Website: http://
www.timewarner.com
Gerald M. Levin, Chairman and
CEO
*Entertainment, publishing*

**TJX**
770 Cochituate Rd.
Framingham, MA 01701
Website: http://www.tjmaxx.com
Bernard Cammarata, Chairman
Edmond J. "Ted" English, President
and CEO
*Specialist retailers*

**Tosco**
72 Cummings Point Rd.
Stamford, CT 06902
Website: http://www.tosco.com
Thomas D. O'Malley, Chairman
and CEO
*Petroleum refining*

**Toys 'R' Us**
461 From Rd.
Paramus, NJ 07652
Website: http://www.amazon.com
Michael Goldstein, Chairman
John H. Eyler Jr., President and
CEO
*Specialist retailers*

**Trans World Airline**
One City Centre
515 N. Sixth St.
St. Louis, MO 63101
Website: http://www.twa.com
Gerald Gitner, Chairman
William F. Compton, President and
CEO
*Airlines*

**Transamerica**
600 Montgomery St.
San Francisco, CA 94111
Website: http://
www.transamerica.com
Frank C. Herringer, Chairman
Donald Shepard, President and
CEO
*Life, and Health (stock) insurance*

**Travelers Property Casualty Corp.**
1 Tower Sq.
Hartford, CT 06183
Robert I. Lipp, Chairman
Jay S. Fishman, President and CEO;
CEO, Commercial Lines
*Insurance*

**Tribune Company**
435 N. Michigan Ave.
Chicago, IL 60611
Website: http://www.tribune.com
John W. Madigan, Chairman,
President, and CEO
*Newspapers, publishing, owns the
Cubs*

**TruServe**
8600 W. Bryn Mawr Ave.
Chicago, IL 60631
Website: http://www.truserv.com
E-mail: email@truserv.com
Donald Hoye, President and CEO
*Specialist retailers*

**Turner Broadcasting Systems**
1 CNN Center, Box 105366
Atlanta, GA 30348
*Website: http://www.turner.com/*
Ted Turner, President
*Operator of cable TV networks*

**Turner Corp.**
Bank of America Plaza
901 Main St., Suite #4900
Dallas, TX 75202
*Website: http://
www.turnerconstruction.com*
Thomas C. Leppert, Chairman and
CEO
*Engineering, construction*

**TRW**
1900 Richmond Rd.
Cleveland, OH 44124
*Website: http://www.trw.com*
Joseph T. Gorman, Chairman and CEO
*Motor vehicles and parts*

**TXU Corp.**
Energy Plaza
1601 Bryan St.
Dallas, TX 75201
*Website: http://www.txu.com*
Erle Nye, Chairman and CEO
*Gas and electric utilities*

**Tyco International**
1 Tyco Park
Exeter, NH 03833
Website: http://www.tycoint.com
L. Dennis Kozlowski, Chairman, President, and CEO
*Metal products*

**Tyson Foods**
2210 W. Oaklawn Dr.
Springdale, AR 72762
Website: http://www.tyson.com
Don Tyson, Senior Chairman
John H. Tyson, Chairman, President, and CEO
*Food producer*

**UAL**
1200 E. Algonquin Rd.
Elk Grove Township, IL 60007
Website: http://www.ual.com
James E. Goodwin, Chairman and CEO
*Airlines*

**Unicom**
10 S. Dearborn St.
Chicago, IL 60603
Website: http://www.exelonenterprises.com
John W. Rowe, Chairman, President, and CEO
*Gas and electric utilities*

**Union Pacific**
1416 Dodge St., Rm. 1230
Omaha, NE 68179
Website: http://www.up.com
Richard K. Davidson, Chairman, President, and CEO
*Railroads*

**Unisource**
6600 Governors Lake Pkwy.
Norcross, GA 30071
Website: http://www.unisourcelink.com
Charles C. Tufano, President
Matthew C. Tyser, VP and CFO
*Wholesalers*

**Unisys**
Unisys Way
Blue Bell, PA 19424
Website: http://www.unisys.com
Lawrence A. Weinbach, Chairman, President, and CEO
*Computer and data services*

**United HealthCare**
9900 Bren Rd. E.
Minnetonka, MN 55343
Website: http://www.unitedhealthcare.com
William W. McGuire, CEO
*Healthcare*

**United Parcel Service**
55 Glenlake Pkwy. N.E.
Atlanta, GA 30328
Website: http://www.ups.com
James P. Kelly, Chairman and CEO
*Mail, package, freight delivery*

**United Services Automobile Assn.
(USAA)**
9800 Fredericksburg Rd., USAA
Bldg.
San Antonio, TX 78288
Website: http://www.usaa.com
Robert G. Davis, Chairman,
President, and CEO
*P and C Insurance (stock)*

**United States Olympic Committee**
One Olympic Plaza
Colorado Springs, CO 80909
Website: http://www.usoc.org
William Hybl, Chairman (President,
internationally)
General Norman P. Blake Jr., CEO
and Secretary

**United Technologies**
1 Financial Plaza
Hartford, CT 06101
Website: http://www.utc.com
George David, Chairman and CEO
*Aerospace*

**Universal Tobacco**
1501 N. Hamilton St.
Richmond, VA 23230
Website: http://
www.universalcorp.com
Henry H. Harrell, Chairman and
CEO
*Tobacco producer*

**Unocal**
2141 Rosecrans Ave., Suite #4000
El Segundo, CA 90505
Website: http://www.unocal.com
Roger C. Beach, Chairman and
CEO
*Mining, crude-oil production*

**US Airways Group**
2345 Crystal Dr.
Arlington, VA 22227
Website: http://
www.usairways.com
Stephen M. Wolf, Chairman
Rakesh Gangwal, President and
CEO
*Airlines*

**U.S. Bancorp**
601 Second Ave. S.
Minneapolis, MN 55402
Website: http://www.usbank.com/
usbsol.html
John F. Grundhofer, Chairman and
CEO
*Commercial bank*

**U.S. Office Products**
1025 T. Jefferson St. NW
Washington, DC 20007
Website: http://www.usop.com
Charles P. Pieper, Chairman
Warren D. Feldberg, CEO
*Wholesalers*

**USF Worldwide, Inc.**
1100 Arlington Heights Rd., Suite
#600
Itasca, IL 60143
Website: http://
www.usfreightways.com
Dan Pera, President
*Transportation*

## USG

125 S. Franklin St., PO Box 6721
Chicago, IL 60606
Website: http://www.usg.com
William C. Foote, Chairman,
President, and CEO
*Building materials, glass*

## USX

600 Grant St.
Pittsburgh, PA 15219
Website: http://www.usx.com
Thomas J. Usher, Chairman and
CEO
*Petroleum refining*

## UtiliCorp United Inc.

20 W. Ninth St.
Kansas City, MO 64105
Website: http://www.utilicorp.com
Richard C. Green Jr., Chairman and
CEO
*Gas and electric utilities*

## Vencor

1 Vencor Place, 680 S. 4th St.
Louisville, KY 40202-2412
Website: http://www.vencor.com
Edward L. Kuntz, Chairman,
President, and CEO
*Healthcare*

## VF

628 Green Valley Rd., Suite #500
Greensboro, NC 27408
Website: http://www.vfc.com
Mackey J. McDonald, Chairman,
President, and CEO
*Apparel*

## Victoria's Secret

Intimate Brands
3 Limited Pkwy.
Columbus, OH 43216
Website: http://
www.victoriassecret.com
Leslie H. Wexner, Chairman,
President, and CEO
*Lingerie*

## Vodafone Group PLC

The Courtyard, 2-4 London Rd.
Newbury, Berkshire RG14 1JX
United Kingdom
Website: http://www.vodafone-
airtouch-plc.com
Lord MacLaurin of Knebworth,
Chairman
Christopher C. Gent, CEO
*Telecommunications*

## Wachovia

100 N. Main St.
Winston-Salem, NC 27150
Website: http://www.wachovia.com
Leslie M. Baker Jr., Chairman and
CEO
*Commercial bank*

## Walgreens

200 Wilmot Rd.
Deerfield, IL 60015
Website: http://
www.walgreens.com
L. Daniel Jorndt, Chairman and
CEO
*Food and drug stores*

**Wal-Mart**
702 S.W. Eighth St.
Bentonville, AR 72716
Website: http://www.wal-mart.com
S. Robson Walton, Chairman
David D. Glass, Chairman of the
Executive Committee
H. Lee Scott Jr., President and CEO
*General merchandisers*

**Walt Disney**
500 S. Buena Vista St.
Burbank, CA 91521
Website: http://www.disney.com
Michael D. Eisner, Chairman and
CEO
*Entertainment*

**Waste Management**
1001 Fannin, Suite #4000
Houston, TX 77002
A. Maurice Myers, Chairman,
President, and CEO
*Waste management*

**WellPoint Health Networks**
1 WellPoint Way
Thousand Oaks, CA 91362
Website: http://www.wellpoint.com
Leonard D. Schaeffer, Chairman
and CEO
*Healthcare*

**Wells Fargo and Co.**
420 Montgomery St.
San Francisco, CA 94163
Website: http://
www.wellsfargo.com
Paul Hazen, CEO
*Commercial bank*

**Western Digital**
8105 Irvine Center Dr.
Irvine, CA 92618
Website: http://
www.westerndigital.com
Thomas E. Pardun, Chairman
Matthew H. Massengill, President
and CEO
*Computer peripherals*

**Westvaco**
299 Park Ave.
New York, NY 10171
Website: http://www.westvaco.com
John A. Luke Jr., Chairman,
President, and CEO
*Forest and paper products*

**Weyerhaeuser**
33663 Weyerhaeuser Way S.
PO Box 2999
Federal Way, WA 98003
Website: http://
www.weyerhaeuser.com
Steven R. Rogel, Chairman,
President, and CEO
*Forest and paper products*

**Whirlpool**
2000 N. M-63
Benton Harbor, MI 49022
Website: http://www.whirlpool.com
David R. Whitwam, Chairman and
CEO
*Electronics, electrical equipment*

**Whitman**
3501 Algonquin Rd.
Rolling Meadows, IL 60008
Website: http://
www.whitmancorp.com
Bruce S. Chelberg, Chairman and
CEO
*Beverages*

**Willamette Industries**
1300 S.W. Fifth Ave.
Portland, OR 97201
Website: http://www.wii.com
William Swindells, Chairman
Duane C. McDougall, President and
CEO
*Forest and paper products*

**The Williams Companies, Inc.**
1 Williams Center
Tulsa, OK 74172
Website: http://www.williams.com
Keith E. Bailey, Chairman,
President, and CEO
*Pipelines, communications*

**Winn-Dixie**
5050 Edgewood Court
Jacksonville, FL 32254
A. Dano Davis, Chairman and CEO
Allen R. Rowland, President and
CEO
*Food and drug stores*

**WorldCom**
500 Clinton Center Dr.
Clinton, MS 39056
Website: http://
www.worldcom.com
Bernard J. Ebbers, President and
CEO
*Telecommunications*

**W. R. Grace**
7500 Grace Dr.
Columbia, MD 21044
Website: http://www.grace.com
Paul J. Norris, Chairman, President
and CEO
*Chemical products*

**WWF (World Wrestling
Federation)**
Titan Tower
1241 East Main St.
PO Box 3857
Stamford, CT 06902

**W. W. Grainger**
100 Grainger Pkwy.
Lake Forest, IL 60045
Website: http://www.grainger.com
David W. Grainger, Senior
Chairman
Richard L. Keyser, Chairman and
CEO
*Wholesalers*

**Xerox**
800 Long Ridge Rd.
Stamford, CT 06904
Website: http://www.xerox.com
Paul A. Allaire, Chairman and CEO
*Computers, copiers, office
equipment*

**Yellow**
10990 Roe Ave.
Overland Park, KS 66211
Website: http://
www.yellowcorp.com
William D. Zollars, Chairman,
President, and CEO
*Trucking*

**York International**
631 S. Richland Ave.
York, PA 17403
Website: http://www.york.com
Michael R. Young, President and
CEO
*Industrial and farm equipment*

# LET'S READ AND EXPLORE

**Angelou, Maya**
104B Wingate Hall
PO Box 7314
Winston-Salem, NC 27109
*Author*

**Archie Comics**
PO Box 419
Mamaroneck, NY 10543
E-mail: archiecom@aol.com
Website: http://
www.Archiecomics.com

**Barker, Clive**
PO Box 691885
Los Angeles, CA 90069
*Author*

**Benedict, Dirk**
PO Box 634
Bigfork, MT 59911
*Author*

**Blyth, Ann**
PO Box 9754
Rancho Santa Fe, CA 92067
*Author*

**Bradbury, Ray**
10265 Cheviot Dr.
Los Angeles, CA 90064
*Author*

**Bradlee, Benjamin**
3014 "N" St. NW
Washington, DC 20007
*Journalist*

**Bradshaw, John**
2412 South Blvd.
Houston, TX 77098
*Lecturer and author of self-improvement books*

**Brown, Helen Gurley**
1 W 81st St., #220
New York, NY 10024
*Magazine editor*

**Bush, Barbara (and Millie)**
10000 Memorial Dr., Suite #900
Houston, TX 77024
*Author and former First Lady*

**Clancy, Tom**
PO Box 800
Huntington, MD 20639
*Author*

**Clark, Mary Higgins**
210 Central Park S.
New York, NY 10019
*Author*

**Clarke, Arthur C.**
4715 Gregory Rd.
Colombo
Sri Lanka
*Science-fiction author*
*Birthday: 12/16/17*

**Collins, Jackie**
PO Box 5473
Glendale, CA 91221
*Author*
*Birthday: 10/4/41*

**Craven, Wes**
2419 Solar Dr.
Los Angeles, CA 90068
*Author*

**Crichton, Michael**
433 N. Camden Dr., #500
Beverly Hills, CA 90210
*Author*

**Dark Horse Comics**
10956 SE Main
Milwaukie, OR 97222
E-mail: dhc@dhorse.com
Website: http://www.dhorse.com
*Mike Richardson, president*

**DC Comics**
1700 Broadway
New York, NY 10019
E-mail: DCWebsite@aol.com
Website: http://www.dccomics.com
*Publishes Superman, Batman, etc.*

**Ellison, Harlan**
PO Box 55548
Sherman Oaks, CA 91423
*Science-fiction author*

**Germond, Jack**
1627 K St., NW, #1100
Washington, DC 20006
*Newspaper columnist*

**GeRue, Gene "Bumpy"**
HC78, Box 1105
Zanoni, MO 65784
Website: http://www.ruralize.com
E-mail: genegerue@ruralize.com
*Author* How to Find Your Ideal
Country Home: Ruralize Your
Dreams

**Grisham, John**
PO Box 1780
Oxford, MS 38655
*Author*

**HarperCollins Publishers**
10 E. 53rd Street
New York, NY 10022
Website: http://
www.harpercollins.com
*Book publisher*

**Highlights for Children**
803 Church St.
Honesdale, PA 18431
*Kent L. Brown, Editor*
Monthly fiction/nonfiction
magazine for kids ages two to
twelve

**Larry Grossman and Associates**
211 South Beverly Dr. #206
Beverly Hills, CA 90212
*Literary agency*

**Guccione, Bob**
2776 Park Ave.
New York, NY 10017
*Magazine publisher*

**Investigative Reporters and
Editors (IRE)**
UMC School of Journalism/26A
University of Missouri
Columbia, MO 65211
Website: http://www.ire.org
E-mail:
jourire@muccmail.missouri.edu
Rosemary Armao, Executive
Director
E-mail: r2croak@aol.com
*A grassroots, nonprofit
organization dedicated to
improving the quality of
investigative reporting within the
field of journalism.*

**Jordan, Robert**
% Tor Books
175 5th Ave.
New York, NY 10010
*Author*

**Kadrey, Richard**
E-mail: kadrey@well.com
*Science-fiction novelist*

**Kehoe, Brendan**
Website: http://www.zen.org/
~brendan/
E-mail: brendan@zen.org
*Author of* Zen and the Art of the
Internet

**Kellner, Mark**
Website: http://
www.markkellner.com/
E-mail: mark@kellner2000.com
*Writer*

**King, Stephen**
49 Flordia Ave.
Bangor, ME 04401
*Author*

**Kinsella, W. P.**
PO Box 2162
Blaine, WA 98231
*Author*

**Koontz, Dean**
PO Box 9529
Newport Beach, CA 92658
*Author*

**Limbaugh, Rush**
366 Madison Ave., #700
New York, NY 10017
*Author and radioshow host*

**Lindsey, George**
% Avon Books
1350 Ave. of the Americas
New York, NY 10019
*Author*

**Lunden, Joan**
77 W. 66 St.
New York, NY 10023
*Author*

***Mad* Magazine**
1700 Broadway
New York, NY 10019
Website:http://www.dccomics.com/
mad/index.html
*Joe Raiola and David Shayne,
Editors*
Comedy magazine of satire and
parody

**Marvel**
Marvel Entertainment Group, Inc.
387 Park Ave. S.
New York, NY 10016
E-mail: mail@marvel.com
Website: http://www.marvel.com
*Joseph Calamari, president and*
*COO, Marvel Entertainment Group*
*Producer of comics, events,*
*movies, specials, and more*

**McMurtry, Larry**
Box 552
Archer City, TX 76351
*Author*

**Miller, Arthur**
Tophet Rd.
Box 320
R #1
Roxbury, CT 06783
*Playwright*

**O'Grady, Captain Scott**
% Doubleday
1540 Broadway
New York, NY 10036
*Author*

**Prussia, Guido**
Guido Prussia Res.
Campo 602
Milano 2
Segrate Milano
Italy
*Italian TV journalist*

**Rushdie, Salman**
% Gillon Aitken
29 Fernshaw Rd.
London SW10 OTG
England
*Author*

**Salinger, JD**
% Harold Ober Assoc.
*425 Madison Ave.*
*New York, NY 10017*
*Author*

**Soap Opera Digest**
Sounding Board
45 W. 25th St.
New York, NY 10010
E-mail addresses:
Editor: SODeditor@aol.com
*Another World* editor:
SODaw@aol.com
Ask Us! (questions):
SODASKUS@aol.com
Sound Off (correspondence):
SODsound@aol.com

**Stern, Howard**
10 East 44th St., #500
New York, NY 10017
*Radio and TV host, author*

**Stine, R. L.**
% Scholastic, Inc.
555 Broadway
New York, NY 10012
*Author*

**TV Guide**
100 Matsonford Rd.
Radnor, PA 19088
Attn: Michael Logan

**Wilson, Katharina**
% Puzzle Publishing
PO Box 230023
Portland, OR 97281
Website: http://
www.alienjigsaw.com/index.html
*Author of* The Alien Jigsaw, *a book*
*about alien abduction*

# WORLD LEADERS

**Afghanistan (Islamic State of)**
Mohammed Rabbani
Chairman of the Ruling Council
Kabul
Afghanistan

**Albania (Republic of)**
Rexhep Kemal Meidani
President i Republikes
Office of the President
Bulevardi Deshmoret e Kombit
Tirane
Albania
Website: http://president.gov.al/
E-mail: presec@presec.tirana.al

Ilir Meta
Prime Minister
Office of the Prime Minister
Bulevardi Deshmoret e Kombit
Tirane
Albania
Website: http://www.tirana.al/
minjash/
E-mail:
postmaster@minjash.tirana.al
(Ministry of Foreign Affairs)

**Algeria (Democratic and Popular
Republic of)**

Abdel-Aziz Bouteflika
Presidence de la Republique
Place Mohamed Seddik Benyahya
El Mouradia
16000 Algiers
Algeria
Website: http://www.mae-dz.org/
E-mail: info@mae-dz.org

Ahmed Benbitour
Premier Ministère
Palais du Gouvernement
Rue du Docteur Saadane
16000 Algiers
Algeria

**Andorra (Principality of)**
M.I. Sr. Marc Forne Molne
Cap de Govern
Carrer Prat de la Geu 62
Andorra la Vella
Andorra
Website: http://www.andorra.ad/
govern/

**Angola (Republic of)**
Jose Eduardo dos Santos
President
Gabinete do Presidente
Luanda

Angola
Website: http://www.angola.org/
index.htm

## Antigua and Barbuda
Lester Bryant Bird
Prime Minister
Office of the Prime Minister
Queen Elizabeth Highway,
Parliament Bldg.
St. John's, Antigua
Antigua and Barbuda
Website: http://www.antigua-
barbuda.com
E-mail: pmo@candw.ag

## Argentina (Argentine Republic)
Dr. Carlos Saul Menem
Presidente de la Republic
Casa de Gobierno
Balcarce 50
1064 Buenos Aires
Argentina
Website: http://www.presidencia.ar

## Armenia (Republic of)
Robert Kocharian
President
President House
Marhshal Baghramyan Ave.
19 Yerevan
Armenia
Website: http://www.president.am/
E-mail: press@president.am

Aram Sargsyan
Prime Minister
1st Government House
Republic Square
10 Yerevan
Armenia

## Australia (Commonwealth of)
Hon. John Winston Howard
Prime Minister
Parliament House, Suite MG8

2600 Canberra, Australian Capital
Territory
Australia
Website: http://www.pm.gov.au/
E-mail: http://www.pm.gov.au/
comments.htm

## Austria (Republic of)
Dr. Thomas Klestil
President
Prasidentschaftskanzlei
Hofburg, Bellariator,
Ballhausplatz 2
A-1010, Wien
Austria
Phone: 43-1-534-22-0
Fax: 43-1-535-6512
Website: http://www.hofburg.at/
E-mail: thomas.klestil@hofburg.at

Wolfgang Schussel
Federal Chancellor
Bundeskanzleramt
Ballhausplatz 2
A-1014, Wien
Austria
Website: http://www.bmaa.gv.at/
index.html.de
E-mail: AbtI3ps@wien.bmaa.gv.at

## Azerbaijan (Azerbaijani Republic)
Heydar Aliyev
President
Office of the President
Ulitsa Levmontova 63
Baku
Azerbaijan
Fax: 994-12-920625
Website: http://www.president.az
E-mail: president@gov.az

Artur Tair oghlu Rasizade
Prime Minister
Council of Ministers
Mermontov Str 68

370066 Baku
Azerbaijan

## Bahamas (The Commonwealth of the)
Rt. Hon. Hubert Ingraham
Prime Minister
Sir Cecil Wallace Whitfield Centre
West Bay St., PO Box CB-10980
Nassau, New Providence
Bahamas
Website: http://
flamingo.bahamas.net.bs/
government/gov4.html
E-mail:
biaphmi@grouper.batelnet.bs

## Bahrain (State of)
Sheikh Hamad ibn 'Isa Al Khalifah
Emir
PO Box 555
The Amiri Court, Rifa's Palace
Rifa
Bahrain

Shaikh Kahlifa bin Salman Al-Kahlifa
Prime Minister
Office of the Prime Minister
PO Box 1000
Manama
Bahrain
Website: http://www.gna.gov.bh/

## Bangladesh (People's Republic of)
Shahabuddin Ahmed
President
Bangabhaban
1000 Dhaka, Dhaka Division
Bangladesh
Website: http://
www.BangladeshGov.org/

Sheikh Hasina Wazed
Prime Minister
Prime Minister's Office

Old Airport Rd. Tejgaon
Dhaka, Dhaka Division
Bangladesh
Website: http://
www.BangladeshGov.org/
E-mail: pm@pmo.bdonline.com

## Belarus (Republic of)
Aleksandr Lukashenko
President
Office of the President
220010 Minsk, Minsk oblast
Belarus
Website: http://president.gov.by/
E-mail: ires@president.gov.by

Uladzimir Yarmoshyn
Premier
Supreme Council
Minsk, Minsk oblast
Belarus

## Belgium (Kingdom of)
King Albert II
Palais Royal
rue de Brederode 16
B-1000 Bruxelles
Belgium

Guy Verhofstadt
Premier Ministre
rue de la Loi 16
B-1000 Brussels
Belgium
Website: http://belgium.fgov.be/

## Belize
Said Musa
Prime Minister
Office of the Prime Minister
New Administrative Building
Belmopan
Belize
Website: http://www.belize.gov.bz/
E-mail: pmbelize@btl.net

**Benin (Republic of)**
Mathieu Kerekou
President
Place de l'Independance
Boite Postale 08 0612
Cotonou
Benin
Website: http://planben.intnet.bj/

**Bhutan (Kingdom of)**
King Jigme Singye Wangchuk
Royal Palace
Thimphu
Bhutan

**Bolivia (Republic of)**
Hugo Banzer Suarez
President
Palacio de Gobierno
Plaza Murillo
La Paz
Bolivia
Website: http://
www.congreso.gov.bo/
indexv3.html
E-mail: mig@comunica.gov.bo

Prime Minister
Office of the Prime Minister
PO Box 1000, Government House
La Paz
Bolivia

**Bosnia and Herzegovina**
Alija Izetbegovic
Presidency of the Republic
Save Kavacevica Ulica 6
71000 Sarajevo
Bosnia and Herzegovina
Website: http://www.mvp.gov.ba/
E-mail: info@mvp.gov.ba

**Botswana (Republic of)**
Festus Mogae
President
State House

Private Bag 001
Gaborone
Botswana
Website: http://www.gov.bw/

**Brazil (Federative Republic of)**
Fernando Henrique Cardoso
President
Oficina do President, Palacio do
Planalto
Praca dos Tres Poderes
70.50 Brasilia
Brazil
Website: http://
www.planalto.gov.br/
E-mail: protocolo@planalto.gov.br

**Brunei (Negara Brunei
Darussalam)**
Sir Muda Hassanal Bolkia
Mu'izzadin Waddaulah
Sultan
Istana Darul Hana
Bandar Seri Begawan Brunei
Maura
Brunei
Website: http://www.brunei.gov.bn/

Bismillahir Rahmanir Rahim
Prime Minister
Prime Minister's Office
Istana Nurul Iman
BA1000 Bandar Seri Begawan
Brunei
Website: http://www.pmo.gov.bn/
Email: page http://
www.pmo.gov.bn/contact.htm

**Bulgaria (Republic of)**
Petar Stoyanov
President
Office of the President
Veliko Narodno Subraine
Sofia 1000
Bulgaria

Website: http://www.president.bg/
E-mail: president@president.bg

Ivan Yordanov Kostov
Prime Minister
Council of Ministers
Boulevard Knjaz Dondukov 1
1000 Sofia
Bulgaria
Website: http://
www.bulgaria.govrn.bg/

**Burkina Faso**
Blaise Compaore
President
Office of the President
03 BP 7030
Ouagadougou 03
Burkina Faso
Website: http://
www.primature.gov.bf/

Kadre Desire Ouedraogo
Prime Minister
03 BP 7027
Ouagadougou 03
Burkina Faso
Website: http://
www.primature.gov.bf/republic/
fgouvernement.htm

**Burundi (Republic of)**
Pierre Buyoya
President
B.P. 1870
Office of the President
Bujumbura
Burundi
Website:http://www.burundi.gov.bi/
presi.htm

Pascal-Firmin Ndimira
Premier Ministre
B.P. 1870
Bujumbura
Burundi

**Cambodia**
Ung Huot
First Prime Minister
Office of the Prime Minister
Phnom Penh, Phnom Penh City
Cambodia

Hun Sen
Second Prime Minister
Office of the Prime Minister
Phnom Penh, Phnom Penh City
Cambodia

**Cameroon (Republic of)**
Paul Biya
President
Office of the President
Yaounde, Centre
Cameroon

**Canada**
Jean Chretien, M.P.
Prime Minister
House of Commons
PO Box 1103
Ottawa, Ontario K1A OA6
Canada
E-mail: *pm@pm.gc.ca*
Website: *http://www.pm.gc.ca/
english.html-ssi*

**Cape Verdi (Republic of)**
Antonio Mascarenhas Montiero
President
Office of the President
Cidade de Praia
Sao Taigo, Praia Concelho
Cape Verde

**Central African Republic**
Ange Felix Patasse
President
Presidence de la Republique
Bangui
Central African Republic

Website: http://
www.socatel.intnet.cf/patasse.htm

**Chad (Republic of Tchad)**
Idriss Deby
President
Office of the President of the
Republic
N'Djamena
Chad
Website: http://www.tit.td/
presidence.html

Nagoum Yamassoum
Prime Minister
Higher Transitional Council
N'Djamena
Chad

**Chile (Republic of)**
Ricardo Lagos
President
Palacio de la Moneda
Oficina de Presidente
Santiago
Chile
Website: http://www.presidencia.cl
E-mail: webmaster@presidencia.cl

**China (People's Republic of)**
Jiang Zemin Guojia Zhuxi
President of the People's Republic
of China
Beijingshi
People's Republic of China

Zhu Rongji
Premier, People's Republic of
China
Guowuyuan
9 Xihuang-chenggen Beijie
Beijingshi 100032
People's Republic of China

Qiao Shi Weiyuanzhang
Chairman, National People's
Congress
Quanguo renmmin Daibiao Dahui
Great Hall of the People
Beijingshi
People's Republic of China

**Colombia (Republic of)**
Andres Pastrana Arango
Presidente
Casa de Narino, Carrera 8a. 7-26
Office of the President
Santa Fe de Bogota
Colombia
Website: http://
www.presidencia.gov.co
E-mail:
pastrana@presidencia.gov.co

**Comoros (Federal Islamic
Republic of the)**
Azali Assoumani
President
Office of the President
B.P. 421
Moroni
Comoros

Azali Assoumani (same as above)
Premier
Mahdi
Moroni
Comoros

**Congo (Democratic Republic of)/
Previously Zaire**
Laurent Desire Kabila
President
Presidence de la Republique
Kinshasa
Democratic Republic of the Congo/
Zaire
Website: http://www.rdcongo.org/
frames/index.html

**Congo (Republic of)**
Denis Sassou-Nguesso
President
Office du President
Palais Presidentiel
Brazzaville
Congo
Website: http://www.congo-
brazza.com/index2.htm

**Costa Rica (Republic of)**
Miguel Angel Rodriguez Echeverria
President
Casa Presidencial, Oficinas
Presidenciales
Apartado 520-2010 Zapoto
San Jose
Costa Rica
Website: http://www.casapres.go.cr/

**Croatia (Republic of)**
Stipe Mesic
President
Predsjednicki dvori
Pantovcak 241
10000 Zagreb, Zagrebacka
Zupanija
Croatia
Website: http://www.predsjednik.hr/
E-mail: www-admin@president.hr

Ivica Racan
Premier
Trg Sv. Marka 2
10000 Zagreb, Zagrebacka
Zupanija
Croatia
Website: http://www.vlada.hr

**Cuba (Republic of)**
Fidel Castro Ruz
President
Palacio de la Revolucion
Havana
Cuba
Website: http://www.cubaweb.cu/
(See NEWS for political info.)

**Cyprus (Republic of)**
H. E Glafcos Clerides
President
Presidential Palace
Nicosia
Cyprus
Website: http://www.pio.gov.cy/
E-mail: pioxx@cytanet.com.cy

**Czech Republic**
Vaclav Havel
President
Office of the President of the C.R.
Hrad (Castle)
119 08 Praha 1
Czech Republic
Website: http://www.hrad.cz/
E-mail: president@hrad.cz

Milos Zeman
Prime Minister
Kancelar prezidenta republiky
Snemouni 4
11908 Praha 1
Czech Republic
Website: http://www.vlada.cz/

**Denmark (Kingdom of)**
Queen Margrethe II
Hofmarskallatet
Det Gule Palae
DK-1256 Copenhagen
Denmark
Website: http://
www.kongehuset.dk/

Poul Nyrup Rasmussen
Prime Minister
Prime Minister's Office
Christiansborg, Prins Jorgens Gaard
11
DK-1218 Copenhagen
Denmark
Website: http://www.stm.dk/
E-mail: stm@stm.dk

**Djibouti (Republic of)**
Ismail Omar Guelleh
President
Presidence de la Republique
Djibouti
Website: http://amb-djibouti.org/
gouverne.htm

S.E.M. Barkat Gourad Hamadou
Premier Ministre
PB 2086, Bureau du Premier
Ministre de la Republique
Djibouti

**Dominica (Commonwealth of)**
Vernon Lorden Shaw
President
President's House
Roseau
Dominica
Website: http://www.dominica.dm/

Rosie Douglas
Prime Minister
Office of the Prime Minister
Government Headquarters,
Kennedy Ave.
Roseau
Dominica
E-mail: pmoffice@cwdom.dm

**Dominican Republic**
Leonel Fernandez Reyna
President
Oficina del Presidente
Santo Domingo, Distrito Nacional
Dominican Republic
Website: http://
www.presidencia.gov.do/
E-mail:
correspondencias@
presidencia.gov.do

**East Timor**
Sergio Vieira de Mello

Special Rep. of the Secretary-
General for East Timor
UNTAET/UN Transitional
Administration for East Timor
Dili
East Timor
Website: http://www.un.org/peace/
etimor/etimor.htm

Xanana Gusmao
President
The National Council of Timorese
Resistance
Dili
East Timor

**Ecuador (Republic of)**
Gustavo Naboa
President
Palacio Nacional
Garcia Moreno 1043
Quito
Ecuador
Website: http://
www.mmrree.gov.ec/minrex/
eminrex.htm
E-mail: webmast@mmrree.gov.ec

**Egypt (Arab Republic of)**
Mohammed Hosni Mubarak
President
Presidential Palace
Abdeen
Cairo
Egypt
Website: http://
www.presidency.gov.eg/
E-mail:
webmaster@presidency.gov.eg/

**El Salvador (Republic of)**
Francisco Guillermo Flores Perez
President
Oficina del Presidente
San Salvador
El Salvador

Website: http://
www.casapres.gob.sv/
E-mail:
webmaster@casapres.gob.sv

**Equatorial Guinea (Republic of)**
Teodoro Obiang Nguema Mbasogo
President
Oficina del Presidente
Malabo
Equatorial Guinea

Angel Serafín Seriche Dougan
Prime Minister
Camara de Representantes del
Pueblo
Malabo
Equatorial Guinea

**Eritrea (State of)**
Issaias Afwerki
President
Office of the President
P.O. Box 257
Asmara
Eritrea
Website: http://www.NetAfrica.org/
eritrea/index.htm

**Estonia (Republic of)**
Lennart Meri
President
Weizenbergi 39, 15050
Office of the President
EE0100 Tallinn
Estonia
Website: http://www.president.ee
E-mail: sekretar@vpk.ee

Mart Laar
Prime Minister
Lossi plats 1a
EE0100 Tallinn
Estonia

Website: http://www.riik.ee/engno/
index.html
E-mail: valitsus@rk.ee

**Ethiopia**
Dr. Nagaso Gidada
President
Office of the President
PO Box 1031
Addis Ababa
Ethiopia

Meles Zenawi
Prime Minister
Office of the Prime Minister
PO Box 1031
Addis Ababa
Ethiopia

**Fiji (Republic of)**
Kamisese Mara
President
Office of the President
Government House
Suva
Fiji

Prime Minister
Government Buildings
Office of the Prime Minister
Suva
Fiji

**Finland (Republic of)**
Paavo Lipponen
Prime Minister
Eduskunta
00102 Helsinki
Finland
Website: *http://www.eduskunta.fin/*
*welcome.html*

Martti Ahtisaari
President
Tasavallan presidentin kanslia
Mariank 2

Finland
E-mail: *presidentti@tpk.fi*
Website: *http://www.tpk.fi/eng/
index.html*

## France (French Republic)
M. Jacques Chirac
President de la Republique
Palais de l'Elysee
55 et 57 rue de Faubourg
Saint-Honore
75008 Paris
France
Website: *http://
www.france.diplomatie.fr*

Lionel Jospin
Prime Minister
57 rue de Varenne
75700 Paris
France
E-mail: *http://
www.premier.ministre.gouv.fr/PM/
Mail.HTM*
Website: *http://www.premier-
ministre.gouv.fr*

## Gabon (Gabonese Republic)
El Hajd Omar Bongo
President
Presidence de la Republique
B.P. 546
Libreville
Gabon
Website: http://www.presidence-
gabon.com/
E-mail: eleusis@mail.eunet.fr

Jean-Francois Ntoutoume
Prime Minister
Cabinet du Premier Ministre
B.P. 91
Libreville
Gabon

## Gambia (Republic of)
Yahya Jammeh
President

Office of the President
State House
Banjul
Gambia
Website: http://www.gambia.com

Permanent Secretary
Ministry for Local Govt. and Lands
The Quadrangle
Banjul, Banjul Division
Gambia

## Georgia (Republic of)
Eduard Shevardnadze
Chairman, State Council
Plekhanova 103
Tbilisi 880064
Georgia
Website: http://
www.presidpress.gov.ge/
E-mail: office@presidpress.gov.ge

## Germany (Federal Republic of)
Johannes Rau
Bundespraesident
Bundespraesidialamt
Schloss Bellevue, Spreeweg 1
10557 Berlin
Germany
Website: http://
www.bundespraesident.de
E-mail: http://
www.bundespraesident.de/
post.htm

Gerhard Schroeder
Bundeskanzler
Bundeskanzleramt der
Bundesregierung
Schlossplatz 1
10178 Berlin
Germany
Website: http://
www.bundesregierung.de/
E-mail:
InternetPost@bundesregierung.de

**Ghana (Republic of)**
Jerry Rawlings
President
Office of the Head of State
The Castle
Accra, Greater Accra
Ghana
Website: http://www.ghana.gov.gh

**Greece (Hellenic Republic)**
Mr. Constantinos Stephanopoulos
President
Presidential Mansion
7 Vas. Georgiou St
106 74 Athens
Greece

Kostas Simitis
Prime Minister
Office of the Prime Minister
Greek Parliament Bldg.,
Constitution Square
Athens
Greece
Fax: 301-671-6183
Website: http://
www.primeminister.gr
E-mail: mail@primeminister.gr

**Greenland**
Prime Minister
Gronlands Hjemmestyre
Postbox 1015
DK-3900 Nuuk/Godthab
Greenland
Website: http://www.gh.gl/
E-mail: homerule@gh.gl

High Commissioner for Greenland
Postbox 1030
DK-3900 Nuuk/Godthab
Greenland

**Grenada**
Keith Mitchell
Prime Minister

Parliament
St. George's
Grenada

**Guatemala (Republic of)**
Alfonso Portillo Cabrera
President
Palacio Nacional, Nivel 2
6 Calle entre 6 y 7 Avenida,
Zona 1
01001 Guatemala Ciudad
Guatemala
Website: http://www.concyt.gob.gt/
sectpub/index.html

**Guinea (Republic of)**
Lansana Conte
President Brigadeer General
Office du President
State House
Conakry
Guinea
Website: http://www.guinea.gov.gn/

**Guinea-Bissau (Republic of)**
Kumba Iala
President
Conselho de Estado
Bissau
Guinea-Bissau

**Guyana (Co-Operative Republic of)**
Bharrat Jagdeo
President
Office of the President
New Garden St. and South Rd.
Georgetown
Guyana

Samuel Hinds
Prime Minister
Office of the Prime Minister
Wight's Lane, Kingston
Georgetown
Guyana

**Haiti (Republic of)**
Rene Preval
President
Palais National, Champ de Mars
Port-au-Prince
Haiti
Website:http://www.haitifocus.com/
haitie/gov.html

Jacques-Edouard Alexis
Premier Ministre
Bureau du Premier Ministre
Villa d'Accueil, Delmas 60
Musseau, Port-au-Prince
Haiti

**Honduras (Republic of)**
Carlos Roberto Flores Facusse
Presidente Constitucional
Casa de Gobierno, Centro Cívico-
Gubernamental, Miraflores Casa
Presid.
Tegucigalpa
Honduras
Website: http://www.sre.hn/

**Hungary (Republic of)**
Ferenc Madl
President
Kossuth Lajos ter 3-5
Office of the President
1055 Budapest, Budapest fovaros
Hungary

Viktor Orban
Prime Minister
Kossuth Lajos ter 1-3
1055 Budapest, Budapest fovaros
Hungary
Website: http://www.meh.hu
E-mail: Viktor.Orban@meh.hu

**Iceland (Republic of)**
Olafur Ragnar Grimsson
President
Office of the President

Stadastad, Soleyjargata 1
101 Reykjavik
Iceland

David Oddsson
Prime Minister
Office of the Prime Minister
Stjornarradshusinu
150 Reykjavik
Iceland
Website: http://brunnur.stjr.is/
interpro/for/for.nsf/pages/for
E-mail: postur@for.stjr.is

**India (Republic of)**
Kocheril Raman Narayanan
President
Rashtrapati Bhavan
110004 New Delhi
India
Website: http://alfa.nic.in/rb/
welcome.htm

Atal Bihari Vajpayee
Prime Minister
152 South Block
110011 New Delhi
India
Website: http://www.nic.in/
indpar.htm
E-mail: page http://164.100.24.8/
feedb.html

**Indonesia (Republic of)**
Abduraman Wahid
President
Office of the President
15 Jalan Merdeka Utara
Jakarta
Indonesia
Website: http://www.dfa-
deplu.go.id/english/govern1.htm

**Iran (Islamic Republic of)**
Seyed Mohammad Khatami
President

Dr. Al Shariati Ave.
% Islamic Republican Party
Tehran
Iran
Website: http://www.gov.ir/
E-mail: page http://
www.president.ir/email/email.htm

**Iraq (Republic of)**
Saddam Hussein At-Takriti
President
Presidential Palace
Karadat Mariam
Baghdad
Iraq
E-mail: irqun@undp.org (Iraq's
Mission to the U.N.)

**Ireland (Eire)**
Mary McAleese
President
Office of the President
Phoenix Park
Dublin 8
Ireland
Website: http://www.irlgov.ie/
E-mail: webmaster@aras.irlgov.ie

Bertie Ahern
Prime Minister/Taoiseach
Office of the Prime Minister
Government Bldg.
Upper Merrion St.
Dublin 2
Ireland
Website: http://www.irlgov.ie/
E-mail:
webmaster@taoiseach.irlgov.ie

**Israel (State of)**
Moshe Katzav
President
Office of the President
3 Hanassi St.
92188 Jerusalem
Israel

Website: http://www.israel-
mfa.gov.il/mfa/

Ariel Sharon
Prime Minister
Kiryat Ben-Gurion
3 Kaplan St., PO Box 187
91919 Jerusalem
Israel
Website: http://www.pmo.gov.il/
E-mail: ask@israel-info.gov.il
Alternate, e-mail:
feedback@pmo.gov.il

**Italy (Italian Republic)**
Carlo Azeglio Ciampi
President
Palazzo del Quirinale
00187 Rome
Italy

Giuliano Amato
Presidenza del Consiglio dei
Ministri (Prime Minister)
Piazza Colonna, 370
00187 Rome
Italy
Website: http://www.palazzochigi.it/
E-mail: page http://
www.palazzochigi.it/contattaci.htm

**Ivory Coast (Republic of Cote
d'Ivoire)**
Robert Guei
President
Presidence de la Republique
Abidjan
Boulevard Clozel
Ivory Coast
Website: http://
www.lacotedivoire.com/

Daniel Kablan Duncan
Prime Minister
Office of the Prime Minister

Abidjan
Ivory Coast

## Jamaica
Percival John Patterson
Prime Minister
Jamaica House
6 Kingston
Jamaica
Website: http://www.jis.gov.jm/
E-mail: jis@jis.gov.jm

## Japan
Emperor Akihito, %
Imperial Household Agency
11 Chiyoda, Chiyoda-ku
100 Tokyo
Japan

Yoshiro Mori
Prime Minister
Prime Minister's Office
6-1, Nagata-cho 1 chome, Chiyoda-Ku
Tokyo
Japan
Website: http://www.kantei.go.jp/
foreign/index-e.html
E-mail: page http://www.iijnet.or.jp/
sorifu/kantei/foreign/comment.html

## Jordan (Hashemite Kingdom of)
H. M. King Abdallah ibn al-Hussein
al-Hashimi
Royal Palace
Amman
Jordan
Website: http://www.nic.gov.jo/
E-mail: info@nic.gov.jo

Ali Abu Ragheb
Prime Minister
PO Box 80
352 Amman
Jordan

## Kazakhstan (Republic of)
Nursultan Nazarbayev
President
Office of the President
Republic Sq.
480091 Almaty
Kazakhstan

Prime Minister
Office of the Prime Minister
Republic Sq.
480091 Almaty
Kazakhstan

## Kenya (Republic of)
Daniel arap Moi
President
Harambee House, Office of the
President
PO Box 30510
Nairobi
Kenya
Website: http://
www.kenyaweb.com/kenyagov/

## Kiribati (Republic of)
Teburoro Tito
President
Office of the President
PO Box 68, Bairiki
Tarawa
Kiribati

## Kosova
Hashim Thaci
Prime Minister/Kryeminister
Website: http://www.kosova.org

## Kuwait (State of)
H. H. Jaber Al-Ahmed Al-Jaber Al-
Sabah
Amir Sheikh
Amiri Diwan
PO Box 799
13008 Safat

Kuwait
Website: http://www.mofa.gov.kw
(Ministry of Foreign Affairs)
H. H. Saad Al-Abdallah Al-Salem Al-
Sabah
Crown Prince Sheikh
Crown Prince Diwan
PO Box 4
13001 Safat
Kuwait

**Kyrgyzstan (Kyrgyz Republic)**
Askar Akayev
President
Office of the President
Ulitsa Kirova 205
Bishkek
Kyrgyzstan
Website: http://gov.bishkek.su/
english/Gov-e.htm

Amangeldy Muraliev
Prime Minister
Zhorgorku Kenesh
Bishkek
Kyrgyzstan

**Laos (Lao People's Democratic
Republic)**
Kanthay Siphandon
President
Office of the President
Lane Xang Ave.
Viangchan
Laos

Sisavat Keobounphan
Prime Minister
Office of the Chairman
Council of Ministers
Viangchan
Laos

**Latvia (Republic of)**
Vaira Vike-Freiberga
President of State

Chancery of the President, Pils
laukums 3
LV-1900 Riga
Latvia
Website: http://www.president.lv/
E-mail: chancery@president.lv

President of Ministers
Cabinet of Ministers of the Republic
of Latvia
Brivibas Blvd. 36
LV-1395 Riga
Latvia

**Lebanon (Republic of)**
Emile Lahoud
President
Baabda Palace
Office of the President
Beirut
Lebanon
Website: http://
www.presidency.gov.lb/
E-mail: http://
www.presidency.gov.lb/write/write/
write.htm

Selim Ahmed Hoss
Prime Minister
Government Palace
Office of the Prime Minister
Beirut
Lebanon
Website: http://www.lp.gov.lb/
E-mail: info@lp.gov.lb

**Lesotho (Kingdom of)**
Letsie III
King
Royal Palace
Maseru
Lesotho

Pakalitha Mosisili
Prime Minister
% The Government Secretary

PO Box 527
Maseru 100
Lesotho

**Liberia (Republic of)**
Dr. Charles Ghankay Taylor
President
Office of the President, Capitol Hill
1000 Monrovia 10
Liberia

**Libya (Socialist People's Libyan Arab Jamahiriya)**
Muammar al-Qaddafi
Colonel
Office of the President
Tripoli
Libya

Mubarak al-Shamekh
General Secretary
General People's Committee
Tripoli
Libya

**Liechtenstein (Principality of)**
H. S. H. Prince Hans Adam II
Schloss
FL-9490 Vaduz
Liechtenstein
Website: http://www.firstlink.li/
fuerst/

Mario Frick
Prime Minister
Regierungsgebaeude
9490 Vaduz
Liechtenstein
Website: http://www.lol.li/

**Lithuania (Republic of)**
Valdas Adamkus
President
Gedimino pr. 53
Office of the President
2026 Vilnius

Lithuania
Website: http://www.president.lt
E-mail: info@president.lt

Andrius Kubilius
Prime Minister
Gedimino 11
2039 Vilnius
Lithuania
Website: http://www.lrvk.lt/
E-mail: kanceliarija@lrvk.lt

**Luxembourg (Grand Duchy of)**
Jean Benoit D'Aviano
Grand Duke
Grand Ducal Place
2013 Luxembourg
Luxembourg

Jean-Claude Juncker
Prime Minister
Ministere d'Etat
4, rue de la Congregation
L-2910 Luxembourg
Luxembourg
Website: http://www.restena.lu/
gover/indexfrench.html
E-mail: http://www.restena.lu:80/
gover/mailbox.html

**Macedonia (Republic of)**
Boris Trajkovski
President
Office of the President
11 Oktomvrii b.b.
91000 Skopje
Macedonia
Phone: 389-91-112-255
Fax: 389-91-237-947

Ljubco Georgievski
Prime Minister
Ilindenska b.b.
91000 Skopje
Macedonia
Phone: 389-91-115-389

Fax: 389-91-119-561
Website: http://www.gov.mk/

**Madagascar (Republic of)**
Didier Ratsiraka
President
Presidence de la Republique
Ambohitsirohitra 101
Antananarivo
Madagascar
Phone: 334-44
Website: http://www.an.online.mg/
E-mail: president.an@online.mg

Tantely Andrianarivo
Prime Minister
Palais de Mahazoarivo
Antananarivo
Madagascar

**Malawi (Republic of)**
H. E. Dr. Bakili Muluzi
President
Office of the President
State House, P.O. Box 40
Zomba
Malawi

Regional Administrator
Private Bag 32
Capital City
Lilongwe 3, Central Region
Malawi

**Malaysia**
Paramount Ruler Sultan Tuanku
Salehuddin Abdul Aziz Shah
Istana Negara
Kuala Lumpur
Malaysia

Dr. Dato Seri Mahathir Mohamad
Prime Minister
Prime Minister's Department
Jalan Dato' Onn
50502 Kuala Lumpur

Malaysia
Website: http://
www.smpke.jpm.my/

**Maldives (Republic of)**
Maumoon Abdul Gayoom
His Excellency the President
Office of the President
Marine Dr.
Male' 20-05
Maldives
Website: http://www.maldives-info.com/
E-mail: admin@foreign.gov.mv

**Mali (Republic of)**
Alpha Oumar Konare
President
Presidence, Koulouba
Bamako
Mali

Mande Sidibe
Prime Minister
Primature
Bamako
Mali

**Malta (Republic of)**
Dr. Guido Demarco
President
The Palace
Office of the President
CMR 02, Valletta
Malta
Website: http://www.magnet.mt

Hon. Dr. Eddie Fenech Adami
Prime Minister
Auberge de Castille
CMR 02, Valletta
Malta
Website: http://www.magnet.mt
E-mail: info@magnet.mt

**Marshall Islands (Republic of)**
Kessai Note
President
Capitol Bldg.
96960 Majuro
Marshall Islands

**Mauritania (Islamic Republic of)**
Maaouya Ould Sidi Ahmed Taya
President
Presidence de la Republique
B.P. 184
Nouakchott
Mauritania
Website: http://www.mauritania.mr/

M. Cheikh El Avia Ould Mohamed
Khouna
Prime Minister
Majlis al-Watani/National Assembly
Nouakchott
Mauritania

**Mauritius (Republic of)**
Cassam Uteem
President
Government House
Port Louis
Mauritius
Phone: 230-454-3021
Fax: 230-464-5370
Website: http://ncb.intnet.mu/
presiden.htm
E-mail: statepas@intnet.mu

Dr. Navinchandra Ramgoolam
Prime Minister
New Government Centre, 6th Floor
Port Louis
Mauritius
Phone: 230-201-1018
Fax: 230-212-9393
Website: http://www.ncb.intnet.mu/
pmo.htm

**Mexico (United Mexican States)**
Ernesto Zedillo Ponce de Leon
President
Palacio Nacional
Patio de Honor, Piso 1, Col. Centro
06067 Mexico City DF
Mexico
Phone: 52-5-395-6700
Fax: 52-5-395-6790
Website: http://
www.presidencia.gob.mx/
E-mail: http://
www.presidencia.gob.mx/pages/
f_forma.html

Gobernador
Palacio de Gobierno 2o.
piso 20000
Aguascalientes, Aguascalientes
Mexico
Website: http://
www.aguascalientes.gob.mx/

**Moldova (Republic of)**
Petru Lucinschi
President
Office of the President
154, Stefan cel Mare Blvd.
Chisinau
Moldova
Website: http://www.moldova.md/

Dumitru Barghis
Prime Minister
Office of the Prime Minister
Chisinau
Moldova
Website: http://www.moldova.md/

**Monaco (Principality of)**
Prince Rainier III
Palais de Monaco
Boit Postal 518
98015 Monte Carlo
Monaco

Michel Leveque
Minister of State
Ministere d'Etat
Monaco

**Mongolia**
Natsagiyn Bagabandi
President
State House
12 Ulaanbaatar
Mongolia
Website: http://www.pmis.gov.mn/

Rinchinnyamiyn Amarjargal
Prime Minister
Office of the Prime Minister
Ulaanbaatar
Mongolia

**Morocco (Kingdom of)**
King Mohammed VI Ibn Al Hassan
Palais Royal
Rabat
Morocco
Website: http://
www.mincom.gov.ma/

M. Abderahmane El Youssoufi
Premier Ministre
Palais Royal, Le Mechouar
Rabat
Morocco

**Mozambique (Republic of)**
His Excellency Joaquim Alberto
Chissano
President
Avenida Julius Nyerere 2000
Caixa Postal 285
Maputo
Mozambique
Website: http://
www.mozambique.mz/

Pascoel Manuel Mocumbi
Prime Minister

Office of the Prime Minister
Praca da Marinha Popular
Maputo
Mozambique

**Myanmar (Union of)/Burma**
Than Shwa
Chairman
State Peace and Development
Council
% Ministry of Defence, Signal
Pagoda Road.
Yangon
Myanmar

**Namibia (Republic of)**
Sam Nujoma
President
State House, Robert Mugabe Ave.
Private Bag 13339
Windhoek
Namibia
Website: http://
www.republicofnamibia.com/
E-mail: http://
www.republicofnamibia.com/.
write.htm

Hage Geingob
Prime Minister
Robert Mugabe Ave., Private Bag
13338
Windhoek
Namibia
Website: http://
www.republicofnamibia.com/
E-mail: http://
www.republicofnamibia.com/
write.htm

**Nauru (Republic of)**
Bernard Dowiyogo
President
Parliament House
Yaren District
Nauru—Central Pacific

**Nepal (Kingdom of)**
King Birendra Bir Bikram Shah Dev
Narayanhity Royal Palace
Kathmandu
Nepal

Girija Prasad Koirala
Prime Minister
Singh Durbar
Kathmandu
Nepal

**Netherlands (Kingdom of)**
Willem Kok
Prime Minister
Binnenhof 20, 2513 AA
Postbus 20001, 2500 EA
The Hague
Netherlands
Website: http://www.postbus51.nl/

**New Zealand**
Helen Clark
Prime Minister
Prime Minister's Office
Parliament House, Executive Wing
Wellington
New Zealand
Phone: 64-4-471-9998
Fax: 64-4-473-7045
Website: http://
www.executive.govt.nz/minister/
pm/index.html
E-mail: pm@ministers.govt.nz

**Nicaragua (Republic of)**
Arnoldo Aleman Lacayo
Presidente
Casa de la Presidencia
Avenida Bolívar y Dupla Sur.
Managua
Nicaragua
Phone: 505-228-2803
Fax: 505-228-2001
Website: http://
www.presidencia.gob.ni

**Niger (Republic of)**
Tandja Mamadou
President
Presidential Palace
Niamey
Niger
Le Prefet du Departement
B.P. 45
Maradi
Niger

President de la Communaute
Urbain
B.P. 258
Niamey
Niger

**Nigeria (Federal Republic of)**
Olusegun Obasanjo
President
Presidential Villa
State House, Aso Rock
Abuja
Nigeria
Website: http://www.nigeriagov.org/
E-mail:
president.obasanjo@nigeriagov.org

**North Cyprus (Turkish Republic of Northern Cyprus)**
H. E. Raul Denktas
President
The Office of the President
Mersin 10
Lefkosa
North Cyprus, Turkey
Website: http://
www.kktc.pubinfo.gov.nc.tr/

Dervis Eroglu
Prime Minister
The Office of the Prime Minister
Mersin 10
Lefkosa
North Cyprus, Turkey

Website: http://www.cm.gov.nc.tr/
E-mail: www@cm.gov.nc.tr

## North Korea (Democratic People's Republic of)
Kim Jong Il
President, Standing Committee
Supreme People's Assembly
Pyongyang
North Korea

## Norway (Kingdom of)
King Harald V
Royal Palace
Det Kgl. Slott, Drammensveien 1
N-0010 Oslo
Norway
Phone: 47-2244-1920
Fax: 47-2255-0880
Website: http://
www.kongehuset.no/
E-mail: http://www.kongehuset.no/
respons.html

Jens Stoltenberg
Prime Minister
Stortinget
Karl Johansgate 22
N-0026 Oslo
Norway
Phone: 47-2224-9832
Fax: 47-2224-2796
Website: http://odin.dep.no/
E-mail:
ap.postmottak@st.dep.telemax.no

## Oman (Sultanate of)
Qabus bin said Al said
Sultan
The Palace
Muscat
Oman
Website: http://www.om.zest.co.ae/
sultofom.html

## Pakistan (Islamic Republic of)
Muhammad Rafiq Tarar
President
Office of the President
Constitution Ave.
Islamabad
Pakistan
Fax: 92-51-811390

Purvaiz Musharraf
General/Chief Executive
Prime Minister's Secretariat
Constitution Ave.
Islamabad
Pakistan
Website: http://www.pak.gov.pk/
E-mail: ce@pak.gov.pk

## Palau
Kumiuro Nakamura
President
Office of the President
PO Box 100
Koror
Palau (Pacific Ocean)

## Palestine
Yasser Arafat
President
Palestinian National Authority
Abu Khadra Bldg.
Omar al-Mukhtar St.
Gaza, via Israel
Website: http://www.pna.org/
E-mail:
postmaster@mininfo.pna.org
(Ministry of Information)

## Panama (Republic of)
Mireya Elisa Moscoso de Arias
President
Palacio de las Garzas
Panama City
Panama
Website: http://
www.presidencia.gob.pa/

**Papua New Guinea (Independent State of)**
The Hon. Mekere Morauta
Prime Minister
Protocol Office, Dept. of Prime Minister
PO Box 6605, Morauta House
N.C.D., Boroko
Papua New Guinea
Website: http://www.pm.gov.pg

**Paraguay (Republic of)**
Luis Angel Gonzalez Macchi
President
Palacio de Lopez
El Paraguayo Independiente y Ayolas
Asuncion
Paraguay
Website: http://www.presidencia.gov.py

**Peru (Republic of)**
Alberto Fujimori Kenyo
President
Ministerio de la Presidencia
Av. Paseo de la República 4297, Surquillo
Lima
Peru
Website: http://www.pres.gob.pe/
E-mail: postmaster@pres.gob.pe

Alberto Bustamante
Prime Minister
Ucayali 363
Lima
Peru

**Philippines (Republic of)**
Joseph Estrada
President
Malacanang Palace
Jose P. Laurel St.
Manila
Philippines

Phone: 63-2-735-6201
Fax: 63-2-742-1641
Website: http://www.erap.com
E-mail: erap@erap.com

**Poland (Republic of)**
Aleksander Kwasniewski
President
Kancelaria Prezydenta RP
ul. Wiejska 10
00-902 Warsaw
Poland
Website: http://www.president.pl or http://www.prezydent.pl
E-mail: listy@prezydent.pl

Jerzy Buzek
Prime Minister
Prime Minister's Office
al. Ujazdowskie 1/3
00-583 Warsaw
Poland
Website: http://www.kprm.gov.pl
E-mail: cirinfo@kprm.gov.pl

**Portugal (Portuguese Republic)**
Jorge Sampaio
President
Presidentia da Republica
Palacio de Belem
1300 Lisboa
Portugal

Antonio Manuel de Oliveira Guterres
Prime Minister
Gabinete do Primeiro-Ministro
Lisboa
Portugal
Website: http://www.primeiro-ministro.gov.pt/
E-mail: pm@pm.gov.pt

President of Regiao Autonoma dos Acores
Palacio de Santana

9500 Ponta Delgada
Sao Miguel, Azores
Portugal

## Qatar (State of)
Sheik Hamad bin Khalifa al-Thani
Emir
The Royal Palace
PO Box 923
Doha
Qatar
Website: http://www.mofa.gov.qa/

## Romania
Emile Constantinescu
President
Palatul Cotroceni
Bd. Geniului 1
Bucharest
Romania
Phone: 401-410-0581
Fax: 401-312-1247
Website: http://www.presidency.ro/
E-mail: presedinte@presidency.ro

Mugur Isarescu
Prime Minister
Palatul Parlamentului
Calea 13 Septembrie 1
Bucharest
Romania
Phone: 401-335-0111
Fax: 401-312-0828
Website: http://domino.kappa.ro/
guvern/home.nsf
E-mail: prim.ministru@gov.ro

## Russia (Russian Federation)
Vladimir Vladimirovich Putin
President
The Kremlin
Moscow
Russia
Website: http://www.gov.ru/
E-mail: president@gov.ru

Prime Minister
Government Offices
Krasnopresnenskaya
2 Moscow
Russia

## Rwanda (Republic of)
Paul Kagame
President
Presidence de la Republique
Kigali
Rwanda

## Saint Kitts and Nevis (Federation of)
The Hon. Dr. Denzil Douglas
Prime Minister
Office of the Prime Minister
Government Headquarters
Basseterre
Saint Kitts and Nevis
Phone: 869-465-2521
Fax: 869-465-1001
Website: http://
www.stkittsnevis.net

## Saint Lucia
Kenny Anthony
Prime Minister
Office of the Prime Minister
Government Headquarters
Castries
Saint Lucia
Website: http://www.stlucia.gov.lc
E-mail: pmoffice@candw.lc

## Saint Vincent and the Grenadines
Rt. Hon. James Fitz-Allen Mitchell
Prime Minister
Office of the Prime Minister
Government Headquarters
Kingstown
Saint Vincent and the Grenadines
Phone: 1-809-456-1703
Fax: 1-809-457-2152

## San Marino (Republic of)
Secretary of State, Political Affairs
San Marino
San Marino-Italy
Website: http://inthenet.sm/
cultur.htm

Secretary of State, Finance
San Marino
San Marino-Italy

Secretary of State, Internal Affairs
San Marino
San Marino-Italy

## Sao Tome and Principe (Democratic Republic of)
Miguel Trovoada
President
Office of the President
C.P. 38
Sao Tome
Sao Tome and Principe

Guilherme Posser da Costa
Prime Minister
Office of the Prime Minister
C.P. 38
Sao Tome
Sao Tome and Principe

## Saudi Arabia (Kingdom of)
King Fahd Bin Abdulaziz Al Saud
Royal Diwan
Riyadh
Saudi Arabia
Phone: 966-1-488-2222

Crown Prince H. R. H. Abdullah
Bin Abdulaziz Al Saud
Royal Court
Riyadh
Saudi Arabia
Phone: 966-1-491-5400

## Senegal (Republic of)
Abdoulaye Wade
President
Office of the President
Avenue Roume, BP 168
Dakar
Senegal
Website: http://www.primature.sn/
president.htm

## Seychelles (Republic of)
France-Albert Rene
President
The State House, PO Box 55
Mahe
Victoria
Seychelles
Phone: 248-224-155
Fax: 248-225-117
Website: http://
www.seychelles-online.com.sc/
E-mail: ppo@seychelles.net

## Sierra Leone (Republic of)
Ahmad Tejankabbah
President
Office of the President
State House, Tower Hill
Freetown
Sierra Leone
Website: http://www.sierra-
leone.org/govt.html

## Singapore (Republic of)
Sellapan Ramanathan Nathan
President
Istana
Orchard Rd.
238823 Singapore
Singapore
Phone: 65-737-5522
Fax: 65-737-9896
Website: http://www.gov.sg/istana/

Goh Chok Tong
Prime Minister

Istana
0923 Singapore
Singapore
Phone: 65-235-8577
Fax: 65-732-4627
Website: http://www.gov.sg/pmo/

## Slovakia (Slovak Republic)
Rudolf Schuster
President/Primacialny palac
Stefanikova 1
810 00 Bratislava
Slovakia
Website: http://www.prezident.sk/

Mikulas Dzurinda
Prime Minister
Nam. Slobody 1
813 70 Bratislava
Slovakia
Website: http://
www.government.gov.sk
E-mail:
prime.minister@
government.gov.sk

## Slovenia (Republic of)
Andrej Bajuk
Prime Minister
Gregorciceva 20
61000 Ljubljana
Slovenia
Website: http://www.sigov.si/
E-mail: alja.brglez@gov.si

Mr. Milan Kucan
President
Erjavceva 17
Office of the President
61000 Ljubljana
Slovenia
Website: http://www.gov.si/up-rs/
enindex.htm
E-mail:
darinka.ilovar@up.sigov.mail.si

## Solomon Islands
Bartholomew Ulufa'alu
Prime Minister
Prime Minister's Office
PO Box G1
Honiara, Guadalcanal
Solomon Islands

## Somalia
Collective Chairmanship
National Salvation Council
Mogadishu
Somalia

## South Africa (Republic of)
Thabo Mvuyelwa Mbeki
President
Office of the President, Private Bag
X1000
Union Buildings, Government Ave.
0001 Pretoria
South Africa
Phone: 27-12-319-1500
Fax: 27-12-323-8246
Website: http://www.gov.za/
president
E-mail: president@po.gov.za

## South Korea (Republic of Korea)
Kim Dae Jung
President
Office of the President (Blue
House)
1 Sejong-ro Chongro-gu
110-050 Seoul
South Korea
Website: http://
www.bluehouse.go.kr/
E-mail: webmaster@cwd.go.kr

Park Tae Joon
Prime Minister
Sindang 4-dong
Chung-ku
340-38 Seoul

South Korea
Website: http://www.opm.go.kr/

**Spain (Kingdom of)**
King Juan Carlos I de Borbon y
Borbon
Palacio de la Zarzuela
28071 Madrid
Spain
Website: http://www.casareal.es/
casareal/

Excmo. Sr. Jose Maria Aznar
Presidente del Gobierno
Complejo de la Moncloa
Edf. Semillas
28071 Madrid
Spain
Phone: 34-1-335-3535
Fax: 34-1-390-0329
Website: http://www.la-moncloa.es

**Sri Lanka (Democratic Socialist
Republic of)**
H. E. Chandrika Bandaranaike
Kumaratunga
President
Presidential Secretarial
Secretarial Building
Colombo, 01
Sri Lanka
Website: http://www.lk/
president.html
E-mail: for_min@sri.lanka.net
(Ministry of Foreign Affairs)

Sirimavo Bandaranaike
Prime Minister
58 Sir Ernest de Silva Mawatha
07 Colombo
Sri Lanka
Website: http://www.lk/
prime_minister.html

**Sudan (Republic of the)**
Omar Hassan Ahmed Al-Bashir

President General
Revolutionary Command Council
Khartoum
Sudan

**Suriname (Republic of)**
Jules Adjodhia
Prime Minister
Nationale Assemblee
Wulfingstraat
Paramaríbo
Suriname

Jules Wijdenbosch
President
Presidentieel Paleis
Onafhankelijkheidsplein
Paramaríbo
Suriname
Website: http://www1.sr.net/
~t100644/
E-mail: burpres@sr.net

**Swaziland (Kingdom of)**
King Mswati III
Royal Palace
Mbabane
Swaziland

H. E. Dr. Barnabas Sibusiso
Dlamini
Prime Minister
PO Box 395
Mbabane
Swaziland
Website http://home.swazi.com/
government/
E-mail: ppcu@realnet.co.sz

**Sweden (Kingdom of)**
King Carl XVI Gustaf
Royal Palace
Kungliga Slottet
S-111 30 Stockholm
Sweden
Website: http://www.royalcourt.se/

Goran Persson
Prime Minister
Statsradsberedningen
Rosenbad 4
103 33 Stockholm
Sweden
Website: http://www.sb.gov.se/
E-mail: regeringen@regeringen.se

**Switzerland (Swiss Confederation)**
Adolf Ogi
President de la Confederation
Bundeshaus West
CH-3003 Bern
Switzerland
Website: http://www.admin.ch/ch/
index.html

**Syria (Syrian Arab Republic)**
Bashar al-Assad
President
Presidential Palace
Abu Rumanah al-Rashid St.
Damascus
Syria

Muhammad Mustafa Miro
Prime Minister
Office of the Prime Minister
Damascus
Syria

Governor's Office
Yousif al-azmeh Square
Damascus Governorate
Syria

**Taiwan (Republic of China)**
Chen Shui-bian
President
Office of the President
Chiehshou Hall
122 Chungking S. Rd., Sec. 1
10036 T'aipei
Taiwan

Website: http://www.oop.gov.tw/
E-mail: public@mail.oop.gov.tw

**Tajikistan (Republic of)**
Imamali Rakhmanov
President
Office of the President
Prospekt Lenina 42
Dushanbe
Tajikistan

**Tanzania (United Republic of)**
Benjamin Mkapa
President
State House
PO Box 9120, Magogoni Rd.
Dar es Salaam
Tanzania
Phone: 116898
Fax: 113425

Frederick Tluway Sumaye
Prime Minister
Office of the Prime Minister
PO Box 980
Dodoma
Tanzania

**Thailand (Kingdom of)**
King Bhumibol Adulyadej
(Rama IX)
Chitralada Villa
Bangkok
Thailand

Chuan Leekpai
Prime Minister
The Secretariat of the Prime
Minister
Government House, Phitsanulok
Rd.
Bangkok 10300
Thailand

**Togo (Republic of)**
Etienne Gnassingbe Eyadema

President
Presidence de la Republique
Lome
Togo
Phone: 228–21–2701
Website: http://
www.republicoftogo.com/

## Tonga (Kingdom of)
King Taufa'ahau Tupou IV
The Palace
PO Box 6
Nuku'alofa
Tonga
Phone: 676–21–000
Fax: 676–24–102

Prince Lavaka'ata Ulukalala
Prime Minister
Office of the Prime Minister
PO Box 62
Nuku 'alofa
Tonga

## Trinidad and Tobago (Republic of)
Arthur Robinson
President
President's House
St. Ann's
Trinidad and Tobago
Website: http://www.nisc.gov.tt/
E-mail: presoftt@carib-link.net

Basdeo Panday
Prime Minister
Office of the Prime Minister
St. Ann's
Trinidad and Tobago
Website: http://www.gov.tt/
E-mail: pmoffice@ttgov.gov.tt

## Tunisia (Republic of)
Zine El Abidine Ben Ali
President

Presidence de la Republique, Palais
de Carthage
2016 Carthage
Tunisia
Website: http://www.ministeres.tn/

## Turkey (Republic of)
Ahmet Necdet Sezer
President
Cumhurbaskanligi Kosku
Cankaya
06100 Ankara
Turkey
Website: http://
www.cankaya.gov.tr
E-mail: cankaya@tccb.gov.tr

Bulent Ecevit
Prime Minister
Office of the Prime Minister
Basbakanlik
06573 Ankara
Turkey

## Turkmenistan
Saparmurad Niyazov
President
Office of the President
Zdaniye Pravitel' stra
Ashkabad
Turkmenistan

## Tuvalu
Hon. Ionatana Ionatana
Prime Minister
Government of Tuvalu
Private Mail Bag, Vaiaku
Funafuti
Tuvalu

## Uganda (Republic of)
Yoweri Kaguta Museveni
President
Office of the President
Parliament Bldgs., PO Box 7168
Kampala

Uganda
Website: http://www.uganda.co.ug/
Govern.htm

Apolo Nsibambi
Prime Minister
Office of the Prime Minister
Post Office Building
St. Clement Hill Rd., PO Box 341
Kampala
Uganda

**Ukraine**
Leonid Kuchma
President
11 Bankova St.
Office of the President
252005, Kiev
Ukraine
E-mail: postmaster@ribbon.kiev.ua

Viktor Yushchenko
Prime Minister
Cabinet of Ministers
12/2 Hrushevskiy St.
252008, Kiev
Ukraine

**United Arab Emirates**
Sheikh Zaid bin Sultan Al Nahayan
President
Amiti Palace
PO Box 280
Abu Dhabi
United Arab Emirates
Website: http://www.fedfin.gov.ae/

Sheikh Maktum ibn Rashid Al
    Maktum
Prime Minister
PO Box 12848
Dubai
United Arab Emirates

**United Kingdom (of Great Britain
and Northern Ireland)**

Her Majesty Queen Elizabeth II
% Private Secretary
Buckingham Palace
SWIA 1AA London
United Kingdom
Website: http://www.royal.gov.uk/

Rt. Hon. Tony Blair
Prime Minister
10 Downing St.
SW1A 2AA London
United Kingdom
Website: http://www.number-
10.gov.uk/

Secretary of State for Northern
Ireland
Stormont
BT4 3ST Belfast, Northern Ireland
United Kingdom
Website: http://www.nics.gov.uk/
E-mail: press.nio@nics.gov.uk

Secretary of State for Scotland
2 Melville Crescent
EH3 7HW Edinburgh, Scotland
United Kingdom
Website: http://
www.scotland.gov.uk/
E-mail: ceu@scotland.gov.uk

Secretary of State for Wales
Cathays Park
CF1 3NQ Cardiff, Wales
United Kingdom
Website: http://www.cymru.gov.uk/
E-mail: webmaster@wales.gov.uk

**United States of America**
George W. Bush
President
The White House
1600 Pennsylvania Ave. NW
Washington, DC 20500
United States of America

Website: http://
www.whitehouse.gov/
E-mail: president@whitehouse.gov

House Majority Leader
House of Representatives
Washington, DC 20515
United States of America
Website: http://www.house.gov/

House Minority Leader
House of Representatives
Washington, DC 20515
United States of America
Website: http://www.house.gov/

Speaker, House of Representatives
House of Representatives
Washington, DC 20515
United States of America
Website: http://www.house.gov/

Senate Majority Leader
U.S. Senate
Washington, DC 20510
United States of America
Website: http://www.senate.gov/

Senate Minority Leader
U.S. Senate
Washington, DC 20510
United States of America
Website: http://www.senate.gov/

**Uruguay (Oriental Republic of)**
Jorge Batlle
President
Av. Dr. Alberto de Herrera 3350
Edificio Libertad Presidencia
Montevideo
Uruguay
Website: http://
www.presidencia.gub.uy/
E-mail:
presidente@presidencia.gub.uy

**Uzbekistan (Republic of)**
Islam Karimov
President
Office of the President
Akhunbabayeva 1
Tashkent
Uzbekistan
Website: http://www.gov.uz/
E-mail: uzinfo@uzinfo.gov.uz

Utkir Sultanov
Prime Minister
Office of the Cabinet Ministers
Government House
700008 Tashkent
Uzbekistan

**Vanuatu (Republic of)**
John Bernard Bani
President
Office of the President
PO Box 110
Port-Vila
Vanuatu

Barak Sope
Prime Minister
Office of the Prime Minister
PMB 053
Port-Vila
Vanuatu

**Vatican City (State of)**
His Holiness John Paul II
Pope
Apostolic Palace
00120
Vatican City, Italy
Website: http://www.vatican.va/

**Venezuela (Republic of)**
Hugo Rafael Chavez Frias
President
Oficina del Presidente
Palacio de Miraflores
Caracas

Venezuela
Website: http://
www.venezuela.gov.ve/

**Vietnam (Socialist Republic of)**
Le Kha Phieu
General Secretary
Council of Ministers
Bac Thao
Hanoi
Vietnam

Phan Van Khai
Prime Minister
1 Hoang Hoa Tham St.
Hanoi
Vietnam

**Western Samoa (Independent State of)**
Malietoa Tanumafili II
King
Government House
Vailima
Apia
Western Samoa, S. Pacific

Tuilaepa Sailele Malielegaoi
Prime Minister
Prime Minister's Office
PO Box L1861
Apia
Western Samoa, S. Pacific
Website: http://
www.interwebinc.com/samoa/

**Yemen (Republic of)**
Ali Abdullah Saleh
President
Office of the President
Sana
Yemen
Website: http://
www.yemeninfo.gov.ye/

**Yugoslavia (Socialist Federal Republic of)**
Slobodan Milosevic
Federal President
Savezna Skupstina
11000 Belgrade, Serbia
Yugoslavia
Website: http://www.gov.yu

Momir Bulatovic
Federal Prime Minister
Office of the Federal Prime Minister
Palace of Federation
Belgrade, Serbia
Yugoslavia

Milan Milutinovic
President
Office of the President
Belgrade, Republic of Serbia
Yugoslavia

Mirko Marjanovic
Prime Minister
Office of the Prime Minister
Belgrade, Republic of Serbia
Yugoslavia

Milo Djukanovic
President
Office of the President
Cetinje, Republic Montenegro
Yugoslavia

Filip Vujanovic
Prime Minister
Office of the Prime Minister
Podgorica, Republic of Montenegro
Yugoslavia
Website: http://www.vlda.cg.yu/
drugi.htm
E-mail: vlada@cg.yu

**Zambia (Republic of)**
Frederick Chiluba
President

Office of the President, State House
Cabinet Office, Box 30208
Lusaka
Zambia
Website: http://
www.statehouse.gov.zm
E-mail: state@zamnet.zm

**Zimbabwe (Republic of)**
Robert Mugabe
Executive President
Office of the President
Private Bag 7700, Causeway
Harare
Zimbabwe
Website: http://www.gta.gov.zw/
E-mail: http://www.gta.gov.zw/
feedback.htm

# WHO'S IN CHARGE

## FIRST FAMILY

**Bush, George Walker Jr.**
The White House
1600 Pennsylvania Ave.
Washington DC 20500
Website: http://
www.president@whitehouse.gov
*Birthday: 7/6/46*

**Bush, Laura Welch**
The White House
1600 Pennsylvania Ave.
Washington, DC 20500
*First Lady of the United States*

## EXECUTIVE DEPARTMENTS

### Department of Agriculture
14th St. and Independence Ave.,
SW
Ann M. Veneman, Secretary
Washington, DC 20250
www.usda.gov

### Department of Commerce
14th St. and Constitution Ave., NW
Washington, DC 20230
Donald L. Evans, Secretary
www.doc.gov

### Department of Defense
The Pentagon
Washington, DC 20301
Donald H. Rumsfeld, Secretary
www.defenselink.mil

### Department of Education
400 Maryland Ave., SW
Washington, DC 20202
Rod Paige, Secretary
www.ed.gov

### Department of Energy
1000 Independence Ave., SW
Washington, DC 20585
Spencer Abraham, Secretary
www.doe.gov

### Department of Health and Human Services
200 Independence Ave., SW
Washington, DC 20201
Tommy Thompson, Secretary
www.dhhs.gov

**Department of Housing and Urban Development**
451 7th St., SW
Washington, DC 20410
Mel Martinez, Secretary
www.hud.gov

**Department of the Interior**
1849 C St., NW
Washington, DC 20240
Gale Norton, Secretary
www.doi.gov

**Department of Justice**
950 Pennsylvania Ave., NW
Washington, DC 20530
John Ashcroft, Attorney General
www.usdoj.gov

**Department of Labor**
200 Constitution Ave., NW
Washington, DC 20210
Elaine L. Chao, Secretary
www.dol.gov

**Department of State**
2201 C St., NW
Washington, DC 20520
Colin Powell, Secretary of State
www.state.gov

**Department of Transportation**
400 7th St., SW
Washington, DC 20590
Norman Y. Mineta, Secretary
www.dot.gov

**Department of the Treasury**
1500 Pennsylvania Ave., NW
Washington, DC 20220
Paul H. O'Neill, Secretary
www.ustreas.gov

**Department of Veteran's Affairs**
810 Vermont Ave., NW
Washington, DC 20420
Anthony J. Principi, Secretary
www.va.gov

## WHITE HOUSE OFFICES AND AGENCIES

**Council of Economic Advisers CEA**
Room 314, Old Executive Office Bldg.
Washington, DC 20501

**Council on Environmental Quality**
Room 360, Old Executive Office Bldg.
Washington, DC 20501

**National Security Council NSC**
Old Executive Office Bldg.
Washington, DC 20503
Chair: The President
National Security Adviser:
Condoleeza Rice
Other Members: Vice President,
Secretary of State, Secretary of
Defense

**Office of Administration**
Old Executive Office Bldg., 725
17th St., N.W.
Washington, DC 20503

**Office of Management and Budget**
Executive Office Bldg.
Washington, DC 20503
Director: Mitchell E. Daniels, Jr.

**Office of National Drug Control Policy**
Executive Office of the President
Washington, DC 20502
Acting Director: Edward H. Jurith

**Office of the United States Trade Representative**
600 17th St., N.W.
Washington, DC 20508

## MAJOR INDEPENDENT AGENCIES

**Central Intelligence Agency (CIA)**
Washington, D.C.
Washington, DC 20505
Director: George J. Tenet

**Consumer Product Safety Commission**
East West Towers
4330 East West Highway,
Bethesda, Md. 20814
Chairperson: Ann Brown

**Corporation for National Service**
1201 New York Ave., N.W.
Washington, DC 20525

**Environmental Protection Agency (EPA)**
401 M St., S.W.
Washington, DC 20460
Director: Christie Whitman

**Equal Employment Opportunity Commission (EEOC)**
1801 L St., N.W.
Washington, DC 20507
Chairwoman: Ida L. Castro

**Farm Credit Administration (FCA)**
1501 Farm Credit Dr.
McLean, Va. 22102
Chair: Michael M. Reyna

**Federal Bureau of Investigation (FBI)**
Press Office
10th and Pennsylvania Ave. NW
#7222
Washington, DC 20535
Director: Ronald L. Dick

**Federal Deposit Insurance Corporation (FDIC)**
550 17th St., N.W.
Washington, DC 20429
Chair: Donna Tanove

**Federal Election Commission (FEC)**
999 E St., N.W.
Washington, DC 20463
Chairman: Danny L. McDonald

**Federal Maritime Commission**
800 North Capitol St., N.W.
Washington, DC 20573

**Federal Mediation and Conciliation Service (FMCS)**
2100 K St., N.W.
Washington, DC 20427
Director: Charles R. Barnes

**Federal Reserve System FRS, Board of Governors of**
20th St. & Constitution Ave., N.W.
Washington, DC 20551
Chair: Alan Greenspan

**Federal Trade Commission (FTC)**
Pennsylvania Ave. at 6th St., N.W.
Washington, DC 20580
Chair: Robert Pitofsky

**General Services Administration (GSA)**
General Services Building, 18th
and F Sts., N.W.
Washington, DC 20405
Acting Administrator: Thurman M.
Davis, Sr.

**House Majority Leader—Dick Armey**
House of Representatives
Washington, DC 20515
Website: http://www.house.gov

**House Minority Leader—Richard A. Gephardt**
House of Representatives
Washington, DC 20515
Website: http://www.house.gov

**National Aeronautics and Space Administration (NASA)**
300 E St., S.W.
Washington, DC 20546
Administrator: Daniel S. Goldin

**National Foundation on the Arts and the Humanities**
1100 Pennsylvania Ave., N.W.
Washington, DC 20506

**National Labor Relations Board (NLRB)**
1099 14th St., N.W.
Washington, DC 20570
Chair: John C. Truesdale

**National Mediation Board**
Suite 250 East, 1301 K. St., N.W.
Washington, DC 20572
Chairman: Francis J. Duggan

**National Science Foundation (NSF)**
4201 Wilson Blvd.
Arlington, Va.
Washington, DC 22230

**National Transportation Safety Board**
490 L'Enfant Plaza, S.W.
Washington, DC 20594
Acting Chariman: Carol J. Carmody

**Nuclear Regulatory Commission (NRC)**
One White Flint North, 11555
Rockville Pike,
Rockville MD 20852
Chairman: Richard A. Meserve

**Office of Personnel Management (OPM)**
1900 E St., N.W.
Washington, DC 20415
Deputy Director: John Sepulveda

**Securities and Exchange Commission (SEC)**
450 5th St., N.W.
Washington, DC 20549
Acting Chairman: Laura S. Unger

**Selective Service System (SSS)**
1515 Wilson Blvd.
Arlington, Va., 22209
Director Gil Coronado

**Senate Majority Leader—Trent Lott**
U.S. Senate
Washington, DC 20510
Website: www://senate.gov

**Senate Minority Leader—Tom Daschle**
U.S. Senate
Washington, DC 20510
Website: www://senate.gov

**Small Business Administration (SBA)**
409 3rd St., S.W.
Washington, DC 20416
Acting Administrator: John D. Whitmore, Jr.

**Tennessee Valley Authority (TVA)**
400 West Summit Hill Drive
Knoxville, TN 37902

**Washington Office:**
One Massachusetts Ave.N.W.
Washington, DC 20444
Chairman: Craven Crowell

**U.S. Arms Control and Disarmament Agency**
320 21st St., N.W.
Washington, DC 20451

**U.S. Commission on Civil Rights**
624 9th St., N.W.
Washington, DC 20425

**U.S. International Trade Commission**
500 E St., S.W.
Washington, DC 20436
Chairman: Steven Koplan

**U.S. Postal Service**
475 L'Enfant Plaza West, S.W.
Washington, DC 20260
Postmaster General: William J. Henderson

**SENATE MAILING ADDRESSES**

**Address Letters to:**
The Honorable (Name of Senator)
United States Senate
Washington, DC 20510

Dear Senator_____

**SENATOR E-MAIL ADDRESSES**

**Steven, Ted (R-AK)**
Senator_Stevens@
stevens.senate.gov

**Murkowski, Frank (R-AK)**
http://murkowski.senate.gov/
webmail.html

**Sessions, Jeff (R-AL)**
senator@sessions.senate.gov

**Shelby, Richard (R-AL)**
senator@shelby.senate.gov

**Lincoln, Blanche (D-AR)**
blanche_lincoln@
lincoln.senate.gov

**Hutchinson, Tim (R-AR)**
Senator.Hutchinson@
hutchinson.senate.gov

**Kyl, Jon (R-AZ)**
info@kyl.senate.gov

**McCain, John (R-AZ)**
John_McCain@mccain.senate.gov

**Boxer, Barbara (D-CA)**
senator@boxer.senate.gov

**Feinstein, Dianne (D-CA)**
senator@feinstein.senate.gov

**Allard, Wayne (R-CO)**
http://www.senate.gov/allard/
webform.html or senator_allard@
exchange.senate.gov

**Campbell, Ben (R-CO)**
administrator@
campbell.senate.gov

**Dodd, Christopher (D-CT)**
senator@dodd.senate.gov

**Lieberman, Joseph (D-CT)**
http://www.senate.gov/member/ct/
lieberman/general/contact.html

**Biden, Joe (D-DE)**
senator@biden.senate.gov

**Carper, Thomas (D-MO)**

**Graham, Bob (D-FL)**
bob_graham@graham.senate.gov

**Nelson, Bill (D-FL)**
senator@billnelson.senate.gov

**Cleland, Max (D-GA)**
http://www.senate.gov/cleland/
webform.html

**Miller, Zell (D-GA)**

**Akaka, Daniel (D-HI)**
senator@akaka.senate.gov

**Inouye, Daniel (D-HI)**
senator@inouye.senate.gov

**Harkin, Tom (D-IA)**
tom_harkin@harkin.senate.gov

**Grassley, Charles (R-IA)**
chuck_grassley@
grassley.senate.gov

**Craig, Larry (R-ID)**
http://craig.senate.gov/
webform.html

**Crapo, Mike (R-ID)**
http://crapo.senate.gov/
webform.html

**Durbin, Richard (D-IL)**
dick@durbin.senate.gov

**Fitzgerald, Peter (R-IL)**
senator_fitzgerald@
fitzgerald.senate.gov

**Bayh, Evan (D-IN)**
http://bayh.senate.gov/
WebMail.html

**Lugar, Richard (R-IN)**
senator_lugar@lugar.senate.gov

**Brownback, Sam (R-KS)**
webmail@brownback.senate.gov

**Roberts, Pat (R-KS)**
pat_roberts@roberts.senate.gov

**Bunning, Jim (R-KY)**
jim_bunning@
bunning.senate.gov

**McConnell, Mitch (R-KY)**
senator@mcconnell.senate.gov

**Breaux, John (D-LA)**
senator@breaux.senate.gov

**Landrieu, Mary (D-LA)**
senator@landrieu.senate.gov

**Kennedy, Ted (D-MA)**
feedback@kennedy.senate.gov

**Kerry, John (D-MA)**
john_kerry@kerry.senate.gov

**Mikulski, Barbara (D-MD)**
senator@mikulski.senate.gov

**Sarbanes, Paul (D-MD)**
senator@sarbanes.senate.gov

**Collins, Susan (R-ME)**
senator@collins.senate.gov

**Snowe, Olympia (R-ME)**
Olympia@snowe.senate.gov

**Levin, Carl (D-MI)**
senator@levin.senate.gov

**Stabenow, Debbie (D-MI)**
senator@stabenow.senate.gov

**Dayton, Mark (D-MN)**

**Wellstone, Paul (D-MN)**
senator@wellstone.senate.gov

**Carnahan, Jean (D-MO)**
senator@carnahan.senate.gov

**Bond, Christopher (R-MO)**
kit_bond@bond.senate.gov

**Cochran, Thad (R-MS)**
senator@cochran.senate.gov

**Lott, Trent (R-MS)**
senatorlott@lott.senate.gov

**Baucus, Max (D-MT)**
http://baucus.senate.gov/
E-mail: Max.htm

**Burns, Conrad (R-MT)**
conrad_burns@burns.senate.gov

**Edwards, John (D-NC)**
Senator@Edwards.senate.gov

**Helms, Jesse (R-NC)**
jesse_helms@helms.senate.gov

**Conrad, Kent (D-ND)**
senator@conrad.senate.gov

**Dorgan, Byron (D-ND)**
senator@dorgan.senate.gov

**Hagel, Chuck (R-NE)**
chuck_hagel@hagel.senate.gov

**Nelson, Ben (D-NE)**

**Gregg, Judd (R-NH)**
mailbox@gregg.senate.gov

**Smith, Bob (R-NH)**
opinion@smith.senate.gov

**Corzine, Jon (D-NY)**

**Torricelli, Robert (D-NJ)**
senator@torricelli.senate.gov or
http://torricelli.senate.gov/
webform.html (preferred)

**Bingaman, Jeff (D-NM)**
Senator_Bingaman@
bingaman.senate.gov

**Domenici, Pete (R-NM)**
senator_domenci@
domenici.senate.gov

**Ensign, John (R-NV)**
senator@ensign.senate.gov

**Reid, Harry (D-NV)**
senator_reid@reid.senate.gov

**Schumer, Charles (D-NY)**
senator@schumer.senate.gov

**Clinton, Hillary (D-NY)**
senator@clinton.senate.gov

**Dewine, Michael (R-OH)**
senator_dewine@
dewine.senate.gov

**Voinovich, George (R-OH)**
senator_voinovich
voinovich.senate.gov or http://
voinovich.senate.gov/
contact_form.html

**Inhofe, James (R-OK)**
jim_inhofe@inhofe.senate.gov

**Nickles, Don (R-OK)**
senator@nickles.senate.gov

**Smith, Gordon (R-OR)**
Oregon@gsmith.senate.gov

**Wyden, Ron (D-OR)**
senator@wyden.senate.gov

**Santorum, Rick (R-PA)**
http://santorum.senate.gov/#email
or
pennstater@santorum.senate.gov

**Specter, Arlen (R-PA)**
senator_specter@
specter.senate.gov

**Reed, Jack (D-RI)**
jack@reed.senate.gov

**Chafee, Lincoln (R-RI)**

**Thurmond, Strom (R-SC)**
senator@thurmond.senate.gov

**Hollings, Ernest (D-SC)**
http://hollings.senate.gov/hollings/
webform.html

**Daschle, Thomas (D-SD)**
tom_daschle@daschle.senate.gov

**Johnson, Tim (D-SD)**
tim@johnson.senate.gov

**Thompson, Fred (R-TN)**
senator_thompson@
thompson.senate.gov

**Frist, Bill (R-TN)**
senator_frist@frist.senate.gov

**Gramm, Phil (R-TX)**
Phil_Gramm@
gramm.senate.gov

**Hutchison, Kay (R-TX)**
senator@hutchison.senate.gov

**Bennett, Robert (R-UT)**
senator@bennett.senate.gov

**Hatch, Orrin (R-UT)**
senator_hatch@hatch.senate.gov

**Allen, George (R-VA)**
senator_allen@allen.senate.gov

**Warner, John (R-VA)**
senator@warner.senate.gov

**Leahy, Patrick (D-VT)**
senator_leahy@leahy.senate.gov

**Jeffords, Jim (R-VT)**
vermont@jeffords.senate.gov

**Murray, Patty (D-WA)**
senator_murray@
murray.senate.gov

**Cantwell, Maria (D-VA)**

**Feingold, Russell (D-WI)**
russell_feingold@
feingold.senate.gov

**Kohl, Herbert (D-WI)**
senator_kohl@kohl.senate.gov

**Byrd, Robert (D-WV)**
senator_byrd@byrd.senate.gov

**Rockfeller, Jay (D-WV)**
senator@rockefeller.senate.gov

**Enzi, Michael (R-WY)**
senator@enzi.senate.gov

**Thomas, Craig (R-WY)**
craig@thomas.senate.gov
Senate Committee on Energy and
Natural Resourceswebmaster@
energy.senate.gov
Senate Committee on Small
Business
committee@small-bus.senate.gov

## HOUSE OF REPRESENTATIVES MAILING ADDRESSES

**The Honorable (Name of Representative)**
U.S. House of Representatives
Washington DC 20515

Dear Representative_____

## UNITED STATES HOUSE OF REPRESENTATIVES E-MAIL ADDRESSES

Representatives may also be
reached by constituents only
through http://www.house.gov/writerep/

**Callahan, Sonny (R-AL, 1st)**
sonny.callahan@mail.house.gov

**Everett, Terry (R-AL, 2nd)**
Terry.Everett@mail.house.gov

**Riley, Bob (R-AL, 3rd)**
bob.riley@mail.house.gov

**Aderholt, Robert (R-AL, 4th)**
robert.aderholt@mail.house.gov

**Cramer, Bud (D-AL, 5th)**
budmail@mail.house.gov

**Bachus, Spencer (R-AL, 6th)**
http://www.house.gov/writerep/

**Hilliard, Earl (D-AL, 7th)**
http://www.house.gov/writerep/

**Young, Don (R-AK, AL)**
Don.Young@mail.house.gov

**Berry, Marion (D-AR, 1st)**
http://www.house.gov/writerep/

**Snyder, Vic (D-AR, 2nd)**
snyder.congress@mail.house.gov

**Hutchinson, Asa (R-AR, 3rd)**
asa.hutchinson@mail.house.gov

**Ross, Mike (D-AR, 4th)**
mike.ross@mail.house.gov

**Faleomavaega, Eni (D-American Samoa AL)**
faleomavaega@mail.house.gov

**Flake, Jeff (R-AZ, 1st)**
jeff.flake@mail.house.gov

**Pastor, Ed (D-AZ, 2nd)**
ed.pastor@mail.house.gov

**Stump, Robert (R-AZ, 3rd)**
http://www.house.gov/writerep

**Shadegg, John (R-AZ, 4th)**
j.shadegg@mail.house.gov

**Kolbe, Jim (R-AZ, 5th)**
jim.kolbe@mail.house.gov or http://
www.house.gov/writerep/

**Hayworth, J. D. (R-AZ, 6th)**
jdhayworth@mail.house.gov

**Thompson, Mike (D-CA, 1st)**
m.thompson@mail.house.gov

**Herger, Walter (R-CA, 2nd)**
http://www.house.gov/writerep/

**Ose, Doug (R-CA, 3rd)**
doug.ose@mail.house.gov

**Doolittle, John (R-CA, 4th)**
doolittle@mail.house.gov

**Matsui, Robert (D-CA, 5th)**
http://www.house.gov/writerep/

**Woolsey, Lynn (D-CA, 6th)**
lynn.woolsey@mail.house.gov

**Miller, George (D-CA, 7th)**
George.Miller@mail.house.gov

**Pelosi, Nancy (D-CA, 8th)**
sf.nancy@mail.house.gov

**Lee, Barbara (D-CA, 9th)**
barbara.lee@mail.house.gov

**Tauscher, Ellen (D-CA, 10th)**
ellen.tauscher@mail.house.gov

**Pombo, Richard (R-CA, 11th)**
rpombo@mail.house.gov

**Lantos, Tom (D-CA, 12th)**
http://www.house.gov/writerep/

**Stark, Pete (D-CA, 13th)**
petemail@stark.house.gov

**Eshoo, Anna (D-CA, 14th)**
annagram@mail.house.gov or http://
www.eshoo.house.gov/ccc.html

**Michael M. Honda (D-CA, 15th)**
michael.honda@mail.house.gov

**Lofgren, Zoe (D-CA, 16th)**
zoe@lofgren.house.gov

**Farr, Sam (D-CA, 17th)**
samfarr@mail.house.gov

**Condit, Gary (D-CA, 18th)**
http://www.house.gov/writerep/

**George Radanovich (R-CA, 19th)**
george.radanovich@
mail.house.gov

**Dooley, Calvin (R-CA, 20th)**
http://www.house.gov/writerep/

**Thomas, Bill (R-CA, 21st)**
http://www.house.gov/writerep/

**Capps, Lois (D-CA, 22nd)**
http://www.house.gov/writerep/

**Gallegly, Elton (R-CA, 23rd)**
http://www.house.gov/writerep/

**Sherman, Brad (D-CA, 24th)**
brad.sherman@mail.house.gov

**McKeon, Howard (R-CA, 25th)**
tellbuck@mail.house.gov or http://
www.house.gov/mckeon/
opinion.htm

**Berman, Howard (D-CA, 26th)**
Howard.Berman@
mail.house.gov

**Schiff, Adam (?-CA, 27th)**
http://www.house.gov/writerep

**Dreier, David (R-CA, 28th)**
http://www.house.gov/dreier/
talkto.htm

**Waxman, Henry (D-CA, 29th)**
http://www.house.gov/writerep/

**Becerra, Xavier (D-CA, 30th)**
http://www.house.gov/writerep/

**Solis, Hilda (D-CA, 31st)**
http://www.house.gov/writerep/

**Roybal-Allard, Lucille (D-CA, 33rd)**
http://www.house.gov/writerep/

**Napolitano, Grace (D-CA, 34th)**
grace@mail.house.gov

**Waters, Maxine (D-CA, 35th)**
http://www.house.gov/waters/
guest.htm

**Harman, Jane (D-CA, 36th)**
http://www.house.gov/writerep/

**Millender-McDonald, Juanita (D-CA, 37th)**
Millender.McDonald@
mail.house.gov

**Horn, Steve (R-CA, 38th)**
Stephen.Horn@mail.house.gov

**Royce, Edward (R-CA, 39th)**
http://www.house.gov/writerep/

**Lewis, Jerry (R-CA, 40th)**
http://www.house.gov/writerep/

**Miller, Gary (R-CA, 41st)**
PublicCA41@mail.house.gov

**Baca, Joe (D-CA, 42nd)**
http://www.house.gov/writerep/

**Calvert, Ken (R-CA, 43rd)**
http://www.house.gov/writerep/

**Bono, Mary (R-CA, 44th)**
http://www.house.gov/writerep/

**Rohrabacher, Dana (R-CA, 45th)**
dana@mail.house.gov

**Sanchez, Loretta (D-CA, 46th)**
loretta@mail.house.gov

**Cox, Christopher (R-CA, 47th)**
christopher.cox@mail.house.gov

**Darrell, E. Issa (R-CA, 48th)**
http://www.house.gov/writerep

**Davis, Susan (D-CA, 49th)**
http://www.house.gov/writerep

**Filner, Bob (D-CA, 50th)**
http://www.house.gov/writerep/

**Cunningham, Randy (R-CA, 51st)**
http://www.house.gov/cunningham/
IMA/get_address3.htm

**Hunter, Duncan (R-CA, 52nd)**
http://www.house.gov/writerep/

**DeGette, Diana (D-CO, 1st)**
degette@mail.house.gov

**Udall, Mark (D-CO, 2nd)**
mark.udall@mail.house.gov

**McInnis, Scott (R-CO, 3rd)**
http://www.house.gov/writerep

**Schaffer, Bob (R-CO, 4th)**
rep.schaffer@mail.house.gov

**Hefley, Joel (R-CO, 5th)**
http://www.house.gov/writerep

**Tancredo, Thomas (R-CO, 6th)**
tom.tancredo@mail.house.gov

**Larson, John (D-CT, 1st)**
http://www.house.gov/writerep/

**Simmons, Rob (R-CT, 2nd)**
http://www.house.gov/writerep

**DeLauro, Rosa (D-CT, 3rd)**
http://www.house.gov/writerep/

**Shays, Christopher (R-CT, 4th)**
rep.shays@mail.house.gov

**Maloney, James (D-CT, 5th)**
http://www.house.gov/writerep/

**Johnson, Nancy (R-CT, 6th)**
http://www.house.gov/writerep/

**Norton, Eleanor (D-DC, AL)**
http://www.house.gov/writerep/

**Castle, Michael (R-DE, AL)**
Delaware@mail.house.gov

**Scarborough, Joe (R-FL, 1st)**
fl01@mail.house.gov

**Boyd, Allen (D-FL, 2nd)**
http://www.house.gov/writerep/

**Brown, Corrine (D-FL, 3rd)**
http://www.house.gov/writerep/

**Crenshaw, Ander (R-FL, 4th)**
http://www.house.gov/writerep

**Thurman, Karen (D-FL, 5th)**
thurman@mail.house.gov

**Stearns, Cliff (R-FL, 6th)**
cstearns@mail.house.gov

**Mica, John (R-FL, 7th)**
John.Mica@mail.house.gov

**Keller, Ric (R-FL, 8th)**
http://www.house.gov/writerep

**Bilirakis, Michael (R-FL, 9th)**
http://www.house.gov/writerep/

**Young, C. W., Bill (R-FL, 10th)**
http://www.house.gov/writerep/

**Davis, Jim (D-FL, 11th)**
http://www.house.gov/writerep/

**Putnam, Adam (R-FL, 12th)**
http://www.house.gov/writerep/

**Miller, Dan (R-FL, 13th)**
http://www.house.gov/writerep/

**Goss, Porter (R-FL, 14th)**
porter.goss@mail.house.gov

**Weldon, Dave (R-FL, 15th)**
http://www.house.gov/writerep/

**Foley, Mark (R-FL, 16th)**
mark.foley@mail.house.gov

**Meek, Carrie (D-FL, 17th)**
cpm@mail.house.gov

**Ros-Lehtinen, Ileana (R-FL, 18th)**
http://www.house.gov/writerep/

**Wexler, Robert (D-FL, 19th)**
http://www.house.gov/writerep/

**Deutsch, Peter (D-FL, 20th)**
http://www.house.gov/writerep/

**Díaz-Balart, Lincoln (R-FL, 21st)**
http://www.house.gov/writerep/

**Shaw, Clay (R-FL, 22nd)**
http://www.house.gov/writerep/

**Hastings, Alcee (D-FL, 23rd)**
alcee.pubhastings@
mail.house.gov

**Kingston, Jack (R-GA, 1st)**
jack.kingston@mail.house.gov

**Bishop, Sanford (D-GA, 2nd)**
bishop.email@mail.house.gov

**Collins, Mac (R-GA, 3rd)**
mac.collins@mail.house.gov

**McKinney, Cynthia (D-GA, 4th)**
cymck@mail.house.gov

**Lewis, John (D-GA, 5th)**
john.lewis@mail.house.gov

**Isakson, Johnny (R-GA, 6th)**
ga06@mail.house.gov

**Barr, Bob (R-GA, 7th)**
http://www.house.gov/barr/
guestlog.htm or
barr.ga@mail.house.gov

**Chambliss, Saxby (R-GA, 8th)**
saxby.chambliss@mail.house.gov

**Deal, Nathan (R-GA, 9th)**
http://www.house.gov/writerep/

**Norwood, Charles (R-GA, 10th)**
http://www.house.gov/writerep/

**Linder, John (R-GA, 11th)**
john.linder@mail.house.gov

**Underwood, Robert (D-Guam)**
guamtodc@mail.house.gov

**Abercrombie, Neil (D-HI, 1st)**
neil.abercrombie@
mail.house.gov

**Mink, Patsy (D-HI, 2nd)**
http://www.house.gov/writerep/

**Leach, Jim (R-IA, 1st)**
talk2jim@mail.house.gov

**Nussle, James (R-IA, 2nd)**
nussleia@mail.house.gov or http://
www.house.gov/writerep/

**Boswell, Leonard (D-IA, 3rd)**
rep.boswell.ia03@mail.house.gov

**Ganske, Greg (R-IA, 4th)**
Rep.Ganske@mail.house.gov

**Latham, Tom (R-IA, 5th)**
latham.ia05@mail.house.gov

**Otter, C. L. "Butch" (R-ID, 1st)**
http://www.house.gov/writerep

**Simpson, Mike (R-ID, 2nd)**
mike.simpson@mail.house.gov

**Rush, Bobby (D-IL, 1st)**
bobby.rush@mail.house.gov

**Jackson, Jesse, Jr. (D-IL, 2nd)**
comments@jessejacksonjr.org

**Lipinski, William (D-IL, 3rd)**
http://www.house.gov/lipinski/

**Gutierrez, Luis (D-IL, 4th)**
luis.gutierrez@mail.house.gov

**Blagojevich, Rod (D-IL, 5th)**
Rod.Blagojevich@mail.house.gov

**Hyde, Henry (R-IL, 6th)**
judiciary@mail.house.gov or http://
www.house.gov/writerep/

**Davis, Danny (D-IL, 7th)**
http://www.house.gov/writerep/

**Crane, Philip (R-IL, 8th)**
http://www.house.gov/writerep/

**Schakowsky, Jan (D-IL, 9th)**
jan.schakowsky@mail.house.gov

**Kirk, Mark (R-IL, 10th)**
http://www.house.gov/writerep/

**Weller, Jerry (R-IL, 11th)**
http://www.house.gov/writerep/

**Costello, Jerry (D-IL, 12th)**
jfc.il12@mail.house.gov

**Biggert, Judy (R-IL, 13th)**
http://www.house.gov/writerep/

**Hastert, Dennis (R-IL, 14th)**
speaker@mail.house.gov

**Johnson, Tim (R-IL, 15th)**
http://www.house.gov/writerep/

**Manzullo, Donald (R-IL, 16th)**
http://www.house.gov/writerep/

**Evans, Lane (D-IL, 17th)**
lane.evans@mail.house.gov

**LaHood, Ray (R-IL, 18th)**
http://www.house.gov/writerep/

**Phelps, David (D-IL, 19th)**
http://www.house.gov/writerep/

**Shimkus, John (R-IL, 20th)**
http://www.house.gov/writerep/

**Visclosky, Peter (D-IN, 1st)**
http://www.house.gov/writerep/

**Pence, Mike (R-IN, 2nd)**
http://www.house.gov/writerep/

**Roemer, Tim (D-IN, 3rd)**
tim.roemer@mail.house.gov

**Souder, Mark (R-IN, 4th)**
souder@mail.house.gov

**Buyer, Steve (R-IN, 5th)**
http://www.house.gov/writerep/

**Burton, Dan (R-IN, 6th)**
http://www.house.gov/writerep/

**Kerns, Brian (R-IN, 7th)**
http://www.house.gov/writerep

**Hostettler, John (R-IN, 8th)**
John.Hostettler@mail.house.gov

**Hill, Baron (D-IN, 9th)**
http://www.house.gov/writerep/

**Carson, Julia (D-IN, 10th)**
rep.carson@mail.house.gov

**Moran, Jerry (R-KS, 1st)**
jerry.moran@mail.house.gov

**Ryun, Jim (R-KS, 2nd)**
http://www.house.gov/writerep/

**Moore, Dennis (D-KS, 3rd)**
dennis.moore@mail.house.gov

**Tiahrt, Todd (R-KS, 4th)**
tiahrt@mail.house.gov or http://
www.house.gov/tiahrt/
guestbook.html

**Whitfield, Ed (R-KY, 1st)**
ed.whitfield@mail.house.gov

**Lewis, Ron (R-KY, 2nd)**
ron.lewis@mail.house.gov

**Northup, Anne (R-KY, 3rd)**
rep.northup@mail.house.gov

**Lucas, Ken (D-KY, 4th)**
write.kenlucas@mail.house.gov

**Rogers, Harold (R-KY, 5th)**
http://www.house.gov/writerep/

**Fletcher, Ernest (R-KY, 6th)**
http://www.house.gov/writerep/

**Vitter, David (R-LA, 1st)**
http://www.house.gov/writerep/

**Jefferson, William (D-LA, 2nd)**
http://www.house.gov/writerep/

**Tauzin, Billy (R-LA, 3rd)**
http://www.house.gov/writerep/

**McCrery, Jim (R-LA, 4th)**
jim.mccrery@mail.house.gov

**Cooksey, John (R-LA, 5th)**
congressman.cooksey@
mail.house.gov

**Baker, Richard (R-LA, 6th)**
http://www.house.gov/writerep/

**John, Christopher (D-LA, 7th)**
christopher.john@mail.house.gov

**Olver, John (D-MA, 1st)**
http://www.house.gov/writerep/

**Neal, Richard (D-MA, 2nd)**
http://www.house.gov/writerep/

**McGovern, Jim (D-MA, 3rd)**
jim.mcgovern@mail.house.gov

**Frank, Barney (D-MA, 4th)**
http://www.house.gov/writerep

**Meehan, Martin (D-MA, 5th)**
martin.meehan@mail.house.gov

**Tierney, John (D-MA, 6th)**
http://www.house.gov/writerep/

**Markey, Edward (D-MA, 7th)**
http://www.house.gov/writerep/

**Capuano, Mike (D-MA, 8th)**
http://www.house.gov/writerep/

**Moakley, Joe (D-MA, 9th)**
joe.moakley@mail.house.gov

**Delahunt, William (D-MA, 10th)**
william.delahunt@mail.house.gov

**Gilchrest, Wayne (R-MD, 1st)**
http://www.house.gov/writerep/

**Ehrlich, Robert (R-MD, 2nd)**
ehrlich@mail.house.gov

**Cardin, Ben (D-MD, 3rd)**
rep.cardin@mail.house.gov

**Wynn, Albert (D-MD, 4th)**
http://www.house.gov/writerep/

**Hoyer, Steny (D-MD, 5th)**
http://www.house.gov/writerep/

**Bartlett, Roscoe (R-MD, 6th)**
http://www.house.gov/writerep/

**Cummings, Elijah (D-MD, 7th)**
Rep.Cummings@mail.house.gov

**Morella, Constance (R-MD, 8th)**
rep.morella@mail.house.gov

**Allen, Thomas (D-ME, 1st)**
rep.tomallen@mail.house.gov

**Baldacci, John (D-ME, 2nd)**
baldacci@me02.house.gov

**Stupak, Bart (D-MI, 1st)**
stupak@mail.house.gov

**Hoekstra, Peter (R-MI, 2nd)**
tellhoek@mail.house.gov

**Ehlers, Vernon (R-MI, 3rd)**
rep.ehlers@mail.house.gov

**Camp, Dave (R-MI, 4th)**
http://www.house.gov/writerep/

**Barcia, James (D-MI, 5th)**
jim.barcia-pub@mail.house.gov

**Upton, Fred (R-MI, 6th)**
talk2.fsu@mail.house.gov

**Smith, Nick (R-MI, 7th)**
rep.smith@mail.house.gov

**Rogers, Mike (R-MI, 8th)**
http://www.house.gov/writerepm

**Kildee, Dale (D-MI, 9th)**
dkildee@mail.house.gov

**Bonior, David (D-MI, 10th)**
david.bonior@mail.house.gov

**Knollenberg, Joe (R-MI, 11th)**
rep.knollenberg@mail.house.gov

**Levin, Sander (D-MI, 12th)**
slevin@mail.house.gov

**Rivers, Lynn (D-MI, 13th)**
http://www.house.gov/writerep/ or
lynn.rivers@mail.house.gov

**Conyers, John (D-MI, 14th)**
john.conyers; camail.house.gov

**Kilpatrick, Carolyn (D-MI, 15th)**
http://www.house.gov/writerep/

**Dingell, John (D-MI, 16th)**
http://www.house.gov/writerep/ or
public.dingell@mail.house.gov

**Gutknecht, Gil (R-MN, 1st)**
gil.gutknecht@mail.house.gov

**Kennedy, Mark (R-MN, 2nd)**
http://www.house.gov/writerep/

**Ramstad, Jim (R-MN, 3rd)**
mn03@mail.house.gov

**McCollum, Betty (D-MN, 4th)**
http://www.house.gov/writerep

**Sabo, Martin (D-MN, 5th)**
martin.sabo@mail.house.gov

**Luther, Bill (D-MN, 6th)**
tell.bill@mail.house.gov

**Peterson, Collin (D-MN, 7th)**
http://www.house.gov/writerep/

**Oberstar, James (D-MN, 8th)**
http://www.house.gov/writerep/

**Clay, William (D-MO, 1st)**
http://www.house.gov/writerep

**Akin, W. Todd (R-MO, 2nd)**
http: house.gov/writerep

**Gephardt, Richard (D-MO, 3rd)**
gephardt@mail.house.gov

**Skelton, Ike (D-MO, 4th)**
ike.skelton@mail.house.gov

**McCarthy, Karen (D-MO, 5th)**
http://www.house.gov/writerep/

**Graves, Sam (R-MO, 6th)**
http://www.house.gov/writerep/

**Blunt, Roy (R-MO, 7th)**
blunt@mail.house.gov

**Emerson, JoAnn (R-MO, 8th)**
joann.emerson@mail.house.gov

**Hulshof, Kenny (R-MO, 9th)**
rep.hulshof@mail.house.gov

**Wicker, Roger (R-MS, 1st)**
http://www.house.gov/wicker/
guestbook.htm or
roger.wicker@mail.house.gov

**Thompson, Bennie (D-MS, 2nd)**
thompsonms2nd@
mail.house.gov

**Pickering, Charles (R-MS, 3rd)**
http://www.house.gov/writerep/

**Shows, Ronnie (D-MS, 4th)**
ronnie.shows@mail.house.gov

**Taylor, Gene (D-MS, 5th)**
http://www.house.gov/writerep/

**Rehberg, Dennis (R-MT, AL)**

**Clayton, Eva (D-NC, 1st)**
EClayton1@mail.house.gov

**Etheridge, Bob (D-NC, 2nd)**
http://www.house.gov/writerep/

**Jones, Walter (R-NC, 3rd)**
congjones@mail.house.gov

**Price, David (D-NC, 4th)**
david.price@mail.house.gov

**Burr, Richard (R-NC, 5th)**
Richard.BurrNC05@
mail.house.gov

**Coble, Howard (R-NC, 6th)**
howard.coble@mail.house.gov

**McIntyre, Mike (D-NC, 7th)**
CongMcIntyre@mail.house.gov

**Hayes, Robin (R-NC, 8th)**
http://www.house.gov/writerep/

**Myrick, Sue (R-NC, 9th)**
myrick@mail.house.gov or http://
www.house.gov/myrick/guest.htm

**Ballenger, Cass (R-NC, 10th)**
cass.ballenger@mail.house.gov

**Taylor, Charles (R-NC, 11th)**
repcharles.taylor@mail.house.gov

**Watt, Mel (D-NC, 12th)**
nc12.public@mail.house.gov

**Pomeroy, Earl (D-ND, AL)**
Rep.Earl.Pomeroy@
mail.house.gov

**Bereuter, Douglas (R-NE, 1st)**
none

**Terry, Lee (R-NE, 2nd)**
talk2lee@mail.house.gov

**Osborne, Tom (R-NE, 3rd)**
http://www.house.gov/writerep/

**Sununu, John (R-NH, 1st)**
Rep.Sununu@mail.house.gov

**Bass, Charlie (R-NH, 2nd)**
cbass@mail.house.gov or http://
www.house.gov/writerep/

**Andrews, Robert (D-NJ, 1st)**
rob.andrews@mail.house.gov

**LoBiondo, Frank (R-NJ, 2nd)**
lobiondo@mail.house.gov

**Saxton, James (R-NJ, 3rd)**
http://www.house.gov/writerep/

**Smith, Christopher (R-NJ, 4th)**
http://www.house.gov/writerep/

**Roukema, Marge (R-NJ, 5th)**
http://www.house.gov/writerep/ or
rep.roukema@mail.house.gov

**Pallone, Frank (D-NJ, 6th)**
frank.pallone@mail.house.gov

**Ferguson, Mike (R-NJ, 7th)**
http://www.house.gov/writerep

**Pascrell, William (D-NJ, 8th)**
bill.pascrell@mail.house.gov

**Rothman, Steven (D-NJ, 9th)**
steven.rothman@mail.house.gov

**Payne, Donald (D-NJ, 10th)**
donald.payne@mail.house.gov

**Frelinghuysen, Rodney (R-NJ, 11th)**
rodney.frelinghuysen@
mail.house.gov

**Holt, Rush (D-NJ, 12th)**
rush.holt@mail.house.gov

**Menendez, Robert (D-NJ, 13th)**
menendez@mail.house.gov

**Wilson, Heather (R-NM, 1st)**
ask.heather@mail.house.gov

**Skeen, Joe (R-NM, 2nd)**
joe.skeen@mail.house.gov

**Udall, Tom (D-NM, 3rd)**
http://www.house.gov/writerep/

**Berkley, Shelley (D-NV, 1st)**
shelley.berkley@mail.house.gov

**Gibbons, Jim (R-NV, 2nd)**
mail.gibbons@mail.house.gov

**Grucci, Felix Jr. (R-NY, 1st)**
http://www.house.gov/writerep

**Israel, Steve (D-NY, 2nd)**
http://www.house.gov/writerep/

**King, Peter (R-NY, 3rd)**
peter.king@mail.house.gov

**McCarthy, Carolyn (D-NY, 4th)**
http://www.house.gov/writerep/

**Ackerman, Gary (D-NY, 5th)**
http://www.house.gov/writerep/

**Meeks, Gregory (D-NY, 6th)**
congmeeks@mail.house.gov

**Crowley, Joseph (D-NY, 7th)**
write2joecrowley@
mail.house.gov

**Nadler, Jerrold (D-NY, 8th)**
jerrold.nadler@mail.house.gov

**Weiner, Anthony (D-NY, 9th)**
http://www.house.gov/writerep/

**Towns, Edolphus (D-NY, 10th)**
http://www.house.gov/writerep/

**Owens, Major (D-NY, 11th)**
major.owens@mail.house.gov

**Velazquez, Nydia (D-NY, 12th)**
http://www.house.gov/writerep/

**Fossella, Vito (R-NY, 13th)**
vito.fossella@mail.house.gov

**Maloney, Carolyn (D-NY, 14th)**
rep.carolyn.maloney@
mail.house.gov

**Rangel, Charles (D-NY, 15th)**
http://www.house.gov/writerep/

**Serrano, Jose (D-NY, 16th)**
jserrano@mail.house.gov

**Engel, Eliot (D-NY, 17th)**
http://www.house.gov/writerep/

**Lowey, Nita (D-NY, 18th)**
nita.lowey@mail.house.gov

**Kelly, Sue (R-NY, 19th)**
dearsue@mail.house.gov

**Gilman, Benjamin (R-NY, 20th)**
http://www.house.gov/writerep/

**McNulty, Michael (D-NY, 21st)**
mike.mcnulty@mail.house.gov

**Sweeney, John (R-NY, 22nd)**
http://www.house.gov/writerep/

**Boehlert, Sherwood (R-NY, 23rd)**
Rep.Boehlert@mail.house.gov

**McHugh, John (R-NY, 24th)**
http://www.house.gov/writerep/

**Walsh, James (R-NY, 25th)**
rep.james.walsh@mail.house.gov

**Hinchey, Maurice (D-NY, 26th)**
mhinchey@mail.house.gov

**Reynolds, Tom (R-NY, 27th)**
http://www.house.gov/writerep/

**Slaughter, Louise (D-NY, 28th)**
louiseny@mail.house.gov

**LaFalce, John (D-NY, 29th)**
http://www.house.gov/writerep/

**Quinn, Jack (R-NY, 30th)**
http://www.house.gov/writerep/

**Houghton, Amory (R-NY, 31st)**
http://www.house.gov/writerep/

**Chabot, Steve (R-OH, 1st)**
http://www.house.gov/writerep/

**Portman, Rob (R-OH, 2nd)**
portmail@mail.house.gov

**Hall, Tony (D-OH, 3rd)**
http://www.house.gov/writerep/

**Oxley, Michael (R-OH, 4th)**
mike.oxley@mail.house.gov

**Gillmor, Paul (R-OH, 5th)**
http://www.house.gov/writerep/

**Strickland, Ted (D-OH, 6th)**
http://www.house.gov/writerep/

**Hobson, David (R-OH, 7th)**
http://www.house.gov/hobson/
formmail.htm

**Boehner, John (R-OH, 8th)**
john.boehner@mail.house.gov

**Kaptur, Marcy (D-OH, 9th)**
rep.kaptur@mail.house.gov

**Kucinich, Dennis (D-OH, 10th)**
http://www.house.gov/writerep/

**Jones, Stephanie (D-OH, 11th)**
stephanie.tubbs.jones@
mail.house.gov

**Tiberi, Patrick (R-OH, 12th)**
http://www.house.gov/writerep

**Brown, Sherrod (D-OH, 13th)**
sherrod@mail.house.gov

**Sawyer, Thomas (D-OH, 14th)**
http://www.house.gov/writerep

**Pryce, Deborah (R-OH, 15th)**
pryce.oh15@mail.house.gov

**Regula, Ralph (R-OH, 16th)**
http://www.house.gov/writerep/

**Traficant, James (D-OH, 17th)**
telljim@mail.house.gov

**Ney, Bob (R-OH, 18th)**
bobney@mail.house.gov

**LaTourette, Steven (R-OH, 19th)**
http://www.house.gov/writerep/ or
steve.latourette@mail.house.gov

**Largent, Steve (R-OK, 1st)**
ok01.largent@mail.house.gov

**Carson, Brad (D-OK, 2nd)**
http://www.house.gov/writerep

**Watkins, Wes (R-OK, 3rd)**
wes.watkins@mail.house.gov

**Watts, J. C. (R-OK, 4th)**
rep.jcwatts@mail.house.gov

**Istook, Ernest, Jr. (R-OK, 5th)**
istook@mail.house.gov or http://
www.house.gov/istook/guest.htm

**Lucas, Frank (R-OK, 6th)**
http://www.house.gov/writerep/ or
replucas@mail.house.gov

**Wu, David (D-OR, 1st)**
david.wu@mail.house.gov

**Walden, Gregory (R-OR, 2nd)**
greg.walden@mail.house.gov

**Blumenauer, Earl (D-OR, 3rd)**
write.earl@mail.house.gov

**DeFazio, Pete (D-OR, 4th)**
http://www.house.gov/writerep/

**Hooley, Darlene (D-OR, 5th)**
darlene@mail.house.gov

**Brady, Robert (D-PA, 1st)**
robert.a.brady@mail.house.gov

**Fattah, Chaka (D-PA, 2nd)**
http://www.house.gov/writerep/

**Borski, Robert (R-PA, 3rd)**
robert.borski@mail.house.gov

**Hart, Melissa (R-PA, 4th)**
http://www.house.gov/writerep/

**Peterson, John (R-PA, 5th)**
http://www.house.gov/writerep/

**Holden, Tim (D-PA, 6th)**
http://www.house.gov/writerep/

**Weldon, Curt (R-PA, 7th)**
curtpa07@mail.house.gov

**Greenwood, Jim (R-PA, 8th)**
http://www.house.gov/writerep/ or
pawizard@mail.house.gov

**Shuster, Bud (R-PA, 9th)**
http://www.house.gov/writerep/

**Sherwood, Donald (R-PA, 10th)**
http://www.house.gov/writerep/

**Kanjorski, Paul (D-PA, 11th)**
paul.kanjorski@mail.house.gov

**Murtha, John (D-PA, 12th)**
murtha@mail.house.gov

**Hoeffel, Joseph (D-PA, 13th)**
http://www.house.gov/writerep/

**Coyne, William (D-PA, 14th)**
http://www.house.gov/writerep/

**Toomey, Patrick (R-PA, 15th)**
rep.toomey.pa15@
mail.house.gov

**Pitts, Joseph (R-PA, 16th)**
pitts.pa16@mail.house.gov or http://
www.house.gov/writerep/

**Gekas, George (R-PA, 17th)**
http://www.house.gov/gekas/
district/survey.html

**Doyle, Mike (D-PA, 18th)**
rep.doyle@mail.house.gov

**Platts, Todd Russell (R-PA, 19th)**
http://www.house.gov/writerep/

**Mascara, Frank (D-PA, 20th)**
http://www.house.gov/writerep/

**English, Phil (R-PA, 21st)**
http://www.house.gov/writerep/

**Acevedo-Vilá, Aníbal (D-Puerto Rico, AL)**
http://www.house.gov/writerep/

**Kennedy, Patrick (D-RI, 1st)**
patrick.kennedy@mail.house.gov

**Langevin, James (D-RI, 2nd)**
http://www.house.gov/writerep

**Brown, Henry Jr. (R-SC, 1st)**
http://www.house.gov/writerep

**Spence, Floyd (R-SC, 2nd)**
http://www.house.gov/writerep/

**Graham, Lindsey (R-SC, 3rd)**
http://www.house.gov/ or graham/
Opinions/opinions.htm

**DeMint, James (R-SC, 4th)**
jim.demint@mail.house.gov or http:
//www.house.gov/writerep/

**Spratt, John D-(D-SC, 5th)**
Rep.Spratt@mail.house.gov

**Clyburn, James (D-SC, 6th)**
jclyburn@mail.house.gov

**Thune, John (R-SD, AL)**
jthune@mail.house.gov

**Jenkins, Bill (R-TN, 1st)**
http://www.house.gov/writerep/

**Duncan, John (R-TN, 2nd)**
http://www.house.gov/writerep/

**Wamp, Zach (R-TN, 3rd)**
http://www.house.gov/writerep/

**Hilleary, Van (R-TN, 4th)**
http://www.house.gov/writerep/

**Clement, Bob (D-TN, 5th)**
bob.clement@mail.house.gov

**Gordon, Bart (D-TN, 6th)**
bart.gordon@mail.house.gov

**Bryant, Ed (R-TN, 7th)**
http://www.house.gov/writerep/

**Tanner, John (D-TN, 8th)**
john.tanner@mail.house.gov

**Ford, Harold, Jr. (D-TN, 9th)**
rep.harold.ford.jr@
mail.house.gov or http://
www.house.gov/writerep/

**Sandlin, Max (D-TX, 1st)**
http://www.house.gov/writerep/

**Turner, Jim (D-TX, 2nd)**
http://www.house.gov/writerep/ or
tx02wyr@mail.house.gov

**Johnson, Sam (R-TX, 3rd)**
http://www.house.gov/samjohnson/
or IMA/get_address.htm

**Hall, Ralph (D-TX, 4th)**
rmhall@mail.house.gov

**Sessions, Pete (R-TX, 5th)**
petes@mail.house.gov

**Barton, Joe (R-TX, 6th)**
http://www.house.gov/barton/
get_address.htm

**Culberson, John (R-TX, 7th)**
http://www.house.gov/writerep/

**Brady, Kevin (R-TX, 8th)**
rep.brady@mail.house.gov

**Lampson, Nick (D-TX, 9th)**
nlmail@mail.house.gov

**Doggett, Lloyd (D-TX, 10th)**
lloyd.doggett@mail.house.gov

**Edwards, Chet (D-TX, 11th)**
http://www.house.gov/writerep/

**Granger, Kay (R-TX, 12th)**
texas.granger@mail.house.gov

**Thornberry, Mac (R-TX, 13th)**
http://www.house.gov/writerep/

**Paul, Ron (R-TX, 14th)**
rep.paul@mail.house.gov

**Hinojosa, Ruben (D-TX, 15th)**
Rep.Hinojosa@mail.house.gov

**Reyes, Silvestre (D-TX, 16th)**
http://www.house.gov/writerep/

**Stenholm, Charles (D-TX, 17th)**
http://www.house.gov/writerep/

**Jackson-Lee, Sheila (D-TX, 18th)**
http://www.house.gov/writerep/

**Combest, Larry (R-TX, 19th)**
http://www.house.gov/writerep/

**Gonzalez, Charlie (D-TX, 20th)**
http://www.house.gov/writerep/

**Smith, Lamar (R-TX, 21st)**
http://www.house.gov/writerep/

**DeLay, Tom (R-TX, 22nd)**
thewhip@mail.house.gov

**Bonilla, Henry (R-TX, 23rd)**
http://www.house.gov/writerep/

**Frost, Martin (D-TX, 24th)**
martin.frost@mail.house.gov

**Bentsen, Ken (D-TX, 25th)**
http://www.house.gov/writerep/

**Armey, Dick (R-TX, 26th)**
http://www.house.gov/writerep/

**Ortiz, Solomon (D-TX, 27th)**
http://www.house.gov/writerep/

**Rodriguez, Ciro (D-TX, 28th)**
http://www.house.gov/writerep/

**Green, Gene (D-TX, 29th)**
ask.gene@mail.house.gov

**Johnson, Eddie Bernice (D-TX, 30th)**
rep.e.b.johnson@mail.house.gov

**Hansen, James (R-UT, 1st)**
http://www.house.gov/writerep/

**Matheson, Jim (D-UT, 2nd)**
http://www.house.gov/writerep

**Cannon, Chris (R-UT, 3rd)**
cannon.ut03@mail.house.gov

**Davis, Jo Ann (R-VA, 1st)**
http://www.house.gov/writerep/

**Schrock Edward (R-VA, 2nd)**
http://www.house.gov/writerep

**Scott, Robert (D-VA, 3rd)**
http://www.house.gov/writerep/

**Sisisky, Norman (D-VA, 4th)**
http://www.house.gov/writerep/

**Goode, Virgil (I-VA, 5th)**
rep.goode@mail.house.gov

**Goodlatte, Bob (R-VA, 6th)**
talk2bob@mail.house.gov

**Cantor, Eric (R-VA, 7th)**
http://www.house.gov/writerep

**Moran, Jim (D-VA, 8th)**
jim.motran@mail.house.gov

**Boucher, Rick (D-VA, 9th)**
ninthnet@mail.house.gov

**Wolf, Frank (R-VA, 10th)**
http://www.house.gov/writerep/

**Davis, Tom (R-VA, 11th)**
tom.davis@mail.house.gov

**Christensen, Donna (D-VI, AL)**
http://www.house.gov/writerep/

**Sanders, Bernie (I-VT, AL)**
bernie@mail.house.gov

**Inslee, Jay (D-WA, 1st)**
jay.inslee@mail.house.gov

**Larsen, Rick (R-WA, 2nd)**
http://www.house.gov/writerep

**Baird, Brian (D-WA, 3rd)**
brian.baird@mail.house.gov

**Hastings, Doc (R-WA, 4th)**
http://www.house.gov/writerep/

**Nethercutt, George (R-WA, 5th)**
george.nethercutt-pub@
mail.house.gov

**Dicks, Norman (D-WA, 6th)**
http://www.house.gov/writerep/

**McDermott, James (D-WA, 7th)**
http://www.house.gov/writerep/

**Dunn, Jennifer (R-WA, 8th)**
dunnwa08@mail.house.gov

**Smith, Adam (D-WA, 9th)**
adam.smith@mail.house.gov

**Ryan, Paul (R-WI, 1st)**
pryan@mail.house.gov

**Baldwin, Tammy (D-WI, 2nd)**
tammy.baldwin@mail.house.gov

**Kind, Ron (D-WI, 3rd)**
ron.kind@mail.house.gov

**Kleczka, Gerald (D-WI, 4th)**
http://www.house.gov/writerep/

**Barrett, Tom (D-WI, 5th)**
telltom@mail.house.gov

**Petri, Tom (R-WI, 6th)**
http://www.house.gov/writerep/

**Obey, David (D-WI, 7th)**
http://www.house.gov/writerep/

**Green, Mark (R-WI, 8th)**
mark.green@mail.house.gov

**Sensenbrenner, James (R-WI, 9th)**
sensen09@mail.house.gov

**Mollohan, Alan (D-WV, 1st)**
http://www.house.gov/writerep

**Capito, Shelley Moore (R-WV, 2nd)**
http://www.house.gov/writerep

**Rahall, Nick (D-WV, 3rd)**
nrahall@mail.house.gov

**Cubin, Barbara (R-WY, AL)**
http://www.house.gov/writerep/ or
cubin.webmaster@
mail.house.gov

## HOUSE OF REPRESENTATIVES COMMITTEE WEBSITES

**House Web Site**
http://www.house.gov/

**House Agriculture**
http://www.house.gov/agriculture/

**House Appropriations**
http://www.house.gov/
appropriations/

**House Banking (All)**
http://www.house.gov/banking/

**House Banking (Democrats)**
http://www.house.gov/banking
democrats/

**House Banking/Subcommittee on Domestic and International**
http://www.house.gov/castle/
banking/

**Monetary House Budget (Republicans)**
http://www.house.gov/budget/

## U.S. GOVERNORS

**Don Siegelman**
Alabama
State Capitol, 600 Dexter Ave.
Montgomery, AL 36130

**Tony Knowles**
Alaska
PO Box 110001
Juneau, AK 99811-0001

**Tauese P. F. Sunia**
American Samoa
Executive Office Bldg.
Pago Pago, AS 96799

**Jane Dee Hull**
Arizona
State Capitol, 1700 West
Washington
Phoenix, AZ 85007

**Mike Huckabee**
Arkansas
250 State Capitol
Little Rock, AR 72201

**Gray Davis**
California
State Capitol
Sacramento, CA 95814

**Bill Owens**
Colorado
136 State Capitol
Denver, CO 80203-1792

**John G. Rowland**
Connecticut
210 Capitol Ave.
Hartford, CT 06106

**Ruth Ann Minner**
Delaware
Tatnall Bldg.
William Penn St.
Dover, DE 19901

**Jeb Bush**
Florida
The Capitol
Tallahassee, FL 32399

**Roy Barnes**
Georgia
203 State Capitol
Atlanta, GA 30334

**Carl T. C. Gutierrez**
Guam
Executive Chamber
PO Box 2950
Agana, GU 96932

**Benjamin J. Cayetano**
Hawaii
State Capitol
Honolulu, HI 96813

**Dirk Kempthorne**
Idaho
State Capitol
PO Box 83720
Boise, ID 83720

**George H. Ryan**
Illinois
State Capitol
Springfield, IL 62706

**Frank O'Bannon**
Indiana
206 State Capitol
Indianapolis, IN 46204

**Tom Vilsack**
Iowa
State Capitol
Des Moines, IA 50319

**Bill Graves**
Kansas
Capitol Building, Second Floor
Topeka, KS 66612–1590

**Paul E. Patton**
Kentucky
State Capitol
700 Capitol Ave.
Frankfort, KY 40601

**Mike Foster**
Louisiana
PO Box 94004
Baton Rouge, LA 70804

**Angus S. King Jr.**
Maine
State House, Station 1
Augusta, ME 04333

**Parris N. Glendening**
Maryland
State House
100 State Circle
Annapolis, MD 21401

**Argeo Paul Cellucci**
Massachusetts
State House, Room 360
Boston, MA 02133

**John Engler**
Michigan
PO Box 30013
Lansing, MI 48909

**Jesse Ventura**
Minnesota
130 State Capitol
75 Constitution Ave.
St. Paul, MN 55155

**Ronnie Musgrove**
Mississippi
PO Box 139
Jackson, MS 39205

**Bob Holden**
Missouri
State Capitol, Room 216
Jefferson City, MO 65101

**Judy Martz**
Montana
PO Box 0801
Helena, Montana 59620

**Mike Johanns**
Nebraska
PO Box 94848
Lincoln, NE 68509-4848

**Kenny C. Guinn**
Nevada
State Capitol
Carson City, NV 89710

**Jeanne Shaheen**
New Hampshire
State House, Room 208
Concord, NH 03301

**Christine T. Whitman**
New Jersey
125 West State St.
PO Box 001
Trenton, NJ 08625

**Gary E. Johnson**
New Mexico
State Capitol, Fourth Floor
Santa Fe, NM 87503

**George E. Pataki**
New York
State Capitol
Albany, NY 12224

**Mike Easley**
North Carolina
State Capitol
116 West Jones St.
Raleigh, NC 27603

**John Hoeven**
North Dakota
600 E. Boulevard Ave.
Bismarck, ND 58505

**Pedro P. Tenorio**
Northern Mariana Is.
Caller Box 10007
Saipan, M. P. 96950

**Bob Taft**
Ohio
77 South High St., 30th Floor
Columbus, OH 43266–0601

**Frank Keating**
Oklahoma
State Capitol Building, Suite #212
Oklahoma City, OK 73105

**John A. Kitzhaber**
Oregon
254 State Capitol
Salem, OR 97310

**Sila Calderon**
Pennsylvania
225 Main Capitol Bldg.
Harrisburg, PA 17120

**Pedro Rosselló**
Puerto Rico
La Fortaleza
San Juan, PR 00901

**Lincoln Almond**
Rhode Island
State House,
Providence, RI 02903

**Jim Hodges**
South Carolina
PO Box 11829
Columbia, SC 29211

**William J. Janklow**
South Dakota
500 East Capitol
Pierre, SD 57501

**Don Sundquist**
Tennessee
State Capitol
Nashville, TN 37243–0001

**Rick Perry**
Texas
PO Box 12428
Austin, TX 78711

**Michael O. Leavitt**
Utah
210 State Capitol
Salt Lake City, UT 84114

**Howard Dean, M. D.**
Vermont
Pavilion Office Building,
109 State St.
Montpelier, VT 05609

**James S. Gilmore III**
Virginia
State Capitol
Richmond, VA 23219

**Charles W. Turnbull**
Virgin Islands
Government House, Charlotte
Amalie
St. Thomas, VI 00802

**Gary Locke**
Washington
PO Box 40002, Legislative Bldg.
Olympia, WA 98504–0002

**Robert E. Wise Jr.**
West Virginia
State Capitol Complex
Charleston, WV 25305

**Tommy G. Thompson**
Wisconsin
State Capitol, PO Box 7863
Madison, WI 53707

**Jim Geringer**
Wyoming
State Capitol Bldg., Room 124
Cheyenne, WY 82002

# NEED A HELPING HAND OR A SYMPATHETIC EAR?

**AboutFace**
PO Box 93
Limekiln, PA 19535
Website: http://www.interlog.com/~abtface
*AboutFace is an international organization which provides information and emotional support to individuals with facial differences and their families.*

**Adoption Center**
1500 Walnut St., #701
Philadelphia, PA 19107
E-mail: nac@adopt.org
Website: http://www.adopt.org
*Helps find loving adoptive families for abused and handicapped children and brothers and sisters who want to stay together.*

**Advocates for Youth**
1025 Vermont Ave., NW Suite #200
Washington, DC 20005
Website: http://www.advocatesforyouth.org/
*Advocates for Youth is a national organization that focuses on adolescents as the critical group to reach with information on reproductive health and family-planning options. Advocates works to increase the opportunities for and abilities of youth to make healthy decisions about sexuality.*

**African American Opportunities Centers (OIC International)**
240 W. Tulpchocken St.
Philadelphia, PA 19144
E-mail: oici@oicinternational.org
Website: http://
www.oicinternational.org
Reverend Leon H. Sullivan,
Founder and Chairman
*The international arm of Reverend Leon H. Sullivan's self-help work skills training movement and job education programs, serving Africa and developing nations worldwide.*

**AIDS Education and Advocacy**
Project Inform
205 13th St., #2001
San Francisco, CA 94103
E-mail: pinform@hooked.net
Website: http://www.projinf.org/
Gregory Horowitz, Chair of the Board
*Provides critical HIV/AIDS treatment information free of charge through publications, a toll-free hot line, home page, and national town meetings.*

**Air Lifeline**
50 Fullerton Court, Suite #200
Sacramento, CA 95825
Website: http://www.airlifeline.org
*Air Lifeline is a nonprofit organization helping patients get to and from medical appointments utilizing volunteer pilots. Patients must be able to walk on their own and be in financial need.*

**Al-anon/Alateen**
1600 Corporate Landing Pkwy.
Virginia Beach, VA 23454
E-mail: WSO@al-anon.org
*The Al-Anon Family Groups are a fellowship of relatives and friends of alcoholics who share their experience, strength, and hope, in order to solve their common problems. We believe alcoholism is a family illness and that changed attitudes can aid recovery.*

**Alcoholics Anonymous**
Grand Central Station
Box 459
New York, NY 10163
*A twelve-step program for alcoholics*

**Alexander Graham Bell Association for the Deaf**
3417 Volta Place, NW
Washington, DC 20007
Website: http://www.agbell.org
*One of the world's largest membership organizations and information centers on pediatric hearing loss and the auditory approach.*

**Alliance for the Prudent Use of Antibiotics**
75 Kneeland St.
Boston, MA 02111
Website: http://
www.healthsci.tufts.edu/apua/
apua.html
*APUA promotes global public health and curbs antibiotic resistance through the education of health providers and consumers, scientific and public health research.*

**The Alzheimer's Association**
919 North Michigan Ave., Suite #1000
Chicago, IL 60611
Website: http://www.alz.org
*The largest national voluntary health organization committed to finding a cure for Alzheimer's and helping those affected by the disease.*

**American Academy of Addiction Psychiatry**
7301 Mission Rd., Suite #252
Prairie Village, KS 66208
Website: http://aaap.org/
*A professional association whose mission is to promote excellence in clinical practice in addiction psychiatry, educate the public to influence public policy regarding addictive illness, and to promote accessibility of quality treatment for all patients.*

**American Association of Certified Orthoptists**
St. Louis Children's Hospital Eye Center
St. Louis, MO 63110
Website: http://www.orthoptics.org/
*Its mission is to promote and advance the professional and educational competence of orthoptists.*

**American Humane Association**
63 Inverness Dr. E.
Englewood, CO 80112
E-mail:
smurphy@amerhumane.org
Website: http://
www.amerhumane.org
Protecting animals and children from cruelty, neglect, and abuse since 1877.

**American Society for Deaf Children**
1820 Tribute Rd., Suite A
Sacramento, CA 95815
Website: http://deafchildren.org

**American Tinnitus Association**
PO Box 5
Portland, OR 97207
Website: http://www.ata.org/
*Dedicated to promoting the relief, prevention, and the eventual cure of tinnitus for the benefit of present and future generations*

**Amnesty International, USA**
322 8th Ave.
New York, NY 10001
Website: http://www.amnesty-usa.org/
E-mail: aimember@aiusa.org
*Founded in 1961, Amnesty International is a grassroots activist organization whose one-million strong members are dedicated to freeing prisoners of conscience, to gaining fair trials for political prisoners, to ending torture, political killings, and "disappearances," and to abolishing the death penalty throughout the world.*

**Amyotrophic Lateral Sclerosis Association**
27001 Agoura Rd., Suite #150
Calabasas Hills, CA 91301
Website: http://www.alsa.org
*The only national nonprofit voluntary health organization dedicated solely to the fight against ALS. Its mission is to find a cure for amyotrophic lateral sclerosis and improve living with ALS.*

## The Arc
500 East Border St., Suite #300
Arlington, TX 76010
Website: http://www.thearc.org
*The national organization of and
for people with mental retardation
and related disabilities and their
families.*

## Assistance Dogs International
% Canine Partners for Life
334 Faggs Manor Rd.
Cochranville, PA 19330
Website: http://www.assistance-
dogs-intl.org/index.html
*This is a membership coalition
representing organizations and
individuals training and placing
Assistance Dogs.*

## Association of Auditory-Verbal International
2121 Eisenhower Ave., Suite #402
Alexandria, VA 22314
Website: http://www.auditory-
verbal.org
*The goal of the Auditory-Verbal
approach is for children who are
deaf or hard of hearing to grow up
in typical learning and living
environments and to become
independent, participating citizens
in mainstream society.*

## Association of Late-Deafened Adults
10310 Main St., #274
Fairfax, VA 22030
Website: http://www.alda.org
*Works collaboratively with other
organizations around the world
serving the needs of late-deafened
people and extends a welcome to
everyone, late-deafened or not,
who supports its goals.*

## A-T Children's Project
668 South Military Trail
Deerfield Beach, FL 33442
Website: http://www.atcp.org/
*The A-T Children's Project was
established to raise funds to
support and coordinate biomedical
research projects, scientific
conferences, and a clinical center
aimed at finding a cure for Ataxia
Telangiectasia, a lethal genetic
disease that attacks children,
causing progressive loss of muscle
control, cancer, and immune
system problems.*

## Autism Society of America
7910 Woodmont Ave., Suite #300
Bethesda, MD 20814
Website: http://www.autism-
society.org
*Promotes lifelong access and
opportunities for persons within
the autism spectrum and their
families, to be fully included,
participating members of their
communities through advocacy,
public awareness, education, and
research related to autism.*

## Bazelon Center for Mental Health Law
1101 15th St. NW, #1212
Washington, DC 20005
Website: http://www.bazelon.org/
E-mail: bazelon@nicom.com
Lee Carty, Communications
Director
*Legal advocacy for the civil rights
and human dignity of people with
mental disability*

## Big Brothers Big Sisters of America

230 N. 13th St.
Philadelphia, PA 19107
E-mail: bbsa@aol.com
Website: http://www.mentoring.org/faboutus.htm/
Thomas McKenna, National Executive Director
*The oldest mentoring organization serving youth in the country.*

## Braille Institute

741 North Vermont Ave.
Los Angeles, CA 90029-3594
Website: http://www.brailleinstitute.org/
*The Braille Institute was founded in 1919 as the Universal Braille Press to provide services to the blind, which now includes production of more than five million Braille pages yearly, preschool services, supplemental academic programs for children, summer camps for children, a youth recreational center, low-priced consumer goods and visual aids, counseling, a career learning center, job placement, social activities, and instruction in basic living skills.*

## The Brain Injury Association

105 N. Alfred St.
Alexandria, VA 22314
Website: http://www.biausa.org
*The mission of the Brain Injury Association is to create a better future through brain injury prevention, research, education, and advocacy.*

## Center on Children + Families

295 Lafayette St., Suite #920
NewYork, NY 10012
Website: http://www.kidsuccess.com/
Beverly Brooks, Executive Director
*Founded in 1919 with a mission to protect children from abuse and neglect, CC+F has evolved to encompass a broad array of programs designed to promote "kid success." With a dedicated staff of 200, CC+F serves over 16,000 children and families each year.*

## A Chance to Grow, Inc.

1800 2nd St., NE
Minneapolis, MN 55418
*A Chance to Grow, Inc., is a nonprofit agency dedicated to accelerating the development of children with learning disabilities and developmental delays, and children and adults with brain injuries.*

## Children and Adults with Attention Deficit Disorder (CHADD)

8181 Professional Place, Suite #201
Landover, MD 20785
Website: http://www.chadd.org
*The national organization representing individuals with AD/HD, for education, advocacy, and support. AD/HD is medically and legally recognized as a treatable yet potentially serious disorder, affecting up to three to five percent of all children and approximately two to four percent of adults.*

**Children of the Night**
14530 Sylvan St.
Van Nuys, CA 91411
E-mail: cotnll@aol.com
Website: http://
www.childrenofthenight.org
*Provides a toll-free, national twenty-four-hour hot line, shelter home, and street program for sexually abused children ages 11–17 who are on the streets.*

**Cochlear Implant Club International**
5335 Wisconsin Ave., NW, Suite #440
Washington, DC 20015
Website: http://www.cici.org
*A nonprofit organization for cochlear implant recipients, their families, professionals, and other individuals interested in cochlear implants.*

**Committee for Children**
2203 Airport Way S, #500
Seattle, WA 98134
Website: http://www.cfchildren.org/
E-mail: webmatron@cfchildren.org
*A nonprofit organization dedicated to the prevention of child abuse and youth violence through the development of educational curricula and original research*

**Educators for Social Responsibility**
23 Garden St.
Cambridge, MA 02138
Website: http://
www.esrnational.org/
E-mail: educators@esrnational.org
*A national nonprofit organization dedicated to helping young people develop the convictions and skills to build a safe, sustainable, and just world*

**Endometriosis Alliance of New York, The**
PO Box 326
Cooper Station
New York, NY 10276
Website: http://
www.monmouth.com/mkatzman/
healing/endo.htm
*A mutual self-help, nonprofit organization providing accurate, current, and independent information about endometriosis*

**Endometriosis Association, The**
8585 North 76th Place
Milwaukee, WI 53223
Website: http://
www.EndometriosisAssn.org/
E-mail:
endo@endometriosisassn.org
*A nonprofit organization that provides support to women and girls, educates the public and medical community, and conducts and promotes research related to endometriosis*

**Families and Work Institute**
330 Seventh Ave. 14th Floor
New York, NY 10001
Website: http://
www.familiesandworkinst.org/
E-mail: ebrownfield@
familiesandwork.org
Ellen Galinsky, President
*A nonprofit organization that addresses the changing nature of work and family life.*

## Families USA Foundation

1334 G St. NW, #300
Washington, DC 20005
Website: http://
www.familiesusa.org/
E-mail: info@familiesusa.org
Philippe Villers, President and Co-
Founder of Families USA
Foundation
*A national nonprofit, nonpartisan
organization dedicated to the
achievement of high-quality,
affordable health and long-term
care for all Americans*

## Family Violence Prevention Fund

383 Rhode Island St., #304
San Francisco, CA 94103
Website: http://www.fvpf.org/
E-mail: fund@fvpf.org
Esta Soler, Executive Director
*A national nonprofit organization
that focuses on domestic violence
education, prevention, and public
policy reform*

## Future Farmers of America

National FFA Center
6060 FFA Dr.
PO Box 68960
Indianapolis, IN 46268
Website: http://
www.agriculture.com/contents/FFA
Bernie Staller, Chief Operating
Officer
E-mail: bstaller@ffa.org
*Building today's youth into
tomorrow's leaders. Over 452,000
members receive education,
motivation, leadership skills,
positive role models and positive
growth; developing community-
oriented adults.*

## Girls Incorporated

120 Wall St., 3rd Floor
New York, NY 10005-3902
E-mail: mekone@aol.com
Website: http://www.girlsinc.org
Regina Montoya, President
*Helps make every girl strong,
smart, and bold. Assists over
350,000 young people nationwide.
Providing teen pregnancy and
substance abuse prevention, math
and science programming.*

## Huntingon's Disease Society of America

158 W. 29th St., 7th Floor
New York, NY 10011-5300
Website: http://neuro-
www2.mgh.harvard.edu/hdsa/
hdsamain.nclk
*Dedicated to finding a cure for
Huntington's Disease (HD) while
providing support and services for
those living with HD and their
families, HDSA promotes and
supports both clinical and basic HD
research, aids families in coping
with the multi-faceted problems
presented by HD, and educates the
families, the public, and healthcare
professionals about Huntington's
Disease.*

## Indian Youth of America

609 Badgerow Bldg.
Sioux City, IA 51101
*Provides opportunities and
experiences that aid Native
American youth in their
educational, physical, career,
cultural, and personal growth while
fostering self-esteem and cultural
pride.*

**International Association of Laryngectomees**
PO Box 2664
Newport News, VA 23609-0664
Website: http://www.larynxlink.com
E-mail: ial@larynxlink.com
*A nonprofit voluntary organization composed of approximately 250 member clubs and recognized regional organizations.*

**International Bone Marrow Transplant Registry/Autologous Blood and Marrow Transplant Registry—North America**
Medical College of Wisconsin
8701 Watertown Plank Rd., PO Box 26509
Milwaukee, WI 53226
Website: http://www.ibmtr.org
*The IBMTR and ABMTR registry aims at improving the success rate of allogeneic and autologous blood and bone marrow transplantation by maintaining a statistical center for the collection and organization of clinical data, disseminating results of analyses of Registry data, and supporting clinical trials using bone marrow transplantation.*

**International Dyslexia Association**
Chester Bldg., Suite #382
8600 LaSalle Rd.
Baltimore, MD 21286-2044
Website: http://www.interdys.org/
International Federation of Hard of Hearing People
Telderssatraat 7
NL-8265 WS Kampen
The Netherlands
*Consists of National Associations of and for hard-of-hearing and late-deafened people and parents' and professional organizations. The board members of IFHOH carry out their work on a voluntary basis.*

**Learning Disabilities Association of America (LDA)**
4156 Library Rd.
Pittsburgh, PA 15234-1349
Website: http://www.ldanatl.org
*The only national organization devoted to defining and finding solutions for the broad spectrum of learning disabilities, LDA is the largest nonprofit volunteer organization advocating for individuals with learning disabilities.*

**Meniere's Network**
% Ear Foundation at Baptist Hospital
1817 Patterson St.
Nashville, TN 37203
*A national network of patient support groups which provide patients with the opportunity to talk to others with Meniere's disease, vestibular disorders, dizziness, or hearing loss; and to share coping strategies.*

**Mexican American Legal Defense and Education Fund (MALDEF)**
634 South Spring St., 11th Floor
Los Angeles, CA 90014
Website: http://www.MALDEF.org/
E-mail: info@maldef.org
Antonia Hernandez, President & General Counsel
*A national nonprofit organization whose mission is to protect and promote the civil rights of the more than 29 million Latinos living in the United States*

**National Alliance for the Mentally Ill**
Colonial Place Three
2107 Wilson Blvd., Suite #300
Arlington, VA 22201-3042
Website: http://www.nami.org/
E-mail: namiofc@aol.com
Laurie M. Flynn, Executive Director
*An organization working with and for persons with mental illnesses and their families*

**National Aphasia Association**
156 Fifth Ave., Suite #707
New York, NY 10010
Website: http://www.aphasia.org
*An organization dedicated to promoting the care, welfare, and rehabilitation of those with aphasia through public education and support of research.*

**National Association of the Deaf**
814 Thayer Ave.
Silver Spring, MD 20910
Website: http://www.nad.org
*The oldest and largest organization representing people with disabilities in the United States. The NAD safeguards the accessibility and civil rights of 28 million deaf and hard-of-hearing Americans in a variety of areas including education, employment, healthcare and social services, and telecommunications.*

**National Black Deaf Advocates**
246 Sycamore St., Suite #100
Decatur, GA 30030
Website: http://www.nbda.org/

**National Council on Stuttering**
1200 W. Harrison St., Suite #2010
Chicago, IL 60607
*Provides information about the prevention and treatment of stuttering*

**National Cued Speech Association**
% Dr. Catherine Quenin
Speech-Language Pathology Department
Nazareth College of Rochester
4245 East Ave.
Rochester, NY 14618
Website: http://www.cuedspeech.org/
*Cued Speech is a sound-based visual communication system which, in English, uses eight handshapes in four different locations ("cues") in combination with the natural mouth movements of speech, to make all the sounds of spoken language look different.*

**National Cystic Fibrosis Foundation**
6931 Arlington Rd.
Bethesda, MD 20814
Website: http://www.cff.org/
*Assures the development of the means to cure and control cystic fibrosis and to improve the quality of life for those with the disease*

**National Easter Seal Society**
230 West Monroe St., Suite #1800
Chicago, IL 60606
Website: http://www.seals.org
*A direct service organization committed to providing world class, quality programs and services to help people with disabilities and their families live with equality, dignity, and independence*

**National Multiple Sclerosis Society**
733 Third Ave., 6th Floor
New York, NY 10017
Website: http://www.nmss.org

**National Parkinson Disease Foundation**
1501 NW 9th Ave.
Miami, FL 33136
Website: http://www.parkinson.org/
*Its goal is to find the cause and cure for Parkinson's disease and related neurodegenerative disorders through research, to educate general medical practitioners to detect the early warning signs of Parkinson's disease, to educate patients, their caregivers, and the general public, to provide diagnostic and therapeutic services, and to improve the quality of life for both patients and their caregivers.*

**National Spasmodic Dysphonia Association, Inc.**
1 East Wacker Dr., Suite #2430
Chicago, IL 60601
Website: http://www.dystonia-foundation.org/
*A nonprofit organization whose main focus is to promote public awareness of Spasmodic Dysphonia (SD) through education in both the public and private sector and provide information, resources, and support to persons with SD and their families.*

**National Stuttering Project**
5100 E. La Palma Ave., Suite #208
Anaheim Hills, CA 92807
Website: http://www.nsastutter.org
*A network of more than 75 active local support groups and programs created to meet the needs of children and adults who stutter.*

**Partnership for a Drug-Free America**
405 Lexington Ave.
New York, NY 10174
E-mail: bob_caruso@drugfree.org
Website: http://www.drugfreeamerica.org
*The Partnership for a Drug-Free America is a private, nonprofit, nonpartisan coalition of professionals from the communications industry.*

**Reading Is Fundamental**
600 Maryland Ave. SW, #600
Washington, DC 20024
E-mail: kmann@rif.si.edu
Dr. William Trueheart, President
*America's largest children's literary organization helps children grow up reading by offering them activities that make reading appealing and giving them free books they choose and keep.*

**The Selective Mutism Foundation**
PO Box 450632
Sunrise, FL 33345


**Self Help for Hard of Hearing People, Inc.**
7910 Woodmont Ave., Suite #1200
Bethesda, MD 20814
Website: http://www.shhh.org
Its goal is to enhance the quality of life for people who are hard of hearing


**Speak Easy International Foundation**
233 Concord Dr.
Paramus, NJ 07652
A supportive self-help mutual aid group for people who stutter. The organization provides a network of friendship and understanding to stutterers and offers encouragement, motivation, and support in dealing with their disfluency.


**Stuttering Foundation of America**
3100 Walnut Grove Rd., Suite #603
PO Box 11749
Memphis, TN 38111-0749
Website: http://www.stuttersfa.org/
The first nonprofit, charitable association in the world to concern itself with the prevention and improved treatment of stuttering, it distributes over a million publications to the public and professionals each year.

**TASH**
29 W. Susquehanna Ave., Suite #210
Baltimore, MD 21204
Website: http://www.tash.org
An international association of people with disabilities, their family members, other advocates, and professionals fighting for a society in which inclusion of all people in all aspects of society is the norm. TASH is an organization of members concerned with human dignity, civil rights, education, and independence for all individuals with disabilities.


**Telecommunications for the Deaf, Inc.**
8630 Fenton St., Suite #604
Silver Spring, MD 20910
Website: http://www.tdi-online.org/
It is an active national advocacy organization focusing its energies and resources to address equal access issues in telecommunications and media for four constituencies in deafness and hearing loss, specifically people who are deaf, hard-of-hearing, late-deafened, or deaf-blind.


**Toys for Tots Foundation (Marine Corps Reserve)**
715 Broadway St.
PO Box 1947
Quantico, VA 22134
E-mail:
brian_murray@marforces.usmcmil
Website: http://www.toysfortots.org
Contact: Brian Murray
The recognized fund-raising and support organization for the Marine Corps Reserve Toys for Tots program, which brings Christmas joy to needy children nationwide.

**United Cerebral Palsy Association, Inc.**
1660 L St., NW, Suite #700
Washington, DC 20036
Website: http://www.ucpa.org
*For 50 years, UCP (a.k.a. United Cerebral Palsy) has been committed to change and progress for persons with disabilities. The national organization and its nationwide network of 135 affiliates strive to ensure the inclusion of persons with disabilities in every facet of society—from the Web to the workplace, from the classroom to the community.*

**Vegetarian Resource Group**
PO Box 1463
Baltimore, MD 21203
E-mail: *vrg@vrg.org*
Website: *http://www.vrg.org*
Reed Mangels, Ph.D., R.D.
*Educates consumers, health professionals, food services, and media about vegetarian, vegan, and low-fat diets—making healthy living easier. Published Vegetarian Journal, Nutrition for Teenagers, and dining guides.*

**YMCA OF THE USA**
101 W. Wacker Dr.
Chicago, IL 60606
E-mail: ymcainfo@ymcausa.org
Website: http://www.ymcanet/
David Mercer, National Executive Director of the YMCA of the USA
*Local YMCAs collectively are the country's largest community service organization, providing values-based experiences that nurture the healthy development of children and teens, support families, and strengthen communities.*

**Youth for Christ/USA**
7670 S. Vaughn Ct.
Englewood, CO 80112
E-mail: *yfc@gospel.com.net*
Website: *http:// www.gospelcom.net/yfc*
*Serving young people in schools, institutions, and neighborhoods through counseling, events, education, and healing relationships; providing love, care, and life skills to youth at risk.*

**YWCA of the USA**
350 Fifth Ave., #301
New York, NY 10118
E-mail: *rcrickmore@ywca.org*
Website: *http://www.ywca.org*
Prema Mathai-Davies, CEO
*Longest and oldest diverse women's membership movement working to empower women and eliminate racism. Advocacy, public policy, health/fitness, child care, leadership, and job training.*

# REACH OUT AND TOUCH SOMEONE WITH YOUR COMPUTER

**Abelson, Amanda**
manda@martingny.ai.mit.edu
*Hypercard programmer*

**Abrams, Rhonda**
rhonda@ideacafe.com
*Business planning expert*

**Aboulela, Amir**
amiraboulela@yahoo.com
*Actor*

**Abramova, Nina**
nina@da.ru
*Fitness, model, body builder*

**Ackroyd, Gayle**
gandj.gibson@sympatico.ca
*Vocalist, musician in the Gayle
Ackroyd Band*

**Adams, Scott**
scottadam@aol.com
*Dilbert creator*

**Aguilera, Christina**
fanmail@christinamail.com
*Singer*

**Aiken, Caroline**
Website: http://songs.com/caroline/
E-mail: caiken@mindspring.com
*Singer, musician*

**Akers, Michelle**
michelle@michelleakers.com
*Soccer player*

**Alcaide, Ruthie**
rwruthie@bunim-murray.com
*MTV's Real World Hawaii*

**Alda, Alan**
Alda@pbs.org
*Actor, director*

**Allard, J.**
jallard@microsoft.com
*Microsoft TCP/IP specialist*

**Allred, Corbin**
Website: http://www.geocities.com/
Hollywood/Boulevard/2710/
corbinallred@juno.com
*Actor*

**Almond, Lincoln**
rigov@gov.state.ri.us
*Governor of Rhode Island*

**Amaya**
rwamaya@bunim-murray.com
*Real World Hawaii*

**Amazing Randi, The**
76702.3507@compuserve.com
*Magician*

**Anderson, Lewis**
andersol@
server2.health.state.mn.us
*Mac shareware author*

**Angry Mob, The**
angrymob@aol.com
*Comedy group*

**Anderson, Bill**
bill@billanderson.com
*Singer, TV host, songwriter*

**Andrews, Andy**
andy@andyandrews.com
*Comedian*

**Angelle, Lisa**
Website: lisaangelle.com
canoesltd@aol.com
*Country singer*

**Anka, Paul**
ankapap@aol.com
*Singer songwriter*

**Ballmer, Steve**
steveb@microsoft.com
*CEO of Microsoft*

**Banks, Tamara**
WB2News@mail.kwgn.com
*Denver TV news anchor*

**Bold & Beautiful, The**
E-mail: yrbb@cbs.com
Website: http://www.cbs.com/
daytime/bb
*TV soap opera.*

**Boy Scouts of America**
Website: http://
www.bsa.scouting.org/
*Provides an educational program
for boys and young adults to build
character, to train in the
responsibilities of participating
citizenship and to develop personal
fitness.*

**Brady, Pat**
pbrady8222@aol.com
*Cartoonist*

**Brown, Dale**
Dale@megafortress.com
*Cartoonist*

**Bugs Bunny Tribute Page**
http://www.voicenet.com/~diann/
bunny.html

**Bush, George, W.**
President@whitehouse.gov

**Caballero, Tara**
Website: http://
www.taracaballeroauthentic.com /
tara@simplyweb.net
*Fitness supermodel*

**Calhoun, Anhon**
acalhoun@wishtv.com
*Sports anchor*

**Callaway, Belle**
belle_online@yahoo.com
*Broadway actress*

**Camozzi, Chris**
jazzd4cc@aol.com
*Musician*

**Calvert, Deforest**
calvert@calvertdeforest.com
*Actor who gained notority from his
Larry Bud Melman character on
David Letterman*

**Cherry, Eagle Ey**
eagle-eye@eagleeyecherry.com
*Musician*

**CNN**
Website: http://www.cnn.com

**Denton, Jamie**
jamiedenton@mydailyplanet.com
*Actress*

**Disney Online**
Website: http://www.disney.com
*A family-oriented website.*

**Eden, Barbara**
barbara@fansource.com
*Actress*

**Evans, Greg**
geluann@aol.com
*Syndicated cartoonist of Luann*

**Fairchiild, Barbara**
Barbara@barbarafairchild.com
*Musician*

**Fisher, Kimberly**
Website: http://
www.kimberlyfisher.com/
kfisher40@aol.com
*Model, actress, Miss Alaska*

**General Hospital**
E-mail: genhosp@ccabc.com
*TV soap opera*

**Geter, Gene**
gg@genegeter.com
*Photographer, interviewer, author*

**Giella, Joe**
tellmary@aol.com
*Syndicated co-cartoonist of Mary
Worth*

**Girl Scouts of the USA**
E-mail: gscomm@gsusa.org
Website: http://www.girlscouts.org
*World's largest organization for
girls*

**Hannot, Augenstein**
AugensteinHannot@bigfoot.com
*Singer, songwriter, poet*

**London, Rick**
thorus1@pearlriver.net or force@c-
gate.net
*Cartoonist*

**Mann, Aimee**
fanmail@aimeemann.com
*Singer*

**National Association of Elvis
Impersonators**
E-mail: NAAEI@aol.com
*Organization of Elvis
impersonators*

**New York Times**
Website: http://www.nytimes.com
*On-line version of the* New York
Times

**O'Brien, Soledad**
sobrien@nbc.com
*Journalist*

**O'Hare, Mark**
ctndawg@aol.com
*Syndicated cartoonist of* Citizen
Dog

**Park, Needham**
needham@fartoojones.com
*Musician*

**Sanchez, Vanessa**
tygress@vanessasanchez.com
*WCW Nitro Girl—Tygress*

**Sanderson, William**
william@williamsanderson.net
*Actor*

**Sansom, Chip**
chipbloser@aol.com
*Syndicated cartoonist of* Born
Loser

**Saturday Night Live**
snl@nbc.com
*Television show*

**Tallman, Patricia**
patricia@patriciatallman.com
*Actress,* Babylon 5—*Lyta
Alexander*

**Today**
E-mail: today@nbc.com
*Television show*

**Valderrama, Wilmer**
wilmer@teenhollywood.com
*Actress* That '70s Show

**Vazquez, Martha**
mvazquez@kvoa.com
*News Anchor—KVOA 4 Tucson,
AZ*

**Von Detten, Erik**
erik@americanteenvideo.com
*Actor*

**Zahn, Paula**
theedge@foxnews.com
*Journalist, broadcaster*

# WRITE TO ME

*The Kid's Address Book* is updated every two years, and you can play an active role in this procedure. If you are notable in any field or know someone who is, send the name, mailing address, and some documentation of the notability (newspaper clippings are effective) for possible inclusion in our next edition.

Also, we are very interested in learning of any success stories resulting from *The Kid's Address Book*.

During the last few years, I have received tens of thousands of letters, ranging from loving to angry, from owners of *The Kid's Address Book*. Despite the overwhelming task of answering this mail, I really enjoy the letters.

But, please, remember a couple of rules if you write:

- Remember to include a self-addressed stamped envelope. For reasons of both time and expense, this is the only way I can respond to mail; so, unfortunately, I've had to draw the line—no SASE, no reply.
- I need your comments. While I confess I'm partial to success stories, comments from purchasers of the book have helped me a great deal for future editions; so fire away.
- Many people have written to request addresses of people not listed in the book. As much as I would like to, I simply can't open up this can of worms. Requests for additional addresses are carefully noted and considered for future editions.
- Most important, send me a photo. That's right, enclose a photo of yourself. After all, from the photo on the back cover, you know what I look like, and I'm rather eager to see you. Receiving a photo from someone who writes adds an entirely new dimension to the letter.

**Michael Levine**
Levine Communications Office
10333 Ashton Ave.
Los Angeles, CA 90024
E-mail: levinepr@earthlink.net

# OTHER BOOKS OF INTEREST

**THE ADDRESS BOOK (10TH EDITION)**
by Michael Levine                    0-399-52667-6/$13.95

The definitive guide to reaching just about anyone: provides mailing address of over 3,500 VIPs and celebrities in every field imaginable.

*A Perigee Trade Paperback*

**THE TEENAGE BODY BOOK** Revised and Updated
**by Kathy McCoy, Ph.D., and Charles Wibbelsman, M.D.**
0-399-52535-1/$17.95

This is the essential handbook for honest, forthright, up-to-date advice in dealing with every dilemma, doubt, and possibility facing teenagers at the threshold of the new century.

*Available September 1999*
*A Perigee Trade Paperback*

**LIFE HAPPENS**
**A Teenager's Guide to Friends, Failure, Sexuality, Love, Rejection, Addiction, Peer Pressure, Families, Loss, Depression, Change, and Other Challenges of Living**

**by Kathy McCoy, Ph.D., and Charles Wibbelsman, M.D.**

0-399-51987-4/$11.00
*A Perigee Trade Paperback*

**TO ORDER CALL: 1-800-788-6262, ext. 1, Refer to Ad #846**

Perigee Books
A division of Penguin Putnam Inc.
375 Hudson Street
New York, New York 10014